# Faces Like Devils

# Faces Like Devils

*The Bald Knobber Vigilantes in the Ozarks*

Matthew J. Hernando

University of Missouri Press
Columbia

Copyright © 2015 by
The Curators of the University of Missouri
University of Missouri Press, Columbia, Missouri 65211
Printed and bound in the United States of America
All rights reserved
First paperback printing, 2019

Cataloging-in-Publication data available from the Library of Congress
ISBN 978-0-8262-2041-7 (hardcover : alk. paper)
ISBN 978-0-8262-2198-8 (paperback : alk. paper)

♾ This paper meets the requirements of the
American National Standard for Permanence of
Paper for Printed Library Materials, Z39.48, 1984.

Typefaces: ITC Legacy Serif, ITC Legacy Sans, Minion Pro

*For my parents, James and Moira Hernando*

# Contents

# Acknowledgments

Anyone who writes a book quickly accumulates a list of personal and professional debts so long that mentioning them all becomes impossible. The people mentioned here, therefore, do not constitute an exhaustive list of all the people who have helped me along the way toward completing this project. First, at Louisiana State University, I would like to thank Gaines M. Foster, David H. Culbert, Charles W. Royster, Paul Paskoff, and especially my advisor William J. Cooper Jr. for his sage advice and consistent encouragement.

Thanks must also go to the trustees and staff of the Missouri State Archives. The archives generously awarded me the William E. Foley research fellowship, which included travel funds for research trips to the archives' facility in Jefferson City. During the many long days that I spent at the archives, the staff members there provided me with invaluable assistance in finding materials needed for my research. I cannot name them all here, but ones who deserve special mention are state archivist John Dougan and Lynn Morrow, the former director of the state archives' Local Records Preservation Program. Both of these men provided me with helpful advice and abundant research assistance. I would also like to thank Robert Neumann and Beverly Johnson of the Greene County Archives in Springfield, Gwen Simmons of the Lyons Memorial Library at the College of the Ozarks in Point Lookout, and John F. Bradbury of the State Historical Society of Missouri Research Center in Rolla.

Lynn Morrow and Dr. Brooks Blevins of Missouri State University both read and critiqued this manuscript, providing me with numerous helpful and insightful comments and suggestions. Dr. Adam Pratt of the University of Scranton also read some earlier drafts of some of my chapters.

Finally, I must thank my family and friends, especially my parents, James and Moira Hernando, whose love and support for my career ambitions over the years have been constant and unflagging. My brothers, Eric and Daniel, and my sisters-in-law, Aimee and Caylin have all served as good-natured listeners as I blathered on endlessly about my work whenever we have been together for holidays or family gatherings. Their kindness and patience has been much appreciated.

Although I have benefited immensely from the assistance of the aforementioned people, they bear no responsibility for any mistakes found in the following pages. This is my work, and I accept full responsibility for any shortcomings.

# List of Tables

# List of Figures

# Faces Like Devils

# Introduction

Sometime in the fall of 1930 Walter Walker of Christian County, Missouri, took his six-year-old son Lloyd into the woods to cut some firewood. It was a common enough chore for young boys in the Ozarks with the colder months coming on, but on this day something happened that young Lloyd would remember for the rest of his life. While in the woods, he and his father met a stranger, an old man, probably in his sixties. His father seemed to know the man, for he told his son to run along and find a friend to play with while he talked to the stranger.

Lloyd later learned that upon arriving in the area the stranger had checked into a motel in nearby Chadwick, Missouri, where he had told people he was a "mineral man" from Oklahoma. He had come to Christian County, he said, to investigate the area's mineral wealth on behalf of his employer. Lloyd never saw the old man doing anything related to mining or minerals, but he did observe the man doing several things that seemed odd. For one thing, the stranger rarely walked on the public roads, preferring to go through the woods as if to avoid detection. He also spent several afternoons visiting with an elderly woman living in that area, whom Lloyd later learned was his sister. She sat with the stranger on her porch for long hours at a time, apparently engrossed in conversation.

After a few weeks of this, when the old man finally took his leave of the area, Lloyd and his father were on hand to see him off. As they watched his retreating figure fade into the distance, Lloyd's father turned to him and asked, "Do you know who that was?" "No, Dad," the boy replied, to which his father responded, "That's the Bald Knobber that escaped from jail in Christian County."[1]

In all likelihood, the man that Lloyd Walker met in the woods so many years ago was Wiley Mathews. By 1930 Mathews had become something of a legend in the Ozark hill country. He was the man who had cheated death some four decades before when he had escaped from the county jail in Ozark, Missouri, on December 28, 1888, just a few months before his scheduled execution date.[2] He had then disappeared, never to be heard from again until he made his surreptitious return trip to visit his sister in 1930. He had good reason for secrecy, for he was still a wanted man because of actions he had taken as a member of a secret organization known as the Bald Knobbers that had thrown much of southwest Missouri into turmoil in the 1880s.

The Bald Knobbers were a vigilance committee that originated in late 1884 or early 1885, in Taney County, Missouri, a sparsely populated rural county located on the border of Missouri and Arkansas. The Bald Knobbers represented themselves as an alliance of taxpayers and law-abiding citizens dedicated to fighting rampant crime in their communities and corruption in their local government. The group's first recorded act of violence occurred on April 15, 1885, when they broke into the county jail in Forsyth and seized two young prisoners, Frank and Tubal Taylor, and hung them from an old oak tree a few miles outside of town.[3] The Bald Knobbers followed this act with a campaign of night riding, whippings, and intimidation designed to purge the area of its criminal element, along with anyone who opposed them. In particular, they targeted members and supporters of the Democratic courthouse ring that had run the local government for most of the preceding decade. Not surprisingly, their actions and methods provoked strong criticism and resistance from many people within their community.

The hostility flared up on February 28, 1886, when the Bald Knobbers' leader, Nathaniel Kinney, shot and killed Andrew Coggburn, a vocal critic of the vigilantes.[4] Coggburn's untimely demise spurred the opponents of the Bald Knobbers into action. Soon an organized opposition group arose, calling themselves the Anti-Bald Knobber or "militia" faction. They petitioned the state government to help them eliminate the vigilante organization in their midst and even formed a militia company for that purpose. In response, Missouri's governor, John S. Marmaduke, sent Adj. Gen. James C. Jamison to

Forsyth to mediate an end to the strife. Jamison's mission resulted in the proclamation of a formal truce between the Bald Knobbers and their opponents. His intervention brought about the official end of organized vigilantism in Taney County, but it did not soothe the bitter hostility between the Bald Knobbers and their enemies. Nor did it long prevent the resumption of bloodshed. On May 9, 1886, Bald Knobber George Washington Middleton shot and killed Anti-Bald Knobber Samuel Snapp in Kirbyville.[5]

In the meantime, the Bald Knobber movement spread north to the adjacent counties of Christian and Douglas, where several members became embroiled in a number of highly publicized court cases following the deaths of William Edens and Charles Greene at the hands of a group of about twenty-five Bald Knobbers on March 11, 1887.[6] Following this tragedy, a legal crackdown commenced in which Christian County authorities brought charges against roughly eighty vigilantes for various crimes. The circuit court convicted several participants in the Edens-Greene killings of murder and sentenced four of them to death. One escaped, but the other three were hanged on May 10, 1889.[7] Federal authorities also participated in the crackdown, charging several dozen Bald Knobbers with intimidating homesteaders, a federal crime under the provisions of the Homestead Act of 1862 and other federal legislation. As a result of these proceedings, the Bald Knobber chapters in Christian and Douglas Counties soon dissolved.

The Bald Knobbers in Taney County came to a less abrupt, but equally bloody end. On August 20, 1888, Anti-Bald Knobber William M. Miles gunned down Nat Kinney inside a general store in Forsyth. While awaiting his trial, Billy Miles was released on bail. He and his brother James attended an Independence Day picnic near Kirbyville. During the festivities Sheriff Galba E. Branson, a Bald Knobber, and a private detective named Edward Funk, whom the Bald Knobbers had allegedly hired to avenge their fallen leader, confronted the Miles brothers. A gunfight ensued in which both Branson and Funk lost their lives.

At the height of their power, the Bald Knobbers numbered an estimated nine hundred men. These numbers made them easily one of the largest vigilante organizations in the United States during the nineteenth century.[8] They were also one of the most violent vigilance committees of that era. Over roughly a four-year period from 1885 to 1889, at least thirteen individuals died as a direct result of Bald Knobber activity in southwest Missouri, including six of the vigilantes and seven nonvigilantes.[9] By comparison, the massive vigilance committees formed in San Francisco, California, in 1851 and 1856, the latter of which numbered roughly six thousand men, killed only four individuals each.[10]

Although often treated solely as a matter of local interest, the bloody history of the Bald Knobber organization informs a broader narrative of vigilante justice that has been a part of American history and culture from the beginning. It is a tradition literally older than the country itself. It goes back to the "Regulator" movements of colonial North Carolina and South Carolina, which became the first vigilante organizations in American history in the 1760s.[11]

The Carolina regulators, like all subsequent American vigilantes, drew inspiration from an idea: the belief that ordinary citizens—not judges, politicians, or policemen, but *ordinary* citizens—retain an inherent right to take direct action to enforce the law as they see fit. This remains one of the distinctive characteristics separating the United States from other nations. It is an idea that finds expression, not only in the historical record, but also in American artistic and literary life. From Owen Wister's western-themed novel *The Virginian*, to Clint Eastwood's *Dirty Harry* movies, to the modern-day *Avengers* film franchise created by Marvel comics, the American public's appetite for the so-called vigilante myth has been nearly insatiable.[12]

Nowhere else has this myth been so pervasive, or so enduring in its effects, than in the United States. Some historians have even gone so far as to describe vigilante justice and lynch-law as uniquely American phenomena,[13] though one need not agree with that contention to agree that no other people have so often indulged the impulse to take the law into their own hands. And certainly in no other nation has the practice persisted for so long.[14]

Recognition of this fact raises an obvious question: Why should this be so? Why should the United States, of all nations, have such a peculiar predilection for such *improvised* methods of dispensing justice? Part of the answer surely lies in American ideological convictions. "We are a rebellious nation," Rev. Theodore Parker once declared, "our whole history is treason . . . our creeds are infidelity to mother church; our constitution treason to our fatherland." That instinctive rebelliousness found its most cogent expression during the American Revolution, which firmly established the people's right to "alter or abolish" their forms of government. A nation so conceived must necessarily retain a strong regard for direct democracy, of which vigilantism is perhaps the most extreme form. Thus, in American history vigilante justice has always been inextricably linked to the concept of popular sovereignty, the conviction that the authority to create new forms and institutions of government rests ultimately with the people. It takes only a short logical step to extrapolate from that conviction the idea that the people have the right to short-circuit established institutions of government in the name of the public will.[15]

Vigilantism may also be a reflection of some ingrained American social values. The historian Richard Maxwell Brown has argued that American vigilantism is fundamentally a socially conservative phenomenon. The "prototypical" vigilance committee, in Brown's view, was committed to preserving respect for law, property rights, and social order. It also defended the three-tiered social hierarchy that he considered the basic structure of American society in the eighteenth and nineteenth centuries. This hierarchy consisted of an upper and middle level, from which vigilante groups usually drew their leadership and rank and file, respectively, and a lower level composed of marginal or alienated people who became the subjects of vigilante action.[16]

The classic example that Brown used to illustrate this thesis was the South Carolina Regulator movement of 1767–69, which grew out of the social turmoil and dislocation in the South Carolina backcountry following the Cherokee War in the early 1760s. Their members came primarily from the respectable, property-owning segment of backcountry society, including modest farmers, planters, and large or small slave owners, while their targets came from the margins of society, including the property-less, outlaws, and vagrants.[17] In these respects, Brown argued, the Regulators set the basic pattern for most subsequent vigilante groups to follow.[18]

On a more practical level, vigilantism was also a response to living conditions on the American frontier, where the regular institutions of law enforcement—the courts, judges, and police—could not always keep up with the furious pace of westward migration and settlement. In the absence of such institutions, American frontiersmen created various *ad hoc* organizations to perform the basic functions of law enforcement. During California's fabled "Gold Rush" of 1848–49, for example, residents of the mining camps set up *ad hoc* "popular tribunals" to administer summary justice to criminals who did not respect the lives and property of others.[19] Likewise, in nearby San Francisco the influx of gold-seeking immigrants in the early 1850s brought with it a burgeoning criminal population. As a result, the city's residents formed two enormous "Committees of Vigilance" in 1851 and again in 1856 to deal with the supposed crime wave. The first of these committees focused exclusively on ridding the city of its criminal element, particularly the so-called Sydney ducks, young male immigrants from the Australian penal colony. The second committee also combatted crime, but had a clear political component as well. It sought to destroy the corrupt political machine of local Democratic boss David C. Broderick, whom the vigilantes blamed for the murder of a local crusading journalist named James King of William.[20]

The San Francisco vigilance committees marked the beginning of a broad trend in which late-nineteenth-century Americans increasingly resorted to collective violence and vigilante justice to solve whatever problems they perceived in their communities. According to one influential study on American vigilantism, the years 1850 to 1889 witnessed the creation of nearly three-fourths of the largest vigilante organizations prior to the twentieth century.[21] In some instances, as in the cases mentioned above, vigilantism was the predictable response to unsettled, frontier-like conditions in areas where regular institutions of law enforcement either did not exist or were too weak to provide an effective crime deterrent. In Montana's Alder Gulch, for example, the discovery of gold in 1863 sparked a massive wave of prospectors into southwest Montana numbering in the thousands. With little formal law enforcement in place, large gangs of outlaws preyed on the weak and vulnerable until local residents formed vigilance committees in the bustling mining towns of Virginia City and Nevada City in late 1863. Within a short period, these groups unified into a single organization and spread throughout the Ruby River region of southwestern

Montana. They successfully purged the area of most outlaw activity, albeit at the cost of dozens of extralegal hangings.[22]

Nor was this type of activity restricted to the frontier, for often late-nineteenth-century Americans resorted to vigilante justice even in places where an established law enforcement apparatus was available. The reasons they might do so varied according to time and place, but Americans of that period had a variety of reasons for relying upon vigilante justice rather than the courts or the police. In some cases, for example, vigilante groups formed in response to the tremendous social turmoil that accompanied the Civil War. The war upset existing social, economic, political, and racial arrangements, which forced people in many parts of the country to create new ones. In the process, they invented extralegal organizations to apply violent solutions to problems they perceived in their society.

In the South, for example, the demise of slavery removed the central institution that had given structure to southern society. In response, many white southerners joined groups like the Ku Klux Klan to reassert white power and overthrow the reconstruction governments installed by the North in the former Confederate states.[23] The Klan's main goals were political—the restoration of southern "home rule" and white supremacy. Its use of violence and intimidation to achieve those goals make it at least as much a terrorist group as a vigilance committee.[24] At the same time, its members considered themselves vigilantes, and they defended their actions using the language of vigilantism. They defined their objectives as the suppression of crime, the projection of life and property, and the defense of the U.S. Constitution and all *constitutional* laws, meaning those laws with which they agreed.[25]

Just as the southern Klan used vigilante tactics to achieve its political ends, there were a variety of groups, particularly in the West, that resorted to vigilante justice for economic reasons as well. In the late nineteenth century, the West became the scene of a series of small, localized conflicts that one historian has called the "Western Civil War of Incorporation." This "war" pitted the supporters of industrialization, big business, and land consolidation against small landholders, cowboys, wage workers, and Native Americans, and both sides resorted to vigilante methods when it suited their purposes.[26]

In some episodes of this conflict, large cattle barons tried to drive out small ranchers, farmers, and homesteaders, either because they were suspected of cattle rustling or simply because the large ranchers wanted their land. This happened during Wyoming's infamous Johnson County War in 1892,[27] the "Fence Cutters War" in Texas from 1883 to 1884,[28] and again during a similar conflict in Custer County, Nebraska, from 1877 to 1878.[29] Other episodes centered on the issue of land consolidation by large corporations. In the 1870s, the Southern Pacific Railroad tried to use litigation to push settlers off of several thousand acres of land claimed by the railroad under a government land grant in the Mussel Slough district of central California. The settlers responded by adopting vigilante tactics to drive out railroad agents and anyone who supported the railroad's land claims, eventually resulting in a bloody gunfight between the pro-railroad and anti-railroad factions in 1880.[30]

While politics and economic considerations motivated many vigilante groups, a significant number drew inspiration from moral or religious concerns. In the late nineteenth century, the forces of modern industrial capitalism—big business, the railroads, timber and mining companies, and so forth—introduced a high degree of economic growth, personal mobility, and social instability to American society. These disruptive forces threw local economies into flux, and undermined traditional social relationships between employer and employee, church and congregant, parents and children. As a result, many people resorted to vigilante actions as a means of reasserting a sense of *control* over their lives by enforcing moral discipline in their societies. Political philosopher Michael Walzer examined a similar dynamic at work in sixteenth-century and seventeenth-century England. The English society that gave birth to Puritanism, writes Walzer, exhibited a high degree of economic growth, social mobility, and instability. The purpose of Puritan politics, therefore, was to "regain control of a changing world" by enforcing moral discipline on society.[31]

What Walzer's puritans did in sixteenth-century England, the "Regulators" did in the North Carolina backcountry in the 1760s. There a diverse coalition of disaffected farmers and religious dissenters combined to challenge the wealthy land speculators and corrupt government officials who exploited them. The North Carolina Regulators, as these agrarian radicals came to be known, drew inspiration from the religious legacy of the Great Awakening, which created an "insurgent climate" that gave small farmers the moral self-assurance necessary to challenge those in positions of authority. The Regulators especially objected to the gradual divergence of traditional Christian morality and the emerging capitalist order, and wanted to create a world where "morality and economics would not be separate."[32]

In the nineteenth century, one pervasive example of this type of moral "regulating" activity was the widespread "whitecapping" phenomenon. It began in southern Indiana in the 1880s and quickly spread to "the four corners of the nation."[33] Whitecapping took a variety of forms, depending on the location and context in which it occurred. In Mississippi, the whitecaps were mainly poor white farmers who persecuted black farm laborers to prevent economic competition.[34] In New Mexico, the whitecaps or *las gorras blancas* were poor Mexican ranchers who resisted the illegal enclosure of common grazing land by wealthy Anglo-American or Mexican landowners.[35]

In its original and most prevalent form, however, whitecapping was "a movement of violent moral regulation by local masked bands," aimed at punishing anyone who transgressed the moral standards of their community.[36] In the 1890s, for example, the whitecaps of Sevier County in eastern Tennessee became notorious for enforcing a stringent moral code on their neighbors, even whipping several women suspected of sexual promiscuity. This practice evoked much enmity toward the vigilantes among their neighbors, which sometimes spilled over into violent opposition.[37] Likewise, the whitecaps of Oklahoma's Indian Territory punished men and women suspected of such offenses as sexual immorality or drunkenness.[38]

In southern Indiana, where the first whitecap group originated, enforcing individual morality became the "overriding concern" of the vigilantes. The offenses they targeted included "neglect of family, wife or child beating, laziness, drunkenness, and improper conduct between men and women."[39] Significantly, the author of the only study on this group links the surge in vigilante activity in the 1880s to the completion of a major railroad line through the area in 1883. In a story remarkably similar to what transpired in the Ozarks around that time, the railroad abruptly drew the region's farmers into the wider commercial network of the United States. In the process, it brought crime and vice into their midst and undermined the economic independence that had previously characterized their lives. Thus, the "intensity of whitecapping in [southern Indiana]" was also a "reaction to the general unsettledness of the times."[40]

Compared to many of these other vigilante organizations, the Bald Knobbers have received relatively little attention from professional historians. This neglect may stem partly from the fact that the organization became the subject of popular fiction long before it received serious historical inquiry. As accounts of the Bald Knobbers circulated in newspapers across the country in the late 1880s, the commercial potential of selling stories about them became readily apparent. In 1887, a troupe of amateur actors based in the town of Sparta in Christian County began performing an eight-act drama titled "The Bald Knob Tragedy of Taney and Christian Counties." Newspaper advertisements for the play, which reportedly showed the history of the organization up to the Edens-Greene murders, touted its "startling situations, assassinations, whippings, secret workings of the clans, etc."[41]

In the early twentieth century, a number of popular novelists published books dealing with the Bald Knobbers. The best known of these writers was the hugely popular Harold Bell Wright. This minister-turned-author of romantic and religious fiction sold more than ten million copies of his books before his death in 1944.[42] Wright's best-selling 1907 novel *The Shepherd of the Hills*, set in the hills of Taney County, caricatured the Bald Knobbers as a gang of outlaws who defied the law and terrorized their neighbors. Their leader, a brutal and semi-animalistic figure named Wash Gibbs, served as the dramatic foil for the novel's main protagonist, a peaceful minister named Daniel Howitt.[43] After Wright's novel became a phenomenal best seller, other writers of popular fiction, including Clyde Edwin Tuck, Anna M. Doling, and Laura Johnson, published works that in one way or another used the Bald Knobbers or vigilante groups like them as cultural symbols of the Ozark region and the traits that the reading public associated with it: backwardness, lawlessness, and violence. More recently, Vonda Wilson Sheets's Bald Knobber–themed novel *Absolution* has continued to tap this rich vein of historical source material, though without some of the negative stereotypes peddled by earlier writers.[44]

The widespread popularity of this literature, especially Wright's *Shepherd*, had the fortuitous effect of promoting a surge in recreational tourism to the Missouri Ozarks, the place people around the nation called the "Shepherd of the Hills country."[45] It also made the Bald Knobbers, or at least an exaggerated caricature of the group, a recognizable symbol of the Ozarks for millions of Americans. So it was that when the Mabe family of Branson, Missouri, decided to open a hillbilly-themed music show in 1959, the name "Baldknobbers" seemed like a natural fit.[46] The popular image of the Bald Knobbers may also have tainted the group with the stigma of sensationalism and provincialism, causing some historians who might otherwise have written about the group to defer from doing so.

The earliest historical accounts of the Bald Knobbers came from men who had belonged to the vigilante order, journalists who covered them, and people who knew them. These contemporary writers usually took sides, either for the Bald Knobbers or against them. For example, Charles H. Groom and D. F. McConckey's 1887 pamphlet *The Bald Knobbers or Citizen's Committee of Taney and Christian Counties* painted a favorable picture of the vigilantes, which hardly seems surprising given that both men belonged to the organization. A. M. Haswell, who did not belong to the organization but knew many people who did, also described the Bald Knobbers as "honest, clean-handed, upstanding, men among men."[47] In the 1930s, Judge William L. Vandeventer, whose father belonged to the vigilantes, wrote a book titled *Justice in the Rough* that presented a mostly sympathetic picture of the Bald Knobbers, although it acknowledged many of their mistakes and crimes.[48] Accounts with a more anti-vigilante perspective include Robert Harper's *Among the Bald Knobbers* and a lengthy investigative exposé on the group published in the *New York Sun* in 1888.[49]

One common element in these early narratives is the theme of gradual decline. The Bald Knobbers, so the traditional story goes, began as an organization for the protection of life and property and the enforcement of social mores. Over time, however, men with less pure motives got into the group and used it for their own purposes. Members used the group to settle personal scores, to gain financial advantage over their neighbors, or to seek political office. According to Haswell, this state of affairs continued until the men who founded the movement "were disgusted to find that the organization which they had formed to drive out law breakers, had itself become a worse law breaker than those it had suppressed, and was rapidly leading to a far worse condition than existed in the beginning."[50] Likewise, Vandeventer wrote that over time men began joining the vigilantes "for the purpose of wreaking private vengeance." In time, the organization no longer confined "its activities to the punishment of law violators," but punished anyone who insulted or offended a member.[51]

There is much truth to the traditional version of the Bald Knobber story and some errors as well. The idea that new and unworthy men got into the organization and corrupted it from within does not square with the available evidence. Many of the most notorious acts attributed to the vigilantes, such as the killings of William Edens, Charles Greene, Andrew Coggburn, and Sam Snapp, involved senior members and leaders of the group. So the supposedly unworthy members were present within the organization from the beginning. Nevertheless, in other ways the *leitmotif* of gradual decline is basically accurate. The Bald Knobbers did eventually stray from their original goals of protecting life and property, and in many cases they used their power to pursue personal grievances and promote their own interests.

In the twentieth century, a second generation of writers without a personal connection to the vigilantes or their opponents began contributing to the literature on the subject. In 1939, Lucille Morris Upton, a journalist and longtime resident of southwest Missouri, published a narrative of the vigilante movement, entitled *Bald Knobbers*, which for many years became the standard work on the subject. Upton's book differed from previous accounts in that she attempted to maintain a neutral stance toward her subject, weighing the various pro-Bald Knobber and Anti-Bald Knobber versions of the story, while insisting that the truth lay somewhere in between. She also drew on a wider array of sources than previous accounts, doing considerable research in local newspapers and other materials.[52] A few years after Upton's book came out, Ozarks folklorist and humorist Vance Randolph penned a small pamphlet on the vigilantes under the pseudonym of Harvey Castleman. Randolph's offering, which he probably intended primarily for a popular audience, contained only a brief sketch of the Bald Knobber history and little original research.[53] Fifty years after Upton's work was published, Elmo Ingenthron, a local historian, schoolteacher, and former superintendent of Taney County's school system, collaborated with Mary Hartman to publish *Bald Knobbers: Vigilantes on the Ozarks Frontier*, the last full-length book on the subject. In their book, Hartman and Ingenthron drew on many of the same sources utilized by Upton, as well as additional research compiled over many years primarily by Ingenthron. This included an extensive body of oral history from "old-timers who either participated on one side or the other or who heard their elders discuss it."[54]

Despite relying on greater resources than their predecessors, the second generation of writers did not go very far beyond the earlier narratives in explaining the underlying causes and motivations behind the Bald Knobber organization and what drove them to take such extreme measures. They reiterated many of the established themes about the Ozarks vigilantes: gradual decline, new members causing corruption from within, and abuses of power leading to the eventual fall of the organization. Upton and Hartman and Ingenthron did observe a link between the Civil War and the events of the Bald Knobber period, but did not elaborate significantly on the nature of that connection.[55] Neither did they say much about how economic conditions, local politics, or religion contributed to the events they described. They also left unexamined many primary sources, including a large body of state and federal court cases, which contain much useful information on this topic. Finally, although both books contain bibliographies, they leave much of their source material undocumented so that it is not always possible to identify their sources.

In the twenty-five years following the release of Hartman and Ingenthron's book, no writer has attempted to recap the history of the Bald Knobbers in its entirety. A small number of historians, however, have contributed short articles and essays on the vigilantes or have dealt with the subject as part of larger treatments of the history of Missouri. For example, in his influential work, *Paths of Resistance*, David Thelen attempted to fit the Bald Knobbers into his broader narrative about how "traditional" Missourians opposed the "new order" of industrial capitalism, which threatened the traditional values of personal autonomy and family and communal ties that many of them held dear. The Bald Knobbers, he argued, depicted themselves "as alternatives to the new order's isolation and individualism."[56] Taking a different approach, local historians Lynn Morrow and Kristin Kalen contend that the Bald Knobbers actually functioned as agents of capitalism and economic modernization. In their view, the vigilantes constituted a "modernizing coalition," which assisted in the development of the local economy by driving out elements of society, particularly criminals, vagabonds, squatters, and open-range stock raisers, who represented an impediment to economic progress.[57]

Despite their different conclusions, the interpretations advanced by Thelen and by Kalen and Morrow both center on a socioeconomic interpretation of the Bald Knobber movement. Other historians have identified partisan politics, rather than economic factors, as the driving force behind the vigilantes' actions. In the fourth volume of the "History of Missouri" series published by the University of Missouri Press, Lawrence Christensen and Gary Kremer included a brief synopsis of the Bald Knobber story. While not denying the existence of other factors, they argued that the vigilantes in Taney County were part of a partisan bid by local Republicans to wrest control of the county government away from their Democratic adversaries.[58] Thomas Spencer expanded on this thesis in his contribution to an anthology of essays on Missouri social history. Spencer argued that the Bald Knobber controversy pitted a faction composed mostly of Republicans and former Unionists against Democrats and former Confederates. Indeed, "when one researches the organization more closely," Spencer asserted, "the entire episode appears to be much more about local politics and regional loyalties than about law and order."[59]

The interpretation advanced in this volume combines many aspects of the previous approaches to this topic, but is essentially different from any of them. First, in order to understand the Bald Knobber movement we must place it in the context of the Civil War and its aftermath in the Missouri Ozarks. The war shattered the social life of southwest Missouri, killing thousands, and touching off an epidemic of internecine violence that forced many more to flee the region. The war also helped create the conditions necessary for vigilante organizations like the Bald Knobbers to flourish by changing people's lives in three main ways. First, it left a legacy of bitterness and mistrust between supporters of the Union and the Confederacy, which continued to affect relations between the two groups for many years to come. Among the Bald Knobbers, Union veterans predominated, while most of those who opposed them had sided with the Confederacy. The war familiarized these men with the use of firearms and military tactics and left many of them with deep grudges against those who fought for the other side. Second, the war polarized the political culture of southwest Missouri, particularly in Taney County where the Bald Knobbers were founded, leading to bitter factional squabbles between Democrats and Republicans in much of the region. Third, the war spawned a surge in criminal activity, as well as an increased societal acceptance of vigilantism and violence as methods of solving problems and deterring crime. In the years following the war, a number of vigilance committees organized across Missouri to deal with the threat posed by ex-bushwhackers and bandits to law-abiding citizens. In southwest Missouri, these included organizations like the Regulators or "Honest Men's League" in Greene County, the Marmiton League in Vernon County, or the Anti-Horse Thief Association in several communities. These groups sought to cope with increased crime and the perceived ineffectiveness of local law enforcement officers in bringing outlaws to justice.[60] In so doing, they established a precedent that the Bald Knobbers would follow in the 1880s.

The second major contention advanced in this book concerns the fundamental distinction that existed between the original vigilance committee in Taney County and its counterparts in Christian and Douglas Counties. The Bald Knobbers in Taney County were an organization very much in line with Brown's prototype of a socially conservative vigilance committee. Their membership consisted of a diverse coalition of middle-class and upper-class men, including people from a variety of professions such as prosperous farmers and stock raisers, merchants, physicians, lawyers, and several politicians. They formed a vigilance committee in response to the perceived deficiencies of local law enforcement, a problem dramatized by a number of high-profile crimes such as the murder of James Everett in Forsyth on September 22, 1883, and the attempted murder of Mr. and Mrs. John T. Dickenson at Taneyville nearly two years later. As men of property and influence they also considered it their duty to promote the economic progress of their community and to encourage further settlement therein. This meant not only combating crime and lawlessness in their county, but also ending corruption in local government, which they identified with the cadre of Democratic officeholders that had governed the county for roughly the previous decade. Thus, the vigilantes had a clear political objective—overthrowing the Democratic courthouse ring—but their motives for doing so stemmed from a desire for social and economic progress rather than mere political partisanship.

The Bald Knobbers in Christian and Douglas Counties shared certain traits in common with the Taney County organization. The most significant of these was a high regard for social order, a willingness to use vigilante tactics to enforce order, and a desire to use the same tactics to advance their own self-interest. The differences between the two groups, however, often overshadowed the similarities. The Bald Knobbers in Christian and Douglas Counties, for example, had neither the social nor economic standing of their comrades to the south. They drew into their ranks mostly poor men, whose occupations were overwhelmingly agricultural. Roughly nine-tenths of the vigilantes in these counties practiced agriculture as their sole or primary occupation. Few of them held any kind of political office. They also differed from the Bald Knobbers in Taney County in terms of their objectives. Whereas the original vigilance committee championed economic progress and encouraged new immigration into their region, the vigilantes in Christian and Douglas Counties reacted to the inequities that such changes produced. They drove out homesteaders whose arrival threatened their access to land and resources from which they derived a livelihood. They attempted to coerce agents of the St. Louis–San Francisco Railroad into giving more favorable terms of employment to local tie hackers from whom they purchased railroad ties. The vigilantes in the two northern counties also emphasized what one might call moral regulation, the punishment of people who violated accepted social mores. Although moral regulation also took place in Taney County, it assumed greater importance in Christian and Douglas Counties. There the vigilantes cracked down on the proprietors of illegal saloons, brothels, and gambling dens, as well as individuals who violated their notions of moral behavior, including polygamists, adulterers, and men who abused or neglected their families. This aspect of Bald Knobber vigilantism grew out of an intensely devout evangelical Christianity that many of the members practiced. The leadership of the Christian County vigilantes included many ministers, lay ministers, and church members, who believed that by reforming the morals of their community they were doing God's work.

The distinctions made here between the two forms of Bald Knobberism that existed in Taney County and Christian and Douglas Counties are important for two reasons. First, they are critical to understanding the Bald Knobber movement as a whole. Many of the shortcomings of prior historical studies on the Bald Knobbers stem from the inability of previous writers to recognize this distinction, so that a generalization made about the vigilantes in Taney County may be perfectly valid, even though it may not accurately describe their counterparts in Christian and Douglas Counties. Second, the distinctions are important because they demonstrate the multifaceted nature of vigilantism as whole. The two groups discussed in this book used the same name, operated simultaneously, and inhabited roughly the same compact geographical area. Yet they exhibited such stark differences in their goals, tactics, and membership that it is sometimes difficult to see how they were considered part of the same group. That two such organizations could exist side by side demonstrates the inherent flexibility of vigilante justice, which could be adapted by any number of persons or groups to achieve objectives they could not accomplish through recourse to the ordinary methods of law enforcement.

## CHAPTER 1

# Southwest Missouri from Settlement to Civil War

The Bald Knobbers of southwest Missouri, like all other American vigilance committees, existed to serve the needs of a particular community, time, and place. It follows that a full understanding of the Bald Knobbers requires an analysis of the people and the land that gave rise to them. The area on which this book focuses—Taney, Christian, and Douglas Counties—comprises part of a region known to geographers as the White River Hills. These hills themselves constitute a subregion of a larger tristate area known as the Ozarks. Shaped somewhat like a parallelogram, the Ozarks consists of roughly 60,000 square miles of terrain in northern Arkansas, southern Missouri, and a small part of Oklahoma. It is a hard land that sometimes gives the appearance of being made for hard people. The dominant geographical characteristics of the Ozarks are its hilly landscape, including "greater relief and steeper slopes than surrounding areas," as well as a tough, rocky soil with large quantities of dolomite, limestone, flint, and chert. An abundance of karstic features, including springs, caves, and sinkholes, formed by the slow erosion of water through rock, also distinguish the Ozarks from neighboring regions.[1]

The White River Hills region consists of a long series of rocky hills and escarpments that envelop the upper portion of the White River. This river, which on the map looks somewhat like a fishhook,

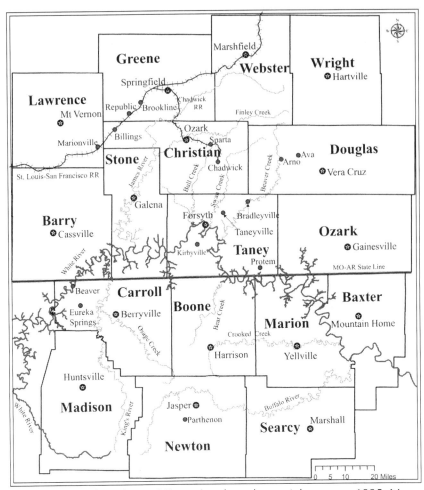

**Fig. 1.1:** Map of southwest Missouri and northwest Arkansas, c. 1885. Map by Dr. Jun Luo, Professor of Geography at Missouri State University.

begins in Madison County in northwest Arkansas and flows north through Barry, Stone, and Taney Counties in Missouri. Then it drops back down through northeast Arkansas and empties into the Mississippi River near the town of De Witt in Arkansas County. The White River's tributaries—including the James River, Finley River, Bull Creek, Swan Creek, Big Beaver Creek, and others—drain rain and groundwater from the surrounding hill country and provide the region with a plentiful source of water for both animals and people. The White River region is conspicuous for its long, narrow ridges and its prominent limestone buttes that jut sharply upward from the earth's surface to form small hills. Often lacking trees near the summit, these small hills are commonly referred to as "knobs" or "balds" (or sometimes "bald knobs").[2]

In 1682 the French explorer René-Robert Cavelier, known to history as the Sieur de La Salle, led an expedition down the length of the Mississippi River. On reaching the terminus of the Mississippi, La Salle and his companions held a formal ceremony on April 9, 1682, in which they claimed possession of the entire Mississippi River Valley, including *all the tributaries* of the Mississippi River, for King Louis XIV of France. La Salle named this new territory "Louisiana," in honor the French monarch. Since the White River emptied into the Mississippi this meant that the lands it traversed also became part of the new French province of Louisiana. Thus, without ever navigating the White River or setting foot in the Ozarks, the French claimed the whole region more than a century before any white settlement of the area had taken place.[3]

The French never did establish permanent settlements in the White River Hills, or any other part of the western Ozarks, primarily because of the area's metallurgical deficiencies. After establishing a permanent settlement at St. Genevieve in southeast Missouri around 1750, the French sent parties of *voyageurs* (i.e., trappers, traders, and woodsmen) into the Ozark hinterland to search for gold, silver, or other precious metals. Although the French found plenty of lead (often a strong indicator of silver deposits) they found no gold or silver. Thus, no white people settled permanently in this area under French rule, and this remained true after the French ceded the colony of Louisiana to Spain in 1762.[4]

Despite European pretensions to "ownership" of the Ozark hinterland, for most of the eighteenth century white people with any knowledge of the region referred to what became southwest Missouri and northwest Arkansas as "Osage Country." The name came from the Osage Indians, an offshoot of the Dhegian-Souian-speaking group that had moved out of the Ohio Valley into the trans-Mississippi region in the early seventeenth century, where they settled near the Missouri, Osage, and Arkansas Rivers. A proud and militant people, the Osage dominated a territory that "was generally considered to be that great body of land embracing the Ozark Plateau."[5]

As the traditional enemies of the Iroquois, the Osage had fought a long and ultimately unsuccessful war to prevent the Iroquois from moving into the Osage's previous homeland in present-day Kentucky. By the early nineteenth century almost all of the Osage had relocated west of the Mississippi River. A small contingent of the tribe made their way up the White River and settled in northwest Arkansas, southwest Missouri, and eastern Oklahoma, while a much larger group followed the Missouri and Osage Rivers and settled in central-western Missouri. The Osage tribe's dominance of the Ozarks did not last long, however. In 1803 the United States purchased the entire Louisiana territory from France. Five years later in 1808 the U.S. Government forced the Osage to sign a treaty ceding control of all of their territory east of a line running from Fort Osage near the Missouri River all the way south to the Arkansas River. This treaty opened up most of the Osage tribe's once vast domain to white settlement.[6]

Although the Osage had officially relinquished control of this territory to the whites, for many years afterward they continued to hunt game east of the line established by the 1808 treaty. These forays brought them into occasional conflict with white settlers moving into the region. In response to white protests, the Osage argued that they had given up only their land, not their hunting rights. Still, in the 1820s and 1830s the federal government gradually compelled the Osage to relinquish control of their remaining territory in the Ozarks and move to reservation land in Kansas.[7]

As the Osage and other Native American tribes slowly moved out of the Ozarks white settlers began to supplant them. In the first decade of the nineteenth century small bands of white Americans gradually moved up the White River planting settlements as they went. One of the first groups to settle in the White River Hills was the famous Coker clan, led by the enterprising pioneer William "Buck" Coker. In the 1630s the Coker family emigrated from County Cork in southern Ireland, and by 1635 they had arrived in Surry County, Virginia, where some of them prospered as tobacco growers. By the late eighteenth century many of them had made their way to present-day Montgomery County, Alabama. Between 1811 and 1815, William Coker led a convoy of his relatives up the White River into the area that became Boone and Marion Counties in Arkansas. In the ensuing years several of William Coker's descendants moved into present-day Taney County and other parts of southwest Missouri.[8]

The first white settlers in southwest Missouri, however, most likely consisted of a group led by John P. Pettijohn, a Revolutionary War veteran born in Virginia. In the early 1800s Pettijohn and his family had settled in Ohio, but in 1818 they decided to leave the Buckeye State and try their luck farther west. After he had lived in Arkansas for a few years, wanderlust again afflicted John Pettijohn. In 1822 he led a small expedition of some two dozen people, including his family and some close friends. They set off by keelboat on a voyage up the White River into present-day southwest Missouri, a land Pettijohn described as flowing with "milk and honey," by which he meant the frontier equivalent: buffalo marrow and bear's grease.[9] Pettijohn and his family settled near the banks of the James River close to the county line between modern Christian and Greene Counties.[10]

Almost as soon as white settlement of southwest Missouri had commenced, however, the process came to an abrupt halt with the arrival of about five hundred members of the Delaware Tribe in the autumn of 1822. In an unusual twist of fate, the Delaware informed the bewildered white residents that they must abandon their new homes because the federal government had given the tribe most of southwest Missouri as a reservation. Not satisfied with this explanation, the whites sent one of their own, Thomas Patterson, to the federal land office in St. Louis to serve as their representative and to inquire as to the validity of the Indians' claim. When Patterson returned he reported that the Indians spoke the truth. As a result, almost all the white settlers who had arrived in the region up to that point departed. The Delaware did allow a few white men, such as the frontier traders William Gillis and James Wilson, to remain among them, either because they rented land from the Indians, sold them valuable goods, or because they had married Indian women. For the next eight years the Delaware Indians remained in possession of their new lands in southwest Missouri. However, in 1830 the U.S. Congress, in response to pressure from white Missourians, changed its mind and ordered the Delaware Indians to move to a new reservation farther west. Despite the capriciousness of this order, the Delaware promptly complied.[11]

The removal of the Delaware signaled the beginning of a new influx of white settlers into the region, including some (like John Pettijohn and his family) who had left the region eight years earlier in order to make way for the Delaware.[12] Other families arriving in southwest Missouri in the years after 1830 would later play key roles in the tumultuous events of the 1880s. For example, in the early 1840s several members of the Layton family of Spotsylvania County, Virginia, arrived in the area. The family patriarch, Horace Layton, had made the family prosperous operating a freight company in eastern Virginia. After his death in 1841 his sons—Charles, John, and Thomas F. Layton—and their families, moved to Greene County, Missouri. As Ozarks pioneers, the Laytons stood out both for their considerable wealth and because they brought with them a few slaves. During the Civil War many of the Laytons, including Thomas F. Layton and his wife, Julia, moved from Greene County to Taney County. Their son, Thomas A. Layton, would become a staunch Anti-Bald Knobber.[13]

Around the same time that the Layton Family arrived in Greene County, Harrison Snapp came to Taney County. Born in 1812 in Rockingham County, Virginia, Harrison Snapp moved to Missouri in 1839 with three of his brothers: Madison, Peachy, and Alexander Snapp. Harrison's brothers ended up living in other parts of Missouri, while he alone settled in Taney County. There he became a substantial landowner. In January 1849, he purchased from the U.S. General Land Office four land patents, totaling roughly 160 acres, on the banks of the White River, followed by two more patents in April 1849 and July 1852 for seventy-one and thirty-four acres, respectively.[14] Snapp married twice and raised nine children. Three of his sons—David J., Lafayette D., and Andrew J. Snapp—fought in the Confederate army. One of his younger sons, Samuel H. Snapp, would die at the hands of the Bald Knobber George Washington Middleton in 1886.[15]

Andrew J. Coggburn, a friend of Samuel Snapp, also met a violent end during the turbulent days of the Bald Knobber strife in the 1880s. His grandparents, James and Jane Coggburn, knew nothing of that when they left their home in Roane County, Tennessee, to seek a new life in Missouri sometime in the early 1840s. By 1845 they had settled in Miller County in central Missouri, where in 1856 James Coggburn purchased a land patent for forty acres. The couple raised a family of ten children, eight of whom accompanied them when they relocated to Taney County in 1865. That year one of their sons, James A. Coggburn, married a Taney County woman named Frances S. Springer, who gave birth to three sons, including the ill-fated Andrew in 1866. James Coggburn did not get to see his children reach adulthood, because in the late 1870s he volunteered to serve as a deputy sheriff of Taney County. In 1879, he led a posse down Bee Creek near the Missouri-Arkansas border in search of a group of horse thieves. When they overtook the thieves, a gunfight ensued in which Coggburn and one other lawman lost their lives.[16]

Aside from their obvious significance as pioneers and trailblazing settlers, families like the Cokers, Pettijohns, Laytons, Coggburns, and Snapps represented a *type* of settler most commonly seen in the early stages of white settlement in the Ozarks. One writer has observed that the "settlement of the Ozarks progressed in three phases." The first phase, the "Old Ozarks Frontier," lasted roughly from the colonial period to the Civil War, with the great bulk of white settlers arriving after the Louisiana Purchase in 1803. This wave of emigrants came overwhelmingly from the upper South—places like Tennessee, Kentucky, North Carolina, and Virginia. Many of these southern emigrants were of Scotch-Irish descent (i.e., Irish Protestants), and most of them were "of the yeoman farmer type, mainly poor, [and] non-slaveholders."[17]

The figures collected for the 1860 and 1870 U.S. Census counts reinforce these observations. For example, in 1870, the first year in which the census office compiled this sort of information, more than thirty-eight hundred residents of Christian, Taney, and Douglas Counties—the future bastions of the Bald Knobber movement—listed the upper South states of Tennessee, Virginia (including West Virginia), and Kentucky as their place of birth. These people represented more than one-quarter of the total population of these counties and by far the largest bloc of those residents not born in Missouri.[18]

The vast majority of people settling in these counties came from poor farm families that relied upon agriculture for their livelihood. Indeed, the 1860 census recorded that only eighty-six people living in Christian, Douglas, and Taney Counties worked in "manufacturing,"

Table 1.1: 1870 Nativity Statistics for Christian, Taney, and Douglas Counties

| County | Born in Missouri (Percent) | Slave States | | | Percent of Non-MO Residents from These Slave States | Free States | | Percent of Non-MO Residents from These Free States | Total Pop. |
| | | W. Virginia & Virginia | Tennessee | Kentucky | | Illinois | Ohio | | |
|---|---|---|---|---|---|---|---|---|---|
| Christian | 3,511 (53%) | 209 | 1,510 | 280 | 63% | 169 | 188 | 11.0% | 6,670 |
| Taney | 2,204 (50%) | 145 | 575 | 216 | 43% | 275 | 121 | 18.0% | 4,385 |
| Douglas | 2,353 (60%) | 71 | 555 | 193 | 53% | 138 | 10 | 9.5% | 3905 |

Source: 1870 U.S. Census

a term that often referred to such occupations as blacksmithing or operating a gristmill or a sawmill.[19] Although some of the remainder worked as shopkeepers, doctors, lawyers, and the like, the majority would have made a living through tilling the soil or stock raising. In 1860, farmers in Christian, Douglas, and Taney Counties grew mainly food staples, including large quantities of corn, wheat, oats, Irish potatoes, and sweet potatoes. Likewise, the stock raisers in these three counties raised substantial herds of dairy cows, beef cattle, sheep, oxen, and especially hogs. As a matter of fact, in 1860 the number of hogs in these counties—approximately thirty thousand—outnumbered the human inhabitants by a ratio of nearly three to one.[20]

A small farmer could make a decent life for himself through farming or raising stock in southwest Missouri, but he probably would not become rich. In a region where the vast majority of farmers owned between ten and ninety-nine acres of land, and none owned more than five hundred acres, traditional husbandry and pastoral pursuits would typically provide enough to live on and not very much else.[21] To supplement their meager incomes, not to mention their meager *diets*, many Ozark Missourians turned to the traditional expedients of hunting and fishing. They discovered that the natural wealth of the Ozark hill country offered a wide variety of fish and game. In the early 1800s small herds of buffalo, sometimes numbering sixty or more, could still be found in the region, as could black bears in much greater numbers. Bears were prized for their pelts, which could be sold, and for their savory meat. A hunter could render bear fat into lard or "bear's grease," which was useful for cooking and as a lubricant, while the fatty meat about the stomach could be cut into strips and cooked as "bear bacon," which some considered a delicacy.[22]

The region's many rivers, streams, and creeks held an abundance of fish—trout, bass, carp, catfish, buffalo fish, suckers, and so on—which required fishermen to use a variety of fishing methods beyond the traditional pole, line, and fishing hook. Some Ozarkers became experts at the art of "gigging," or spearfishing, for which they made one, three, or even five-pronged spears, or "gigs." Others learned how to hunt fish with bows and arrows, a pastime referred to as "bowin' and spikin'." Still others built wooden fish traps that they placed in narrow shoals or streams to trap larger fish for the fisherman to collect later. But perhaps the most adventurous fishing method was "noodling," which involved wading into a stream or creek looking for the crevices beneath large rocks or fallen timbers in which large catfish were known to lurk. When the "noodler" found a promising hole, he would stick his hand down in it, hoping to entice the catfish to bite his hand or fingers, after which he would drag the fish out by hand.[23]

The poverty of southwest Missouri manifested itself in other ways as well. For example, it impacted public expenditures on services like education. In 1858 teachers in Douglas County and Taney County earned less than half the average yearly pay for teachers in Missouri of roughly $115.[24] It also affected labor relations, particularly in the relative scarcity of slaves in southwest Missouri as compared to the rest of Missouri and the southern United States. Despite their heavy reliance on agriculture, most southwest Missourians earned their daily bread without the assistance of slaves. In 1860 only about 3,900 slaves lived in a twelve-county area stretching across the southwestern corner of the state, or roughly 5 percent of the 78,000 people living there. Moreover, more than 40 percent of these slaves (1,668) lived in Greene County, easily the wealthiest county in all of southwest Missouri and home to the city of Springfield, the commercial center of the Ozarks region. More typical of the Ozarks in this respect were Christian, Taney, and Douglas Counties. Christian County had only 229 slaves in 1860 (4.4 percent of its population), while Taney County had 82 slaves (2.3 percent), and Douglas County had none at all.[25]

The scarcity of slaves in this area stemmed from a variety of factors, including the relative poverty of most of the early settlers and

Table 1.2: Slaves in Southwest Missouri in 1860

| County | Total Slaves | Total Population | Percent Slaves |
|---|---|---|---|
| Jasper | 335 | 6,883 | 4.9% |
| Newton | 426 | 9,319 | 4.6% |
| McDonald | 72 | 4,038 | 1.8% |
| Dade | 346 | 7,072 | 4.9% |
| Lawrence | 284 | 8,846 | 3.2% |
| Barry | 247 | 7,995 | 3.1% |
| Greene | 1,668 | 13,186 | 12.6% |
| Christian | 229 | 5,491 | 4.2% |
| Stone | 16 | 2,400 | 0.7% |
| Taney | 82 | 3,576 | 2.3% |
| Webster | 220 | 7,099 | 3.1% |
| Douglas | 0 | 2,414 | 0.0% |
| Total Figures | 3,925 | 78,319 | 5.0% |

Source: 1860 U.S. Census

the absence of most of the crops that ordinarily involved the use of slave labor. Farmers in Christian, Taney, and Douglas Counties grew no hemp and ginned no cotton in 1860. They did grow modest quantities of tobacco, but probably just enough for local consumption.[26]

Given the social and economic characteristics of the early settlements of southwest Missouri—the settlers' sturdy yeoman heritage, their upper South backgrounds, and the scarcity of slaves among them—it hardly comes as a surprise that they took a cautious view of the sectional crisis that confronted the nation in 1860-61. No less an authority on political matters than Abraham Lincoln observed that the secession issue had divided Missourians into a bewildering array of camps. As Lincoln put it, even pro-Union Missourians broke down into at least four groups: "those who are for the Union with, but not without, slavery; those for it without, but not with; those for it with or without, but prefer it with; and those for it with but prefer it without."[27] Perhaps because they understood their own deep divisions on the subject, most Missourians preferred to remain neutral as long as possible. As one contemporary observer put it, they believed that they should "do nothing to bring on a war, and should do nothing to help it along should one break out."[28]

Missourians had three separate opportunities to voice their opinion on sectional issues at the ballot box: the state gubernatorial election held in August 1860, the November 1860 presidential election, and a special election held in February 1861, to choose delegates to a state convention to consider the issue of secession.[29] Each time the people of southwest Missouri joined the majority in expressing their preference for moderation and preserving the Union. Missouri's gubernatorial election held in August 1860 pitted a pair of Democrats, Claiborne Fox Jackson and Hancock Jackson, against a Republican, James B. Gardenhire, and an independent, Sample Orr. During this election the Missouri Democratic Party split between the supporters of Stephen Douglas, who favored sectional conciliation and compromise, and the supporters of John C. Breckinridge, who took a much harder, pro-southern position on sectional issues. At first, Claiborne Fox Jackson, the Democratic front-runner, attempted to straddle the fence between the Douglas and Breckinridge camps within his party. When he had to choose a side, however, he shrewdly picked the Douglas Democrats, the stronger of the two factions. Thereafter, the Breckinridge men backed Hancock Jackson. Thus, even though Claiborne Fox Jackson would become an ardent secessionist following his inauguration as governor, in the 1860 gubernatorial race most voters considered him the "moderate" Democratic candidate.[30]

As it turned out, the main opposition to Jackson's candidacy came not from his fellow Democrat, nor even the Republican Gardenhire, but rather Sample Orr. A little-known probate judge from Greene County, Orr began his campaign as an independent. Later he received the endorsement of Missouri's nascent Constitutional Union Party when the party's original nominee declined to run. Orr did not look the part of a politician. One contemporary described him as a slightly built man of medium height and weight with freckles and a shock of bright red hair that complimented "keen blue eyes, white eyelashes, nervous, short step, sloping shoulders, long neck—another Icabod Crane." His opponents mockingly referred to him as "nobody's nominee" and "one of the ugliest men in the state of Missouri." Orr astonished his critics by waging a vigorous campaign across the state in which he fiercely proclaimed his uncompromising loyalty to the Union. He finished second in the race with 65,583 votes to Claiborne Fox Jackson's 74,446 votes. Hancock Jackson and Gardenhire finished a distant third and fourth place with 11,415 votes and 6,135 votes, respectively.[31] Orr did even better in southwest Missouri, where he carried several counties, including his native Greene County, which he won by 835 votes over Claiborne Fox Jackson, as well as Christian, Lawrence, and Ozark Counties by somewhat smaller margins. He did

Table 1.3: 1860 Presidential Election in Southwest Missouri

| County | Douglas | Bell | Breckinridge | Lincoln |
|---|---|---|---|---|
| Barry | 257 | 333 | 286 | 1 |
| Christian | 120 | 342 | 308 | 0 |
| Dade | 283 | 406 | 305 | 8 |
| Douglas* | 0 | 0 | 0 | 0 |
| Greene | 298 | 986 | 414 | 42 |
| Jasper | 407 | 424 | 192 | 38 |
| Lawrence | 138 | 445 | 516 | 59 |
| McDonald | 206 | 138 | 194 | 3 |
| Newton | 654 | 406 | 255 | 22 |
| Stone | 83 | 31 | 112 | 0 |
| Taney | 97 | 43 | 287 | 0 |
| Webster | 172 | 335 | 376 | 7 |
| Totals | 2,715 | 3,889 | 3,245 | 180 |

* No votes recorded for Douglas County.

Source: Goodspeed's *History of Southeast Missouri, 1888*

lose Stone and Taney Counties, but even there the Breckinridge supporter Hancock Jackson failed to finish anywhere near the lead. These results demonstrated the inherent conservatism of the people of southwest Missouri, who preferred moderate unionism or even uncompromising unionism to anything that smacked of disunion.[32]

The 1860 presidential election featured a four-way contest between the northern Democrat Stephen Douglas, the southern Democrat John C. Breckinridge, the Republican Abraham Lincoln, and the Constitutional Union Party candidate John Bell.

Once again Missouri voters spoke strongly in favor of the candidates who represented unionism and sectional conciliation. They gave Douglas a narrow victory over Bell, with 58,801 votes to Bell's 58,372 votes, with Breckinridge and Lincoln pulling up the rear at 31,317 votes and 17,028 votes, respectively.[33] Once again, the votes in southwest Missouri closely paralleled the statewide results. The election returns for a twelve-county swath stretching from Jasper, Newton, and McDonald to Webster, Douglas, and Taney Counties, show that Bell won five of those counties while Douglas won two. Breckinridge won four of those counties, but only in Taney did he win an outright majority. Together, Bell and Douglas finished with 6,604 votes, or nearly two-thirds of the 10,029 votes cast in these counties.[34]

On January 3, 1861, Gov. Claiborne Fox Jackson took the oath of office. Just two weeks prior South Carolina had seceded from the Union, an action that would precipitate the secession of six more southern states by February 1. Reacting to these events, Jackson recommended that the Missouri General Assembly call a state convention to consider what course of action Missouri should take, possibly including secession. The General Assembly approved his request, and on February 18 Missourians went to the polls to elect delegates. The election resulted in a lopsided victory for Missouri's unionists. Candidates who ran as either "conditional" or "unconditional" unionists received roughly 110,000 out of 140,000 votes cast, while secessionist or "states' rights" candidates received the remainder.[35] In southwest Missouri the unionist forces did even better. For example, in Missouri's Nineteenth Congressional District (comprising Greene, Christian, Stone, Taney, and Webster Counties) no secessionist candidates appeared on the ballot. Instead, a slate of three unconditional unionist delegates led by Sample Orr trounced a slate of conditional unionists. The unconditional unionists received between 3,316 and 3,430 votes each, while the conditional unionists received between 775 and 859 votes each.[36]

As the preceding elections returns suggest, the people of southwest Missouri desperately wanted to avoid the outbreak of hostilities between the North and South. They must have known, given their precarious position at the southern boundary of a border state, that war would mean special hardships for them. And so it did, even though southwest Missouri did not witness many formal battles between large numbers of combatants; the few that did occur involved at most a few thousand men. For example, on July 5, 1861, a brigade of German-American troops under the command of Col. Franz Sigel attempted to cut off the retreat of roughly 4,000 Missouri State Guardsmen under the command of Gov. Claiborne Fox Jackson, who had recently fled the state capital at Jefferson City in advance of Brig. Gen. Nathaniel Lyon's Union army. In a closely fought contest near the town of Carthage in Jasper County, Jackson's men defeated the much smaller Union force, and continued their retreat southward.[37] About a month later a Confederate army of roughly 10,000 men under the command of Gen. Sterling Price and Brig. Gen. Benjamin McCulloch moved into southwest Missouri from Arkansas with the intention of capturing Springfield, and then recapturing the state capital. On August 10 General Lyon, with a force of about 5,400 men, launched a surprise attack on the rebel army at Wilson's Creek near the county line between Greene and Christian Counties. The Confederates repelled the attack, and later occupied Springfield, but sustained such heavy casualties (roughly 12 percent of their total force) that they could not follow up their victory, and soon lost the territory they had gained.[38]

The last major Confederate incursion into southwest Missouri came in the winter of 1862–63. Following the rebel defeat at the Battle of Prairie Grove in Arkansas (December 7, 1862), Lt. Gen. Theophilus Holmes ordered a general withdrawal of Confederate forces south of the Arkansas River. At the same time, he ordered Brig. Gen. John S. Marmaduke to lead a cavalry expedition into Missouri to threaten Union supply and communication lines, thereby providing cover for the Confederate withdrawal. Marmaduke's command of about 2,000 cavalrymen crossed the Missouri-Arkansas border on December 31, 1862, and proceeded north through Taney, Christian, and Greene Counties. They destroyed a small Union outpost at Ozark on January 7. The following day Marmaduke attempted to capture the important federal fortifications and supply depot at Springfield, but Brig. Gen. E. B. Brown and the city's garrison successfully defended the city. Marmaduke's men withdrew west through Webster and Wright Counties, and fought a minor battle near the town of Hartville before returning to Arkansas.[39]

Marmaduke's defeat at the Battle of Springfield and retreat into Arkansas assured Union military hegemony in southwest Missouri for the duration of the war. Indeed, with the exception of Gen. Sterling Price's brief and ill-fated incursion into Missouri in the fall of 1864, the Confederacy never again seriously challenged the Union for control in any part of the state. The Union triumph did not, however, end the *guerrilla* warfare in the Show-Me State. Indeed, the long, bitter, and intensely personal conflict between unionists and rebels continued and intensified in the second half of the war.

Civil War historians have already given ample attention to the phenomenon of guerrilla warfare in Missouri, and it would serve no purpose to try to revise or improve upon that work.[40] For two reasons, however, this study does require some general observations about the nature of guerrilla warfare in southwest Missouri. First, most studies of the guerrilla warfare in Missouri have tended to focus on the central-western part of the state, particularly the western counties bordering Kansas such as Jackson, Cass, Bates, and Vernon. This was the area subjected to the infamous General Order Number 11 requiring the removal of most of the civilian inhabitants. For years afterward people referred to it as the "Burnt District" because of the plundering and despoiling that occurred during the war.[41] Historians rightly emphasize this area because it was the main hotbed of the Confederate guerrilla activity in the state, and the home turf of many of the war's most legendary (or infamous) characters: William C. Quantrill and William "Bloody Bill" Anderson. Nevertheless, partisan violence characterized the war in southwest Missouri just as much as in west-central Missouri.

Second, for many members of the Bald Knobber movement, and their Anti-Bald Knobber opponents, the Civil War constituted the seminal event of their lives. Twelve of the forty-two Taney County Bald Knobbers who can be identified by name fought for the Union in some capacity.[42] Furthermore, a number of senior leaders of the Bald Knobbers, men like Capt. Madison Day of the Fourteenth Missouri State Militia Cavalry and Alexander C. Kissee of the Seventy-Second Enrolled Missouri Militia, fought in militia units that spent most of their time fighting Confederate guerrillas. By contrast, those Anti-Bald Knobbers old enough to have served during the Civil War usually sided with the South. Some of them may have fought as guerrillas, while others enlisted in conventional units. Moreover, the younger men in both the Bald Knobber and Anti-Bald Knobber camps often had relatives who had served in the war.[43]

Whereas in other parts of the country political ideology and patriotic sentiment often motivated military service, for the men engaged in guerrilla warfare on both sides of the conflict in the Missouri Ozarks, revenge and plunder served as the primary motivations. In war-torn southwest Missouri, where employment and economic opportunities were scarce, service in one of the many small "independent companies" often seemed a good way to make a living. The soldiers who fought this kind of war went by diverse and (often) interchangeable names.[44] On the rebel side these unconventional soldiers commonly referred to themselves as "guerrillas," while their enemies often called them "bushwhackers." The rebels commonly called irregular Union troops "jayhawkers," a term usually used to refer to the Kansas militiamen who made raids into Missouri, but sometimes applied to other Union troops as well. The closest Union equivalents of the guerrillas were the so-called Mountain Feds. These small bands of Union sympathizers, usually few in number, roamed the hills of southern Missouri and northern Arkansas wreaking vengeance on their enemies. Most of the anti-guerrilla fighting fell to the Provisional Enrolled Missouri Militia, a sort of auxiliary to the regular Union army tasked with guarding supply lines and important military installations and hunting down guerrilla units.[45] By whatever name they went, these irregular fighting units killed and plundered wherever they went.

Faced with the widespread violence and dislocation that attended the war, the ordinary civil authorities quickly found themselves unable to cope with the problems of law enforcement. Consequently, the U.S. Army's provost marshal system stepped in to fill the gap and became "the basic police power within the state."[46] Thus, the provost marshal papers for Missouri contain numerous examples of the pilfering nature of guerrilla warfare. In March 1862 Union loyalist Thomas Baker of Christian County received a visit from a party of twelve guerrillas including William Reed, whom the U.S. military later captured. The guerrillas confiscated two of Baker's horses. Next they raided his corncrib and forced him to give them some meat and flour for their supper. After finishing their meal, one of the men took a mare belonging to Baker and rode away. The rest stayed at Baker's house overnight and forced him to prepare their dinner and serve them. While there they candidly informed him that they were "not in the service of the C.S.A." Instead, they had formed an independent company and "paid themselves in property taken from Union men."[47]

Horse theft represented the most common type of property crime in southwest Missouri during the Civil War, mostly because bandits found horses easy to steal and easy to exchange for cash or other goods. The war left many parts of southwest Missouri virtually depopulated of horses. For example, the U.S. Census Office reported that Taney and Ozark Counties had more than 1,600 and 900 horses, respectively. By 1867, however, a report by Missouri's commissioner of statistics found only 548 and 298 horses in these counties. These and neighboring counties suffered similar declines in other forms of livestock as well.[48]

The lawless bands of armed men who roamed the countryside during this period stole anything small enough and light enough to carry away by hand, horse, or wagon. The case of Nelson Burkhart, a prosperous farmer from Christian County, illustrates the rapaciousness of the guerrilla bands operating in that part of the country. Shortly after the war ended, Burkhart brought suit against several dozen men, beginning with one Samuel Miller. According to Burkhart, these men, ostensibly a Confederate raiding party led by Miller, came to his home in September 1862. They seized Burkhart, beat him severely, and then carried off or destroyed a huge amount of property, which he claimed amounted to $75,000. Burkhart's lawsuit lists an impressive variety of goods stolen or destroyed. A partial list of the damages found in the court records included the following:

> One iron gray mare of the value of two hundred (200) dollars, one bay horse of the value of one hundred and fifty dollars, three mules worth six hundred dollars, one wagon and gearing of the value of one hundred and fifty dollars, bed clothing of the value of fifty dollars, seventy-five head of cattle of the value of fifteen-hundred dollars, forty head of sheep worth one hundred and twenty dollars, [an article] of leather of the value of fifty dollars, stove vessels of the value of five dollars, corn of the value of one hundred dollars, hay of the value of fifty dollars, oats of the value of one hundred dollars, fruit of the value of two hundred dollars, and destroyed an orchard of fruit trees worth ten thousand dollars, destroyed shade trees in the yard worth two thousand dollars, 44 head of cattle worth 800 dollars, household furniture and goods of the value of fifteen hundred dollars. Also [the defendants] did burn and destroy [the] blacksmith shop and tools worth . . . three hundred dollars and dwelling house of the value of two thousand dollars, [and] also other houses of the value of three thousand dollars.[49]

As the preceding examples indicate, Missouri's Civil War guerrilla fighters would steal anything of value from anyone. Since the

Union army prevailed in the war, it comes as no surprise that most of the cases that the provost marshal system or the civil courts handled stemmed from complaints made by Union sympathizers. Sufficient evidence exists, however, to show that Missouri's pro-Union fighting men could behave with as much avarice and callousness as their rebel counterparts.

In January 1863, Mrs. L. A. Vance of Taney County received an unwelcome visit from three federal cavalrymen who asked to see her husband. She told them that her husband had gone to Arkansas, although she did not specify why he left (which might indicate that he served in the rebel army or an independent company). After a while, two of the three soldiers left. The one that remained offered her money to have sex with him. When she refused, he attacked her, choked her severely, then raped her, despite the presence of her child in the room. After the attack, Mrs. Vance sought refuge and solace at a neighbor's house. When she returned home the next morning she discovered, to her horror, that her attacker had robbed her, and that "everything I had had been carried off."[50]

In addition to cases involving obvious abuse and theft, many of the Union outrages upon rebel sympathizers were cloaked in a veneer of legality. In wartime Missouri, Union authorities could find any number of legal excuses to confiscate the property of those who supported the Confederacy. For example, during the war pro-Union bankers foreclosed on the estates of thousands of individuals who had signed promissory notes for loans from state banks intended to fund Confederate military units in Missouri. The state government under Gov. Claiborne Fox Jackson had wanted to use these funds to wage war against the federal government. When Jackson's government fell in June 1862, however, a wave of foreclosures commenced. The property confiscated in this manner eventually amounted to more than 350,000 acres of land, most of which the banks disposed of at sheriff's auctions.[51]

Another common method of expropriation of property was to force southerners to sign bonds to ensure loyal behavior in the future. If federal authorities caught or even suspected a person of rendering a service to the rebel soldiers or guerrillas, they could force him or her to sign a "loyalty oath." These oaths pledged the oath taker to support the Union, abstain from disloyal behavior, and inform federal officials of "any hostile movement, gathering, or conspiracy" against the government of the United States. Often they contained a clause pledging the oath taker to remain in a particular area for the duration of hostilities.[52] As security for these oaths, those who took them had to sign a bond in which they agreed that federal authorities could seize a portion of their property (usually between $1,000 and $2,000) if they violated their oaths. Since many people did not have enough property to cover the amount stipulated in their bonds, they often had to ask friends, neighbors, or relatives to co-sign their bonds, which made the co-signer's property also liable to seizure.

The case of Thomas F. Layton of Greene County illustrates how easily southern sympathizers could lose their property under the loyalty oath system. In February 1862 Thomas F. Layton, father of the future Anti-Bald Knobber leader, Thomas A. Layton, left his home in Springfield, Missouri, with Gen. Sterling Price and his retreating Confederate army. Although Layton claimed that he never formally belonged to the rebel army, he admitted that he "participated with them at the Battle of Pea Ridge" in Arkansas (March 7–8, 1862) where Union forces captured him. After spending a couple of months at a federal prison in Alton, Illinois, Layton secured his release by taking a loyalty oath and signing a bond in the amount of $1,000. He then returned home to Springfield.[53]

Shortly after Layton returned home, federal authorities arrested him again. They alleged that he had sheltered rebel soldiers in his home and tried to send one of his two slaves, a black woman named Sally, south to rebel territory. Layton vigorously denied both of these allegations. His wife, Julia, and their houseguest at that time, Julia's sister Cordelia Richards, both swore out statements in support of his denial. However, Mrs. Layton's testimony does indicate that the Laytons feared that Sally might run away with her husband, who was most likely a free black man living nearby.[54]

We do not know whether the Layton family was guilty of the specific offenses charged to them or if the government actually expropriated their property. Their family history, however, suggests that they continued to assist the rebel cause covertly from Springfield, with Julia Layton and Cordelia Richards making trips across Union lines at Forsyth carrying badly needed supplies to the Missouri troops in Arkansas, including horseshoe iron and "dolls stuffed with quinine." Thus, they certainly might have sheltered rebel troops at their home as well. Moreover, during the war Thomas and Julia Layton moved from Springfield to Taney County, so it seems probable that they lost their property in Springfield.[55]

In addition to plunder, vengeance and the desire to inflict pain and suffering on one's adversaries also fueled the partisan conflict in the Missouri Ozarks. In light of their prewar history of unionism and political moderation, the ferocity with which the people of this region waged war against one another might seem strange, but the war had the effect of forcing people to choose sides. As one historian has observed, as the war progressed "neither guerrillas nor Unionists permitted neutralism, seeing it as a service, however meekly given, to the enemy."[56] Men who attempted to remain neutral earned the mistrust of both factions, and they soon discovered that neutrality would not spare them from robbery or violence.[57] Capt. William Monks, a Union militia officer, summed up the prevailing attitude on both sides when he told a Howell County man who wanted to remain neutral "you must choose between the two powers; and if you are more afraid of the rebels than you are of me you will have to take your chances . . . This day you must settle in your own mind whom you will obey."[58]

Such uncompromising attitudes produced acts of violence shocking in their frequency and ferocity. In September 1862, a company of thirty rebel guerrillas under the command of Dave Hilliard visited the home of Jacob Aleshire, a Union sympathizer living in Christian County. They robbed Aleshire of some store goods, women's clothing and shoes, and a tablecloth. They also kidnapped a man named Thomas Budd, who had chosen the wrong time to visit Aleshire's residence. Three days later Aleshire and a search party discovered Budd's horribly disfigured body lying next to a nearby creek. According to Aleshire, Budd had "been shot and burned; he was considerable [sic] disfigured, his ears and nose being cut off."[59]

Cruel acts such as the Budd murder happened frequently in the Missouri Ozarks. On both sides of the conflict certain deranged individuals, whom sane people would have shunned in peacetime, became leaders of men and elevated sadism to an art form. One such individual, the rebel guerrilla leader Alfred Bolin, stands out as an extreme example of the savagery that the war created. Capt. Madison Day, a federal officer and a future Bald Knobber, knew Bolin before the war and recalled that for many years he had made a living as a highwayman operating in the White River region.[60] Bolin declared his allegiance to the Confederate cause and soon gained a following as commander of a guerrilla company. Bolin and his company operated primarily in the White River Hills along the road between Forsyth, Missouri, and Carrolton, Arkansas. One of their favorite haunts was a large, boulder-topped hill located about four miles south of Kirbyville in Taney County, which bore the appropriate nickname of "Murder Rock."[61]

From the security of their base in the hills, the Bolin gang preyed upon Union patrols, pro-Union civilians, and anyone else whose life or property they wished to take. Bolin perfected the art of bushwhacking, or firing from cover. According to one local historian, his "specialty was the murder of Union men at home on furloughs." This usually involved waiting alongside some "lonely road he knew his victim traveled" and picking off his victim "as he traveled to or from his home."[62] Although Bolin claimed to be a southern patriot fighting for the Confederacy, many of his killings lacked any military justification at all. These included the murder of a twelve-year-old boy named Bill Willis, whom Bolin gunned down near Roark Creek in Taney County, and an eighty-year-old man from Christian County whom the Bolin Gang murdered near Hensley's ferry on the White River.[63]

Although the Union army put a price on Bolin's head, all its attempts to capture him failed. One of the Union officers tasked with hunting Bolin down was Lt. Willis Kissee of the Seventy-Third Infantry, Enrolled Missouri Militia, a young officer who by the end of the war claimed to have killed thirty-two rebels in the service of his country. Although a tough guerrilla fighter himself, Kissee never did catch Bolin, who narrowly evaded him on a number of occasions. Twenty years after the war Alexander C. Kissee, Willis Kissee's brother, would play an important role in the Bald Knobber organization of Taney County.[64]

The federals finally managed to kill Bolin when they sent Zachariah E. Thomas, a young private from the First Iowa Cavalry, disguised as a Confederate soldier to find and kill Bolin. Thomas caught up with Bolin on February 1, 1863, at the homestead of a southern family near Forsyth, Missouri. He managed to convince the bushwhacker that he was a sick Confederate soldier headed home on furlough. Later that evening, as Bolin stooped next to the fireplace to light his pipe, Thomas smashed his skull with a blunt instrument. (Depending on the source, he used either a poker or a plow coulter.) Federal troops brought Bolin's body to Forsyth, where Madison Day identified his remains, and then to Ozark. At some point along the way the soldiers cut off the guerrilla leader's head, which they fastened to the top of a pole and displayed publicly in Ozark as a gruesome warning to other bushwhackers.[65]

If any man could have called himself the Union counterpart to Alfred Bolin, that dubious distinction probably belongs to John R. Kelso. Among the men who earned a warrior's reputation in the Missouri Ozarks, Kelso stands out for his extraordinary intellect coupled with political fanaticism and a merciless attitude toward rebel soldiers and southern sympathizers. Before the war Kelso made a living as a schoolteacher in Ozark, Missouri. There he acquired a reputation as a formidable, albeit self-taught, scholar. He excelled in science and mathematics, and had reportedly attained fluency in five different languages with a particular aptitude for Latin and Greek. His contemporaries also remembered him as a cold and aloof man who "formed no friendships and had no companions."[66]

For the first few months of his military career Kelso served in the Dallas County Home Guards. Subsequently, he became a lieutenant in the Fourteenth Missouri Cavalry Militia under the command of another famous guerrilla fighter, Capt. Milton Burch. Finally, he joined the Eighth Missouri State Militia where he achieved the rank of captain.[67] During his time serving with Captain Burch, Kelso participated in several small-scale military operations typical of the war in southwest Missouri. One such episode occurred on August 1, 1862, when Confederate colonel Robert R. Lawther, with about fifty-five of his Missouri Partisan Rangers, attempted a surprise attack on Captain Burch encamped near Ozark with about eighty men from the Fourteenth Missouri Cavalry, including Lieutenant Kelso. After receiving news of the approaching rebels, Burch and company repulsed their attackers and pursued them south into Taney County. They caught up to Lawther's men on August 3 near the Snapp family farm just south of the White River. They attacked and scattered them, inflicting light casualties and capturing several horses and mules along with some supplies.[68] In another significant military operation in Marion County, Arkansas, Kelso played an important role in capturing and destroying the Confederate saltpeter works at Bean Cave near Dubuque. These works had cost the Confederate $30,000 to build and could accommodate up to one hundred workers at a time. Their destruction deprived rebel forces in the area of an important source of gunpowder.[69]

Small actions such as the skirmishes at Ozark, Snapp's farm, and Bean Cave served as Kelso's "apprenticeship" in the ways of Ozarks warfare. After joining the Eighth Missouri State Militia he would earn a reputation as one of the Union's most fearless guerilla fighters. Kelso's fanaticism proved an asset in this respect. He believed fervently in the Union cause, and "held all Confederates to be traitors, guilty of treason and deserving death." This conviction allowed him to fight the rebel guerrillas with a ferocity that shocked even his comrades. Like Bolin, he perfected the art of ambush from cover, often lying for hours in the brush "with a Latin grammar in one hand and a cocked pistol in the other" as he waited for a victim to appear. According to one report, one night he stumbled upon the camp of three sleeping guerrillas. Creeping into their camp, he noticed that they slept under a large quilt with an attractive design. Not wanting to soil the quilt with their blood, he deftly removed it from their sleeping forms and then quietly slaughtered them with his knife.[70]

Kelso's military career ended more happily than Bolin's. In 1864 he decided to run for Congress in Missouri's Fourth Congressional District. His major opponent in the race was the incumbent congressman and fellow Republican Sempronius H. ("Pony") Boyd. A colorful orator and prominent lawyer from Springfield, Missouri, Boyd would later gain recognition as one of the lead attorneys representing the Bald Knobbers charged with the murder of Charles Green and William Edens in 1887. Kelso defeated Boyd and a few other minor candidates with a healthy plurality of the votes cast in the 1864 general election. As a congressman (1865–67) he became identified with the radical wing of the Republican caucus in the House of

Representatives and advocated a strict federal Reconstruction policy toward the South.[71]

Alfred Cook, another famous guerrilla leader who operated in southwest Missouri, lived in Taney County before the war where he farmed and raised six children with his wife, Rebecca. At the beginning of the war Cook tried to remain neutral, but the fact that he and his wife came from Kentucky, and that he owned a few slaves, made his family a target of the county's unionists. Faced with the threat of violence and robbery, Cook and his family fled across the border into Marion County, Arkansas. However, they found the situation there no better than the one they had left. Finally, Cook and about a dozen like-minded men formed their own independent company to protect themselves and seek vengeance against their enemies.[72]

In the waning months of the war, the Cook band launched a series of fierce retaliatory raids against Unionists in Missouri and Arkansas, which prompted federal authorities to take action against them. In January 1865, Capt. William L. Fenex of the Seventy-Third Infantry sent Lt. Willis Kissee with a detachment of twenty-five men to find and destroy Cook's company. While scouting in Boone County, Arkansas, Lieutenant Kissee received a tip that Cook and his men often hid in a nearby cave. Not knowing the cave's location, Kissee captured Cook's son, described as a "small boy," and then forced him, by unspecified means, to reveal the location of his father's hiding place. After Lieutenant Kissee and his men found the cave and surrounded its entrance, he asked Cook's men to surrender. Nine of the fourteen men inside accepted his request. When the remainder, including Cook, Ed Brown, and Hiram Russell, refused to leave the cave, Kissee had a large fire built on the ledge overlooking its mouth. He then ordered the burning timber thrown down in front of the cave to smoke out the remaining men. As the three choking guerrillas stumbled out of the cave, Kissee's men gave them "their Southern rights," meaning they shot them dead. The federal soldiers placed their bodies in an ox wagon and took them a short distance away before burying them side by side in a common grave.[73]

Guerrilla warfare in southwest Missouri exposed the people of that region to a uniquely brutal and personal kind of fighting, which impacted the daily lives of ordinary people in the area in a variety of ways. First, the war subjected them to immense suffering and deprivation. Not surprisingly, the war forced large numbers of farmers to leave southwest Missouri, which temporarily interrupted agricultural production in the region. For example, in 1860 farmers in Christian and Taney Counties reported 23,800 and 12,600 acres of improved farmland, respectively. Just two years after the war a special report by Missouri's commissioner of statistics showed only 18,900 and 3,800 acres of improved land in those counties, although these figures would improve markedly by 1870.[74] Those who remained at home during the war faced the prospect of repeated robbery, which left many on the brink of starvation.[75] Some even resorted to eating wild onions, wild salad, or flat cakes made from ground tree bark in lieu of bread.[76]

The war drove thousands of people away from their homes. Vera Cruz, the seat of Douglas County, burned down during the war, as did Rock Bridge, the seat of Ozark County. When Col. William Monks returned home to West Plains, the seat of Howell County, he found that rebel troops had burned down every building except "an old school house . . . which was used for a court house." Likewise, on April 22, 1863, Union troops burned down Forsyth, the seat of Taney County, prior to evacuating it.[77] Greene County, because of the large federal garrison stationed in Springfield, remained relatively stable during the second half of the war. Consequently, it became choked with refugees, many of them female relatives of soldiers on either side who had no one to protect them at home. At the close of the war an unofficial census listed 476 "refugees" living in the county, a number that likely understated the problem.[78]

In addition to the deprivation and displacement that the residents of southwest Missouri experienced during the war, in the postwar years they also saw a dramatic increase in crime and lawlessness. One historian has described the years immediately following the Civil War in Missouri as a "reign of terror" in which crime and violence became rampant. Many of the criminals, who had military experience as soldiers or guerrillas, used the skills they learned in wartime to make a new livelihood for themselves as outlaws. In response to this crime problem, Missouri's law-abiding citizens began turning to vigilante justice. Out of 229 documented lynchings in Missouri's history, 112 of them occurred in a twenty-year period from 1866 through

1885.[79] Missourians also formed many local vigilance committees, calling their organizations "Honest Men's Leagues," "Anti-Horse Thief Associations," or "Regulators."[80] For example, David McKee, a former Union officer, founded the Anti-Horse Thief Association (AHTA) in Clark County in northeast Missouri, a group dedicated to stamping out the gangs of horse thieves that plagued that part of the state. By the mid-1880s the AHTA had expanded across the state, boasting strong chapters in several southwest Missouri communities, such as Springfield, Joplin, and Webb City.[81] The first such organization in southwest Missouri, the Greene County Regulators, formed in 1866 in response to a rash of robberies, horse theft, and murder. Although the Regulators lasted only a few months, they hung three suspected criminals and shot a fourth.[82] From 1866 through 1867 a similar organization operated in Vernon County, calling itself the "Marmiton League." Not much is known about this organization, other than that it broke up a "band of supposed horse thieves and desperadoes" operating in the area, shot one of the outlaws in the process, and expelled several people suspected of "concealing and harboring the criminals."[83] In 1875 a group in Stone County calling itself the "Sons of Honor" attempted to enforce its own idea of law and order there. In the process, it created so many problems for the legitimate local government that Missouri governor Charles H. Hardin sent his adjutant general, the famous artist George Caleb Bingham, to the county to mediate an end to the strife.[84] Vigilance committees like these gave residents of southwest Missouri a foretaste of the tumultuous years to come in the 1880s.

## CHAPTER 2

# Taney County from the Civil War to the Bald Knobbers

Although many details concerning the history of the Bald Knobbers remain in dispute, such as the total number of members, the number of their victims, and the date on which they disbanded, the group does have a definite place and time of origin. All the sources agree that the Bald Knobbers first organized in the town of Forsyth in Taney County, Missouri, sometime in late 1884 or early 1885.[1] As we have already seen, the date of their founding placed the Ozark vigilantes squarely in the context of a broad late-nineteenth-century trend in which Americans became increasingly willing to use collective violence and vigilante tactics to solve whatever problems they perceived in their communities.

For the most part, the Taney County Bald Knobbers fit the basic socioeconomic model of vigilantism described by Richard Maxwell Brown. As we shall see, most of their leadership and rank and file came from upper- or middle-class backgrounds, including several lawyers, merchants, businessmen, and political officeholders. Many of their victims, like the outlaws Frank and Tubal Taylor or local ruffians like Andrew Coggburn, were the very sort of socially marginalized people whom Brown expected vigilantes to target. Although the Bald Knobbers would not have articulated their goals in terms of preserving a social hierarchy or class structure, they clearly did have their own economic interests in mind. Their goals included establishing an honest and thrifty local government and making the county safe for immigration, new businesses, and investment.

This agenda did not originate *ex nihilo*. Rather it resulted from a specific set of social, economic, and political circumstances arising in Taney County during the generation following the Civil War. During this period the county underwent a series of four dramatic changes. First, the demographic landscape began to change as a continuous stream of settlers from midwestern states and other parts of Missouri began to challenge southerners as the dominant demographic group in the county by the end of the century. Second, in the postwar period residents of Taney County and the White River region became increasingly affected by the presence of industrialization, capital formation, market-based agriculture, and other such harbingers of economic modernization. This was not strictly a new phenomenon, but rather a continuation of long-standing trends that intensified toward the later stages of the nineteenth century. Third, the postwar period witnessed an intense political competition between the local Republican and Democratic Parties for control of the county's government, a struggle that often centered on the issues of crime and an expanding county debt. Finally, a strong surge in criminal activity over the two decades following the Civil War angered many residents in the area and caused them to consider alternatives to traditional law enforcement practices.

Prior to the Civil War the vast majority of the early settlers of the Ozarks came from upper South states like Tennessee, Virginia, and Kentucky. In the years following the Civil War, however, the Ozarks entered a second settlement phase in which states such as Ohio, Illinois, Indiana, Iowa, and Kansas became the primary source of new immigrants to the Ozarks.[2] The census figures for Taney County illustrate this trend. In 1870 native-born Tennesseans, Virginians, and Kentuckians accounted for 936 of the county's 4,385 residents. This represented more than one-fifth of the total population and 43 percent of those not born in Missouri. By 1900 the population of Taney County had more than doubled to roughly 10,000 inhabitants. Most of this growth came from native-born Missourians, who nearly tripled their numbers in the county. The contingent of people from

**Table 2.1:** 1870–1900 Nativity Statistics for Taney County

| Year | Born in MO | Not Born in MO | VA | TN | KY | VA, KY, & TN | % of Those Not Born in MO | IL | OH | IN | IA | KS | IL, OH, IN, IA, & KS | % of Those Not Born in MO | Total Pop. |
|---|---|---|---|---|---|---|---|---|---|---|---|---|---|---|---|
| 1870 | 2,204 | 2,181 | 145 | 575 | 216 | 936 | 43% | 275 | 121 | 169 | 69 | 29 | 663 | 30% | 4,385 |
| 1880 | 3,379 | 2,220 | 100 | 434 | 239 | 773 | 35% | 257 | 88 | 197 | 68 | 66 | 676 | 30% | 5,599 |
| 1900 | 6,557 | 3,570 | 136 | 352 | 413 | 901 | 25% | 383 | 167 | 205 | 184 | 204 | 1,143 | 32% | 10,127 |

Source: 1870, 1880, and 1900 U.S. Censuses.

Tennessee, Virginia, and Kentucky actually declined to 901, or about 25 percent of those not born in Missouri. Meanwhile, the number of residents from nonsouthern states like Ohio, Illinois, Indiana, Iowa, and Kansas all modestly increased, as did their share of the county's population born outside of Missouri.[3]

Taken together, these numbers indicate that by 1900 nonsoutherners had surpassed southerners as the primary source of new immigrants to the county.

Some of the new arrivals, like their predecessors, were farmers and stock raisers, but they also included people of diverse backgrounds and occupations: clerks, businessmen, entrepreneurs, Civil War veterans, merchants, and land speculators. These people became the "carriers of the New South culture" of economic modernization, political reform, and prosperity based on free markets and free labor.[4] They were predominantly middle-class and upper-class people who wanted not merely to scratch out a living as their predecessors had done, but to reform and modernize the Ozarks, bringing to the region roads, bridges, railroads, banks, greater social stability, and opportunities for profitable business.

Many of the new residents of Taney County fit this basic pattern of settlement. For example, in 1866 Barnett Parrish, a native Illinoisan and a widower, moved to Taney County bringing with him eight of his children including his thirteen-year-old son Joseph Calvin ("Cal") Parrish. An energetic and enterprising man, Barnett Parrish quickly established a farm and later became involved in the hotel business.[5] Cal Parrish soon surpassed his father in energy and industry. He first rented and then purchased his own land, and by age thirty-five he owned a fine sixty-acre farm. He also operated a merchandising company in Forsyth with one of his brothers and became co-owner of a drugstore there. In 1891 he helped establish the Taney County Bank and became one of its largest shareholders. A shrewd businessman, Parrish knew how to make contacts with the right people and use them to his advantage. In 1875 he married Mary Jennings, the granddaughter of a state legislator, with whom he had eight children. Parrish also joined the Republican Party, the Free Masons (he held several offices in the local Masonic lodge in Forsyth), and eventually the Bald Knobbers.[6]

Like the Parrishes, Sylvanus and Semira Groom, born in New York and Indiana, respectively, moved to Missouri from Indiana in 1859. They eventually settled in Holt County where Semira gave birth to their son, Charles H. Groom, in 1861. During the war Sylvanus Groom fought for the Union in the Thirteenth and Twenty-Fifth Missouri Infantry regiments. After the war he farmed and practiced medicine near the town of Fillmore in Andrew County. At the age of ten Charles Groom moved to Forsyth in Taney County where he began an apprenticeship as a printer. In 1882 Groom married Tremandria L. Jennings, the daughter of Taney County politician Lysander H. Jennings. Like many of his friends and associates, Groom belonged to the Bald Knobbers and the Republican Party in the 1880s. In 1884, the voters elected the twenty-three-year-old Groom as county treasurer, thereby making him the youngest man ever to hold county office up to that point. The following year, the Taney County courthouse burned down, but Groom managed to rescue enough of the county's tax records to furnish the county with a new set of tax books. In 1886 he began studying law. Five years later he passed the bar exam and opened a practice in Forsyth.[7]

Alexander C. Kissee, a native of Illinois and resident of Christian County where his parents had lived since the 1840s, fought for the Union during the Civil War in the Seventy-Second Enrolled Missouri Militia. Four years after the war ended, Kissee moved to the present site of Kissee Mills in Taney County. There he purchased "a large tract of land, all well improved," which he farmed. The following year Kissee became postmaster of the Kissee Mills post office, a position that he kept for several years. Within a few years he owned or co-owned several local businesses, including "two stores, a grist mill, [and] a saw mill."

He also owned a cotton gin, about which I will say more later on in this chapter. In addition to joining the Bald Knobbers in the 1880s, Kissee belonged to the Free Masons and the Republican Party.[8]

In 1855, Alexander Kissee married Catherine McHaffie, the sister of James K. Polk McHaffie, who later became one of Kissee's business partners. Catherine gave birth to ten children from the time of her marriage to Kissee to her death in 1876. Kissee remarried that same year, this time to Cordelia Davis of Greene County, who bore eleven children during her marriage.[9] After Cordelia's death, Alexander Kissee remarried three more times. In 1899 he married a teenage girl named Rose, whom he divorced the same year.[10] In 1900 he married Emma Thomas, who died the following year, and in 1902 he got remarried to Sarah J. Bryant. These last two women bore him five more children, giving this remarkable Ozarks progenitor a total of at least twenty-six offspring.[11]

Kissee's brother-in-law, James K. Polk McHaffie, was born in Greene County in 1846. His parents, David and Catherine McHaffie, moved from Knox County in eastern Tennessee to Greene County, Missouri, in 1835. They settled first in Springfield and then moved to a new homestead south of there within the present limits of Christian County. James McHaffie moved to Taney County in 1873 and settled at Kissee Mills, where he partnered with Alexander Kissee in a merchandising operation. He later sold his interest in the business to his partner and started a farm on Beaver Creek where he eventually owned about "500 acres of rich bottom land." His father, David McHaffie, had belonged to the Democratic Party before the Civil War, but later joined the Republicans. James McHaffie also joined the Republican Party and belonged to the Free Masons.[12]

One of the more interesting characters to move to Taney County in the late 1800s was John T. Dickenson. Unlike the other individuals mentioned here, Dickenson was a foreigner; he came to the United States from England in 1879, bringing with him his wife, Mary, and son John.[13] The Dickenson family arrived in Taney County in 1882, part of a small colony of English socialists who founded the town of Eglinton, a little hamlet located about five miles northeast of Forsyth, near present-day Taneyville. They wanted to turn their colony into a socialist utopia in the heart of the American wilderness, owning all property and sharing all profits in common. The colony did not long survive, but some of its members remained, including the Dickenson family. Mr. Dickenson gradually came to question the socialist ideology of his fellow colonists, and he eventually broke with them altogether. He became a prominent local businessman, owner of a successful general store, a postmaster, and a probate judge.[14]

In 1880, Alonzo S. Prather moved with his wife, Mirah, and their six children, from Kansas to Taney County, apparently with a brief sojourn in Springfield along the way.[15] A native of Indiana, Prather served during the Civil War in the Sixth Indiana Volunteers, along with his father Hiram and several of his brothers. After the war, Alonzo Prather made a living as a Republican official in Arkansas, winning appointments as the Madison County prosecuting attorney, the superintendent of public education for Arkansas's Fourth Judicial District, which encompassed most of northwest Arkansas, and the receiver at the U.S. Land Office in Harrison, Arkansas. While serving as Madison County prosecutor, Prather (according to a family story recounted by his grandson) risked his life by raising the American flag on the flagpole outside the county courthouse in Huntsville, Arkansas, on the Fourth of July. No one had done this since before the war. To make his point, he stood guard on the courthouse steps armed with a shotgun and a revolver in order to prevent anyone from taking it down.[16]

Sometime in the late 1870s, the Prather family went to Kansas where they settled near a town called Mulverd. They relocated to Taney County in 1880, where Prather practiced law for many years. He also published a small weekly newspaper, the *Taney County Home and Farm*, from 1881 to 1886, and served five nonconsecutive terms as a state representative in the Missouri General Assembly between 1888 and 1910. Like many of his associates, Prather became an active member of the Grand Army of the Republic (GAR), a Union veterans' organization, and a Bald Knobber.[17]

Like Alonzo Prather, Nathaniel N. Kinney came to Taney County by way of Kansas, although the man who would become the chieftain of the Bald Knobbers in Taney County had lived an adventurous and well-traveled life by the time he brought his family there in 1883. Born around the year 1845 in modern-day West Virginia, Kinney fought for

**Fig. 2.1:** Nathaniel Kinney. Source: William L. Vandeventer, *Justice in the Rough,* 1937. Used by permission of the State Historical Society of Missouri Research Center, Rolla, MO.

the Union during the Civil War in the Sixth West Virginia Infantry.[18] Although he later claimed to have held the rank of captain, he really spent the entire war as a private.[19] After the war Kinney lived in Indiana, Colorado, and eventually Kansas. Along the way he married Margaret Delong, widow of a U.S. Army officer who had perished during the war. The year 1875 saw Kinney living in Topeka, Kansas, where the city directory listed him working as a hackman (i.e., carriage driver). Two years later he had found employment as a "superintendent" with the "Topeka Line Company" (probably the Atchison, Topeka, and Santa Fe Railroad).[20]

While in Topeka, Kinney maintained a busy social calendar. In 1877 he became a lodge officer in the Ancient Order of United Workmen, a "fraternal and beneficial organization composed of men of all useful professions and occupations."[21] The following year Kinney joined the Topeka Rifles, a local militia company which the Atchison, Topeka, and Santa Fe Railroad created to counter widespread labor unrest in the wake of the massive railroad strikes that had paralyzed much of the nation's railroad network in 1877. Because of his enormous size (variously estimated at between six feet, two inches and six feet, seven inches) and charismatic personality, Kinney's militia comrades made him their color sergeant.[22]

In 1880, Kinney and his family, including his wife, Margaret, his son Paul and daughter Georgia, and his stepdaughters Mary and Eva Delong, left Kansas and moved to Springfield, Missouri. Most likely, his stepson James A. Delong accompanied them or else followed along later.[23] In Springfield Kinney took a job as a saloon keeper at a notoriously violent local saloon situated on the city square.[24] The owner of the saloon, J. C. F. Kinney, shared his employee's last name but no records indicate a family relationship between them. In 1883, the family moved again to Taney County, where Kinney purchased a farm a few miles north of Kirbyville where he raised cattle, sheep, and pigs, which earned him a decent income of roughly $800 to $1,000 per year. Unlike most of his associates in the Bald Knobbers, Kinney actively supported the Democratic Party, although he also belonged to many other organizations such as the Grand Army of the Republic and the Grange.[25]

Why did ambitious and energetic men like Parrish, Groom, Kissee, McHaffie, Dickenson, Prather, and Kinney choose to make Taney County their home in the years following the war? They had a variety of reasons for their decision. After the war Missouri's state government, private associations, railroads, and the press all encouraged prospective settlers to move to the state, and many people responded. Missouri's State Board of Immigration spearheaded this promotional effort, sending agents to the eastern United States and abroad to encourage potential immigrants to move to Missouri.[26] The state agency also worked in conjunction with private immigration organizations, such as southwest Missouri's "Emigrant Association," which residents of the region founded in 1870 to publicize the benefits of settlement in their section of the state. The Atlantic and Pacific Railroad, which completed its line to Springfield in 1870, contributed to the effort by advertising in Europe for new settlers.[27]

All of this promotional work paid off. By the late 1860s popular travel guides lauded southwest Missouri as the "Garden of the West," a place with good soil, temperate weather, plentiful timber and mineral resources, streams full of "pure, clear, running water," and game of every description including "deer, geese, turkey's [sic], prairie chickens, raccoons, quails, opossums, otter, beaver, mink, etc."[28] Similarly, the Susquehanna Valley Emigrating Association of Oswego, New York, encouraged residents of the Empire State to move to southwest Missouri. The association cited the "salubrity" of its climate, as a result of which "consumption and asthmatic complaints never originate here, and are often cured by the climate."[29] Although such promotional literature exaggerated the region's benefits, it had the desired impact.

Moreover, many of the new settlers had visited the White River country in person as federal soldiers during the war and had gained an appreciation for the commercial potential of the area. They would probably have noticed the region's many streams and creeks, abundant timber, and plentiful fish, fowl, and other game for hunting. They definitely took notice of the large amount of cheap or unclaimed land in Taney and other surrounding counties, a situation which the ravages of war exacerbated by forcing many residents to flee the area. In the late 1860s the U.S. Land Office at Springfield had about 300,000 acres of public land in Taney County to dispose of, or roughly three-quarters of the county's entire acreage. Similar quantities of public land existed in neighboring counties. Some of it the government would sell at the standard rate of $1.25 per acre, while the rest it made available under the provisions of the Homestead Act of 1862 for the nominal fee of $16 per 160 acres.[30] Many of the ambitious young men who began settling in Taney County at the close of the Civil War quickly took advantage of the federal government's real estate largesse. Among these, at least nineteen known Bald Knobbers in Taney County, most of them recent immigrants to the area, took out homestead patents in the period from the end of the war through the early twentieth century.[31]

In addition to the abundance of available land, the White River itself served as a major attraction to new settlers. In the 1830s steamboats began plying the lower portion of the river in northern Arkansas, though prior to the 1850s no steamboat advanced farther up river than Elbow Shoal at the Arkansas-Missouri line. Before that time most goods shipped down river from southwest Missouri had to go by keelboat, flatboat, or on large wooden rafts that the owners sold for timber and lumber upon reaching their destination.[32] In 1851, the Missouri legislature appropriated $8,000 to make improvements in the upper White River "so as to make it navigable for steamboats and other water craft," and appointed a three-member river commission to handle the matter. Several private citizens also chipped in for the improvement project.[33] Using these funds, the river commission hired Harrison Snapp to dig a channel at Elbow Shoal wide enough for a steamboat to pass through. The following year the *Yahogony* became the first steam-powered vessel to reach Forsyth. For the remainder of the decade steamboats made intermittent trips up the White River into Missouri, but navigation of the upper White River, with its many snags, shoals, fallen trees, and treacherous bends, remained a dangerous proposition and several vessels wrecked making the attempt.[34]

The Civil War interrupted commerce on the White River, but following the war the steamboats resumed making their trips. The vessels carried freight up river to sell to Ozarks merchants. On the return trip they carried the products of southwest Missouri and northwest Arkansas, primarily lead ore, cotton, and other agricultural produce, down the White River to the Mississippi. From there these products reached markets throughout the United States. Taney County's location at the northernmost bend in the river put it in an ideal position to capitalize on this trade.

It also helped spark another interesting development—a miniature "cotton boom" in Taney County and neighboring counties. As mentioned in the previous chapter, farmers produced hardly any cotton in the White River hills during the antebellum period.[35] Part of the reason for this stemmed from the soil itself: most of the rough and rocky hill country was poorly suited for cotton growing. But in the rich bottomlands adjacent to the White River and several of the creeks that feed into it, farmers could cultivate some cotton. They did not do so prior to the Civil War mainly because of the lack of adequate transportation. Following the war the improvements made to the White River and the extension of the Atlantic and Pacific Railroad to Springfield in 1870 helped resolve that difficulty. Thereafter, cotton production in the White River region grew steadily until the turn of the century. In 1879, Taney County farmers devoted 1,400 acres to cotton cultivation on which they grew 760 bales of cotton. The neighboring counties of Stone and Ozark produced similar quantities.[36] The *Taney County Times* estimated in 1887 that the county had produced roughly $100,000 of cotton that year.[37] By 1890, cotton cultivation in Taney County had increased to nearly 3,000 acres and more than 900 bales.[38]

In the larger geographic context, of course, the postwar cotton boom in the White River valley was a fairly minor development. Neither Taney County nor any other part of Missouri ever became a "cotton kingdom" in the sense in which historians generally use that term. The entire state of Missouri produced fewer bales of cotton in 1890, roughly 16,000, than several *counties* in Mississippi.[39] Those local farmers who did plant cotton generally sold a few bales a year to supplement their income. It did not become their sole livelihood. Nevertheless, the growth in cotton production symbolized several larger trends affecting Taney County at this time. These included the county's increasing connection to larger national markets and the continuing desire of many citizens for economic modernization. Not surprisingly, then, several Bald Knobbers became involved in the cotton trade. William Connor built a cotton gin on the White River south of Forsyth in the middle 1870s. Likewise, the Kissee family built a water-powered cotton gin at Kissee Mills on Beaver Creek in 1890, and James B. Rice established a cotton gin on Cedar Creek.[40]

Nor did the trend toward greater economic modernization stop at the cotton trade. By the late nineteenth century, liquor distilling had become an integral part of the local economy. At first, the production of spirits remained the domain of small-scale producers who sold to local customers. Many distillery owners also operated gristmills, which provided the corn mash used to make whiskey. The owners sold their product to customers at the rate of a gallon of whiskey for a bushel of corn.[41] Then in 1884 four local entrepreneurs, including Samuel W. Boswell and William Peck, and the Bald Knobbers Calvin Parrish and Reuben S. Branson, founded the largest distillery in Taney County at Forsyth. By the 1890s this distillery produced about 3,000 gallons of whiskey per year, and according to one observer, "these men are doing a paying business."[42]

For a time, it looked like mining might also become a vital bulwark of Taney County's economy. In the late nineteenth century, several counties in southwest Missouri saw a rapid expansion of mining for lead and zinc. In 1880 Christian, Greene, Dade, Newton, and Jasper Counties all produced substantial quantities of lead, and four of the five mined zinc as well.[43] Alas, Taney County did not immediately share in its neighbors' good fortune. In that county very little mining activity occurred prior to the 1890s.[44] Then, in 1891, reports of new

lead and zinc finds resulted in a surge of interest in mining in Taney
County. For example, a mining convention held in Springfield that
year drew a delegation comprised of some of the most prominent men
in Taney County, including three former Bald Knobbers: Alexander
Kissee, James B. Rice, and James R. Vanzandt. Another Bald Knobber,
John Lafayette Cook, the president of the White River Real Estate
and Mining Company, took advantage of the mining fever by selling
and leasing land to "capitalists and others desirous of buying or leasing mineral land in the White River Country." Moreover, several new
mines opened up including the King Solomon Mine near Kirbyville,
the Gibralter Mine near Hercules, and the Golden Eagle Mine near
Protem. By the turn of the century, one contemporary writer noted
that "lead prospecting has been accompanied with some success"
along several major creeks in western Taney County. Nevertheless,
mining did not enjoy prolonged success there. Most of the lead and
zinc deposits proved too small and too scarce to sustain profitable
mining operations. By the end of World War I, declining lead and zinc
prices brought an end to mining in the county.[45]

Despite the significant progress Taney County made in the generation following the Civil War, its improvement had occurred in fits and
starts, and in many ways the county remained one of the poorest and
most underdeveloped counties in southwest Missouri. Its population
grew steadily between 1860 and 1890 from nearly 3,600 to roughly
8,000. Nevertheless, its rate of population growth over that time span
lagged far behind neighboring counties, some of which tripled or qua-
drupled their populations over the same period.[46] Taney County also
fell behind neighboring areas in terms of economic and infrastructural
development. While the total value of farms in the county increased
from roughly $210,000 in 1860 to $837,000 in 1890, Taney County
still trailed far behind Greene ($9.5 million), Christian ($2.8 million),
and Douglas ($1.4 million) Counties, and about even with Stone and
Ozark Counties.[47] While the Atlantic and Pacific Railroad reached
Greene County in 1870, and Christian County received railroad service in 1883, Taney County had to wait until 1906 for the completion
of the White River Railway, which for the first time brought regular
railroad transportation to the county.[48]

Many factors contributed to this disparity of fortunes, including the lingering effects of the Civil War, Taney County's remote location, the late arrival of railroad transportation, and the relatively poor condition of much of its soil. Regardless, by the 1880s, many inhabitants had begun to blame their misfortune on corruption in local government and crime. The dissatisfaction that many of the area's residents felt toward their government grew directly out of the tumultuous political history of the county between the end of the Civil War and the mid-1880s.

The Civil War ended with the Republican Party firmly in power, both at the state level in Jefferson City, and at the local level in Taney County. At the war's conclusion John R. Kelso represented Missouri's Fourth Congressional District, which included Taney County, in Congress. Francis M. Gideon represented the county in the state house, and William Yandell served as county judge. All three men belonged to the Republican Party. Former Confederate sympathizers found this situation intolerable. One of them, John Haggard, wrote to a friend that southerners had "no more chance for to get justice in Taney County than a cat in hell without claws."[49] The Republicans dominated politics in the county for two main reasons. First, many of the county's former residents (mostly Democrats) had left during the war. Second, the state government had disfranchised most of the remaining Democrats as Confederate sympathizers. In the election of 1864, only twenty-nine voters cast ballots in Taney County. Most of these votes probably came from a garrison of Union soldiers under the command of Capt. William L. Fennix, a Republican, whom Gov. Thomas C. Fletcher later appointed county and circuit clerk. Not surprisingly, they voted unanimously for Abraham Lincoln for president and F. M. Gideon for state representative.[50]

After the war, Missouri Republicans controlled the state legislature and called for a constitutional convention in 1865 to draft a new charter for the state. Charles D. Drake, a Radical Republican from St. Louis, whom the city's *Daily Dispatch* referred to as "dogmatical [*sic*] and not infrequently overbearing," emerged as the dominant figure at the convention.[51] Drake pushed for the convention to include strong provisions in the new constitution disfranchising former Confederates and ensuring Republican hegemony. On May 1, 1865, the delegates to the convention followed Drake's lead and passed an "ousting ordinance," which expelled from office roughly eight hundred officials whose loyalty they deemed suspect. The act vacated the offices of all the justices and clerks for the "Supreme Court of Missouri, the circuit courts, the county courts, and the special courts of record and of all county recorders and circuit attorneys." Republican governor Fletcher then replaced most of them with Republicans.[52] In Taney County this act resulted in the appointment of a whole new slate of officials, including a new sheriff, three justices of the county court, and a new county clerk and circuit clerk.[53]

The convention also passed a provision of the new constitution that required that anyone who voted or ran for office must take an oath swearing that they had never "been in armed hostility to the United States," had never aided or supported "persons engaged in any such hostility," and had never disloyally communicated with enemies of the state. This provision, called the "Ironclad Oath," effectively disfranchised almost all ex-Confederates. In order to enforce disfranchisement, the constitution included "Registry Acts," which divided Missouri into voting districts and required all citizens who wished to vote to register in their districts and take the Ironclad Oath. Moreover, certain professional groups including attorneys, educators, and some corporate officers also found themselves subjected to the Ironclad Oath. This provision even applied to members of the clergy. Radical Republicans often blamed rebel clergy for encouraging sedition and disloyalty within their congregations. Consequently, they too had to take the oath in order to practice their profession.[54]

The intended purpose of these provisions in the 1865 constitution, in addition to punishing former rebels, was to ensure Republican dominance in Missouri politics by disfranchising most of the people who would have voted the Democratic ticket. In Taney County, as in many other Missouri communities, they accomplished that purpose efficiently. For example, in the 1868 presidential election the Republican candidate, Ulysses S. Grant, defeated Democrat Horatio Seymour in Taney County with 208 votes to 52 votes. That same year the Republican candidates in all the major statewide races won Taney County by similar margins. In the state senate race Republican S. W. Headley beat Democrat L. T. Watson by a four votes to one margin, and in the state representative race Republican Jesse Jennings prevailed over fellow Republican Willis Kissee and Democrat J. W. Wyatt with a majority of the total votes cast.[55] Republicans also won most, if not all, of the county offices. For example, Larkin Adamson won the election for sheriff; Levi Boswell won the race for county treasurer; James Keithley became public administrator; and Enos Stanley became the new probate judge.[56]

Republican dominance in Taney County continued until the early 1870s, when intraparty discord between Liberal Republicans and Radical Republicans undermined the party's control of Missouri politics. The Liberal Republicans, led by party dissidents such as Carl Schurz and Benjamin Gratz Brown, revolted against their party leadership for a variety of reasons. For one, they objected to the corruption of the Grant administration, epitomized by the Whiskey Ring scandal in St. Louis in which a group of major distilleries and public officials defrauded the government of millions of dollars in taxes.[57] The Liberal Republicans also opposed, on both moral and philosophical grounds, the continued disfranchisement of former rebels. For this reason, in the party's 1870 convention the Liberals supported a resolution pledging the party's support for constitutional amendments "removing all disqualifications from the disfranchised people of Missouri and conferring equal political rights on all classes."[58]

The Radicals, who drew their strongest support from the rural northern and southwestern parts of Missouri where guerrilla fighting had taken the heaviest toll on the pro-Union population, bitterly opposed this resolution. They argued that enfranchising former Confederates would reward treason and undermine the party's control of the state. Senator Charles Drake, in a bitter speech attacking fellow senator Carl Shurz for his treachery against the Republican Party, predicted that once the voters passed constitutional amendments reenfranchising the state's ex-rebels, "you might bid goodbye to Missouri as a Republican state."[59] The majority of delegates to the 1870 convention agreed with him. When the full convention voted down the resolution favoring reenfranchisement, the Liberals walked out of the convention and nominated Benjamin Gratz Brown for governor of Missouri.[60]

Thus, the 1870 gubernatorial election became a strange fratricidal struggle between Radicals and Liberal Republicans. The Democrats, sensing an opportunity to exploit their opponents' discord, cast their lot in with the Liberal Republicans and Brown. They calculated that if he helped repeal the voting restrictions they would surely win the following election. That November Brown easily defeated the Radical nominee, Joseph W. McClurg, in the race for governor. The Liberal Republican triumph appeared complete. In a sign of things to come, however, Brown won with slightly less than half of his support coming from the Liberal Republicans and the rest from Democrats.[61]

In the same election that elevated Brown to the governor's mansion, Missouri voters approved a constitutional amendment repealing the Ironclad Oath. The following year the new governor, true to his word, supported legislation overturning the Registry Acts, thereby completing the end of disfranchisement in Missouri. Unfortunately for the Liberal Republicans, the dire predictions of the Radicals that the reenfranchisement of former rebels would lead to a Democratic resurgence proved accurate. In the next gubernatorial election in 1872, Silas Woodson swept into office with the support of tens of thousands of newly registered Democratic voters. Woodson's victory initiated a period of Democratic dominance in state government lasting nearly forty years.[62]

The dramatic political changes occurring at the statehouse also had huge ramifications for Taney County. Most of the local Republicans in this rural border county in southwest Missouri, the scene of vicious guerrilla fighting during the war, sided naturally with the Radicals during the political insurgency of 1870. That year Taney County gave a large majority of its votes (231 out of 314 votes cast) to the Radical Republican Joseph W. McClurg for governor. It also helped elect the Radical Harrison Eugene Havens to the first of two terms in the U.S. Congress by a similarly large margin.[63]

The 1870 election marked the last occasion on which Taney County Republicans would enjoy such untrammeled dominance in county politics. With the end of disfranchisement, the 1870s witnessed a resurgence of the local Democratic Party that brought the two parties into approximate parity. This allowed the Democrats to wrest control of local government from the Republicans for the next several years. The change in the county's electoral make-up became apparent almost immediately. In the presidential election of 1872, Ulysses S. Grant still carried Taney County, but by a much smaller margin than in 1868. In addition, his opponent, the Liberal Republican-Democratic candidate Horace Greeley, received four times as many votes (201) as Horatio Seymour had earned in the previous election.[64] Likewise, the Democratic candidates for governor, lieutenant governor, and all the other major state offices increased their vote totals over the previous election by similar margins. Further down the ticket, the Democrats did even better. Rev. Jordan M. Haworth, a Democrat and future Anti-Bald Knobber, came within a whisker of winning the race for sheriff, losing by only twenty votes. John J. Brown, a Republican and future Bald Knobber, barely survived in his race for prosecuting attorney against B. F. Dilley, winning by just eight votes.[65]

Because of a number of resignations, governor's appointments, and special elections in the early 1870s, combined with the uncertainty of determining the party affiliation of certain officials, it is not exactly certain which party held the balance of power in Taney County's local government between 1872 and 1874. It is clear, however, that in the 1874 elections the Democrats scored a victory in the local elections. That year Democrat Thomas F. Layton replaced Lysander H. Jennings as county and circuit clerk; Rufus V. Burns replaced J. J. Brown as prosecuting attorney; and William L. Peck took over the job of sheriff and collector of revenue from James C. Johnson. The Democrats also elected J. J. Reynolds and Jordan M. Haworth to the county court, where they joined Republican and U.S. Army veteran C. C. Owens, which gave the Democrats two out of the three members of that body.[66]

The Democrats never dominated local politics in the 1870s the way that Republicans had in the late 1860s, but for the most part they controlled county government for the balance of the decade. A small cadre of officeholders, which the Bald Knobbers later referred to contemptuously as the "old county ring," comprised the core of the local party leadership.[67] This core consisted of William L. Peck, who served as sheriff and collector of revenue from 1874 to 1880, John Moseley, who succeeded Peck in that position from 1880 to 1884, John J. Reynolds, who won two elections for probate judge in 1874 and 1878, and Thomas C. Spellings, who served as the county prosecutor for five months in 1880 and a full term from 1882 to 1884. It also included

several members of the Layton family, such as Thomas F. Layton, who
served four years as circuit and county clerk from 1874 to 1878, his
son Thomas A. Layton, who succeeded him in that position in 1878
and won a second four-year term in 1882, and Albert S. Layton, who
served as coroner from 1878 to 1880.[68]

The period of Democratic ascendancy in Taney County, which
lasted until 1884, also coincided with a strange development in the
county's finances. For reasons which remain unclear, during the 1870s
the county amassed more than $42,000 in bonded debt, which many
residents in those days considered a startling figure. Whatever reasons
Taney County officials had for borrowing this money, or however
they spent it, the fact remains that the public debt became a political
bone of contention among residents of the county. This intensified
the atmosphere of mistrust in local government, which contributed
to the rise of vigilantism in the middle 1880s.[69]

The story of Taney County's debt problem began just prior to the
Civil War. In the 1850s, the county needed a new courthouse. At the
time, the county's narrow property base—residents owned only about
5 percent of the land in fee simple—limited the local government's
ability to borrow the money necessary to build the structure. In 1855
the Missouri General Assembly passed a law allowing the county to
borrow roughly $3,600 from the state's internal improvements fund
and to repay the state with bonds, which the county would pay down
over time by raising taxes. Taney County's small tax base must have
made repayment of the debt a serious burden on local taxpayers. In
1861, just prior to the outbreak of the Civil War, the state forgave the
county's outstanding debt, thereby allowing it to eliminate the taxes
raised for that purpose.[70]

Unfortunately for the residents, their brand-new courthouse did
not escape the war unscathed. Much of it was destroyed in the course
of a Federal assault on Forsyth in 1861.[71] Nor did the war spare the
county's finances. In the years 1863 and 1864 the county government,
like many other counties in southwest Missouri, found itself unable
to collect taxes of any kind.[72] The problems with tax collection did not
cease with the end of the war. In an 1867 report to the state government, the county assessor E. W. Meyers remarked that many residents
"are jealous of everything tending to show the wealth of the county,

believing it to be a scheme of government to ascertain their income preparatory to assessing a national revenue tax." He also observed that under present circumstances, the county could rarely find enough qualified men to fill all the county offices.[73]

Then in the early 1870s, something quite strange happened. Between January 1871 and March 31, 1872, Taney County issued some $17,650 in bonds. That in itself does not seem suspicious. Other counties also increased their indebtedness by similar amounts or more. The biannual state auditor's report, however, shows that during that period the total acreage in Taney County subject to taxation expanded dramatically, from roughly 35,000 acres valued at $142,000 in 1871 to nearly 360,000 acres valued at $500,000 in 1872. To put it another way, according to these figures in one year the total amount of land owned in fee simple expanded tenfold, and total property values increased roughly 350 percent. This seems highly improbable, especially since by 1875 Taney County's taxable acreage figures had dropped back down to pre-1872 levels, and even by the end of the decade residents owned only 72,000 acres in fee simple valued at roughly $177,000.[74]

The most reasonable interpretation of this evidence is that Taney County's officials intentionally inflated their property and property value statistics in order to secure the loans they needed for public works projects, particularly a new courthouse. I cannot identify the exact person(s) responsible for this dubious financial maneuver. It seems probable, however, that at least Lysander Jennings, the county clerk, and Elias Cleavenger, the surveyor, would have known about it. Both men won elections in 1870, prior to the official end of disfranchisement, and therefore almost certainly belonged to the Republican Party. Thus, the first expansion of county debt occurred on the Republican watch.[75]

The Democrats, however, did not prove themselves any better stewards of county finances. In July 1880, Taney County carried roughly $32,000 in bonded debt, reportedly for the purpose of "funding old bonds and warrants." By January 1, 1883, the figure stood at more than $28,000. The state auditor's report for that year noted that the vast majority of this debt, roughly $27,000, came in the form of ten-year bonds with a 10 percent rate of interest. The county had issued these bonds in 1874 and sold them to the Greene County National

Bank in Springfield and the St. Louis National Bank in St. Louis. The report also noted that the county had not made prompt interest payments on its debt, and had only $422,000 in taxable wealth. By comparison, two of Taney County's equally poor neighbors, Douglas and Ozark Counties, carried just $15,000 and $10,000 in debt, and neighboring Christian County had no debt at all. Finally, in November 1883, the county refinanced part of its debt by issuing $33,000 in new five- to twenty-year bonds with a 6 percent rate of interest, sold to the Third National Bank in St. Louis. This act brought the county's total indebtedness to the then staggering figure of $42,600. Thus, the Democratic ring that controlled county government for much of the 1870s and early 1880s raised the county's bonded indebtedness by approximately $25,000.[76]

Paltry as these figures might seem today, people living in a small, rural section of southwest Missouri in the late nineteenth century had plenty of reasons to consider a debt burden of that size a significant problem. For one thing, it meant paying higher taxes in order to pay down the debt. By the late 1880s the property tax rate had reached $2.10 per $100 of assessed property, of which $1.35 went to interest payments and paying down the debt.[77] Moreover, failure to make interest payments, which became an issue for Taney County, could damage a county's credit and hinder its ability to borrow money for other necessary projects.

Equally important, however, is the question of how all of this money was spent, and for that there does not appear to be a satisfactory answer. From the end of the Civil War to the beginning of the Bald Knobber period, the only major public works project undertaken by the county government was to repair the old bombed-out courthouse. Although precise information about the cost of those repairs is unavailable, evidence from neighboring counties suggests that it should not have come to anything like $42,000. For example, in 1886 Crawford County built a modest, two-story brick courthouse similar to the one found in Taney County for $7,500, and in 1882 Texas County renovated its courthouse at a cost of $4,300. Indeed, Taney County itself would later have to build another courthouse after a fire in 1885 rendered the old one unusable. The cost in this case, $5,000, was picked up by the state.[78]

It is hardly surprising, therefore, that in the 1880s many local residents looked at their public finances and wondered where all this money had gone. It was not an unreasonable question, since local governments in late-nineteenth-century Missouri, from big cities down to small rural counties, had a well-developed reputation for corruption. Commonplace problems included bribery, graft, county courts issuing bonds to pay for the construction of railroads that were never built, and "loans" of public monies to friends of local officials without ever collecting on them.[79] While it may be impossible to definitely prove that these things happened in Taney County, widespread suspicions of fiscal malfeasance helped make the county debt an important political issue in the ongoing struggle between Democrats and Republicans there. The Republicans, forgetting their own role in creating the problem, happily blamed the burgeoning debt on the Democrats.[80] Taney County's finances also became a potent symbol of the corruption and inadequacy of local government that the men who started the Bald Knobber movement found so offensive. For example, the Bald Knobber chieftain Nathaniel Kinney recalled his shock upon arriving in Taney County and learning that "the county was $42,000 in debt, and had not even a plank to show for it. The money had simply been stolen."[81]

Whether due to theft or not, the miserable state of county finances became one of two major focal points of Republican and Bald Knobber dissatisfaction with the Democratic regime running local government. By the 1880s, however, the crime problem easily eclipsed the debt problem in the public's consciousness. Before discussing the issue of crime in Taney County, one must add that the postwar surge in lawlessness that the county experienced was neither unprecedented nor unusual in the context of postwar Missouri. As discussed in chapter 1, the years following the Civil War witnessed a dramatic increase in crime and lawlessness, sometimes referred to as a "reign of terror."[82] The impact of this crime surge swelled the state's prison population. The number of inmates in Missouri's prisons increased from 286 in 1860 to 1,623 in 1870, and further increased to 2,041 in 1880.[83] Many of the outlaws—most notably the members of the infamous James-Younger gang—gained a sort of apprenticeship in the outlaw trade while fighting as soldiers or guerrillas in the Civil War.[84]

The inhabitants of Taney County experienced more than their share of this crime surge. While an unfortunate courthouse fire in 1885 prevents an exact accounting of the number of homicides in the county, numerous newspapers and contemporary accounts from the 1880s suggest that murder became more common after the war than before. Most of these sources put the number of murders in Taney County from the Civil War to the Bald Knobber period at between thirty and forty. For example, in their apologetic narrative of the Bald Knobber movement, Charles Groom and D. F. McConkey state that prior to the Civil War only three murders took place in Taney County, but since that time "there has been near thirty murders committed" with only one successful prosecution of the culprit.[85] The *Jefferson City Daily Tribune* reported that over the same period there "had been thirty-eight willful murders" with no convictions, a figure with which the editors of the *Taney County News* concurred. Similarly, the *New York Sun* reported that the number of homicides "is estimated all the way from thirty-two to forty-two . . . and no one punished for them" even with prison terms.[86]

It is important to remember, however, that these figures represent only the best estimates of journalists relying on information gleaned from interviews with local residents. By the late 1880s the Bald Knobbers had become a sensationalized topic in the press, and the tendency of journalists to exaggerate may have inflated the number of homicides that actually took place. Although it is impossible to examine the circuit court records for Taney County between 1865 and 1885, an analysis of the records for neighboring Christian County over the same period provides some perspective on the state of violent crime in that area. The records show that Christian County witnessed no fewer than fifteen murders during the years in question, along with dozens of cases of assault and battery or assault with intent to kill.[87] To be sure, some violent crimes probably escaped the attention of local authorities, but the homicides documented in court records represent a solid basis from which to start. Given that social conditions in the two counties were basically similar, and that Christian County had its own vigilance committee starting in 1886, it seems reasonable to assume that the number of murders in each county were roughly equal. For that reason, we may cautiously estimate that Taney County had around fifteen to twenty murders between the end of the Civil War and the beginning of the Bald Knobber period, or about half the numbers usually cited by contemporary journalists.

Whatever the actual homicide figures may have been, the evidence taken together presents a picture of Taney County as a community beset by crime, with the legal authorities struggling to cope with an aggressive criminal element. Moreover, the lawmen themselves often took grave risks in attempting to enforce the law. For example, in 1879 Taney County deputy marshals James Coggburn and J. W. Dawson led a posse in pursuit of a band of horse thieves, catching up with them at a house located on Bee Creek in the southern part of the county. In the ensuing gunfight James Coggburn, and one other man, William Bates, lost their lives.[88]

In addition to investigating homicides, the law officers of Taney County also had to deal with widespread property theft, particularly of horses and livestock. Gangs of horse thieves and cattle rustlers inundated the county, taking full advantage of the "open range" system of stock raising practiced at that time. In those days, most farmers allowed their hogs and cattle to run freely in Taney County's densely forested hills, grazing wherever they wished.[89] The large proportion of unclaimed or government-owned land provided stock raisers with plenty of open territory on which to fatten their cattle. At the same time, however, this system made cattle theft relatively easy. A thief had only to catch an unbranded cow out of sight of its owner and mark it with his own brand. Because the thieves operated exclusively in the county's hills and forests, they could almost always evade detection. The Bald Knobber Joe McGill, who had returned to Taney County in 1881 after living for several years in Texas, recalled that the sheriff at the time, John Moseley, made hardly any arrests at all. For the most part, the criminals simply ignored the lawmen or taunted them, saying that their "'authority reaches only to the bluffs,' and when they were once in the hills and brush, they defied the law—nothing and nobody were safe."[90]

One band of criminals that worked these hills was the notorious Taylor Gang, so called because several brothers named Taylor belonged to it. The Taylor family had come to Missouri from Kentucky and settled about five miles from Forsyth on a hill called Nubbin Ridge.

According to newspaper reports, the Taylor gang, led by the brothers Frank and Tubal, engaged in a variety of petty crimes including brawling, carrying concealed weapons, discharging firearms in public thoroughfares, and stealing cattle or chickens. The Taylors often publicly flaunted their disregard for the law by riding into Forsyth loaded with cash and inviting "the whole town to drink at their expense, remarking that they didn't work for their money."[91] They also had the ugly habit of mutilating other people's cattle for sport. One of their enemies, Alexander Kissee, made the mistake of speaking ill of them in public. For this transgression they took three of his finest cows, cut their tongues out, and left the poor beasts to starve.[92]

By the 1880s, many residents of Taney County found their communities, in the laconic words of Joe McGill, "in a bad way." Their local government "was bankrupt and in the hands of a party clique." Criminals ran roughshod over their neighborhoods, exposing their property to theft and their lives to danger, and the officers of the law appeared either unable or unwilling to stop them.[93] The men who would create the Bald Knobber organization found this situation intolerable. Most of them had arrived in Taney County after the Civil War expecting to build new lives and new fortunes there. They had moved their families to a war-torn region and invested years of their lives and most of their capital to make their new home a success. As former soldiers, many of them yearned to take matters into their own hands. They only needed a spark or provocation to push them into action.

The first spark came on September 22, 1883, with the murder of local businessman James M. Everett. Everett descended from the Everett clan of Marion County in north Arkansas. In the mid-1840s, his family had become notorious for their role in the infamous "Tutt and Everett War," a local political dispute that had degenerated into a bitter family feud that left several members of the Tutt and Everett families dead. In the wake of that dispute, several members of the Everett family had moved north into Missouri.[94] James Everett's friends, including Nathaniel Kinney and many others who later became Bald Knobbers, described him as "a prominent merchant of the town, in the liquor business." He owned a store in Forsyth located on the east side of the town square, which also served as a billiard hall and saloon. One back room contained a billiard table, and a front room housed Everett's merchandise and a bar. Everett managed his saloon with the help of his brother, Barton, whom most people called "Yell" Everett on account of his penchant for speaking louder than necessary. In their establishment the brothers sold a type of whiskey generally called "forty rod," or extremely potent whiskey.[95]

On the day in question, two young men, Albert G. Layton (commonly called "Al"), a local roughneck of bad reputation, and his friend Sam Hull, went to Everett's establishment for drinks and a few games of pool. While playing their game they had an argument of some kind that quickly escalated to blows. In the heat of the moment, Layton attempted to draw his revolver, at which point James Everett intervened. He grappled with Layton, wrestled him out of the saloon, and threw him down onto the porch outside. Those present recalled that Everett told the younger man, "I don't low to hurt ye," as he held him pinned to the floor, but "I aim to keep ye out of trouble." A small crowd of spectators gathered around the prostrate pair, some of them urging Layton to give up his weapon in exchange for promises of safety, which the young man refused to do. Then someone suggested that Everett had better let him up, which the saloon keeper unwisely did. Once released, Layton reportedly dusted off his clothes, and then without warning he raised his revolver and fired two shots into Everett's body, killing him instantly. Next he turned and shot Everett's brother Barton "through the right shoulder, making him yell louder than he had ever done before." Before those present had time to react, Layton ran to his horse and galloped away.[96]

Shortly after making his escape, Al Layton surrendered to Sheriff John Moseley and posted bond. Given the generally dismal record of county law officers at apprehending fugitives, Layton might well have tried his luck on the run. The young man also had good reasons, however, to hope for a favorable outcome in court. He belonged to one of the oldest and best-known families in the county, and his cousin, Thomas A. Layton, held the offices of county and circuit clerk. Most of the county officers, including Prosecutor T. C. Spellings and Sheriff Moseley, were friends and political allies of his family. Moreover, local juries had a reputation for acquitting criminals, in part because jurors had to consider the potential consequences of convicting men among whose relatives they had to live. Whatever role these calculations may have played, a grand jury, which ironically included Nathaniel Kinney, indicted Layton for murder. The circuit court granted Layton a continuance and set the date of his trial for October 1884, more than a year after the shooting took place.[97]

In the interval, another notorious crime took place. On October 7, 1884, a young man named Newton Herrell killed Amos Ring, a man alternately described as his stepfather or his "mother's lover." Mr. Ring had recently begun living with Herrell's mother, a widow living in a cabin a short distance from Forsyth. Their domestic arrangement did not include the benefit of clergy. Herrell took offense at this affront to his mother's reputation. On the day in question he went to his mother's home and exchanged harsh words with her beau. Taking offense at this treatment, Ring retrieved a piece of wood from the stove and advanced on Herrell intending to teach him a lesson. Herrell quickly seized the opportunity to settle his score with Ring and drew his revolver and shot the older man dead.[98]

The murders of James Everett and Amos Ring infuriated many local residents, who saw them as symptomatic of the larger problems that had afflicted Taney County for some time. The friends of the deceased James Everett, in particular, looked toward the upcoming trial of Al Layton as a test case to see if the courts would sustain the law and punish the guilty. Many of them believed that "if murder, robbing, arson, horse stealing, petty thieving, and other crimes were to continue and go unpunished, it was time that the law-abiding citizens organize to combat lawlessness."[99] So it must have come as an unpleasant shock to them when the jury in the Layton murder trial returned a verdict of not guilty on October 22, 1884. Charges of foul play flew back and forth. Some alleged that Prosecutor T. C. Spellings had accepted a bribe in exchange for sabotaging the case against Layton. Still others accused county clerk Thomas A. Layton of using his influence on behalf of his cousin, and still others accused the defense of plying the jury with alcohol. No hard evidence exists to substantiate any of these claims, although according to one newspaper report "it is admitted that the jury got drunk."[100]

The reaction to Layton's acquittal came in two forms. First, it helped galvanize the political opposition to the Democratic clique running the local government at that time. In the elections held the following month, the Republicans had their best showing, and the Democrats their worst, in roughly a decade. At the top of the ticket, Republican presidential candidate James G. Blaine handily won Taney County with 646 votes to Grover Cleveland's 460 votes.[101] In the governor's race, Nicholas Ford, the "Fusion" candidate representing the Republican Party and the Greenback Labor Party, defeated Democrat John Sappington Marmaduke in Taney County by a similar margin.[102]

More significantly, several Republicans (including some who became prominent Bald Knobbers) won election to local offices, defeating the Democrats who had held those positions. James K. Polk McHaffie defeated John Moseley in the race for sheriff and collector of revenue; Reuben S. Branson defeated incumbent Thomas F. Compton in the race for county assessor; and Charles H. Groom won the election for treasurer. All three men belonged to the Republican Party, and all three would also join the Bald Knobbers. Additionally, Republicans Francis M. Keithley and J. W. Underwood won election to the county court. Prosecutor T. C. Spellings, who had drawn criticism for his role in the Layton trial, lost his job to Rufus V. Burns, who was most likely a fellow Democrat. County clerk Thomas Layton kept his office, but only because his four-year term did not end until 1886.[103] The one Bald Knobber who lost an election in 1884, Nathaniel Kinney, ran for state representative as a Democrat against Republican James C. Johnson and Greenbacker James R. Vanzandt. Johnson prevailed in the contest with a modest majority.[104]

In addition to the political backlash of 1884, the controversy surrounding the Layton trial also prompted several leading citizens to begin meeting about the possibility of forming a vigilance committee. The available sources disagree about the exact date of the first meeting, but it happened either shortly before or shortly after the verdict in the Layton trial, possibly as late as January 1885. It took place in Forsyth, in the store formerly belonging to James Everett but subsequently managed by his brother Barton. Thirteen men attended the meeting, including Nathaniel N. Kinney, Alonzo S. Prather, Barton Y. Everett, James B. Rice, Thomas W. Phillips, James R. Vanzandt, Patterson F. Fickle, J. J. Brown, Galba E. Branson, James K. Polk McHaffie, James A. Delong, Charles H. Groom, and Benjamin B. Price. Kinney chaired the meeting, and the participants appointed Brown, a prominent attorney in Forsyth, to draw up a series of resolutions that the participants signed. The resolutions established a vigilance committee, officially named the "Committee for Law and Order," for the purpose of assisting local law enforcement officers in the performance of their duties. They pledged that the signers "would at all times respond to the call of the officers to enforce obedience to the law."[105] The vigilantes had no specific rules concerning masks, and in Taney County the members of the committee rarely, if ever, wore them. The only insignia the vigilantes wore was a small badge made of red silk, approximately five by two inches, with the words "Stand Up for Taney County and Law and Order" stitched onto them.[106]

The participants also decided to make the vigilance committee a secret organization, so as to ensure the safety of its members, and they asked Brown and Kinney to draw up a constitution and bylaws and a membership oath to administer to new recruits. No copies of the constitution and bylaws survive, since to preserve their secrecy the members of the group later decided to destroy them.[107] Several versions of the membership oath survive, however, including one that the *New York Sun* later reprinted. The oath represented the basic sentiments and purpose of the organization:

Do you, in the presence of God and these witnesses, solemnly swear that you will never reveal any of the secrets of this order nor communicate any part of it to any person or persons in the known world, unless you are satisfied by a strict test, or in some legal way, that they are lawfully entitled to receive them; that you will conform and abide by the rules and regulations of this order, and obey all orders of your superior officers or any brother officer under whose jurisdiction you may be at the time attached; nor will you propose for membership or sanction the admission of anyone whom you have reason to believe is not worthy of being a member, nor will you oppose the admission of anyone solely on a personal matter. You shall report all theft that is made known to you, and you shall not leave unreported any thief on account of his being a blood relation of yours; nor will you willfully report anyone through personal enmity. You shall recognize and answer all signs made by lawful brothers and render them such assistance as they may be in need of, so far as you are able or the interest of your family will permit; nor will you willfully wrong or defraud a brother, or permit it if in your power to prevent it. Should you willfully and knowingly violate this oath in any way, you subject yourself to the jurisdiction of twelve members of this order, even if their decision should be to hang you by the neck until you are dead, dead, dead. So help me God.[108]

Despite the sense of urgency that the language of the oath seemed to convey, at this point the vigilance committee remained in its infancy stage. For the first few months of its existence the organization did not do much either to enforce the law or to apprehend or punish criminals. In order to have the impact they desired the vigilantes needed greater numbers and better organization.

To accomplish those ends, the vigilantes held their first large-scale organizational meeting on April 5, 1885. It took place on a large treeless ridge (a "bald knob" in local parlance) located near Kirbyville, a place known as "Snapp's Bald." The vigilantes selected this location because it gave them a clear view of the surrounding countryside, which provided security in case someone wished to spy on the proceedings or ambush them. According to James A. Delong, Nathaniel Kinney's stepson, early that morning Kinney went to the meeting place alone, ostensibly to ensure its security. The vigilante leaders had invited those they wished to recruit into the organization ahead of time. As the morning broke, a small handful of men approached the meeting place in "terror lest they should be led into a trap." At the clearing at the top of the hill they met Kinney, who greeted them all as they arrived.[109]

As the day wore on more men arrived, eventually bringing the total to roughly one hundred. When it looked like no more would come, Kinney stood up to address the crowd. He gave what witnesses described as "a blood-stirring oration over the bloody shirt of J. M. Everett." No one preserved the exact text of Kinney's speech, but according to one newspaper account it ended as follows: "What will become of our sons and daughters? Our lives, our property, and our liberty are at stake. I appeal to you, as citizens of Taney County, to say what we shall do. Shall we organize ourselves into a vigilant committee and see that when crimes are committed the laws are enforced, or shall we sit down and fold our arms and quietly submit?" At this point some men in the crowd shouted, "Boy, she pops!" This phrase, a common colloquialism among the hill folk at that time, replaced the traditional "aye" at future Bald Knobber gatherings.[110]

After voting to organize themselves into a vigilance committee, the new recruits took the membership oath and received instruction concerning the rules and secrets of the order. The members also voted to elect Nathaniel Kinney as the leader, or "chieftain," of the group. One of the first rules that Kinney imposed forbade the use of written records of any kind in order to preserve the secrecy of the organization. They also adopted a semi-military structure, which subdivided the organization into separate companies, or "legions," each with a captain commanding it. For example, James Delong, Kinney's stepson, commanded a legion that eventually numbered more than forty men.[111]

The first public act associated with the Bald Knobbers occurred shortly thereafter, on April 7, 1885, at Forsyth. Somewhere between ten o'clock in the evening and one o'clock in the morning a company of between sixty and one hundred armed men rode into town. They surrounded the county jail, apparently intending to take from it the prisoner Newton Herrell, who had sat there awaiting trial for the murder of Amos Ring seven months before. When he heard the commotion outside, Herrell, who probably realized the crowd's intention, began shouting for help. The riders demanded the keys to the jail, but Sheriff McHaffie, himself a charter member of the Bald Knobbers, denied their request. The riders backed down this time, but before leaving town they entered the courthouse and placed on the judge's bench a length of rope tied into a noose, presumably to signal their desire that the court convict Herrell and punish him accordingly.[112]

Sheriff McHaffie's refusal to give the vigilantes the keys to the jail raises some interesting questions. First, it calls into question whether the Bald Knobbers had really reached a consensus among themselves about how to punish lawbreakers. Second, it raises the possibility that a conflict had already arisen among members of the Bald Knobber leadership. Given Kinney's election as chieftain just two days prior, it seems safe to assume that he approved the raid on the jail. Sheriff

McHaffie evidently did not. One newspaper account suggests that the riders only intended to scare Herrell, not to lynch him.[113] If true, that would mean the vigilantes staged the entire affair as an elaborate ruse to frighten a prisoner and project their own authority. It hardly seems likely, however, that the Bald Knobbers would have gone to all that trouble to scare a man who would soon stand trial for murder. In any event, their escapade did not have the desired effect. In response to the night's events, the circuit judge granted Newton Herrell a continuance of his trial and sent him to the Greene County jail in Springfield for his safe keeping.[114] Several months later, on November 2, Herrell escaped from jail and promptly disappeared. He managed to evade recapture for two years, until lawmen finally caught up with him at Golden City, Missouri, on September 6, 1887.[115]

Despite the inconclusive end to the Bald Knobbers' first raid on Forsyth, it sent a signal that the vigilantes intended to bring real change to Taney County and that they would no longer tolerate lawlessness in their communities. About a week after the near lynching of Herrell, Alonzo Prather wrote an editorial in his newspaper, the *Home and Farm*, which justified the action and explained what the people could expect from the vigilantes in the future. Prather noted that for the preceding two or three weeks "small squads of men" had been meeting at various places in the county to discuss the crime situation in their community. The "demonstration in Forsyth on Monday night of last week," he said, had showed that now "something more than talk is likely to be done toward enforcing the law." This demonstration was a response to the prevailing condition of lawlessness in Taney County, where for several years the lawful authorities had allowed criminals to run rampant while decent citizens had "to keep under cover and pay the bills." Henceforth a "combination of law-abiding citizens" would assist law officers in enforcing the law and apprehending criminals. This new organization, Prather promised, would ensure that "the law will be enforced hereafter in Taney County—not mob law, but there will be force enough to sustain the courts and the officers."[116]

The Bald Knobbers soon had another opportunity to demonstrate what kind of force they could bring to bear in order to enforce the law and punish criminals. On April 7, 1885, the same day as the

Bald Knobbers' attempted lynching of Herrell, Frank Taylor visited John T. Dickenson's general store at Eglinton. Taylor attempted to purchase a pair of boots and other items on credit. Since Dickenson had already extended credit to Taylor without receiving payment he refused to comply with this request. An argument broke out, which culminated with Taylor's cursing and threatening Dickenson. He also wrecked the store and left merchandise strewn across the floor, before he walked out.[117]

A few hours after the confrontation at Dickenson's store, Frank Taylor rode into Forsyth where his brother Tubal had recently surrendered to the authorities on the charge of maiming Alexander Kissee's cattle. For some reason, Sheriff McHaffie had placed Tubal in the temporary custody of a deputy rather than locking him up in the jail. When Frank Taylor arrived in town, he found Tubal and his guardian on the porch of the Everett saloon. Frank dismounted in front of the saloon, and without any warning Tubal jumped into the saddle and rode away.[118]

The following day, April 8, John Dickenson went to Forsyth. Dickenson naturally resented the treatment he had received from Frank Taylor. In earlier days he might have let Taylor's insults and abuses pass. Dickenson had recently joined the Bald Knobbers, however, and perhaps this new association emboldened him. He swore out an indictment against Frank Taylor on the charge of disturbing the peace. The grand jury indicted Taylor, but he quickly posted bond to secure his release.[119]

Two days later, on April 10, 1885, Frank Taylor, his brother Tubal, and a friend named Elijah Sublett returned to the Dickenson store. They brought with them a large "black-snake" whip, with the apparent intent of horsewhipping the storekeeper for having Frank indicted. Upon entering the store Frank Taylor sat down next to Mr. Dickenson and exchanged the customary "good evening." Suddenly, Taylor seized the older man by the throat. Dickenson tried to free himself, and the two men struggled with each other until Taylor pulled out his revolver and shot Dickenson in the mouth, knocking out several teeth and a part of his left jawbone. Hearing the commotion, Mrs. Dickenson attempted to intervene on her husband's behalf. In the ensuing commotion the Taylor brothers and Sublett fired at least four more shots, wounding Mr. Dickenson in the right shoulder and inflicting slight wounds to Mrs. Dickenson. Neither person's wounds proved fatal.[120]

The shooting of Mr. and Mrs. Dickenson touched off a huge manhunt. A large search party said to number "several hundred strong," including Bald Knobbers and other citizens, turned out to search for the perpetrators.[121] The vigilantes especially wanted the Taylors, whose many transgressions made them primary targets for the vigilantes' wrath. In the end, however, the Taylor brothers gave themselves up when they learned that their victims had not succumbed to their wounds. Given the county's long history of acquitting criminals, the brothers may have thought that they could win an acquittal as Al Layton had done. Or perhaps they thought that they had better take their chances with the law rather than risk running into a company of Bald Knobbers. Still another version of this story suggests that when the Taylors heard about a reward offered for their capture they devised a plan to enrich themselves. According to this scenario, they would enlist some of their friends to hand them over to Sheriff McHaffie. After the Taylors posted bonds to secure their release, "their friends were to collect the reward and divide [it] with them."[122]

Whatever intentions they may have had, the brothers clearly miscalculated the situation. On April 15, 1885, they sent a message to Sheriff McHaffie that they wished to surrender in return for a promise of protection. Two of the sheriff's deputies took the Taylor boys into custody and locked them up in the county jail. At about ten o'clock that evening a company of between seventy-five and one hundred armed men rode into Forsyth and surrounded the jail. Although the men reportedly wore no masks, none of them was identified afterward, save for Nathaniel Kinney, whose size made him unmistakable. This time no one interfered with their work. Using two sledgehammers procured from a local blacksmith shop, the men battered down the door to the jail and broke into the cell holding the Taylors.[123]

The men seized the Taylors and took them from the jail. The brothers now realized their danger and "begged piteously for their lives but all to no purpose." As the Taylors rode out of town with their captors, Frank Taylor reportedly noticed a young woman named Jennie Lunce watching from the home of J. S. B. Berry where she worked. He had once courted her, and so as he passed by the house he bid farewell to her.[124] The next morning Deputy T. H. Toney and another man named A. L. Parrish discovered the bodies of the Taylor brothers hanging from the limb of a scrub oak tree roughly two and a half miles outside of Forsyth. Attached to Tubal Taylor's shirt they found a placard, with the following message inscribed upon it: "Beware! These are the first victims to the wrath of outraged citizens. More will follow. The Bald Knobbers."[125] Despite this rather obvious clue, the coroner's inquest held concerning the Taylor brothers' deaths concluded simply that the men had died "by hanging at the hands of about one hundred men to this jury unknown."[126]

The hanging of the Taylor brothers came at a crucial juncture in the history of Taney County and southwest Missouri. During this period the forces of economic modernization, improved transportation, and mass immigration steadily wore away the foundations of the traditional rural and communal society in the Ozarks. At the vanguard of this new social order came a group of men determined to remake Ozarks society in their own image. Although their backgrounds varied significantly, they did share certain traits. They were predominantly middle-class and upper-class men, many of whom came from states in the North or the Midwest. Several of them had served in the Union army, or else belonged to families that had supported the Union during the Civil War, and most of the veterans continued to identify with the Union cause through participation in organizations such as the Grand Army of the Republic. A majority of them belonged to the Republican Party, although there were significant exceptions (e.g., Kinney). Most important, they shared a common vision of the kind of society they wanted to build in the Ozarks, which included new roads, bridges, banks, railroads, responsible local government, and prosperity based on free markets and free labor. The Bald Knobber movement championed this vision and drew into its ranks those who believed in it. They identified the enemies of their cause as the numerous outlaws and petty criminals who had long plagued their communities, and the corrupt courthouse ring of Democratic politicians whom they believed had burdened them with an outrageous public debt. The lynching of the Taylor brothers demonstrated their willingness to use violent force to remove these obstacles to progress.

## CHAPTER 3

# The Purging of Taney County

The lynching of Frank and Tubal Taylor set off a chain of events that few of the Bald Knobbers who participated in the hangings could have predicted. These included the emergence of an organized opposition to the vigilantes, an escalation of violence between them and their opponents, and the eventual intervention by the state government. The initial response to the lynchings, however, was widespread apprehension about what might come next. Following the Taylor brothers' untimely demise, at least a few members of the vigilance committee began to have second thoughts about their activities. Some members promptly quit the group, including Jim Parnell and Emmett Everett (who may have recalled his family's tragic experiences during the Tutt-Everett conflict in Arkansas). These dropouts felt that they had joined the organization to enforce the law and to assist legitimate law officers, not to subvert or take the law into their own hands.[1]

For most of the band, however, the real concern was whether their action would meet with the approval of their fellow citizens, on whose sentiments their survival depended. Over the next couple of weeks, the Bald Knobbers held meetings to discuss the mood of the public. They took heart when they learned that most of their neighbors approved of the Taylor lynching, and few wanted to see the men who took part in it prosecuted.[2] In fact, their actions brought more recruits into their ranks, which according to some sources soon swelled to at least three hundred men.[3]

With support from their community, the emboldened Bald Knobbers began purging Taney County, driving out criminals and other people whose presence they considered undesirable. Contemporary observers reported a general exodus of the county's outlaw population who discovered "that while horses were getting wilder, more skittish and harder to catch after dark, the farmers were raising more hemp than ever before." The possibility of receiving a visit from "the dreaded Bald Knobbers recalled to their memories the fact that it was a long time since they had seen their kinfolks in Arkansas, and they generally took the trip forthwith."[4] Among the first people to leave were Francis and Matilda Taylor, the parents of Frank and Tubal Taylor whom the Knobbers had so recently dangled from their ropes. The Taylors moved the remainder of their family to Marionville in Lawrence County. Frank and Tubal's brother, William Taylor, enrolled in Marionville College, where he joined the Methodist Episcopal Church and taught Sunday School. William Taylor would himself later play a role in the Bald Knobber story the following year.[5]

Over the next several months many other families and individuals followed the Taylors out of Taney County. No one knows exactly how many people the Bald Knobbers drove out, but enough examples exist to suggest that scores of people left, if not hundreds. The Bald Knobbers commonly referred to their method of eviction as "warning out." It involved a night-time visit to the victim's home by a group of riders. Often the riders fired a few shots into the air to announce their presence, followed by a stern warning to the transgressor to flee or face dire consequences. Frequently the riders left a bundle of hickory switches at the doorstep of the evictee. The number of switches represented the number of days the victim had to depart before the Bald Knobbers would pay him a return visit.[6]

A resident named Ben Boyd received one of the first of these visits from the vigilantes. Boyd lived with his family across the White River from Forsyth. By the fall of 1885 he had gained a reputation for "larcenous proclivities"; several of his neighbors complained about his alleged thefts. The Bald Knobbers decided to expel him from Taney County. One night Charles Groom led a small group of four riders to

Boyd's house. As they approached the home, Boyd's dog alerted him to their arrival, and he quickly took refuge underneath the structure. As they arrived, the men called for Boyd to come out to meet them. He refused and asked them what they wanted. Groom replied that they had received complaints "that you have difficulty in distinguishing your property from that of your neighbors, and consequently your neighbors are objecting to your residing longer in the community." Groom went on to say that Boyd had ten days to leave before they paid him another visit. Upon realizing that they did not intend to punish him that night, a relieved Boyd replied, "Hell, I'll give you back nearly all that time." He promised to leave the county by 10 o'clock the next morning. True to his word, Boyd and his family departed for Arkansas the next day.[7]

Several members of the Pruitt clan received similar warnings from the Bald Knobbers. The family of William H. Pruitt received the following notice: "W. H. Pruitt, you have fooled with the wrong end of the mule, and you have 30 days to leave the county." As if to emphasize their point, the note contained a picture of a tree with a noose hanging from it. The families of Reuben Pruitt, Wade Pruitt, and James Pruitt received similar messages. According to the Anti-Bald Knobber Sampson Barker, a band of about sixty-five Bald Knobbers paid a nocturnal visit to the home of one of the Pruitt men (he did not specify which one). During the course of the raid the vigilantes "abused his half idiotic wife and poor little bare headed, bare-footed, and semi-naked girl children," killed the family dog, and "shot into the walls of the poor miserable log hut in which they were camped."[8]

J. F. Grant and his family, including his wife and three children, also received an eviction order from the Bald Knobbers, as did three of the Orr brothers and their families. The Bald Knobbers also paid night-time visits to the homes of Robert Patterson, Frank Grand, and James Coffer, an "old inoffensive man" who never quarreled with anybody and who was "almost a pauper" at the time of his eviction. On another occasion, the Bald Knobbers seized a man named Edward Tuttle and kept him prisoner for a whole day and night. They told the terrified man that they wanted to hang him, and they even forced him to make out a will. In the end Tuttle saved himself from a lynching only by promising to sell his farm and leave the county immediately.

Tuttle sold his farm at a considerable loss and moved his family to Christian County.[9]

The Bald Knobbers targeted some people on the suspicion of criminal activity. Others had to go because they were connected in some way to the Democratic political machine that the voters had recently deposed in the 1884 election. Still others the Bald Knobbers forced out simply because they somehow had managed to anger, annoy, or inconvenience the vigilantes. Examples of such coercion abound. The Bald Knobbers expelled Jerome Winslow, a young man described in newspaper accounts as "well connected" and a "friend of the Taylors." They also warned out Jefferson Weaver, the son-in-law of ex-sheriff John Moseley, possibly to keep him from testifying against a Bald Knobber who was on trial for felonious assault. A man named Jonathan Brooks received a warning from the Bald Knobbers that he had built a fence on a public road. The fence inconvenienced some of his Bald Knobber neighbors, who ordered him to move it. When he failed to comply, they destroyed it at night. He wisely decided not to rebuild it. Another man drew the Bald Knobbers' ire during a dispute with a widow concerning the possession of a farm. The Bald Knobbers sent him a written note telling him "politely but firmly" not to "meddle with Mrs. S_____ or her business; let her alone in possession of her homestead; don't make any more threats to send a mob to drive her away from home. You will also allow her to cultivate the crop that her husband planted. Don't misunderstand this note, but obey it to the letter, or we will use you in our way of doing."[10]

Neither political connections nor social stature protected those who attracted the Bald Knobbers' wrath. For example, the justice of the peace in Oliver Township had to leave Taney County because, according to one newspaper account, "He could do no business. He was not a Bald Knobber." The same article reported that a band of about forty Bald Knobbers arrested "two young men named Coggburn" without a warrant and took them before a judge who "fined them $25.00 for carrying concealed weapons." The father of these young men was most likely John S. Coggburn, whom the newspaper called "one of the best citizens of the county" as well as the treasurer of the local Masonic Lodge. John S. Coggburn was also the uncle of Andrew Coggburn, who within a few months would die at the hands of Nathaniel Kinney.[11]

The Bald Knobbers also paid visits to the homes of John H. Haworth and M. P. Boyd and fired gunshots into their houses in an attempt to intimidate them and drive them away. John Haworth's uncle, Jordan M. Haworth, was a prominent minister in the community who had served a term as the presiding judge of the county court and as the county's representative in the Missouri General Assembly. John Haworth himself belonged to the Forsyth Lodge, Number 453, of the Free Masons and had cofounded (with his uncle) the first Christian Church in Taney County.[12] Many years later Haworth wrote an account of his experiences during the Bald Knobber years in which he recalled that the raid on his house stemmed from his decision to rent a farm about ten miles south of Forsyth. Apparently, several Bald Knobbers wanted to purchase the place, but as long as Haworth held the lease they could not do so. On the night in question a party of about twenty Bald Knobbers led by a man named McGill (probably Joe McGill) came to his home. McGill asked him if he intended to keep his lease. Haworth replied that he did even if "every ear of corn cost me a dollar." McGill warned that if he did so "we will crack your neck." Several of the Bald Knobbers then fired shots into the roof of Haworth's house, after which they turned around and rode off.[13]

As the preceding episodes demonstrate, in addition to enforcing the law, the Bald Knobbers were not above using their power to intervene in private disputes between neighbors. Many of them apparently felt that their authority also extended to matters of private morality and vice. If the Bald Knobbers believed a man had abused his wife or neglected to support his family, he could find himself the recipient of an unwelcome visit from a "dark assemblage" that would "take him from his bed, and mete out justice to him with a full-grown sapling."[14] The Bald Knobbers took special notice of any public disruptions made during religious services. Nathaniel Kinney, a very religious man, used to teach a Sunday School at the Oak Grove schoolhouse near Kirbyville. Kinney's reputation for stern religiosity drew scorn from many of the young roughnecks with whom he so frequently clashed as a vigilante leader. Richard Prather, who attended Kinney's Sunday School as a boy, recalled that one Sunday a group of "wild young hellions" sitting in the back row disrupted Kinney's lesson. The enormous Kinney walked back to where the "young scamps" were sitting and towering over them declared, "One more peep out of you and I'll throw you out of the window." In the face of this furious giant the scamps wisely left the church and rode off firing their pistols into the air in defiance.[15]

Not all of the roughnecks showed such discretion. In September 1885, local authorities issued a warrant for the arrest of two of the three Mercer brothers on the charge of disturbing public worship. On September 29, Deputy Sheriff Arter Kissee, a Bald Knobber and a brother of Alexander Kissee, took the warrant to the Mercer family's cabin on Nubbin Ridge. There he found Buck Mercer, one of the two men named in the warrant. Kissee entered the cabin from the back door. When Mercer saw the officer coming toward him he ducked out the front door. On his way out Mercer grabbed his shotgun, which he discovered was unloaded. He ran around the back of the house intending to grab his other gun, which he had left leaning against the rear wall of the cabin. Kissee met him coming out the back door and fired a shot into the man's chest, killing him instantly.[16]

One of the young hellions who delighted in disrupting Kinney's Sunday School was Andrew Coggburn, nephew of John S. Coggburn and cousin to the two young men whom the Bald Knobbers had arrested for carrying concealed weapons. In the summer of 1885, Kinney's congregation held a Sunday School convention at their church. One morning the participants opened the door to find that someone had left a coat in the church. The coat had a placard on it marked with a skull and crossbones and the words "Captain Kinney's," a reference to the Bald Knobber leader.[17] Affixed to the front door of the church they also found a miniature coffin with a buckshot ball and a note inside. The note read: "To old Kinney, pisen [sic] and death is his favorite role." Several of the Coggburn boys, including Andrew Coggburn, and their sisters attended the church that morning. The Coggburns evidently found it amusing to observe the discomfort their actions had caused. Kinney later recalled that when he saw the coffin with the ominous note he "called everybody up to see it, and said, pointing my finger at Coggburn, 'the man who did this is here and he will need a box before I do.'"[18] The Coggburn boys carried no weapons with them, so no violence occurred at that time, but someone later said that their sisters had revolvers concealed under their dresses in case their men needed them. After that day Kinney and the Coggburns "were like tigers, each watching the other lest he might pounce on him unawares."[19]

Kinney's stern warning to Andrew Coggburn evidently did not deter the younger man from continuing to antagonize the Bald Knobber chieftain and his followers. At some point he decided upon a rather innovative method of expressing his disrespect for the vigilante leader. He wrote a satirical song titled "The Ballad of the Bald Knobbers" sung to the tune of the popular old ditty "My Name Is Charles Guiteau." The song, which Coggburn and his friends enjoyed singing whenever they wanted to annoy the Bald Knobbers, mocked the vigilantes for their pride, greed, and abuses of power. At least two different versions of the song exist, indicating that it may have gone through multiple revisions and redactions over time, but both versions contain a verse aimed directly at Nathaniel Kinney:

> There is one big Bald Knobber
> Whose Name I will Expose,
> His Name is Nat N. Kinney,
> And he wears his federal clothes.
> He tries to boss the people
> And make them do his will.
> There's some that does not fear him,
> But others mind him still.[20]

The disturbances surrounding Nathaniel Kinney's church, and the feud between Kinney and the Coggburn family, underscored the escalating tensions between the Bald Knobbers and those who found their tactics heavy handed and unjust. Those tensions only increased when, on December 19, 1885, the Taney County courthouse mysteriously burned down. Only two sets of records survived the fire. The county treasurer Charles Groom, a Bald Knobber, managed to rescue enough of Taney County's tax records to furnish the county with a new set of tax books. The county clerk Thomas A. Layton, an Anti-Bald Knobber who still held office by virtue of winning a four-year term in 1882, managed to rescue a book containing the abstracts of Taney County's land titles.[21]

The actual cause of the fire remains unknown, but the people of Taney County had no shortage of theories on the matter. The Bald Knobbers blamed the fire on their enemies, particularly the members of the old Democratic courthouse ring that the voters had thrown out in the election of 1884. This included former sheriff John Moseley, former prosecutor T. C. Spellings, former county judge J. J. Reynolds, and Thomas A. Layton, the current county clerk who still held office because he was not up for reelection until 1886. After retaking the county courthouse, the new Republican regime petitioned the circuit court to appoint an independent investigator to go over the county's books, presumably to uncover evidence of their predecessors' financial misdeeds. The Democratic officials declared that they had nothing to hide and that an investigation would only vindicate them. Before any investigation could proceed, however, the courthouse burned down. The Bald Knobbers claimed that the members of the old regime had burned down the courthouse in an attempt to cover their tracks. Their opponents, by contrast, claimed that the vigilantes themselves had set the fire, possibly to destroy the county's land records so as to allow the Bald Knobbers to push property owners off their land. Vance Randolph, in his historical narrative of the Bald Knobbers, wrote that one unnamed vigilante "made a great deal of money over a long period of time, which he could not have made if the county records had been preserved."[22]

The accusations of arson were not without foundation or merit. The tactic of destroying evidence via courthouse burning had considerable precedent in the Ozarks at this time. The following year in Douglas County, for example, the county treasurer burned down his own courthouse to destroy evidence of embezzlement, despite which he ultimately served five years in a state penitentiary for arson. Likewise, arsonists destroyed courthouses in Christian County in 1865, Reynolds County in 1871, and Shannon County in 1895. Given this background, the arson explanation remains a distinct possibility.[23]

Even so, there are reasons to suspect a more innocent explanation for the fire. For one thing, the courthouse could certainly have burned down accidentally rather than because of arson. Indeed, nineteenth-century courthouses had a notorious propensity for going up in flames, since they were typically constructed of wood, packed full with paper and other flammable material, and heated using woodstoves or open fireplaces.[24] Moreover, the question of motive for arson remains somewhat murky. If the Bald Knobbers, for example, had wanted to start the blaze, they must surely have realized that the cost of replacing the courthouse would add to the county's already large debt burden, which as taxpayers they wanted to eliminate. Shortly after the fire, the voters defeated a bond issue that would have added $4,000 to the county's debt to pay for a new courthouse. Then in 1890, state representative Alonzo Prather managed to convince the General Assembly to underwrite the construction of a new courthouse, but in 1885 no one could have known that the state would pay the bill.[25]

Given the impending investigation into the county's finances, the possibility of arson by the departing Democratic officeholders seems more plausible. On the other hand, if the former county officials whom the Bald Knobbers accused of starting the fire wanted to destroy evidence of financial malfeasance, why risk committing arson? Why not destroy any incriminating evidence before leaving office? Moreover, why wait a full year after their electoral defeat in 1884 before taking action? Thus, the blaze that destroyed the Taney County courthouse may have had an innocent explanation, and this seems more probable than either of the competing arson theories. In the tense and suspicious atmosphere of 1885 and 1886, however, few people gave their neighbors from the "other side" the benefit of the doubt.

Following the courthouse fire of 1885, two events took place that helped push the Bald Knobbers and their opponents perilously close to open violence against one another. The first was the murder of Mack Dimmock, a young mentally retarded man from Marionville in Lawrence County, who died in a gulch near the Boston Road (also called the "Wilderness Road") which ran through Taney County. Many of the Bald Knobbers assigned the blame for this terrible crime to William Taylor, the brother of Frank and Tubal Taylor who had perished the previous April.

In late February 1886, William Taylor hired Mack Dimmock, who owned a horse and buggy and a wagon, to take him on a short trip into Taney County, ostensibly to purchase a load of timber there.

About five days later Taylor returned to Marionville, with the horse, buggy, wagon, and lumber, but without Dimmock. He had a bill of sale that he acknowledged writing, but claimed that Dimmock had signed it, selling him the horse and other equipment for $60 in cash and a promissory note for another $60. Taylor claimed that during their journey Dimmock left him at a place called Camp Spring in Taney County. Dimmock, he explained, intended to go to Springfield and take a train to Illinois to see his mother, who had recently moved there. Many people had suspicions about the accuracy of this story, but no one investigated the matter until Mrs. Dimmock, anxious over not hearing from her son, wrote from Illinois to Deputy Sheriff S. R. Stafford in Marionville asking him to find the young man. Stafford set out for Taney County retracing the route Taylor and Dimmock had followed. In Taney County he met some men who told him they had seen the body of a young man in a deep gulch not far from the road. The lawman found the body and brought it back to Marionville, where someone identified the remains of the unfortunate victim as young Mack Dimmock. Stafford then filed formal charges against William Taylor for murder.[26]

Since the murder had taken place in Taney County, the authorities there issued a warrant for Taylor's arrest on March 30, 1886. They intended to have him brought back to Taney County to await trial there. Not surprisingly, William Taylor feared to return to Taney County lest he should die at the end of a rope like his brothers. So he made an impassioned appeal to the authorities in his own county to send him to the Greene County jail in Springfield instead, where at least he would have protection from the Bald Knobbers' brand of justice. In his appeal he cited the death of his brothers "who were disposed of by the Taney County mob" as proof that he would not survive if sent there. In view of his brothers' unfortunate end, the authorities in Lawrence County granted Taylor's request and sent him to Springfield. He remained there until the next term of the circuit court in Forsyth held in April 1886.[27]

Around the same time that Taylor allegedly murdered Mack Dimmock, another tragic event took place in Taney County, at the Oak Grove schoolhouse near Kirbyville where Nathaniel Kinney's Sunday School met. On Sunday, February 28, Nathaniel Kinney took his young son Paul to the schoolhouse to attend an evening service held by the Reverend H. C. Dennison. He met Andrew Coggburn and Samuel H. Snapp outside the doors of the schoolhouse. The exact sequence of events that followed became the subject of much debate in the ensuing months, but this much remains clear: moments after meeting him at the schoolhouse Nathaniel Kinney shot and killed Andrew Coggburn.[28] The rest of the story depends largely on which narrative one chooses to believe.

According to the pro-Bald Knobber version of the event, the service had already started by the time that Kinney arrived. One of Kinney's friends, most likely Deputy Sheriff Galba Branson, noticed Coggburn and Snapp in attendance and ran to warn the Bald Knobber chieftain to take precautions in case they meant harm to him. Kinney strapped on his revolver and headed toward the church. When they arrived at their destination, Kinney and his son tied their horses about a hundred feet from the schoolhouse door and cautiously approached on foot. According to Richard Prather, Kinney's son Paul later told him that his father made him walk behind his huge frame for protection. As they approached the building Kinney made out the figures of two men standing in the shadows on either side of the door. According to Paul Kinney, it seemed at the time like a deliberate attempt to ambush his father. Kinney stopped, drew his revolver, and called out to the two men to raise their hands and come into the light. Andrew Coggburn stepped into the light and raised his left hand, but with his right he attempted to draw his own revolver, at which point Kinney shot him once in the body causing him to fall backward onto the ground. As he died, Coggburn tossed up his pistol into the air and it nearly landed at Paul Kinney's feet. Turning to Sam Snapp, Kinney leveled his gun and asked him what he intended to do. Snapp replied that he had no weapon and would do nothing, so Kinney sent him back inside the schoolhouse to wait for the authorities to arrive.[29]

Kinney then went to the doorway of the building and instructed everyone inside to wait until he told them they could leave. He picked out several men from the crowd whom he knew personally and asked them to come outside and build a fire in order to provide some light at the crime scene. When his men had finished this task, Kinney allowed the congregants to leave the building one at a time, keeping the "bad ones covered all the time until they were well out of sight." Then he surrendered to Deputy Sheriff Branson, who took him into custody until a coroner's inquest held the following morning declared the killing a justifiable homicide and cleared Kinney of all charges.[30] Some people doubted the validity of this conclusion, given the fact that Kinney and several of his supporters showed up at the hearing heavily armed with firearms and other weapons, ostensibly to protect Kinney from retaliation by Coggburn's relatives or friends. Kinney himself carried a revolver and a double-barreled shotgun, despite the fact that the county's law officers still officially held him under arrest.[31] The coroner's jury examined only one witness, a man named John Davis, who had attended the service that night. Neither Paul Kinney nor Sam Snapp testified, even though they were the only actual eyewitnesses to the killing.[32]

Those hostile to the Bald Knobbers told a very different version of the story. What the Bald Knobbers described as a simple case of self-defense, their enemies portrayed as a cold-blooded murder. The basic details of this version of the event came from Sam Snapp, the only Anti-Bald Knobber present at the scene of the killing. He told his story to Adj. Gen. James C. Jamison about six weeks after Coggburn's death. According to Snapp, he and Coggburn had gone to the schoolhouse together simply to attend the service. They got up to leave the service, and as they exited the building they saw Nathaniel Kinney walking toward the door. Coggburn turned to Snapp and asked, "Do you think they will hurt me?" By this Snapp understood him to mean Reuben Branson and the other Bald Knobbers present at the service. "No, I think not," Snapp replied. Coggburn then stepped forward and called out to Kinney, "How are you, Cap?" Kinney immediately drew his weapon and commanded Coggburn to "throw up your hands!" He repeated the command three times, to which Coggburn replied, "I have my hands up." After the third command Kinney fired his revolver and "Coggburn fell dead, exclaiming, 'Oh, I'm killed.'" In his statement before Jamison, Snapp did not specifically say whether Coggburn was armed at the time of his death (other anti-Bald Knobber accounts suggest he was not). He was quite adamant, however, that Coggburn had no weapon in his hands when he died, and that he did not "draw or attempt to draw a pistol." When Kinney shot Coggburn, the younger man had both hands "raised up above his head and there was no pistol or other weapon in them."[33]

Kinney then turned toward Snapp and asked him if he had a weapon. Snapp assured him that he did not, and Kinney ordered the frightened man to go back into the church. A party of armed Bald Knobbers soon gathered and kept the doors to the building closed for roughly a half an hour and did not allow anyone to go in or out. When the Bald Knobbers finally allowed the crowd of worshipers to go home, Snapp noticed a Bald Knobber named Hensley (probably Augustus or William P. Hensley) "feeling in and about the clothing of the dead man Coggburn." Snapp maintained that he did not testify before the coroner's jury because he never received a subpoena ordering him to do so, even though at the time the inquest took place he was "at home all the time, or nearby chopping wood, not over 100 yards from the public road and in plain view of it all the time . . . and could have been subpoenaed if they had wanted my testimony."[34]

No one will ever know exactly what happened outside the Oak Grove Church that February night, but having summarized the two competing narratives of this event, it is worth pointing out that both stories contain serious flaws. For one thing, it seems unlikely that either Andrew Coggburn or Sam Snapp went to the church service that night intending to assassinate Nathaniel Kinney. Everything about Coggburn's behavior up to that point—including his disruptions at Kinney's Sunday School, his threats against the Bald Knobber chieftain, and his Anti-Bald Knobber song—paints him more as a juvenile agitator rather than a calculating killer. His casual greeting to Kinney moments before his death ("How are you, Cap?") does not fit the typical pattern of an Ozarks ambush: bushwhackers did not greet their victims before killing them.[35] Nor does it seem probable that either Coggburn or Snapp would risk ambushing Kinney outside a church where they knew other Bald Knobbers attended services. It seems more likely, therefore, that the two men went to the church service merely to antagonize Kinney and the other Bald Knobbers, as Coggburn had often done before.

For several reasons, it is also unlikely that Nathaniel Kinney murdered Andrew Coggburn in cold blood. First, Kinney saw himself as the leader of a vigilance committee, not an outlaw. Whatever one may think of the Bald Knobber chieftain's actions, Kinney clearly believed that he enforced law and order in his community. Intentionally murdering someone outside a church service would have seriously undermined that self-image, not to mention his reputation among his neighbors and peers. Moreover, with his young son present, Kinney would have felt reluctant to do anything that could escalate the crisis into a violent confrontation. Yet, if he believed that the situation posed a threat to his life or that of his son, he might well have felt compelled to act preemptively. In the dark Kinney might not have been able to tell whether Coggburn carried a weapon, and even if he did not have one in his hands or on his person, Kinney probably assumed that he did. A lifetime of violent encounters, first during the Civil War and then as a member of a militia company in Kansas, would have taught him to suspect a possible ambush and act accordingly.

In the long run, however, it did not matter exactly how Coggburn died. The larger significance of his death is that it hardened the positions of both the Bald Knobbers and their opponents. As a result of the killing, an organized Anti-Bald Knobber opposition faction began to take shape. The opposition aimed to end vigilante justice using public protest, political agitation, and potentially violent force. For the first time it became possible to speak of the Anti-Bald Knobbers as a specific group of people rather than an ill-defined collection of dissidents. The names of at least twenty-six of these anti-vigilantes can be identified using newspaper accounts, their letters to public officials, and other primary and secondary sources. Using a similar array of sources, the names of at least forty-two Bald Knobbers can also be identified.[36]

An investigation into the backgrounds of these men makes it possible to offer certain general observations about each group and suggests several points of comparison between the two. First, the Anti-Bald Knobbers came from very similar geographic backgrounds. All but two of the twenty-six anti-vigilantes can be found in U.S. Census records. Nearly half of the remainder, eleven of twenty-four, were born in Missouri, four were born in Tennessee, three in Virginia, one in Kentucky, one in Arkansas, and one in North Carolina. Only three hailed from outside of the South, including one from Indiana and two from Illinois.[37] Thus, the Anti-Bald Knobber cause seemed to draw recruits primarily from the county's southern inhabitants. They also attracted people with deep family roots in the community. As seen in chapter 1, many of the supporters of the anti-vigilante cause came from families that had moved to southwest Missouri very early in the settlement period, often before the Civil War. Such families included the Laytons, the Snapps, and the Coggburns.[38] Additionally, Dr. K. L. Burdette and Jordan M. Haworth arrived in southwest Missouri before the Civil War.[39]

By contrast, the Bald Knobbers drew recruits from more wide-spread geographical backgrounds. Once again, census records can be found for all but two of the vigilantes. Only twelve of the remaining forty vigilantes, or three-tenths, claimed Missouri as their birth state, while ten hailed from Tennessee, three from Arkansas, two from Virginia, one from North Carolina, and one from West Virginia. Interestingly, at least ten of them, or one-quarter, came from places outside of the South, including three from Illinois, two from Indiana, and one each from Ohio, New York, Massachusetts, and Kansas. One Bald Knobber, John T. Dickenson, came from as far away as England. Moreover, while it is not always possible to tell exactly when someone arrived, several leading vigilantes settled in Taney County after the Civil War, many of them in the last ten or fifteen years before the Bald Knobber period. For example, Nathaniel Kinney brought his family to the county in 1883; Alonzo Prather arrived with his family in 1880; Augustus Hensley moved there with his family in 1878; James K. Polk McHaffie settled there in 1873; and Charles Groom came to the county as a young boy in 1871.[40]

In keeping with their predominantly southern backgrounds, most of the Anti-Bald Knobbers old enough to have served in the Civil War sided with the Confederacy, and many others had family connections that tied them to the southern cause. Eight of the anti-vigilantes fought in the Confederate army, compared with only two who fought for the Union. At least six other anti-vigilantes had fathers who served in the Confederate army, while just one had a father who had served the Union. Additionally, one Anti-Bald Knobber, Sam Snapp, had three brothers who fought for the Confederacy.[41] As we shall see later in this chapter, many southerners considered their service to the South a point of pride, and used it to appeal to Gov.

Table 3.1: 1870 Military Backgrounds of Taney County Bald Knobbers and Anti-Bald Knobbers

| Bald Knobber Veterans | | Anti-Bald Knobber Veterans | |
|---|---|---|---|
| Fought for the Union | 12 | Fought for the Union | 2 |
| Fought for the CSA | 3 | Fought for the CSA | 8 |
| Fathers who fought for the Union | 9 | Fathers who fought for the Union | 1 |
| Fathers who fought for the CSA | 0 | Fathers who fought for the CSA | 6 |
| **Total Number** | **42** | **Total Number** | **26** |

Source: 1870, 1880, and 1890 Censuses; Alexander Street Press, LLC, "The American Civil War Research Database," and Ancestry.com, "Civil War Collection"

John S. Marmaduke, Missouri's first ex-Confederate governor, for help against the Bald Knobbers. By contrast, the Bald Knobbers and their families sided overwhelmingly with the Union during the Civil War. As mentioned in chapter 1, twelve of the vigilantes fought in the U.S. Army, while only three fought for the Confederacy. Another nine vigilantes had fathers who had fought for the Union.[42]

Civil War loyalties do not, by themselves, explain the conflict between the two groups. It is interesting to note, however, the differences between the military backgrounds of the two factions, and this in turn suggests that wartime loyalties played a role in determining which side many men chose to support. It also helps to explain their readiness to resort to violence to resolve their disputes. Nine of the Bald Knobber veterans and four of the Anti-Bald Knobber veterans served in Missouri units, meaning that they witnessed and participated in some of the cruelest and ugliest fighting in the war. As a result, they had little reason to feel sympathy or show compassion for people on the other side.

The two camps also differed in terms of their occupational pursuits. A clear majority of people on both sides engaged in some form of agriculture, which in Taney County generally included farming and stock raising. Among the Anti-Bald Knobbers found in census records, eighteen out of twenty-four, or three-fourths, reported themselves as farmers on census returns. Among the Bald Knobbers just a little more than half, twenty-three out of forty, practiced agriculture as their profession. Where they differed was that the Bald Knobbers had more members who practiced different occupations, or had other professions *in addition to* farming, while the great majority of Anti-Bald Knobbers pursued farming as their sole occupation.[43]

Among the Anti-Bald Knobbers, nine individuals had jobs other than farming around the time of the Bald Knobber conflict. They included the county clerk, Thomas Layton, along with two ministers, two schoolteachers, one mill operator, one physician, one storekeeper, and one carpenter. Among the Bald Knobbers, twenty-nine individuals had jobs other than, or in addition to, farming. They included eight lawyers, three schoolteachers, three postmasters, three mill operators, two storekeepers, two merchants, two newspaper publishers, one ferryman, one minister, one clerk, one physician, and one carpenter.[44]

A surprising number of the Bald Knobbers also served in local political offices. Between 1886 and 1892, four Bald Knobbers occupied the office of sheriff: James K. Polk McHaffie, Galba Branson, Reuben Isaacs, and John Lafayette Cook. Two of the vigilantes, Galba Branson and Arter Kissee, became sheriff's deputies. Charles Groom served as county treasurer from 1884 to 1886. Reuben Branson held the assessor's office from 1884 to 1886, and then replaced Anti-Bald Knobber Thomas Layton as county clerk, in which post he served from 1886 to 1888. Madison Day held the position of county coroner from 1886 to 1890. James A. Delong and Benjamin Price occupied the office of county prosecutor from 1888 to 1890 and 1892 to 1894, respectively.[45] As discussed earlier in this chapter, the Anti-Bald Knobbers also had several officeholders in their ranks, although most of these were former Democratic officials who had lost their positions following the Republican takeover in 1884. These included John Moseley, the former sheriff, Jordan M. Haworth, a former state representative and justice of the county court, Thomas A. Layton, the sitting county clerk, and John J. Reynolds and Enos Stanley, both former probate judges.[46]

The greater diversity of occupations among the Bald Knobbers, as well as the greater number of nonagricultural pursuits that many of them practiced reinforced their commitment to a future of economic modernization, improved infrastructure, and responsible local government. The predominantly agrarian Anti-Bald Knobbers, however, remained committed to the traditional rural and agricultural values of the Ozarks. They resented being driven from power in local government and chaffed at the Bald Knobbers' high-handed methods and interference in their personal affairs. They viewed the vigilantes as greedy usurpers, busybodies, and untrustworthy newcomers. But if they wanted to defeat their vigilante oppressors, they would need to enlist the power of the state government. To do that they would have to wage a vigorous public relations campaign to make their grievances known to a wider audience and to the authorities in Jefferson City.

Even before Coggburn's death, the Bald Knobbers' enemies had tried to make their grievances known by speaking out through the press. They received first-rate publicity on November 10, 1885, when Missouri's long-serving secretary of state, Michael K. McGrath, published an editorial in the *Jefferson City Daily Tribune*, one of the state's most influential Democratic organs. In this editorial McGrath aired many of the Anti-Bald Knobbers' complaints against the vigilantes. As a partisan politician, McGrath also attempted to link the Taney County Bald Knobbers to the Republican Party. He described them as a "ku-klux organization composed of Republican officeholders," and noted that "several of the county officers" belonged to the Bald Knobbers, and that all of the county officers save two were "Radicals," a pejorative term for Republicans.[47] McGrath may have been sincere, but his Anti-Bald Knobber comments were also part of a larger game of rhetorical one-upmanship between Republicans and Democrats. In the 1870s and 1880s, Missouri Republicans had routinely denounced the politically ascendant Democrats for being "soft on crime" and used the exploits of such notorious outlaws as Frank and Jesse James to embarrass their opponents.[48] Thus, by blaming the Bald Knobbers on the Republicans, the secretary of state delivered some payback to Republicans for blaming the James gang on the Democrats.

Even so, McGrath had the story partially correct. As seen in chapter 2, most of the Bald Knobbers supported the Republican Party, and the emergence of the Bald Knobbers coincided with the ascendance of the Republican Party in Taney County around 1884. McGrath neglected to mention, however, that the Bald Knobbers' leader, Nathaniel Kinney, not only belonged to the Democratic Party, but chaired the local Democratic Party committee in 1886.[49] Democrats John Lafayette Cook and James R. Vanzandt also joined the vigilante ranks.[50] Thus, the Bald Knobbers did not act merely as a cohort of the

Republican Party, but rather as a bipartisan organization, which had opposed the old Democratic courthouse ring because they associated it with high crime rates and political corruption.

After Andrew Coggburn's death, the Anti-Bald Knobbers stepped up their publicity campaign against the vigilantes. Since the newspapers in Taney County usually supported the Bald Knobbers, the Anti-Bald Knobbers mostly aired their grievances in newspapers in nearby Springfield and other parts of the state. For example, on March 6, 1886, a column by an anonymous "Citizen of Taney" appeared in the *Springfield Daily Herald*, which described the Coggburn killing as "but an outburst of the malice and hatred deep-seated and long-cherished in the hearts of an organized clan" that dominated the county.[51] Ten days later the *Herald* published another broadside from an anonymous "Citizen of Taney County" that lambasted the Bald Knobbers as "an organized clan of marauders, outlaws, and murderers . . . whose very name is a symbol of vindictiveness, treachery, and outrage, and whose dark deeds and dangerous menaces hold a reign of force and terror over every citizen not a member of this invisible Sanhedrin." The editorialist also took aim at Nathaniel Kinney, whom the writer accused of hunting down "Joe Cogburn [sic], whom he found and shot down at church, in a most brutal and cowardly manner, and who 'packed' the coroner's jury with 'Bald Knobbers' and . . . by dint of menaces and threats bulldozed the jury into acquitting him."[52]

The Anti-Bald Knobbers also had objectives that went beyond merely publicizing their grievances. On the Monday following Andrew Coggburn's death, a group of around forty people opposed to the Bald Knobbers met in Forsyth. There they drafted and signed a petition to the governor of Missouri, John S. Marmaduke, asking him to intervene on their behalf. The petitioners wanted official permission to establish a company of militia in their community and weapons with which they would protect themselves and oppose the Bald Knobbers. The participants at the meeting appointed a committee of three, including J. J. Reynolds, Jordan M. Haworth, and Dr. Kenneth L. Burdette, to carry their petition to the governor in Jefferson City. The following day, Kinney and several of his followers appeared in Forsyth and made public "threats against those who had attended the meeting on Monday." Concerning the participants in the meeting,

Kinney reportedly declared, "We have spotted all of them; revenge is ours, and we will have it." In the face of such intimidation, Haworth and Burdette backed out of the trip to Jefferson City, leaving only J. J. Reynolds to carry the petition to the governor, which he did on March 5, 1886.[53]

Although only Reynolds risked making the trip to Jefferson City, several other Anti-Bald Knobbers supported the petition effort by writing letters to the governor and other state officials affirming the need for state intervention. For example, on March 1, county clerk Thomas A. Layton, the only Anti-Bald Knobber still in office in 1886, wrote to the governor begging him to heed the Anti-Bald Knobber petition that "Dr. K. L. Burdett and J. M. Heaworth [sic]" would soon bring to Jefferson City. The petition would ask the governor to use "the power of the state to quell the lawlessness" in Taney County. Layton wrote that the county's residents needed state intervention because the sheriff, James K. Polk McHaffie, "is in sympathy with the 'mob,'" along with most of the "civil authorities" in the area.[54] When it became apparent that Burdette and Haworth would not arrive as scheduled, Layton wrote another letter, this time to Secretary of State McGrath, begging the state's patience in the matter. He explained that Burdette and Haworth had not yet left because they "were watched by the Gang of outlaws [and] they were afraid to go." According to Layton, Haworth had become so afraid of the Bald Knobbers that he left his own house and had gone to stay at his brother-in-law's home instead. Layton begged McGrath to tell the governor to "send the Adjutant General down to inquire into matters here." He warned that "something terrible" would happen if the governor did nothing, because the "opponents to this 'Bald Knob Gang' are now preparing to defend themselves."[55]

This subtle allusion to preparations for self-defense referred to some early steps that the Anti-Bald Knobbers had taken toward organizing a militia company, to which they hoped the governor would give his approval. J. J. Reynolds returned home after his meeting with Governor Marmaduke, having received a vague promise from the governor to send a representative to Taney County who would "get the facts on both sides."[56] After his return from Jefferson City, Reynolds and fellow Anti-Bald Knobber, William H. Miles, the father of the man who would later kill Nathaniel Kinney, began organizing a militia company. Although it remains unclear whether Governor Marmaduke actually gave them permission to do so, within a few days Reynolds wrote to the governor to report on the progress of the militia company, which he predicted would soon reach a full strength of eighty men by March 15.[57] Their progress at recruiting came to a halt, however, when on March 11 the Bald Knobbers held a mass meeting of their own in Forsyth attended by between 154 and 300 men. Nathaniel Kinney chaired the meeting, and most of the Bald Knobber leadership attended it, including Sheriff McHaffie, Alonzo S. Prather, Benjamin B. Price, James A. Delong, and many others.[58] The purpose of the meeting, according to the vigilantes' opponents, was to awe and intimidate those Anti-Bald Knobbers involved in organizing a militia company. It apparently succeeded, for the following day Reynolds wrote to Secretary of State McGrath telling him he would have already filled the roster of the militia company "had not [the] Nobers [*sic*] . . . made their demonstrations" and scared off potential recruits.[59]

The vigilantes may well have intended to intimidate their opponents and thwart the organization of a militia company. Their stated purpose, however, was to draft a series of resolutions that condemned the creation of a militia company. A six-member committee, including Alonzo S. Prather, James A. Delong, W. H. Pollard, Elverton C. Claflin, William G. Connor, and T. W. Price, drew up the resolutions, which urged Governor Marmaduke not to intervene in their local affairs, and opposed the creation of "any militia company . . . believing that it will have a tendency to incite turmoil and cause serious trouble in the county." The antimilitia resolutions stated that no need for a militia existed because "the constituted authorities of the county are able and willing to enforce the civil law" and that J. J. Reynolds and his fellow Anti-Bald Knobbers had based their case for a militia "upon a false representation of alleged lawlessness" in the county. The meeting's participants also selected a three-member committee including Sheriff James K. Polk McHaffie, Thomas W. Phillips, and Benjamin B. Price to bring a copy of these resolutions to the governor, along with a list of some 234 signatures of people who endorsed their message.[60] Not everyone who signed this vigilante counter-petition necessarily belonged to the Bald Knobbers. Many people may have signed it because they felt pressured to do so or because they objected to the cost of creating a militia company, which legally Taney County would have to bear. Nevertheless, the number of signatures on the antimilitia resolutions, compared to the forty-odd signatures on the promilitia petition submitted to the governor, indicates that the Bald Knobbers enjoyed sympathy from the greater number of the Taney County's citizens.

The competing appeals from the Bald Knobber and Anti-Bald Knobber factions created a difficult dilemma for Governor Marmaduke. If he intervened in Taney County on behalf of the Anti-Bald Knobbers there, he ran the risk of provoking an outbreak of violence for which the public would hold him responsible. As a former Confederate officer during the Civil War, Marmaduke had participated in some of the bitter fighting in southern Missouri and northern Arkansas. Thus, he would not have relished the thought of a new round of bloodletting in the Ozarks. On the contrary, as the Anti-Bald Knobbers persistently warned him, if he did nothing, violence might still occur. Then the public would blame him for his inaction. Moreover, many of the people trying to organize the anti-vigilante militia company were fellow Democrats and his political supporters. As Sampson Barker reminded the governor in one his letters, he had supported the governor's election and had always been a faithful "defender of your administration." As a supporter, therefore, he urged the governor to "carefully consider our grievances, give the matter the attention that is due as to its merits or demerits."[61] Another militia supporter, William H. Lunceford, put it in even blunter terms when he wrote to remind the governor that he had "voted for you as governor of the state believing that you would discharge the duties of the Chief Executive with credit to yourself." Now he asked Marmaduke to fulfill his obligation to "extend the protection that is due a law loving and law abiding citizen" by suppressing the Bald Knobbers, "this lawless black midnight organization," which met under cover of darkness and terrorized anyone brave enough to oppose them.[62]

As though these political considerations did not carry enough weight, many of the militia supporters could also appeal to the governor on an emotional level, citing their shared experiences in the Confederate military as a reason he should help them now. Sampson

Barker pointed out that one of the militia commanders, William H. Miles, had served as a lieutenant in the Confederate army and "more than once won the praise of his superiors for his bravery and magnanimity." Barker himself hailed from a family of proud servicemen. Both of his grandfathers served in the Revolutionary War, while his father fought in the War of 1812, and his brother served in the Mexican War. Barker himself "served in the C.S. Army under T. J. Jackson and R. E. Lee." These experiences, wrote Barker, had taught him that "the great bulwark of American liberty lies in the powers of our Citizen Soldiers." With that in mind, how could "any law abiding citizen be opposed to the organization of our citizens into military companies?"[63]

Faced with this difficult dilemma, Governor Marmaduke needed a way to make the problem go away without causing any more bloodshed. To accomplish this he turned to one of his most trusted lieutenants, Adj. Gen. James C. Jamison, the commander of Missouri's militia forces. By 1886 Jamison had already lived a colorful and adventurous life. Born in 1830 in Pike County, Missouri, Jamison spent much of the 1850s in California prospecting for gold. In 1855, he set out for Nicaragua, where he fought under William Walker in one of his famous filibustering expeditions to Central America. After Walker fled Nicaragua following his defeat at the hands of a Costa Rican army, Jamison returned to Missouri.[64] When the Civil War broke out Jamison fought for the Confederacy, serving under Gen. Sterling Price at the Battle of Lexington in Missouri. As adjutant general from 1885 to 1889, Jamison had proved himself a useful lieutenant to Missouri's chief executive. In 1885 and 1886, the governor asked him to use state troops to help control labor unrest among Missouri railroad workers and coal miners. Jamison also helped negotiate an end to a bitter strike that temporarily halted transportation and shipping along several railroad lines running through Missouri and Kansas.[65] Faced with another potential crisis, Governor Marmaduke turned once again to his favorite "fixer" to handle the Bald Knobber situation.

According to the official adjutant general's report for 1886, Jamison arrived in Forsyth on April 8, 1886, and the following day he convened a meeting with people from both sides in the dispute. He delivered a short speech in which he told the people that the state government intended "to enforce obedience to the civil law in Taney County" and urged the "prompt disbandment of the citizen's committee," an organization also known as the Bald Knobbers.[66] The same day he also met with several of the leading Anti-Bald Knobbers and Bald Knobbers in the area. During the course of these conferences he received a promise from Nathaniel Kinney and other vigilante leaders to disband the Bald Knobbers. According to Joe McGill, who attended these meetings, Jamison laid down an ultimatum to the vigilantes: if they disbanded and ceased their activities the state would "make no more trouble about it—just let it drop." But if they did not disband, the state "would be compelled to send the state militia at our expense, to bring about peace and order."[67] The adjutant general's demand forced the Bald Knobbers to face a difficult decision. Not all of them wanted to break up their organization. According to Richard Prather, a moderate faction led by his father, Alonzo, advocated disbanding the group, arguing that it had "served its purpose." Nathaniel Kinney and some of his followers wanted to continue as before. This disagreement caused a rift within the Bald Knobber leadership and between the two men and their families. Richard Prather noted that for a time "Paul and I were estranged . . . [b]ut my father's counsel prevailed" and most of the vigilantes agreed to disband.[68]

On the following day, April 10, a large crowd of about five hundred men met on the public square in Forsyth. They appointed a committee to draft a series of resolutions that publicly disbanded the Bald Knobber organization, declaring that the need for a vigilante group had come to an end, and that the "civil authorities and courts of our county can and will guarantee protection to life, liberty, and property."[69] Since that time, wrote Jamison, although "a few lawless acts" had occurred in the county, for the most part the people had known "comparative peace and order."[70]

Thus, on the surface, Jamison's visit seemed to have resolved the problem. In his private correspondence with the governor, however, the adjutant general painted a less optimistic picture. His summary of the interviews he conducted at Forsyth show that not everyone anticipated an immediate return to "comparative peace and order." Most of the Anti-Bald Knobbers interviewed believed that peace would return so long as the Bald Knobbers kept their promise to disband their organization. For example, Dr. Kenneth L. Burdette told Jamison that he no longer thought it "advisable to arm the militia company recently raised in this county," and that the government should give the Bald Knobbers a chance to "make good on their promise of disbanding, which, if done in good faith will end our troubles." Yet, he worried about the Bald Knobber leader, Nathaniel Kinney, whom he did not trust to keep the peace. Although he hoped that "the disbanding of the Bald Knobbers will result in the restoration of peace," he had "no confidence in the public promises made by Cap Kinney to you today."[71] Another Anti-Bald Knobber, Henry C. Everett, echoed Burdette's sentiments, telling Jamison that if "Kinney's band is broken up, as he publically promised you today, I believe it will end the trouble." But he too expressed concerns over Kinney's influence over his followers.[72] Still other Anti-Bald Knobbers wished that Kinney would stand trial for killing Andrew Coggburn. According to William Blunk and Enos Stanley, two members of the local grand jury, this seemed unlikely since the other members of the grand jury sympathized with the vigilantes and "would not find any bills against anyone who was a Bald Knobber."[73]

Aside from the bitterness toward Kinney, another issue had the potential to disturb the uneasy truce that Jamison had hammered out. Around the same time that Jamison arrived in Forsyth, William Taylor went on trial for the murder of Mack Dimmock. Many of the Anti-Bald Knobbers feared that the vigilantes would lynch Taylor just as they had done to his brothers the year before. If that happened, the tenuous peace would not last. To assuage these fears, the Bald Knobbers addressed the case in their resolutions of disbandment, in which they pledged to give "William Taylor, who is charged with murder, a fair and impartial trial by a jury of his peers."[74] Likewise, R. V. Burns, the county prosecutor whom Jamison described as a "neutral" in the factional conflict within Taney County, told the adjutant general that he expected Taylor to remain unmolested until his trial and sentencing. Burns believed that the vigilantes had no reason to lynch Taylor, since the evidence against him appeared "so strong that hardly a doubt remains of his guilt."[75]

On this point, the Bald Knobbers made good on their promise, for they did not lynch William Taylor. One of the vigilantes, attorney

John J. Brown, even agreed to represent him in court. On April 8, the circuit court delayed his trial by granting his motion for a continuance, which he filed on the grounds that he needed more time to prepare his defense. When the court reconvened in October, Taylor again filed a motion for a continuance on the grounds that he had not yet located two witnesses essential to his defense, William Timbers and James Rothdell, and could not proceed to trial without them.[76] Many of the Bald Knobbers scornfully referred to these men as "fictitious witnesses," whom William Taylor had invented in order to delay the proceedings. In any event, the court denied the second motion for a continuance and the case went to trial, but in a surprise ruling the jury found Taylor not guilty. Immediately after his acquittal, William Taylor wisely decided to leave Forsyth. He walked about twenty-five miles to Chadwick, a railroad depot in Christian County, and from there he went back to his hometown of Marionville. When he returned the people of that town shunned him, since many of them entertained doubts about his innocence. Taylor eventually left Marionville and settled in Howell County, Missouri.[77]

Many Bald Knobbers claimed that they never took part in any vigilante activity after the Bald Knobbers disbanded and that the formal ceremony held at Forsyth on April 10 marked the end of the group's history in Taney County. For example, about a week after the ceremony, the *Springfield Daily Herald* published an editorial from an anonymous pro-vigilante resident of Taney County. The writer declared that peace now reigned in Taney County: "The Bald Knobbers are *non est*—if that word means that they are in their fields plowing, trying to make an honest living. The militia have beat their imaginary guns into plowshares and are also quietly at work."[78] Likewise, August C. Hensley wrote that the "regular organization disbanded that day and never met again," even though many subsequent misdeeds were later attributed to the Bald Knobbers, who then "got a bad reputation that didn't belong to them all over the country."[79] Joe McGill concurred, writing that "the original organization that was called the Bald Knobbers disbanded that day . . . and never met afterwards." McGill then added the cryptic qualifier that "some who had been members of the original organization did meet" and continued to use the name "Bald Knobbers."[80]

There is no reason to doubt either man's veracity, and it seems likely that many of the Bald Knobbers kept their word to the adjutant general to remain disbanded. It appears equally certain, however, that not all of the vigilantes abided by the agreement they had made with the government. Some continued to enforce their own brand of law and order, and incidents of night riding and intimidation continued after Jamison departed. On Saturday night, May 1, 1886, someone shot a horse belonging to Thomas A. Layton and set fire to a fence on his property. The flames consumed "about 40 panels before the neighbors could stop it." The following week a barn belonging to someone referred to as "Dr. Anderson" also burned down.[81] Some Anti-Bald Knobbers charged that the vigilantes continued their policy of forced evictions. According to John J. Reynolds, they ran off two men named Kur and Brannan, and even expelled a widow "with her small children" from their home.[82] Nor did the truce long prevent the resumption of bloodshed. On Sunday, May 9, George Washington ("Wash") Middleton, a Bald Knobber who had sometimes served as Nat Kinney's bodyguard, shot and killed Samuel H. Snapp in Kirbyville, Missouri.[83]

Unlike the killing of Andrew Coggburn, where the competing stories told by the Bald Knobber and Anti-Bald Knobber factions obscured the truth, the basic facts surrounding the death of Sam Snapp are fairly clear. On the day of the killing, witness Ben Prather observed Sam Snapp and Wash Middleton sitting on boxes and talking in front of John Kintrea's General Store in Kirbyville. Prather himself sat outside the store reading a newspaper and failed to take notice of anything out of the ordinary. He later described their tone as "mild and compromising," rather than bitter or angry. At some point he heard Middleton call Snapp a liar. Then the two men stood, and Middleton pulled out his gun and began firing. As Middleton opened fire, Snapp continued to retreat, making no attempt to draw or fire a weapon. Claude Layton, another witness, said he heard two shots before looking up to see Middleton firing a third shot, which finally finished Snapp off. He also recalled that at the time Middleton fired his third shot Snapp had retreated several paces, apparently trying to get out of Middleton's line of fire.[84]

The two men seemed to have had a history of hostility toward each other. George W. Gibson recalled that a few days before the

shooting he heard Wash Middleton threaten and verbally abuse Sam
Snapp, saying that he would kill him. Likewise, William Ellison said
that several hours before the shooting he saw Middleton and Snapp
arguing, and that Middleton called Snapp a "damn bushwhacker."[85]
According to Alonzo Prather, who at the request of Adjutant General
Jamison wrote a letter describing the shooting, the hostility between
the two men may have originated when Middleton attempted to join
the local chapter of the Agricultural Wheel, an organization similar
to the Farmer's Alliance. Snapp, who already belonged to the group,
blocked Middleton's membership because of the role he had taken
in the "Bald Knob business." This rejection angered Middleton, who
never forgave Snapp for the slight. On the day of the shooting, Sam
Snapp and William Ellison met up with Middleton on the road outside Kirbyville. Both men had spent the weekend drinking. Upon seeing Middleton, Snapp made the fateful error of singing the anti-Bald
Knobber song composed by the late Andrew Coggburn. Middleton
remarked that it was "a nice song for a bushwhacker" to sing, to which
Snapp replied, "you bet your boots" and rode on. Prather believed that
"the singing of that song caused Snapp's death. If he had kept quiet
. . . he would be alive today."[86]

Later that day the two men met again outside John Kintrea's
store, and an argument broke out, which led to Snapp's death. On
this point Prather's account differed from the court testimony, which
clearly depicted Middleton as the aggressor. Prather wrote that Snapp
confronted Middleton and demanded to know what Middleton meant
by calling him a bushwhacker. Middleton replied that he called Snapp
a bushwhacker because of "the company he kept," at which point
Snapp challenged Middleton to "settle the matter" right there. Prather
did not explicitly say whether Snapp carried a weapon, although
Middleton obviously did. Prather did mention, however, that both of
them usually went about armed, as did "everybody else for that matter." He also pointed out the physical inequality between the two men.
Snapp was a young man in the prime of life and weighed roughly 200
pounds, while Middleton had advanced beyond fifty years in age and
weighed around 140 pounds. Nevertheless, Middleton was far from
helpless. During the Civil War he had served as a scout for the U.S.

Army, and had "the reputation of being a 'killer' and it is said [he] killed several men since the war."[87]

Middleton's choice of the term "bushwhacker," the common unionist pejorative for a rebel guerrilla, is curious on a number of levels. As a veteran himself, Middleton would have known that Snapp, at about thirty years of age, was too young to have fought in the Civil War. His explanation that he called him a bushwhacker because of "the company he kept" was probably a reference to Snapp's association with the Anti-Bald Knobber faction. Thus, Middleton's insult indicates that the grizzled guerrilla fighter had transferred the enmity he felt for his old Confederate foes to the Anti-Bald Knobbers as a group.

The murder of Sam Snapp set off another firestorm of protest against the Bald Knobbers, much of it in the form of letters to Jefferson City and Adjutant General Jamison. Over the course of the next week, Jamison received letters from the Anti-Bald Knobbers W. H. Jones, John J. Reynolds, and K. L. Burdette, as well as the wife of Anti-Bald Knobber James S. B. Berry. All of them referenced the Snapp killing as proof that the vigilantes had broken their promise to keep the peace. Mrs. Berry called the killing a "cold blooded murder" and bemoaned the fact that the death of Snapp, a widower, had made orphans of his "five small children."[88] According to Reynolds, the death of Snapp proved that the "disbanding [of the Bald Knobbers] is as I thought it would be a farce."[89] Jones and Burdette both pointed out that Sam Snapp had witnessed the killing of Andrew Coggburn and implied that vigilantes may have eliminated Snapp in order to keep him silent.[90] On this point the Anti-Bald Knobbers probably misinterpreted the evidence. The coroner's inquest held two months earlier had declared Nat Kinney's killing of Andrew Coggburn a case of self-defense, and with Bald Knobber-friendly officials in power in the local government Kinney had little reason to fear any trouble from the law. Alonzo Prather made essentially the same point in his letter to Jamison when he dismissed the notion of a "conspiracy" to kill Sam Snapp, and observed that since the grand jury had already declined to indict Kinney "there was no necessity to 'remove' Snapp."[91]

If Middleton expected the pro-Bald Knobber local officials to protect him as they had Kinney, he was soon disappointed. After a series of legal maneuvers by the lawyers on both sides delayed the start of his trial by more than a year, a jury found Middleton guilty of murder in the second degree and sentenced him to a term of forty years in the state penitentiary, which a circuit judge, Walter D. Hubbard, later reduced to fifteen years.[92]

Sheriff McHaffie and his deputies never had a chance to transport Middleton to the state penitentiary; on October 16, 1887, he escaped from the county jail in Forsyth and fled to Arkansas.[93] Following Middleton's escape, accusations flew back and forth concerning who had been responsible for letting Middleton go. Some of the Anti-Bald Knobbers accused Sheriff McHaffie of letting the convict escape, while others believed that the Bald Knobbers had broken into the jail and freed their comrade. One former Bald Knobber, George Brazeal, even said the vigilantes had given Middleton a horse and saddle, a Winchester rifle, and fifty dollars to facilitate his flight.[94] Not surprisingly, the Bald Knobbers tended to assign blame for the jailbreak to other parties. After the escape, Nathaniel Kinney told a reporter for a Springfield newspaper that one of Middleton's sons came up from Arkansas and broke his father out of jail.[95] No hard evidence exists to substantiate any of these theories. Nevertheless, it does not appear that the Bald Knobbers eagerly anticipated Middleton's recapture. As Kinney nonchalantly explained to the Springfield reporter, Middleton's extensive knowledge of the Ozark hill country made his recapture unlikely. He added somewhat cryptically that "if [Middleton] is ever taken at all it will be more the result of accident than of design."[96]

Kinney's prediction proved inaccurate, however, for Wash Middleton spent the remaining eight months of his life on the run from the law. The Snapp family offered a sizable reward for Middleton's capture, to which the county court added a bounty of one hundred dollars. Additionally, Governor Marmaduke offered three hundred dollars of the state's money "for the arrest and delivery of said George Middleton to the warden of the Missouri State Penitentiary" in Jefferson City.[97] These incentives apparently had the desired effect, for in February 1888, a posse led by Charles Richardson caught up with Middleton in Boone County, Arkansas. In the ensuing gunfight, Middleton managed to kill Richardson before making his escape.[98] By the following summer, his luck had run out. On July 4, Detective James L. Holt attempted to apprehend Wash Middleton at an Independence Day picnic in Newton County. When Middleton resisted arrest, Holt shot and killed him right there. Middleton's body was buried in an unmarked grave in the Little Buffalo cemetery near the town of Parthenon, Arkansas.[99]

The Middleton-Snapp shooting marked the beginning of an extended lull in hostilities between the vigilantes and anti-vigilantes in Taney County. After Sam Snapp's body hit the ground in Kirbyville on May 9, 1886, more than two years elapsed before another homicide related to the Bald Knobber troubles occurred. The 1886 election resulted in another Republican victory, and the voters elevated three of the ex-vigilantes to the important positions of sheriff, county clerk, and coroner. Ironically, the only vigilante candidate who did not win his race that year was Nat Kinney, who lost a second bid for state representative, probably because he once again ran as a Democrat.[100] With a pro-Bald Knobber local government the vigilantes, for the most part, seemed content to run the county through the legitimate channels of power. The appeals to the state government for assistance following the killing of Sam Snapp fell on deaf ears. Adjutant General Jamison's official report to the governor in 1887 had declared that "comparative peace and order" now reigned in the county, and the state government did not seem anxious to reopen the issue.[101] Without support from the state government, the Anti-Bald Knobbers could do little to loosen their enemies' grip on power, or to avenge the wrongs they had suffered. In time, the old hostility between the two groups would flare up again in renewed bloodshed. But for the time being, at least, an uneasy peace settled over the county.

## CHAPTER 4

# Righteous Devils:
# The Bald Knobbers in Christian
# and Douglas Counties

A s the Bald Knobber troubles in Taney County subsided into a welcome, though still uneasy, truce between the vigilante and anti-vigilante factions, many hoped that Bald Knobber vigilantism would soon become a thing of the past. That was not to be, however, because certain ongoing events in the two counties immediately northward would soon make the Ozark vigilantes even more notorious than previously. The Bald Knobber chapters in Christian and Douglas Counties, which form the focus of this chapter, evolved out of the original organization in Taney County. Apart from their name, the northern vigilantes shared several significant characteristics with the first vigilance committee, especially in the areas of organization and ritual. They also differed from the parent group in a number of fundamental ways, including their basic objectives, the causes that motivated them to organize, and the type of men who joined their ranks. The northern vigilantes tended to be poorer and less socially prominent than their southern counterparts, and took a dimmer view of the economic changes affecting the Ozarks, which so many of the original committee enthusiastically promoted. They also tended to be more religiously devout and more inclined to use vigilante tactics to regulate the morals of their neighbors. Finally, unlike the Taney County vigilantes who generally avoided prosecution for their actions, the excesses of the Bald Knobbers in Christian and Douglas Counties eventually landed scores of them in court on various charges.

The differences between the two groups seem all the more striking considering that they operated almost simultaneously. Within months of the Bald Knobbers' founding in Taney County, new chapters of the group began sprouting up in other parts of southwest Missouri. During the summer of 1885, the Bald Knobbers organized in Douglas County. Joseph Walker, a farmer living in the vicinity of Ava, became the leader of the group there. Walker had plans for bringing the Bald Knobbers to neighboring Christian County, so he invited Nathaniel Kinney to come up from Kirbyville to help establish a new chapter of the organization. Sometime in the fall of 1885, Joseph Walker and Nathaniel Kinney held an organizational meeting in the town of Chadwick. Aside from this initial cooperation, however, the Taney County vigilantes do not appear to have interacted with their northern counterparts on a regular basis. The meeting resulted in the creation of a new chapter of the Bald Knobbers. Joseph's brother, David Walker, took command as the chieftain of the vigilante group in Christian County.[1]

Dave Walker had fought for the Union during the Civil War, serving in the Sixteenth Missouri Cavalry (originally the Sixth Enrolled Missouri Militia), a unit which spent most of the war fighting in southwest Missouri.[2] He worked a modest farm near the breaks of Bull Creek, which earned him the nickname "Bull Creek Dave."

His son, William Walker, though only a teenager at the time, soon rose to a position of leadership within the Bald Knobbers and functioned as second in command or "assistant chief" to his father.[3] Following the custom established by Kinney's vigilantes, the Bald Knobbers in Christian County subdivided into multiple companies or "legions," each based in a particular town or township. Dave Walker himself took command of the legion based in Chadwick. Samuel Preston Sr. commanded the company based in Sparta. James M. ("Bud") Gann led the legion based in Shady Grove; Martin T. Humble commanded the company in Buckhorn; John James led the legion

**Fig. 4.1:** Dave Walker. Source: William L. Vandeventer, *Justice in the Rough*, 1937. Used by permission of the State Historical Society of Missouri Research Center, Rolla, MO.

in Garrison; and Sylvanus Kissee took command of the company in Finley Township.[4]

Other men who seemed to play a leadership role in the organization, based on the frequency with which they later appeared in indictments, included John Mathews, Wiley Mathews, Charles O. Simmons, and Gilbert Applegate.[5] John Mathews was a small farmer and a Baptist deacon who enjoyed a reputation as one of the finest marksmen in the hills.⁶ The Reverend Charles O. Simmons (whom contemporaries called "C. O. Simmons") worked a farm and preached at a Baptist church in Chadwick, Missouri.⁷ Like many of their vigilante compatriots, Mathews and Simmons were devout Christians and active in the religious life of their communities. Nevertheless, both of them would face charges for various crimes including their role in the murders of Charles Greene and William Edens, for which Mathews received a death sentence and Simmons spent a term of twelve years in the state penitentiary.⁸

John Mathews's nephew, Wiley Mathews, was a young man in his early twenties when the Bald Knobbers first organized. The younger Mathews was born in Arkansas around the year 1863. In 1880, he lived with his parents, Lefford and Elizabeth Mathews, and worked on their farm.⁹ Born in Arkansas in 1845, Gilbert Applegate came to Missouri with his parents Joseph and Elizabeth Applegate before the Civil War. The Applegate family moved around frequently. They lived in Greene County in 1850, but by 1860 they had relocated to Taney County.¹⁰ Applegate fought for the Union during the Civil War, serving in the Sixteenth Missouri Cavalry, and also earned a reputation as a pro-Union bushwhacker. He reportedly murdered a Confederate prisoner named Fulbright, even though local Union militia already had him in custody. Applegate waited near a road for the militia troops transporting the captive to pass, and then fired two shots, the second piercing his victim's skull.¹¹ In the 1880s, Gilbert Applegate actually lived in Douglas County, but as a Bald Knobber he participated with Bald Knobbers in Christian County in several vigilante actions across the county line.¹²

In addition to Christian and Douglas Counties, some circumstantial evidence suggests that the Bald Knobbers, or organizations similar to them, sprouted up in other parts of Missouri and even Arkansas. In the spring of 1887, newspaper reports alleged that the "spirit of the Bald Knobbers" had infected Callaway County near St. Louis. They cited as evidence of their claim the brutal flogging of a man named Turner, possibly because he was suspected of having extramarital relations with a neighbor's wife. The same articles pointed to other vigilante activities, such as the flogging of one black man and the shooting death of another, as proof that Bald Knob-style vigilantism had come to Callaway County.[13]

Similar anecdotal evidence from newspapers suggests that Bald Knobbers or other groups like them spread from southwest Missouri to northwest Arkansas in the middle 1880s. When a party of night riders murdered Phillip Clayton and severely wounded his teenage son in Marion County in December 1886, one newspaper account suggested that the perpetrators targeted Clayton because he belonged to the "Bald Knobbers," an organization that was "numerically strong in the border counties of Arkansas and Missouri."[14] The following year in September a dispute over the ownership of a drove of hogs led to the murder of John Hardcastle, a farmer living in Stone County, Arkansas. Five assassins shot and killed Hardcastle as he attempted to leave the area with his family. In the wake of the shooting, rumors circulated that the killers belonged to "an organization similar to the Bald Knobbers of Missouri."[15] Other newspaper accounts also reported that the Bald Knobbers had become numerous in northern Arkansas and that while most of the vigilantes in that part of the country were good citizens and church-goers, they were "emphatic with those who disagree with them" and they "regulated morals in their own way."[16]

In addition, some Bald Knobber activity may have occurred in nearby Webster and Wright Counties. In September 1887, in Webster County, a group of around fifty masked men rode into Marshfield and conducted a public demonstration. They left threatening messages at the county courthouse advising the officers of the court including circuit judge Washington I. Wallace not to prosecute any Bald Knobbers for misdeeds they had allegedly done in that county.[17] In Wright County, federal authorities prosecuted a man named Granville Vanbiber for threatening and intimidating a homesteader named A. J. Symmes and driving him from his home. The case file itself does not prove that Vanbiber was a Bald Knobber, for he apparently acted alone, unlike the defendants in the other cases of this nature. Attached to the file, however, is a small handwritten note from the United States land commissioner to U.S. attorney Maceanas E. Benton calling the case "a very good Bald Knob case" and recommending that he investigate it.[18] It remains unclear whether the commissioner used that description because he knew that Vanbiber actually belonged to the Bald Knobbers or because the case shared similar characteristics with other Bald Knobber cases involving homesteaders.

A few Bald Knobbers may also have been active in Greene County, Missouri. On October 1, 1887, a Springfield newspaper ran a story about a "shiftless" Greene County man named John Loney who received a threatening note, supposedly from the Bald Knobbers, warning him to leave the county. The note accompanied a bundle of hickory switches, a well-known Bald Knobber calling card. It scared Loney enough to cause him to leave the area immediately. Another man named James Robinson received a similar message after he allegedly stole some German carp from a neighbor's fishpond. Robinson awoke one morning to find a threatening message posted on his door. It included the following poetic passage describing his crimes: "A mess of fish now and then, occasionally a big fat hen, or a bushel of wheat from some man's pen." The signature on the paper read "Bald Knobbers." A few days later, when Robinson still had not left the area, he received a second, more direct note telling him to leave within ten days or face the consequences. The signature at the bottom read "Citizens."[19] The people behind these threats may have belonged to an actual Bald Knobber organization, or they may have simply copied their methods in order to rid themselves of troublesome neighbors. Either way, their actions showed that the Bald Knobbers had become a potent symbol of vigilante justice in southwest Missouri, even in areas where they did not have significant numerical strength.

An abundance of documentary evidence demonstrates the existence of a strong Bald Knobber movement in Christian and Douglas Counties. Beginning in the summer of 1886, the Bald Knobbers in this area conducted a campaign of night riding and intimidation. In the main, they targeted people whose lives failed to measure up to the exacting moral standards of the vigilantes, as well as recently settled homesteaders whose arrival cut off the vigilantes' access to land and resources they wished to utilize. One of their first recorded acts of violence occurred on the evening of July 30, 1886, when a group of masked Bald Knobbers went to the home of E. P. Helms, a thirty-four-year-old homesteader with a wife and six children who had settled in the eastern part of Christian County the previous year.

The vigilantes broke into Helms's home, dragged him outside, put a rope around his neck, whipped him severely, and warned him to leave the country. Helms apparently did not take the lesson to heart, for he stubbornly remained on his land. In March of the following year, the Bald Knobbers returned to Helms's place and repeated the process all over again. This second visit finally convinced him to leave the area and resettle near Springfield, Missouri.[20]

As soon as he was out of his enemies' grasp, Helms filed charges against the Bald Knobbers for what they had done to him. As a result, several vigilantes faced prosecution, both in the circuit court for assault and battery, and in federal court for intimidating homesteaders, which was a federal crime under the provisions of the Homestead Act of 1862 and other federal legislation.[21] During one of the federal trials stemming from this case, the Bald Knobbers' attorney, S. H. Boyd, claimed that the vigilantes had whipped Helms for keeping "lewd women" in his home. Not surprisingly, Helms had a different take on the situation. He stated that the men whipped him because he had testified against Bald Knobbers in court, because he refused to sell his land to the Bald Knobber Amos Jones, and because Helms had cut some timber on his own land to make railroad ties. Helms's wife testified that several of the vigilantes warned him to "steal nobody's timber but your own," which may indicate that they thought he had taken timber from his neighbors' land as well.[22]

Another Christian County man, Greene Walker, provoked the anger of the Bald Knobbers for more salacious reasons. People throughout the Ozark hill country knew of Walker as a notorious polygamist, in that he kept more than one woman as his wife. His unconventional lifestyle did not sit well with the moralistic Bald Knobbers. In August 1886, Dave Walker led a group of at least nineteen vigilantes to Greene Walker's house. They seized the unfortunate man, took him from his home, and beat him "upon the body . . . with sticks and large switches," which they had brought for that purpose.[23] After beating him, the vigilantes advised Walker to discontinue his misconduct. He failed to heed their warning, however, and a party of night riders led by Michael M. Humble (brother of Martin Humble) returned and beat him a second time, after which he left the area.[24]

In addition to whipping people who violated accepted sexual mores, the Bald Knobbers also punished men who in their judgment abused or neglected their families. According to William L. Vandeventer, if a man became known for behaving abusively toward his children he might some evening receive a bundle of switches and a note warning him to change his ways. One unnamed individual who unwisely failed to comply with such a demand had the Bald Knobbers visit his home and apply "hickory switches with unsparing hands" to his body. This had the desired effect of persuading him to leave the county.[25] Similarly, on August 15, 1886, a band of around fifteen vigilantes led by Michael Humble visited the home of Horace Johnson, a shiftless man described as "too lazy to support his family."[26] They dragged him from his house and beat him "on the back, legs, and body . . . with sticks and large switches."[27]

Finally, the Bald Knobbers punished those who made a public nuisance of themselves, or disturbed the peace of their communities. For example, in August 1886, a group of around ten or fifteen Bald Knobbers stopped a local man named Clayton Whiteacre on a public road, pulled him off his horse, and beat him severely with their guns. They told Whiteacre that the alleged offense for which they punished him was disturbing the peace by firing his gun in public and throwing rocks at people passing by on a public road.[28]

In the minds of many Bald Knobbers, the saloons and gambling dens in the small railroad town of Chadwick represented an even graver threat to the peace and happiness of local families than did public nuisances or lazy and shiftless husbands. Prior to 1883, Chadwick did not even exist on the county map. That year the Springfield and Southern Railroad Company, a subsidiary of the St. Louis and San Francisco Railroad, completed a feeder line into Christian County. The railroad first built the town as a camp to house its workers and then made it the line's terminal depot.[29] The railroad used Chadwick primarily as a shipping center from which to purchase and ship the railroad ties it needed for laying new tracks elsewhere. The county's immense forests helped meet the railroad's demand for timber.[30]

Within a few years timber cutting, or "tie-hacking" as the locals called it, became an integral part of the local economy. Hundreds of the county's farmers and stock raisers took up tie hacking as a means of supplementing their incomes. The men would cut down a straight-trunked oak or hickory tree using a crosscut saw and then use broad axes to hew the trunks into eight-foot lengths of timber for use as ties. In this manner a man might make eight or ten railroad ties in a typical workday. Next they loaded their ties into wagons and hauled them to Chadwick, where purchasing agents paid for them in cash, usually about twenty cents per tie.[31]

That might seem like a paltry wage, but in the poor, cash-strapped rural communities of southwest Missouri the two dollars a day that a farmer might earn hacking ties could mean the difference between bare subsistence and a more comfortable existence. One of the men who relied upon tie hacking was the Bald Knobber chieftain, David Walker. In the spring of 1886 Walker mailed a letter from the Chadwick post office to his brother Joseph in Douglas County. In it he indicated the changes that tie hacking had brought to the local economy, telling his brother that "Will and I have been making ties till this morning" and that "times is tolerably Good here now [that] work is Plenty and money [is] Ready."[32]

With a steady stream of money flowing in and out of Chadwick, a local vice industry soon developed there that was designed to siphon off the tie hackers' hard-earned income. Though the town numbered only around one hundred inhabitants in its early years, there quickly sprang up a number of ramshackle saloons and gambling dens where men could drink hard liquor or lose their earnings at the card tables if they chose to do so. These establishments became known as "blind tigers" in the local parlance and soon drew the ire of the Bald Knobbers. The vigilantes blamed the saloon keepers, the "agents for the devil" as one contemporary writer called them, for corrupting the morals of the tie hackers, whom they taught "games; trickery, and all imaginable indecency and wicked vices." The vigilantes understandably believed that the money lost through these pursuits should have gone to supporting the men's families at home.[33]

In the evening of November 9, 1886, Dave Walker led a band of around forty Bald Knobbers into Chadwick. They broke into a saloon belonging to John Rhodes and Russell McCauley, both of whom had previously appeared before the circuit court to face charges for selling liquor without a license.[34] Rhodes and McCauley put up a brief fight, and they exchanged a few shots with the night riders before beating a hasty retreat out of town. The vigilantes then entered the saloon and busted it up, breaking all the furniture and pouring out the proprietors' stock of beer and whiskey.[35]

The saloon keepers apparently proved more recalcitrant than the vigilantes anticipated, because two days later another party of one hundred or so night riders rode into Chadwick again, intending to repeat the deeds of the previous raid. As they performed their task, however, several citizens of Chadwick began firing on them from adjacent buildings. In short order the "shooting became general, more than 100 shots being exchanged," and the Bald Knobbers "stampeded" out of Chadwick ahead of a hail of bullets. Amazingly, only one vigilante fell "seriously wounded" in the fray, and his comrades managed to get him out of town safely.[36]

Not surprisingly, such methods infuriated people who did not appreciate the vigilantes intruding on their personal affairs. An organized opposition to the Bald Knobbers never developed in Christian and Douglas Counties as it had in Taney County, likely because the vigilantes in the northern counties never exercised the same degree of power in local politics. Nevertheless, many people still chaffed under their coercion, and some even dared to speak out against them. The vigilantes contemptuously referred to their enemies as "slickers," a term redolent of the history of Missouri vigilantism. In antebellum Missouri, the term "slicking" referred to the customary practice of whipping some petty criminal, especially a counterfeiter, with a hickory switch that had been roasted over a fire to toughen it. Sometimes this rough form of justice could leave behind lingering resentments between victims and perpetrators that could erupt into outright blood feuds, such as the famous "Slicker War" in Benton and Hickory Counties, where "slicker" and "anti-slicker" factions battled each other from 1841 to 1843.[37]

Like many of those earlier vigilantes, the Bald Knobbers punished anyone impudent enough to speak against them. In November 1886, they visited the home of Bob Patterson to warn him not to talk about them anymore. When Patterson answered the door one of the Bald Knobbers pistol whipped the unlucky man "inflicting a very dangerous and ugly wound."[38] Around the same time they visited George

Baty, who had been "talking too much" about them, whipped him with switches, and pummeled him with their fists.[39]

Ultimately, the Bald Knobbers' intolerance of criticism led to tragic and unforeseen consequences, both for them and their critics. About a year before his death at the hands of the vigilantes, William Edens got into an accidental scuffle with a group of Bald Knobbers when they came to his home in search of his brother-in-law, John Evans, who lived with him at that time. The men wanted to whip Evans because he had reportedly disturbed a Sunday worship service by showing up drunk at church. Afterward he returned home, firing his pistol into the air and swearing. When the vigilantes came to whip him, William Edens attempted to protect his brother-in-law and got between him and the men whipping him. As a result, the men "struck him a few licks" before Dave Walker yelled at them to stop.[40]

After that incident, William Edens hated the Bald Knobbers because of the indignity done to him and his relative, and he frequently spoke out against them. On one occasion he boasted publicly that if the night riders ever tried to whip him they would have to return the next morning "when it is light and count their dead around my house." When the Bald Knobbers heard about this threat, Dave and William Walker led a group of vigilantes to William Edens's home and dragged him out of the house. They stripped him, tied him to an oak tree, and beat him bloody with sticks and switches. When they had finished, they mocked him as they departed, telling him that in the morning he should get up and "see how many dead Bald Knobbers you can count."[41]

The Bald Knobbers in the two northern counties shared a number of traits in common with the original organization in Taney County. Perhaps their greatest similarity was a high regard for social order, as well as a willingness to use vigilante tactics to enforce that order, and to advance their own self-interests. As we shall see, however, the ways they defined these values and expressed them in action could differ quite markedly.

They shared some more mundane traits as well. As described above, both used the same semimilitary style of organization, with a head man or "chieftain" at the top, and several companies or "legions" based in various parts of each county. In practice, however, the northern vigilantes did not exhibit much formal discipline within their ranks. Although contemporary estimates put the strength of the Christian County Bald Knobbers at between two hundred and eight hundred men,[42] most of the vigilante acts attributed to the group involved at most a few dozen members. Dave Walker's Chadwick legion was apparently very active, a fact reflected in the number of times Walker's name made its way onto indictments, but other legions seem to have done fairly little. Dave Walker himself apparently did not have great confidence in his authority within the organization. During the trials for the murders of Charles Greene and William Edens, he told an interviewer, "They call me the chief but I don't know as I am eny more 'an eny of 'em." He was rather just one of the "best men" of his section, who had joined together to "punish them rascally chaps who did this theivin' an' who was always a treatin' their women-folks mean."[43] One might well infer from this explanation that Walker wanted to minimize his responsibility for other people's misdeeds. His words also indicate, however, that he exercised less influence over his followers than Nat Kinney did over his men. For example, after his arrest, Walker tried to convince his fellow Bald Knobbers not to testify against each other, but his pleas did not prevent a number of them from turning state's evidence.[44]

The vigilantes in the two northern counties also had a membership oath that closely replicated the pledge used by their counterparts to the south. A descendant of Joseph Walker has preserved a copy of the oath used in Douglas County. The initiate who took it pledged "never to reveal the secrets of this order" and to obey the commands of his superiors within it. Significantly, the new member promised to observe all the rules of his order, and of any "sister order under whose jurisdiction I may at the time be attached." This provision indicated that some members transferred their membership from one county organization to another whenever they moved and that members often participated in Bald Knobber activities across county lines. The new member also pledged not to sponsor anyone for membership who did not deserve it, nor to oppose the membership of any person out of personal hostility, and to report all crimes of which he became aware, even if a blood relative committed them. Finally, the initiate promised that he would never defraud fellow members and that if he betrayed the oath he would submit to the judgment of his comrades, even if they decided to hang him "by the neck until dead!"[45]

Despite these similarities, the type of men recruited into the vigilante ranks in the two northern counties differed in significant ways from the composition of the group in Taney County. As seen in chapter 3, the original organization included not only a large proportion of farmers, but an equally significant number of lawyers, schoolteachers, merchants, storekeepers, and other professions not related to agriculture. They came from diverse geographical backgrounds; about half of them listed either Missouri or Tennessee as their birthplace, while the rest came from different parts of the country, including Virginia, West Virginia, Arkansas, North Carolina, Illinois, Indiana, Ohio, New York, Massachusetts, and Kansas. One even emigrated from England. They were predominantly older or middle-age men, averaging nearly forty years old apiece, and more than a quarter of them had fought for the Union during the Civil War.

By contrast, the members of the Bald Knobbers in Christian and Douglas Counties were overwhelmingly farmers. Out of ninety-five vigilantes in these counties for whom census records are available, roughly nine-tenths of them engaged in agriculture as their sole or primary profession. This usually meant that they classified themselves as "farmers," "farm laborers," "farm hands," or some related designation on the federal census returns. They tended to be much younger men, averaging around thirty years in age, with many members in their teens or early twenties. As a result, nearly six-tenths of them were born in Missouri, while most of the rest came from the neighboring states of Tennessee, Arkansas, and Illinois, with a smattering of members from other states.[46]

Fewer of them were old enough to have seen military service during the Civil War, but of that group at least twelve fought for the Union and two fought for the Confederacy.[47]

Moreover, the Christian County Bald Knobbers usually came from humbler economic circumstances than their counterparts to the south. Although tax assessment records for both counties are spotty at best, some general observations can be gleaned from them. First, the vigilantes in Christian County tended to have less wealth in land than their brethren in Taney County. The land assessment records

Table 4.1: Christian and Douglas County Bald Knobbers — Occupation, Age Distribution, and Place of Birth

| Occupations | | Place of Birth | |
|---|---|---|---|
| Farmer | 88 | Missouri | 55 |
| Other Occupations | 8 | Tennessee | 14 |
| Political Officials | 3 | Arkansas | 11 |
| Unknown | 12 | Illinois | 5 |
| Total Individuals* | 106 | Kentucky | 4 |
| Age Distribution | | Virginia | 2 |
| Average Age in 1885 | 30.1 | Indiana | 2 |
| 50 Years and Over | 4 | New York | 1 |
| 20 Years and Under | 17 | Ohio | 1 |

* Some individuals had more than one occupation.

for Christian County in 1885 contain the names of at least thirty-one Bald Knobbers. Twenty-two of these, or more than two-thirds, owned land assessed at less than $500, while just nine owned more than $500 of real estate, and only one owned land worth more than $1,000. By contrast, the land assessment records for Taney County in 1886 contain the names of at least nineteen Bald Knobbers. More than half of these, eleven, owned land valued at more than $500, while just eight owned less than $500 in real estate. Five of them had land valued at more than $1,000. Second, the wealthiest vigilantes in Taney County far outstripped those in Christian County. Four Bald Knobbers in Taney County—John J. Brown, James K. Polk McHaffie, Alexander C. Kissee, and his brother Arter Kissee, owned land valued in excess of $1,800, while the wealthiest vigilante in Christian County, William Johns, had approximately $1,200 in real estate. Finally, the Bald Knobbers in Taney County were far more likely to own property in towns, particularly the county seat at Forsyth, while those in Christian County mainly owned property in rural areas. For example, John J. Brown owned dozens of lots in Forsyth, and several other Bald Knobbers including McHaffie, George Washington Middleton, James B. Rice, Charles H. Groom, Reuben S. Branson, and John L. Cook owned property in Forsyth and other nearby towns as well.[48]

The vigilantes in Christian County did not follow the custom of meeting on the large tree-less hills, or "bald knobs," favored by their brethren to the south. These convenient geographical features did not exist there, so instead they held many of their meetings in caves. When the group first organized in the county, Dave Walker suggested that they meet in a cave he knew of about two miles from his house. The cavern was located in a deep gulch beneath a high, overhanging cliff face that provided the vigilantes with natural seclusion from prying eyes. The mouth of the opening was broad and spacious enough to accommodate many men. In view of these advantages, the vigilantes made the cavern a regular meeting place.[49]

Another custom that set the Bald Knobbers in the northern counties apart from their southern counterparts was their penchant for hideous and terrifying masks. The members of the original organization in Taney County rarely, if ever, wore masks during their vigilante excursions.[50] They had no need to, since their members essentially controlled the county government from the middle to late 1880s. In the two northern counties, however, the vigilantes did not have that luxury. The sources currently available indicate that only one local official in Christian County, Judge Reuben L. Hale of the county court, may have belonged to the Bald Knobbers.[51] In Douglas County, Constable George L. Sanders and Justice of the Peace Joel Casad likely belonged to the Bald Knobbers, but no other public officials did.[52]

Thus, the vigilantes in these counties adopted the practice of wearing elaborate masks to hide their identity. The members typically used black cambric or calico material to make their masks. The masks covered the whole head and face, with holes cut out for the eyes and mouth. The men stitched around the edges of the holes with red thread, which created a "button-hole" appearance. From the top of each mask extended two cloth cones or "horns," made of the same material. Plugs made of wood or cork held the cones upright, and the point of each protrusion had a tassel of red thread on it. Lastly, they drew circles of white paint around the face holes to give the masks a ghostly aspect.[53] One may readily imagine the psychological impact that such masks had, particularly on those unfortunate enough to face a party of riders wearing them in the dead of night. The vigilantes who disguised themselves in this manner wanted to look like "hideous, horrid creatures" that possessed "[f]orms like men but faces like devils."[54]

**Fig. 4.2:** A man wearing a Bald Knobber mask. Source: William L. Vandeventer, *Justice in the Rough*, 1937. Used by permission of the State Historical Society of Missouri Research Center, Rolla, MO.

Yet the men who wore the masks did not see themselves as devils, but as righteous men fighting for justice and morality in their communities. The moral fervor of these "righteous devils" stemmed in large part from the devout brand of evangelical Christianity that many of them shared. Although sufficient records do not exist to determine the church membership status of most Bald Knobbers, contemporary observers frequently referred to the strong religiosity of many of the vigilantes from Christian and Douglas Counties. After the Edens-Greene killings one observer noted that fourteen of the twenty-five individuals arrested in connection with that crime belonged to Baptist congregations.[55] Around the same time, a Georgia newspaper reported that several members of the vigilante movement then incarcerated, including Dave Walker, Joseph Hyde, William Abbott, and C. O. Simmons, all belonged to the Baptist church.[56]

The social order that these vigilantes attempted to create depend-ed upon the strict moral regulation of their neighborhoods, a fact that did not go unnoticed by their contemporaries. In comparing the Bald Knobbers to other vigilante groups of the day, the *Jefferson City Daily Tribune* conceded that vigilantes sometimes performed a useful function by tracking down horse thieves and other criminals. On the other hand, the paper noted that the "desirability of an organization which shall go into the houses of their neighbors to tell them how to live, or to intimidate neighbors for any purpose whatever, is very doubtful."[57] Years after the Edens-Greene murder trials, Judge Walter D. Hubbard, the jurist who presided over the trials, joined with several other prominent Springfield attorneys in requesting Gov. Lawrence V. Stephens to commute the sentences of Amos Jones and William Stanley. Hubbard argued that these men bore less responsibility for the tragic deaths of Charles Greene and William Edens than other parties involved in the incident and said that he did not believe they "were bad men at heart." Rather, they had "imbibed a kind of Joan of Arc sentiment, and being ignorant, thought that they had a right to go out and make humanity do right according to their notions of right."[58]

Even some Bald Knobbers from Taney County felt that their northern brothers had gone too far in their attempt to regulate the morals of their neighbors. In their short history of the Bald Knobber movement, Charles Groom and D. F. McConkey drew a sharp distinc-tion between themselves and their more fanatical brethren in Christian County, who erred in trying to "force those who would not by per-suasion or of their own account be what the God of nature designed they should be."[59] Groom and McConkey pointed to the whipping of the polygamist Greene Walker and the raid on John Rhodes's and Russell McCauley's saloon as evidence that their northern cousins had interfered too much in the private lives of other people.[60] Indeed, the harsh attitude of the northern Bald Knobbers toward liquor diverged substantially from the more relaxed attitude of their southern coun-terparts on the subject. As seen in chapter 2, the southern vigilantes elected as their chieftain the former saloon keeper, Nat Kinney, and two of their more prominent members, Reuben Branson and Calvin

Parrish, owned a large distillery producing thousands of gallons of whiskey per year.[61]

The northern Bald Knobbers emphasized moral regulation in part because they wanted to protect their family members from the pernicious influences that accompanied the emergence of modern industrial capitalism in the Ozarks. In the wake of the railroad and timber companies came brothels, blind tigers, gambling dens, and various purveyors of vice who challenged the traditional social mores of the hill country. The vigilantes reacted to these changes by using violent force to impose moral discipline on their community. In so doing they regained a sense of control over their destinies that the combined stresses of social and economic change had undermined, even if that control came at the expense of those weaker than them.

In that respect, the Bald Knobbers' closest contemporaries were the various "whitecap" groups that flourished in places like eastern Tennessee, southern Indiana, and Oklahoma's Indian Territory. As discussed in the introduction, residents of these places responded to challenges to traditional morality and social mores by using vigilante tactics to crack down on those who violated their community's standards of behavior. Their victims varied depending on place or circumstance, but they typically included drunkards, adulterers, and fornicators, people who disrespected houses of worship, and men who abused or neglected their families.[62]

Unlike the aforementioned whitecaps, however, the vigilantes of the Ozarks clashed with the agents of economic change on matters of dollars and cents as well. For example, in the mid-1880s, one of the most powerful economic entities in southwest Missouri was the J. L. Lee Tie and Timber Company of Springfield, Missouri, which later merged into the Hobart-Lee Tie Company. This firm engaged in a variety of lumbering operations throughout the region. One of its primary businesses was the purchase and transport of railroad ties, which it bought from local tie hackers and resold to the St. Louis and San Francisco Railroad and other customers. In 1886 the founder of this corporation, Joshua L. Lee, sent his nineteen-year-old son Robert E. Lee (named after the famous general) to Sparta to take over the company's commissary there.[63]

As commissary, part of Robert Lee's job was to inspect and purchase railroad ties from local tie hackers and to "cull" or reject any
inferior ties they brought him. This brought him in close contact with
many of the county's residents, including Bald Knobbers. Years later,
in an interview with journalist Lucille Morris Upton, Lee estimated
that around six hundred Bald Knobbers worked for the timber company as tie hackers. This figure, though probably greatly exaggerated,
indicated how important timber had become to the local economy.
Lee also remembered that sometime after his arrival in Sparta a band
of night riders visited his father at the company's office in Chadwick.
The riders demanded that the elder Lee raise the price of railroad
ties and tell his tie inspector not to cull so many of their ties before
purchase. They threatened to burn down the company's commissary
if he did not meet their demands. Lee recalled that his father refused
their request, telling them that he treated them as fairly as he could,
and that if they harmed him or destroyed company property they
would only drive him away and lose jobs and wages. A short time later
a company inspector found a note attached to a load of ties cut by
Dave and William Walker. The note warned him that if he culled any
ties "the Bald Knobbers will call on you."[64]

Neither of these threats resulted in actual violence against the
company or its representatives, likely because the vigilantes realized
the legal and economic consequences of following through on their
threats. They did show, however, that like the Taney County Bald
Knobbers, some Christian County Bald Knobbers considered it perfectly appropriate to use vigilante methods to advance their collective
economic interests. In Christian County, however, that meant chal-
lenging one of the more powerful corporations in their community,
as opposed to the Taney County group's preference for promoting
new immigration and investment.

In that respect, the Christian County organization's closest contemporaries may have been the so-called night riders of the "black
patch" region of western Kentucky and Tennessee. In the early 1900s
a coalition of tobacco farmers and planters in this region frequently resorted to vigilante tactics to combat agents of the "Tobacco
Trust," an alliance of major tobacco manufacturers. The black patch

vigilantes believed the trust was guilty of unfair (and illegal) price fixing. They retaliated by harassing purchasing agents, burning down company warehouses, and intimidating farmers who sold their tobacco to the trust.[65]

The economic vigilantism of the Christian and Douglas Counties Bald Knobbers extended beyond harassing timber companies and their employees. Many of the Ozark vigilantes now wanted to stop new homesteaders from settling in their region as well. As the Bald Knobber movement gained momentum and spread to different areas of southwest Missouri, it began to attract the attention of federal officeholders who worried that such activities could retard the socioeconomic development of the region. On October 1, 1886, U.S. commissioner McLain Jones wrote to federal judge Arnold Krekel expressing his concern about "a body of men called Bald Knobbers, who ride around the country doing as they please, giving people notice to leave the country, whipping them, etc." Jones believed that these men did "a great deal of harm" to the region by "keeping back emigration, etc." He pointed out a recent case in New York in which federal authorities had prosecuted several people for attempting to deprive homesteaders of their right to live on and develop their land. He went on to suggest that the same strategy might apply in southwest Missouri.[66]

The commissioner's prediction proved correct. From 1887 through 1888 dozens of Bald Knobbers from Christian and Douglas Counties stood trial in federal court for intimidating homesteaders and running them off their land. The most successful of these cases, in terms of the number of persons prosecuted, stemmed from the two whippings of the Christian County homesteader E. P. Helms in July 1886 and March 1887. Twenty vigilantes faced charges in federal court in connection with these two beatings.[67] About four months after Helms's first beating, Bald Knobber captain John James led a band of armed and masked men to the residence of homesteader Perry Hursh in Christian County. They called him out of his house and ordered him to leave the county within thirty days or they would hang him. Faced with this unattractive alternative, Hursh wisely decided to move on.[68]

The vigilantes' hostility to homesteaders extended even to those who helped them settle in the area. In November 1886, Bald Knobber John Denny led a party of night riders to the home of Hugh Ratliff, a homesteader in Douglas County. They found Ratliff in bed asleep with his wife. Suddenly the men broke the door down and burst into the house. A furious struggle ensued as the vigilantes attempted to seize Ratliff and put a noose around his neck. He fought back, and in the course of their struggle the men broke down the bed where he lay. Ratliff's wife tried to intervene, but her arm became caught between the bed railing and one of the attacker's knees. The young infant she carried in her arms was nearly crushed as a result of the fighting, but the men let her up when she cried out that "they were killing the child."[69]

The men finally wrestled Ratliff out of the house. They took him to an old tree stump where they held him down and proceeded to whip him. As they administered this punishment, Ratliff asked them why they were treating him this way. The men replied that they wanted him to "pay your just and honest debts and tend to your own business, and furnish no more money to homesteaders in this country." Ratliff later explained in his statement that he had loaned money to one Caleb Atwood, another homesteader who had recently arrived in the area, in order to help him get established.[70] The U.S. marshals, acting under orders from Commissioner Jones, began rounding up the men involved in this case in December 1886.[71] They eventually charged ten vigilantes with intimidating Ratliff and Atwood and forcing them to leave the county. The attorney for these men, S. H. Boyd, brokered a deal with U.S. attorney Maceanas E. Benton whereby they pled guilty in exchange for relatively mild sentences of between two and six months in prison for their role in evicting these men.[72]

Although the efforts of officials such as McLain Jones and Maceanas Benton met with great success, the federal government's anti-Bald Knobber campaign did not immediately eliminate the threat to homesteaders. In April 1887, a band of ten to fifteen armed and masked men visited the homestead of Robert Ellis in Douglas County. When the men arrived, Ellis and his friend Joseph Bacorn heard them approach. Realizing the danger, Ellis and Bacorn ran outside and hid in some brush nearby. When vigilantes entered the house they questioned Ellis's brother, George Ellis, but he refused to tell them where his brother had gone. The men told George that his brother had twenty days to leave the county or they would kill him. As the vigilantes prepared to leave, Bacorn heard one of them say they intended to visit his homestead next. The following day he returned home to find a bundle of switches and a note ordering him to leave. Although the men wore masks, Ellis and Bacorn could identify at least four of them from their body types and voices, including J. L. Garrison, David H. Hunter, John F. Stout, and W. W. Wagoner. Additionally, Stout's wife later testified against her husband, informing the authorities that he belonged to the Bald Knobbers and had taken part in the raid.[73]

Around the same time as the Ellis raid, a party of men including David Hunter, whom witnesses recognized because of his long white beard visible underneath his mask, went to the homestead of Noah O'Connell and ordered him to leave the area. When he did not comply with their order, they burned down his house. The following January a group of Bald Knobbers, including David Hunter, paid a return visit to Robert Ellis's home and ordered him, in front of his family, to leave his homestead "under penalty of death." They also left a note to that effect, advising him that "[s]ix feet of land will be your worth if you don't heed this warning."[74]

Some homestead intimidation cases had no definitive connection to the Bald Knobbers even though they had many of the earmarks of their other actions. One such case involved homesteader Daniel A. Skeens of Douglas County. Skeens took out a homestead patent in September 1886 and settled with his family on his new land. He found it difficult to earn a living there, however, and in early 1887 he left his family and his land to find work elsewhere. In the meantime, one of his neighbors, Uriah Pruitt, filed a lawsuit against Skeens, seeking to appropriate his homestead on the ground that he had abandoned it. The suit went before officials in the local U.S. land office in Springfield, who ruled in Pruitt's favor. Skeens immediately appealed the decision to the General Land Office in Washington. In the interval U.S. attorney Benton wrote to all parties involved informing them that Skeens had the right to remain on his homestead until authorities in Washington reached a final decision. Acting in defiance of these instructions, local constable George L. Sanders went to the homestead with a party of men and forcibly evicted Skeens and his family from their home. Pruitt and his friends also had the support of local Justice of the Peace Joel Casad, who issued an order allowing Sanders to evict Skeens, even though the land office in Springfield warned him that he had no authority to do so. Furthermore, Casad refused to allow Skeens to "introduce any papers from the land office at all in his court," which would have upheld his right to the land.[75]

Nothing in the court records related to the Skeens case conclusively proves that the men who evicted him belonged to the Bald Knobbers, although the timing, location, and methods that these men employed all suggest such a connection. A similar case occurred in Stone County, where James W. Carr harassed and intimidated one Coe Holley, an elderly homesteader in that area. Carr lived in Christian County at the time of the federal census in 1880. He had been cutting some cedar timber from government land in the vicinity of Holley's homestead, a crime for which he had previously faced charges in federal court. At some point Carr must have decided to access the timber on Holley's land, for in June 1887, he and an accomplice named Jacob Horn made two attempts to drive Holley from his property. One night Carr shot into Holley's tent while he and his family lay asleep. Later, when Holley began erecting a log house on his property, Carr tried unsuccessfully to burn it down.[76] Nothing in the case file directly substantiates a link to the Bald Knobbers, but once again the timing, location, and nature of the crime suggest the strong possibility of a connection.

The precise reasons for the Bald Knobber hostility to homesteaders require some effort to sort out, in part because the court documents do not always explain why the vigilantes targeted particular individuals. Certain homesteaders may have earned the vigilantes' enmity through theft or immoral behavior. Nevertheless, the frequency of these cases, and the strong federal response they elicited, suggest that the vigilantes had an underlying motive for wanting to exclude homesteaders from the area in the 1880s. In some cases, homesteaders may have inadvertently intruded on existing land arrangements. In the Ozarks at that time the custom of "squatting" remained fairly prevalent, and many homesteaders may have taken up land that some-body else had long held without ever acquiring formal title.[77] Attorney S. H. Boyd, who represented dozens of the vigilantes in various causes, probably had this in mind when he remarked in the course of one trial that the "Homestead law was a constant source of annoyance and cost to the Government, and it would be better if it did not exist."[78]

At the same time, some of the Bald Knobbers themselves filed for homesteads with the federal government, including such prominent members as David Walker, Gilbert Applegate, and Bud Gann.[79] So clearly the vigilantes did not object to homesteaders in general, but rather to individual homesteaders who somehow provoked them. Access to timber likely played a role in the decision to target particular homesteaders. As previously discussed, after the new railroad line to Chadwick opened in 1883, tie hacking became a significant part of the local economy, and access to good timberland became extremely important. Judge William L. Vandeventer, whose own father faced charges in connection with the case involving Perry Hursh, wrote that the vigilantes especially disliked "squatters" who would settle on vacant land, and "erect for themselves a log cabin, and proceed to appropriate the 'tie timber' thereon."[80] Obviously, homesteaders were not the same thing as "squatters," but Vandeventer probably used the term pejoratively to describe those who only came to the area to harvest the timber.

In the 1880s, a troupe of amateur actors based in Sparta per-formed a historical drama titled "The Bald Knob Tragedy," which included a scene based on just such a situation involving a home-steader and timber theft. In the scene, the Bald Knobbers went at night to the home of their intended victim, a man named McCormack, and called him out of his house. They informed him that "you have been stealing timber for the past year and it has got to be stoppen [sic], you dirty old rascal." McCormack, they said, practiced no occupation besides "stealing government timber" and would often cover his theft by reporting it to the authorities as the work of some innocent person. For these crimes the vigilantes gave him fifty lashes "well laid on."[81] Although the incident represented in the play is probably fictional, it supports the notion that the Bald Knobbers targeted homesteaders who took timber that the vigilantes wanted for themselves.

The cases involving E. P. Helms and Coe Holley offer further support for the contention that access to timber played a signifi- cant role in the Bald Knobbers' antihomesteader campaign. The vigilantes claimed that they whipped Helms because of his moral deficiencies. Both Helms and his wife, however, testified that the men targeted him because one of them, Amos Jones, wanted to acquire his land, and because they desired the timber thereon.[82] Likewise, James Carr tried to drive Coe Holley off his land in order to harvest the timber on it. Even if Carr did not belong to the Bald Knobbers, which remains uncertain one way or the other, his actions illustrate the lengths to which some residents would go to obtain precious timber resources.[83]

By aggressively prosecuting vigilantes who harassed or intimi- dated homesteaders, the federal government dealt a severe blow to the Bald Knobber movement in southwest Missouri. Over a period of roughly two years beginning with the first arrests in late 1886, federal authorities tried and convicted nearly three dozen known or suspected Bald Knobbers in Christian and Douglas Counties for violating home- steaders' rights. It remains uncertain, however, whether the federal legal offensive would have exerted sufficient force to collapse the vigi- lante organization had not events at a small cabin in Christian County on March 11, 1887, turned the power of public opinion and the full weight of local and state authorities decidedly against the vigilantes.

That cabin belonged to James Edens, the father of William Edens, who had so unwisely antagonized the Bald Knobbers. The elder Edens lived in a small, one-room cabin approximately 16 by 18 feet, with doors on the east and west sides, and a small window to the right of the western door. His house lay alongside the railroad line that ran south to Chadwick, approximately two miles southeast of Sparta. A three-cornered fence enclosed the yard about the house. It was shaped that way because the railroad cut off part of the yard. At its closest point, the railroad passed about forty yards from the house.[84]

On the night in question, James Edens had two of his adult children staying with him. His daughter Melvina had recently given birth to a child and since that time had experienced a bout with the measles. Her husband, Charles Greene, had taken her and their two young children to stay with her parents so they could help nurse her back to health. James Edens stayed up until about ten o'clock that evening, sitting with his daughter Melvina and administering her medicine. His son William, who lived about a quarter mile northwest of him, had also come to his parents' house for a visit along with his wife, Emma.[85] Earlier that day, William had visited Sparta where he once again publicly antagonized the vigilantes by comparing a Bald Knobber to a "sheep killing dog" and implying that he had as much right to kill one as the other. This insult had apparently reached the ears of young William Walker, who vowed revenge on the impertinent Edens.[86]

Around the time that the Edens and Greene families had settled down to bed, Dave Walker and a group of about twenty-five to thirty Bald Knobbers began holding a meeting.[87] The specific purpose of the meeting remains somewhat vague. Judge Vandeventer and Robert Harper both wrote that Dave Walker, who had grown wary of the group's increasingly violent activities, called the meeting in order to disband the organization.[88] In his testimony in Dave Walker's trial, Gilbert Applegate confirmed that the day before the meeting at the old smelter Walker told him that he wanted to disband his group, and he wanted Applegate to attend because he had taken part in disbanding some of the Bald Knobber legions in Douglas County. Once at the smelter, however, Dave Walker did not attempt to disband the group, and according to Applegate "if he made any proposition to disband his men I didn't hear it."[89]

The meeting commenced around eight o'clock in the evening and lasted for roughly two hours. It took place in an isolated location called the "old smelter," located in a deep ravine or "holler" about two miles southeast of Sparta and roughly a mile west of Dave Walker's home. The smelter was located in the northwest quarter of section 6, township 26, and range 19.[90] The meeting itself does not appear to have been especially well organized or purposeful. James McGuire, who attended the assembly, testified that members continued to drift in for roughly an hour after the meeting began, and some men got bored and left early. As the members arrived, most of them congregated beneath a tree next to the road running through that place. The night air must have felt cold, however, for someone had built a fire about twenty-five or thirty feet from the tree, and during the meeting men would get up and "pass back and forth from the tree to the fire." Several of them carried weapons, mostly pistols, rifles, and shotguns. For example, William Newton later recalled that Wiley Mathews carried a double-barreled shotgun, and John Mathews had a Winchester rifle, while Newton himself carried a pistol and a shotgun. Most of the men wore the distinctive Bald Knobber mask of black cambric or calico cloth with horns and tassels of white or red thread.[91]

The men present discussed a variety of topics, much of it unrelated to any kind of vigilante business. Gilbert Applegate recalled that they talked about "shooting, and making ties, and so-on . . . and bragging on their guns and one thing and another." Some of the men suggested whipping various individuals, but most of those present rejected these proposals. Then someone proposed that they go pour out some whiskey belonging to a local moonshiner named William ("Bucky Bill") Roberts, to which Dave Walker agreed. Around ten o'clock that evening the meeting broke up. Some of the men parted ways with the others and returned to their homes, but at least half of the crowd followed Dave Walker as he led them out of the holler. A few of the vigilantes, including Dave Walker, rode horses, but most of the crowd proceeded on foot. The group following Walker headed in a northeast direction, passing the homes of Thomas Day and Judge Reuben L. Hale, before reaching the tracks of the railroad line to Chadwick. They crossed the tracks at a railroad crossing built for the convenience of tie hackers and timber haulers. At this point, some of them must have realized that they were very close to William Edens's home, for a group of about ten or twelve of them led by William Walker broke away from the rest, ran toward the house, and entered it. Finding William Edens absent, the men decided to search for him at his father's house, located about a quarter of a mile to the southwest. They ran back to the railroad, and then followed the tracks at a rapid pace down toward James Edens's residence. This action apparently took the rest of the vigilantes, including Dave Walker, Joe Inman, Gilbert Applegate, and James R. McGuire, completely by surprise. When he saw the men rushing toward James Edens's house, Joe Inman hollered to his chieftain

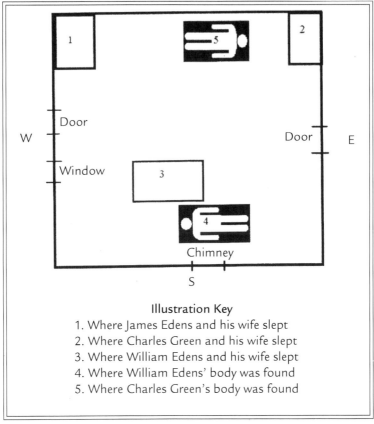

**Illustration Key**

1. Where James Edens and his wife slept
2. Where Charles Green and his wife slept
3. Where William Edens and his wife slept
4. Where William Edens' body was found
5. Where Charles Green's body was found

**Fig. 4.3:** Author's diagram of James Edens's cabin. This author's sketch is based on a similar diagram found in *State of Missouri vs. David Walker,* 1888, MSA, Missouri Supreme Court Files, Box 1144, Case 4.

to stop them or they would get themselves into trouble. Walker called out to his men, yelling, "hold up there, boys," but they either did not hear him or chose to ignore the order.[92]

A great deal of confusion and sometimes contradictory testimony surrounds the events that happened next, but the following facts are clear. After the crowd of about ten or twelve Bald Knobbers reached the Edens cabin one of them called out, presumably to William Edens, something to the effect of "Get out of there, God damn you, or we will kill you!" William awoke suddenly when he heard the commotion outside. As he sprang out of bed and pulled up his pants, he shouted to his father, "Get up, pap, the Bald Knobbers are here!" The elder

Edens jumped out of bed and felt for his pistol in the pocket of the coat that he had left hanging over the bed. He called to his wife, who said she had the weapon, and he grabbed it from her. About that time someone on the outside shattered the window on the western side of the house and fired three shots into it.[93]

The next moment the two doors on either side of the house crashed open. Wiley Mathews used an axe he found in the yard outside to break down the western door, while someone else, possibly William Walker, kicked in the door on the other side. Suddenly, eight or ten men surged into the house, setting off a chaotic struggle inside of it. Three of them seized James Edens, who had just laid hold of his pistol, and attempted to pry the weapon away from him. With a strength born of desperation, Edens managed to break loose of two of his assailants just long enough to raise his pistol and fire a round, which struck William Walker in the leg. At the same time he saw what appeared to be an axe coming at his head. He managed to turn his head just enough to avoid taking the full force of the axe on his skull, but still suffered a glancing blow. At roughly the same time someone fired a shot that ripped through the side of his neck, creating a wound that Coroner J. P. Ralston later described as "large enough that I could introduce my index finger very readily for quite a distance." James Edens lost consciousness immediately and fell across his daughter-in-law Emma onto one of the beds in the house. He did not wake up until the following day.[94]

As the elder Edens struggled with his assailants, his son and son-in-law faced mortal danger. One of the masked men ordered William Edens to raise his hands, and he immediately complied. But an instant later another of the vigilantes, most likely Wiley Mathews, shot him in the back with a shotgun at point-blank range. Several of the pellets pierced his heart, and others tore all the way through his torso. As Edens fell to the floor in front of the fireplace, someone else shot him in the back of the head with a rifle. The bullet entered the back of his skull and exited underneath his chin. Meanwhile, another vigilante shot Charles Greene in the side of his head. The bullet entered his left temple and pierced his brain, but it did not come out the other side. Instead, it left an impression in his skull that could be "distinctly felt just back of the right ear." When Melvina Greene saw her brother killed, she jumped out of bed. One of the vigilantes raised his gun as if to shoot her, but she got her hand up in time to deflect the muzzle of the weapon. When the gun discharged, the bullet tore off the tip of the little finger on her left hand, and the blast from the front of the weapon caught her dress on fire. The woman briefly grappled with her assailant and managed to pull the mask partly off his face. She noticed that he had no beard, which in those days usually indicated a young man.[95]

After the shooting subsided, the Bald Knobbers quickly exited the house. Emma Edens managed to extricate herself from beneath her father-in-law's unconscious body and went to check on her husband. Before she got to him, however, she saw two of the vigilantes standing out in the yard a few feet from the door. One of them said to the other one, "put it to him again." The other man, who later testimony revealed was most likely William Walker, raised his gun and fired a last shot into the house. Then the men turned and left. To Emma Edens's surprise, she found her husband still breathing when she got to him, but he drew only a few short breaths before he expired.[96]

The tragic events that took place inside James Edens's cabin lasted only a few minutes, but they fundamentally altered the entire course of the Bald Knobber movement. Overnight the vigilantes had transformed themselves from righteous defenders of the law and Christian morality into murderers, outlaws, and social pariahs, an outcome that surely surprised many of them. The Bald Knobbers thought of themselves as dutiful citizens fighting against crime and immoral behavior that the railroads, industry, and social change had brought to their communities. They also considered themselves protectors of poor families from what they perceived as the unfair policies of corporations like the J. L. Lee Tie and Timber Company and unfair competition from homesteaders who used federal law to deprive them of resources they saw as their own. The incident at James Edens's cabin changed all that.

## CHAPTER 5

# The Crackdown: Southwest Missouri Reacts to the Edens-Greene Killings

The Edens-Greene murders constituted a watershed moment that dramatically altered the history of the Bald Knobber movement in southwest Missouri. The homicides prompted a harsh reaction, both from the public at large and from local law enforcement officials, particularly Christian County sheriff Zachariah A. Johnson, whose task it became to track down those responsible for the killings and bring them to justice.

Even before the slayings of William Edens and Charles Greene, some people had called for swift action to put down the Bald Knobber movement in southwest Missouri. In addition to the anti–Bald Knobber protests originating in Taney County, the actions of the vigilantes in Christian County and other places began drawing unfavorable attention in the press. About three months prior to the tragedy at the Edens cabin, the *St. Louis Republican* denounced the organization as a "tyrannical and criminal conspiracy against the peace of [Missouri]" that was "bringing the state into disrepute."[1] Springfield's *Leader* seconded the *Republican*'s sentiment, and added that the Bald Knobbers posed an obstacle to the socioeconomic progress of southwest Missouri, because "[e]migration and capital cannot be expected to go into counties where mob law rules." The city of Springfield had an interest in the affairs of the counties where the Bald Knobbers held sway, argued the *Leader*, because "Taney and Christian and other counties are directly tributary to Springfield, and influences which retard the development of those counties are influences directly inimical to Springfield's interests."[2]

These arguments seemed to carry weight with federal authorities. As discussed in the previous chapter, federal officeholders in southwest Missouri began cracking down on the Bald Knobbers in late 1886, primarily by prosecuting vigilantes who violated the rights of homesteaders to live on and develop their property. The men who spearheaded this effort included officials such as U.S. commissioner McLain Jones and district attorney Maceanas E. Benton, both of whom worked assiduously to bring to justice as many Bald Knobbers as possible. By contrast, prior to March 1887, no Bald Knobbers faced charges in Christian County for crimes related to vigilante activity, and local officials in that county and elsewhere seemed to have little interest in prosecuting these men. Some of the officials, like Sheriff Zach Johnson, knew the vigilantes as friends, neighbors, and political supporters,[3] while others like county judge Reuben L. Hale may have belonged to the organization themselves. Most of them probably feared the consequences of attacking an organization that exercised such great influence in their neighborhoods. Journalistic critics of the night riders decried this apparent apathy, arguing that the "laws of the state have suffered the most, and the conspiracy cannot be broken up unless the state laws are enforced." To that end, the *Leader* urged authorities in Christian, Taney, and Douglas Counties to "look after this subject" at the next session of the circuit court in their respective districts.[4]

Ultimately, it took more than prodding by newspapers to convince reluctant officeholders to take action against the Ozarks' fearsome night riders. Some galvanizing event would have to take place, which would turn public opinion against the vigilantes and force local officials into action. The murders of William Edens and Charles Greene provided just such a tipping point. News of the homicides spread rapidly from "neighbor to neighbor; from village to village" throughout the area,[5] arousing the "intense indignation" of the public against the vigilantes.[6] On March 13, the citizens of Ozark held a public meeting at the courthouse where they passed resolutions condemning the Bald Knobbers and urging county officials to act swiftly against them.[7] The public also demonstrated its anger by their attitude toward county judge Reuben L. Hale. During the course of the investigation into the Edens-Greene affair, it became known that Judge Hale probably belonged to the Bald Knobbers. Although he had played no role in that night's unfortunate events, nor in any other vigilante outrage as far as anyone knew, angry citizens petitioned Hale to resign his position on the county court immediately.[8] Hale did not resign, and he actually won another term in the same office in 1888,[9] but the initial backlash against him revealed the public's hostility toward the vigilantes in the weeks following the murders.

The first official to view the scene of the crime was the county coroner J. P. Ralston, who went to James Edens's cabin the morning after the killings. He examined the two corpses and made notes about the wounds. He also examined James Edens, who had been seriously wounded in the attack but would eventually recover.[10] Ralston left the crime scene as he had found it and went to assemble a coroner's jury, which returned to the crime scene and interviewed the survivors, including the wives of the deceased, Emma Edens and Melvina Greene. Neither woman could positively identify the attackers, since all of them wore masks, but they did give the names of six men whom they thought they had recognized, including Samuel Preston Sr., Samuel Preston Jr., James Preston, William J. ("Bud") Ray, William Roberts, and Joseph Inman. The women swore out affidavits against these men, and arrest warrants were issued.[11] Mrs. Greene identified young Bud Ray as the man with whom she had struggled in the cabin. She had managed to pry her assailant's mask partly off his face, and thought she could identify Ray from his beardless face, which in those days usually indicated a young man. Subsequent testimony, however, later exonerated him.[12]

The responsibility for tracking down the Bald Knobbers who participated in the Edens-Greene affair fell to Sheriff Johnson. The sheriff, a native of Indiana, had moved to Ozark in Christian County as a young man in 1873. He eventually settled down there, married, and raised a family. Johnson became active in county politics, and in

**Fig. 5.1:** Sheriff Zachariah Johnson. Source: William L. Vandeventer, Justice in the Rough, 1937. Used by permission of the State Historical Society of Missouri Research Center, Rolla, MO.

1886 he received an appointment from Gov. John S. Marmaduke to fill the office of sheriff, which had fallen vacant after the death of the incumbent William Gardner.[13]

In response to the Edens-Greene killings, Johnson quickly assembled a posse and went in search of the perpetrators. Acting on the information obtained from the widows of Greene and Edens, the sheriff quickly arrested Samuel Preston Sr., his son, Bud Ray, and William Roberts.[14] He then caught an important break. Acting on a tip from an anonymous source, he managed to locate and arrest Joe Inman, who became the first Bald Knobber to break down and make a full confession, naming everyone he knew of who had been involved in the events of that tragic night.[15] Using this information, Sheriff

Johnson quickly apprehended almost all of the vigilantes who had either attended the meeting at the old smelter or had taken part in the killings. By March 16, he had sworn affidavits against twenty-two of his suspects and had already arrested thirteen of them, including several of the leaders like Dave Walker, John Mathews, Wiley Mathews, and C. O. Simmons.[16] The following day the sheriff had nineteen men in custody and moved Inman to the Greene County jail in Springfield for his own protection.[17] By March 18, Johnson had in addition netted Andrew Adams, Jesse Robertson, Gilbert Applegate, Peter Davis, Lewis Davis, and James McGuire, which brought the total number of suspects incarcerated to twenty-five.[18]

Thus, in about a week, Sheriff Johnson managed to round up nearly all of the parties suspected of taking part in the Edens-Greene affair. His swift response to the situation earned him name recognition in newspapers across the country[19] and effusive praise from journalists, one of whom referred to the sheriff's performance as the "quickest capture of murderers on record in the Southwest."[20] Of the suspects, only William Walker, the assistant chief and son of the vigilante chieftain Dave Walker, remained at large. The younger Walker had suffered a wound in his leg during the fray at the Edens cabin, which caused his father to take him into Douglas County where he could hide with his relatives and recuperate. Sheriff Johnson would later invent a cunning stratagem to apprehend the young man, but for the moment he remained outside of the law's reach.

In the meantime, the excitement occasioned by the Bald Knobber murders and the ensuing manhunt began to fray the nerves both of the county officials and the public at large. About ten days after the murders, ex-county clerk J. C. Rogers, who had "been on his feet almost constantly . . . since the Bald Knob campaign began," reported that he had lost nearly ten pounds during that period. Similarly, county recorder W. M. Wade spent so much time guarding Bald Knobber prisoners that he had to catch up on his paperwork on a Sunday. He sheepishly told a reporter that he "hoped his religious friends would not blame him" for this infraction.[21] The stress of the situation particularly impacted the citizens of Ozark, the county seat. They felt especially uneasy because of the large number of Bald Knobbers incarcerated in their courthouse and because the jail was too small and dilapidated to accommodate so many. Such great fear did the night riders engender in that part of the county that many townsfolk assumed that the vigilantes would raid their community in a rescue effort. It appeared as though their worst fears had come true on the evening of March 17, when reports reached Ozark of gunfire coming from the direction of Sparta. In their heightened state of fear, many residents assumed that a Bald Knobber rescue party approached their town. Alarms went out, and soon a large body of armed citizens assembled at the courthouse ready to repel the anticipated raiding party. Wild rumors began circulating; one man ran into town and reported that around twenty men had died in fighting between Bald Knobbers and citizens at Sparta. It turned out, however, that the object of their fears was nothing more than a boisterous wedding charivari. The noise they heard happened to be a party of friends and well-wishers serenading a newly married couple with songs, anvil shooting, and dozens of gunshots aimed at the sky.[22]

The public's anxiety, coupled with legitimate concerns about the security of the prisoners confined to the courthouse, forced local officials to consider other means of housing them. On March 19, Sheriff Johnson and two deputies took fifteen Bald Knobber prisoners to Springfield by train and placed them in the county jail there "for greater security."[23] The removal of the greater number of their prisoners to Springfield allowed county officials to focus on the task of gathering evidence and preparing for the trials that would inevitably ensue. In late March, Judge Walter D. Hubbard of the circuit court called for "a special term of the court to be held at Ozark on the 19th of April" to deal with the Bald Knobbers connected to the Edens-Greene homicides.[24]

In the meantime, Sheriff Johnson and his deputies continued their search for William Walker, the last remaining vigilante who had eluded their grasp. Walker's capture had symbolic significance, not only because of his prominent role in the Edens-Greene killings, but also because he had served as the assistant chief of the Bald Knobbers in Christian County. For this reason, the county government and Governor Marmaduke together put up a reward of three hundred dollars for information leading to his apprehension.[25] The problem was that William Walker seemed to have disappeared into the hills. Some reports circulated that he had gone into hiding "in the woods near Chadwick," while others stated that he had already died and his friends had buried him.[26] Joe Inman told authorities that the young man lost a lot of blood from his gunshot wound, which Inman believed "will in all probability prove fatal."[27]

William Walker did not die. He went into Douglas County where his father Dave had taken him to stay with his uncle, Charles Gatson ("Gat") Walker, until he recuperated. As long as he remained safe in the hills among his relatives, it seemed unlikely that the law could reach him. Sheriff Johnson did have one asset, however, which he exploited to the fullest possible advantage. He had in his custody one William Newton, a Bald Knobber arrested in connection with the Edens-Greene affair. Newton's sister, Lois, was William Walker's sweetheart and quite possibly his fiancée.[28]

William Newton's brother, Joseph Newton, also belonged to the Bald Knobbers, but had not yet been arrested for anything. Joe wanted to help his brother in any way he could, so he approached Sheriff Johnson with an offer to help him capture William Walker. The sheriff told Joe Newton that if he helped capture William Walker he would do whatever he could do for Joe's brother.[29] Joe first visited his brother in jail and urged him to testify for the state, which was advice he wisely decided to follow.[30] Next he visited Dave Walker and convinced the vigilante chieftain that he wanted to help his son get far away from southwest Missouri where he could be safe from capture. Dave Walker agreed and told Joe Newton about his son's whereabouts. He even wrote a letter of introduction for Newton to use in locating his son. About two weeks after the murders, Joe Newton left for Douglas County in a wagon, taking with him his sister Lois and William Walker's sister Ellen. He apparently intended to use the women as bait to earn William Walker's trust, though he did not disclose his true intentions to them at the time. When they arrived at Gat Walker's home in Douglas County, they discovered that William had already crossed the state line into Baxter County, Arkansas. Gat Walker told Newton he could find the young fugitive at his uncle John Walker's house in Arkansas. A lame horse prevented Newton from taking the women any farther in the wagon, so he sent them back to Christian County. He then set off for Arkansas accompanied by Joseph Walker, another one of William's uncles.[31]

When Joe Newton arrived at John Walker's home in Baxter County, he found William Walker still hobbling around on crutches because of his wounded leg and an outlaw named Frank Bean who had recently escaped from the Greene County jail in Springfield. Newton persuaded both men to accompany him across the border to West Plains, Missouri, on the pretext of helping them escape capture. From West Plains they could catch a train down to Jonesboro, Arkansas, from whence they would enter the hill country surrounding Batesville. There they could hide out in greater security, he argued, than at their current location. The two fugitives agreed and followed Newton to West Plains.[32]

While en route, Newton and Walker discussed the fateful night of the Edens-Greene killings. According to Newton, Walker told him that he blamed the botched raid on the many inexperienced "tenderfoots" among the vigilantes that night. Walker told Newton that he had struggled with Charles Greene because he had pulled a pistol and tried to wrestle the weapon away from him. In all probability it was actually James Edens with whom Walker had grappled, but he would not have known that at the time. Walker also mentioned that one of women (probably Melvina Greene) attacked him and tore off part of his mask and that he would have "killed her dead as hell" had she not put her hand up in time to deflect his pistol. When the men arrived at their destination, they decided to camp for the night just outside of town. Joe Newton took the first opportunity to go into town and send a telegram to Sheriff Johnson in Ozark, telling him to come to West Plains immediately. The sheriff gathered his deputies and did as instructed, arriving in West Plains in time to arrest William Walker and Frank Bean before they could board another train back to Arkansas. The lawmen also arrested Joe Newton, but only to keep the other two from suspecting his role in their capture, which only became public knowledge about a year later at the trial of William Walker, where Newton testified against Walker and explained his role in the assistant chief's capture.[33]

The arrest of William Walker brought to twenty-six the number of vigilantes arrested in connection with the Edens-Greene murders. As impressive as the performance of Sheriff Johnson and his deputies had been, there still remained the hard work of gathering information that the county prosecutor, Gustavus A. Watson, could use to build cases against them—a task easier said than done. The men who raided the Edens cabin had worn masks, the house was dark, and the chaotic struggle inside lasted only a few moments. Emma Edens and Melvina Greene, who had witnessed and survived the attack, could only guess the identity of those attackers whom they thought they recognized. Thus, if the prosecution wanted to build a case against any of the vigilantes, it would have to obtain information from the Bald Knobbers themselves. As long as the vigilantes kept their oaths and refused to divulge any secrets regarding their order, the prosecution would find it extremely difficult, if not impossible, to prove any charges against them. If one or more of them broke, however, the entire Bald Knobber band could end up in prison. Dave Walker foresaw this danger and tried to convince his fellow vigilantes to stonewall the authorities and withhold any useful facts from them. Shortly after the Edens-Greene killings, Walker conferred with his followers and told them to keep that night's events to themselves. He instructed them to invent alibis that they could corroborate for each other. For example, Walker told Charles Graves, Joseph Inman, Gilbert Applegate, and James McGuire to say that they spent the evening playing cards at Inman's house until 11 o'clock, around the time of the murders.[34] Likewise, during the court proceedings the following month several witnesses said that after being arrested Walker tried to convince them not to divulge information. One witness said that the chieftain went so far as to come up to him in the courthouse and tell him to "Die with the whole thing in you." Rumors circulated among the prisoners that their comrades outside stood ready to "inflict the full penalty of the oath on anyone who might give anything away."[35]

These rumors and threats notwithstanding, the Bald Knobbers did not prove very disciplined when it came to obstructing prosecutors and resisting interrogation. Over the next few weeks and months, a veritable wave of confessions took place. In securing these confessions, the prosecution received vital assistance from Sheriff Johnson and his deputies, who proved ruthlessly inventive in devising ways to apply pressure to their prisoners. During their confinement, many Bald Knobbers complained that those who turned state's evidence received better treatment, while those who held out could expect their sufferings to multiply. In a letter to his brother, Dave Walker groused that "the Breakers" (i.e., those who had divulged information) were allowed outside of their cells to exercise their limbs, while "the Best" were confined at all times. Moreover, the men who had kept their oaths rarely received "anything fit to eat and only half enough at that," and were seldom allowed to warm themselves next to the "one little stove" the jail kept for heating.[36] Likewise, Amos Jones wrote to his brother that Sheriff Johnson "feeds William Newton cake and sausage"—Newton was one of the "breakers"—while other prisoners had to subsist on bread, molasses, and undercooked beef.[37]

In the face of these tactics, many vigilantes forgot their oaths of secrecy and looked for an opportunity to curry favor with the prosecution by telling whatever they knew. Like a series of dominos falling, each new confession led to others, as men realized that if their comrades had already started talking they had little to gain from silence. As mentioned above, the first such domino to fall was Joseph Inman, one of the Bald Knobbers who had attended the meeting at the smelter and witnessed, but did not directly participate in, the Edens-Greene killings. Inman gave a description of the night's events, including the meeting at the old smelter and the eventual attack on the Edens cabin. He gave the names of several men whom he had recognized at either place, and he identified William Walker as the one who led the small band of vigilantes to James Edens's home, and who suffered a wound in the fray. Perhaps most damning of all, Inman reported that shortly after the killings Dave Walker had conferred with John Mathews and suggested that if someone would take care of his son he would lead a group back to the house to "finish killing them women," thereby silencing any witnesses.[38]

Shortly after Inman's confession, James McGuire also agreed to testify. McGuire was a young man who was boarding at Joe Inman's house at the time of the killing. He had joined the Bald Knobbers earlier that day. The assistant chief, William Walker, administered the oath to him and also showed him the special hand grips and passwords by which vigilantes identified each other. In most respects McGuire's testimony concerning the fateful night's events corroborated Inman's version. He said that when the meeting at the smelter broke up he thought the participants were going home. McGuire did not participate in the raid on James Edens's house, and said that he did not even realize whose house it was until after the attack occurred. He also said that Dave Walker gave him a pistol with one round in it as they left the smelter ground.[39]

Like James McGuire, William Abbott displayed especially bad timing when he decided to join the Bald Knobbers. On the invitation of Joseph Hyde, Abbott attended the final meeting at the old smelter and took the oath of membership that very night. He apparently did not know much about the organization when he joined. When asked in court what the purpose of the Bald Knobbers was, Abbott replied that it "didn't have any object as I know of; they didn't tell me what their object was." Abbott did not accompany the crowd to James Edens's house and therefore did not testify concerning the murders. He did, however, talk about what transpired at the meeting at the smelter. He gave the names of several of the vigilantes present and explained how they equipped themselves, including weapons and masks.[40]

The testimony of another Bald Knobber, Charles Graves, also significantly affected subsequent murder trials. Graves's evidence proved particularly devastating to Wiley Mathews and Dave Walker. Graves recalled that after the raid on James Edens's cabin Wiley Mathews spoke to him about what transpired in the cabin. Mathews told him that he had killed William Edens that night "to save his uncle John that he shot him in the back with a shot gun."[41] Graves also corroborated Joe Inman's claim that Dave Walker wanted to eliminate any witnesses to the murders. The chieftain, said Graves, proposed to "go back and kill the women and children" and burn down James Edens's cabin, so as to remove any trace of the crime.[42] In addition to testifying about the events surrounding the Edens-Greene killings, Graves actually took Sheriff Johnson to the crime scene and helped him recover evidence, including some Bald Knobber masks, weapons, and a dark lantern that the vigilantes had hidden following the murders.[43]

Shortly after Charles Graves agreed to testify, Reverend C. O. Simmons and William Newton both expressed their desire to turn state's evidence. At first the prosecution rejected their request, saying that they already had enough testimony. In Newton's case, however, they must have changed their minds, for they later dropped their case against him in order to use him as a witness in subsequent trials.[44] Although a witness for the state, Newton's testimony, along with that of Charles Graves, proved pivotal in acquitting Gilbert Applegate, the first Bald Knobber to stand trial for murder.[45] Newton did, however, help convict several other Bald Knobbers of murder. For example, he testified that he saw Wiley Mathews batter down the western door of James Edens's cabin with an ax, and that he witnessed William Walker fire the last shot into the Edens cabin as he stood outside the door of the house. Finally, he swore that after the killings, Wiley Mathews told him that he had an empty gun, which indicated that he had fired it in the house.[46]

The preceding examples represent a few of the more prominent instances in which the Bald Knobbers themselves provided the prosecution with the evidence necessary to build a case against the parties responsible for the Edens-Greene murders. By the time the special term of the circuit court began on April 19, 1887, Prosecutor Watson had enough evidence to pursue indictments against sixteen of the twenty-six men originally arrested in the case. On April 21, the grand jury handed down indictments for first-degree murder against twelve men for the killing of William Edens. These included David Walker, William Walker, Wiley Mathews, John Mathews, C. O. Simmons, Gilbert Applegate, William Stanley, William Newton, Charles Graves, Joe Inman, Amos Jones, and Andrew Adams. Two days later the grand jury delivered indictments for murder against the same individuals and four others—James Mathews, Joe Hyde, Lewis Davis, and Peter Davis—for the killing of Charles Greene.[47] The defendants charged in each of these indictments pled not guilty and quickly filed for a continuance on the basis that they had not had sufficient time to prepare for their defense. Since many of them were relatively poor men, they also needed time to raise the necessary funds to pay their attorney's fees. Judge Hubbard granted the request for a continuance until the next regular term of the circuit court scheduled to begin on August 22, 1887.[48]

In addition to handling the murder cases, the grand jury also used the special session of the court to issue indictments against those implicated in other Bald Knobber-related crimes. Over the next week, the grand jurors handed down indictments against roughly 80 individuals on approximately 250 separate charges.[49] For example, on April 26 the grand jury indicted twenty-seven vigilantes for participating on November 9, 1886, in the raid on the Chadwick tavern belonging to John Rhodes and Russell McCauley.[50] At the same time, the grand jurors filed indictments against nineteen individuals involved in the whipping of the polygamist Greene Walker on August 21, 1886.[51] Likewise, they indicted nine vigilantes for the beating of the now-deceased William Edens, who had publically criticized them,[52] nine for the flogging of homesteader E. P. Helms,[53] and fifteen for the flogging of Horace Johnson for failing to support his family.[54] The grand jury also indicted nine Bald Knobbers for whipping George Baty for speaking against them,[55] six more for conspiring to whip Samuel Daves,[56] and another six for stopping Clate Whiteacre on a public road, knocking him off his horse, and beating him with their guns.[57]

In addition to charging everyone who had participated in Bald Knobber raids or whippings, the grand jury also filed indictments for unlawful assembly against anyone who had attended a Bald Knobber meeting, particularly when those meetings led to acts of violence. For example, the twenty-seven people whom the grand jury indicted for raiding Rhodes and McCauley's tavern in Chadwick also faced charges for participating in an unlawful assembly, which in this case meant a meeting held for the purpose of planning or carrying out a criminal act.[58] Likewise, the men who whipped William Edens faced charges not only for the assault itself, but also for participating in an unlawful assembly,[59] as did those who whipped Horace Johnson, Greene Walker, Samuel Daves, and so on.[60] As we have already seen, in order to assemble the evidence necessary to prove these charges, local authorities had to rely heavily on information obtained from the vigilantes themselves. For that reason, the grand jury took a dim view of anyone who attempted to give them false or misleading information.

For example, they indicted Thomas B. Daugherty for perjury for providing false testimony regarding the beating of Horace Johnson,[61] and they indicted Joseph Garrison for doing essentially the same thing in the Greene Walker whipping case.[62]

The implicit purpose of all these indictments was not only to tie as many charges to as many Bald Knobbers as possible, but also to send a message that local officials would no longer tolerate vigilante activity in Christian County. At the beginning of the special session, Judge Hubbard delivered a "charge to the grand jury" that encouraged the jurors to take a strong stand against "Bald Knobbism" by issuing tough indictments against the vigilantes. Most of the public heartily endorsed the judge's message.[63] The actions of the grand jurors over the following week showed that they agreed with the judge and wanted to follow his lead in stamping out the Bald Knobber organization in their communities. The vigilantes themselves seemed to understand that message, because those who could do so fled the area rather than face prosecution or testify against their friends. In late April, a correspondent for the *Kansas City Star* reported that a merchant based in Sparta told him that between forty and fifty people had "left the county since the grand jury began its investigations."[64] The same paper had earlier reported on a "general exodus" of vigilantes from "the Bald Knob section about Chadwick" in response to the prosecution of Bald Knobbers.[65] Likewise, the *St. Louis Post-Dispatch* reported that many people had left the state even before the grand jury began its session.[66]

Those who fled often did so to avoid the economic costs of a long trial and incarceration as well as to evade a conviction and possible prison sentence. Several of the indicted men were extremely poor, so that their families sometimes found themselves in dire straits, having to sell "their life's accumulations" in order to "retain lawyers to defend their misguided sons." Many people expected the cost of the trials to "nearly bankrupt the community."[67] For example, when Joe Inman found no one willing to lend him money to pay for his defense, he turned to his father whom he begged to mortgage a farm the family owned in Greene County in order to pay for his legal bills.[68]

The Bald Knobber trials also created logistical and security problems for the authorities in Christian County. The townspeople in

Ozark had expected the Bald Knobber prisoners held in the Springfield jail to return on August 22, a Monday. Sheriff Johnson, however, feared for the security of the prisoners if they arrived on schedule. So on Saturday he and a couple of his deputies went in secret to Springfield, gathered their charges, and on Sunday morning took them by train back down to Ozark. They placed their prisoners in the county's new brick jail, completed just in time for the next term of the circuit court in Ozark.[69] The court opened with great fanfare. Large crowds including spectators, lawyers, witnesses, jurors, defendants, the families of the accused, and many journalists descended on this small town of fewer than five hundred inhabitants.[70] Newspaper reports estimated the multitudes, probably with some exaggeration, at between one to two thousand people.[71] The crowds became so large that they quickly exceeded the town's capacity to handle them all, and Ozark's few available hotel rooms soon became "overrun with people from all over the country."[72] Many people in the crowd were relatives of the accused Bald Knobbers being held in jail. These people mainly camped out on the outskirts of town in wagons and tents. So numerous did they become that at night Ozark was "illuminated by the numerous camp fires that completely surrounded the town."[73] The families of the Bald Knobbers came to support their loved ones, and Sheriff Johnson allowed them to bring the prisoners gifts of food, clothing, tobacco, fruit, and whatever other creature comforts they could obtain. One woman even brought an apron full of "old fashioned ginger cakes" to her husband in jail.[74]

The presence of so many relatives of the jailed vigilantes added a tragic aspect to the court proceedings. Many of the Bald Knobber families were very poor, and had to make tough financial sacrifices to abandon their farms during the court session. One newspaper estimated that "work has been suspended on half of the farms in the county" because of the trials.[75] In the camps outside of town some people made extra money by selling watermelons to bystanders looking to beat the summer's heat.[76] During the court session the families of the prisoners frequently crowded into the town's Methodist church to pray for their men. For example, on Thursday evening, August 25, the church held a candle light service which so many people attended that "many were turned away for want of standing room."[77]

Judge Hubbard opened the court session at one o'clock on Monday afternoon. The first day the court handled mostly minor business. Several motions to quash various indictments were heard and rejected. John Wilson, a Bald Knobber and Baptist preacher, pled guilty to taking part in the whipping of Greene Walker. Later that afternoon the proceedings were interrupted when the wife of William Stanley, one of the Bald Knobbers indicted for the Edens-Greene murders, had what appeared to be a nervous breakdown. She had fallen ill with a fever that morning, and had gone to bed for rest. When she awoke, however, she rushed toward the jail yelling wildly and praying to heaven to spare her husband's life. Her "frantic shrieks" disturbed the crowd gathered around the jail and courthouse and interrupted court proceedings until her friends could lead her away.[78]

For the balance of the week, the court dealt mainly with cases involving small offenses such as whippings, raids, and unlawful assemblies. On Tuesday, August 23, the court heard confessions from dozens of Bald Knobbers who admitted participating in a variety of crimes including the first and second floggings of Greene Walker, the whipping of Horace Johnson, and the raid on the Rhodes and McCauley saloon in Chadwick. Many of the same men confessed to taking part in unlawful assemblies.[79] The next couple of days brought more of the same. On Wednesday and Thursday, the court heard testimony from victims of Bald Knobber outrages, including people like Greene Walker, Horace Johnson, and E. P. Helms. It also heard more confessions from the vigilantes accused of unlawful assembly, and dealt with other cases involving small offenses such as carrying concealed weapons, disturbing the peace, and assault and battery. For example, the Bald Knobbers John Carter and Isaac Garrison pled guilty to beating Greene Walker and raiding the Rhodes-McCauley saloon in Chadwick. Moreover, on Thursday, several Bald Knobbers accused of the Edens-Greene murders filed a motion (which they later withdrew) for a change of venue based on the severe "prejudice" against them on the part of their neighbors.[80]

The following day the attorneys for eight of the Bald Knobbers indicted for the Edens-Greene murders tried another tactic. They filed an application for a second continuance until the circuit court's next regular term scheduled to begin the following February. They based

this request on the grounds that they had not yet located two witnesses supposedly critical to their defense: Gat Walker, Dave Walker's
brother, and another man named Missouri Bond. Gat Walker had
recently moved to Memphis, Tennessee, and Bond to Baxter Springs,
Kansas. The applications stated that Bond, if present, would testify
that on the morning after the shooting, James Edens told him that
his son William was actually responsible for the shooting because he
had fired the first three or four shots through the window of the cabin
at the men outside, which "was the cause of the whole trouble . . . no
one was to be blamed for what occurred there but William Edens."
Gat Walker, if present, would testify that within a day or two of the
shooting he overheard Emma Edens, William Edens's widow, say that
her husband, Charles Greene, and James Edens started the trouble
by firing at the men on the road outside, and that when these men
entered the house she did not recognize any of them.[81]

Although Judge Hubbard decided to grant the request for a
second continuance, the facts alleged in the application seem dubious for several reasons. First, they directly contradicted the sworn
testimony of James Edens and Emma Edens themselves.[82] Second,
Gat Walker hardly qualified as a credible witness. He belonged to
the Bald Knobbers himself, had sheltered William Walker while he
was on the run from the law, and had been indicted for the beating
of homesteader E. P. Helms.[83] Third, Missouri Bond, if he ever spoke
to James Edens at all, could not have done so the morning after the
shooting because at that time Edens was lying unconscious in his
home having sustained serious injuries the night before.[84] Fourth,
multiple witnesses who saw the crime scene said that the glass shards
from the broken window in the Edens cabin were found only inside
the house. If someone inside the house had fired through the window
first the shards would have fallen outside the house.[85] Finally, Walker
and Bond never did testify in any of the subsequent murder trials,
which suggests that the defense only asked for a second continuance
to buy extra time. Why did Judge Hubbard grant their request? He
probably did so because the court already had a backlog of cases (one
newspaper estimated around a thousand) far greater than it normally
handled in any given term, of which about a quarter involved the
Bald Knobbers.[86]

One Bald Knobber did not want to delay the proceedings. Against the advice of his lawyers, Gilbert Applegate asked that his trial begin as soon as possible. The court agreed, and Applegate's trial began on September 2.[87] It attracted much attention, both from spectators and the press, because many saw it as a dry run for the murder trials that would proceed during the next term. Indeed, almost all of the key witnesses who testified in this case also testified in the trials of Dave Walker, William Walker, Wiley Mathews, and John Mathews.[88] The case differed from the others, however, in a few important ways. First, unlike the other men who attended the meeting at the old smelter, Applegate did not belong to Dave Walker's Chadwick legion. He came from Douglas County and had joined the Bald Knobbers there. According to Applegate's own testimony in Dave Walker's trial, he only attended the meeting that night because he thought Dave Walker wanted his help in disbanding the vigilante group in Christian County.[89] Moreover, none of the state's witnesses testified that Applegate actually entered James Edens's house, or that he had conspired with any of the other men to kill or injure William Edens and Charles Greene, or even that he had encouraged the others to do so. In light of these facts, on September 7, 1887, a jury found Gilbert Applegate "not guilty" on the charge of first-degree murder.[90] For the prosecution this failure ultimately proved to be a blessing in disguise, because Gilbert Applegate later testified for the state in cases involving other persons charged with the same crime.

Even as the court dealt with the Applegate case, it proceeded to wrap up the other Bald Knobber cases on its docket. Although the local officials like Prosecutor G. A. Watson and the attorneys assisting him aggressively pursued the vigilantes responsible for the Edens-Greene murders, as a rule they showed leniency toward vigilantes who had not taken part in the killings. This pattern of selective leniency held true for the many individuals who pled guilty or were convicted of participating in whippings, raids, and unlawful assemblies. For example, on August 27 the court handed down fines to roughly two dozen vigilantes for these minor offenses. The fines varied in amounts based on the number and severity of offenses, but overall they averaged between $20 and $30. The highest went to Hiram Anderson who received four fines for a total of $100, while several individuals paid only a single fine of $12.50. Those receiving the fines also had to give bonds, ranging from $100 to $300, to ensure that they would "keep the peace" in the future. As lenient as these penalties were, however, some of the vigilantes still had no money to pay and had to go to jail. The individuals confined to jail for nonpayment of fines included Reuben Shipman, Matt Shipman, J. H. Shipman, Isaac Garrison, and Thomas ("Tandy") Dalton.[91] These men later filed appeals to have their fines commuted.[92]

Shortly after the Applegate trial the circuit court adjourned its August session and departed Ozark. It would not return until its next session scheduled for late February. After Applegate's acquittal, the court still had only dealt with one of the cases involving those responsible for the Edens-Greene murders. On September 7, 1887, the court granted bail to seven of these men including Andrew Adams, Joe Inman, Joe Hyde, Charles Graves, Lewis Davis, Peter Davis, and the recently acquitted Gilbert Applegate, who still faced indictments on other charges. The nine men who remained incarcerated included Dave Walker, William Walker, Wiley Mathews, John Mathews, James Mathews, C. O. Simmons, Amos Jones, William Newton, and William Stanley. Some people interpreted the move as an indication of whom the prosecution would target the following term. When he saw the other men being released, Dave Walker reportedly remarked, "Well boys, you see now whose necks are to be broken."[93]

The chieftain's appraisal of the situation proved basically accurate. Four of the seven men released from jail—the Davis brothers, Joe Inman, and Charles Graves—testified as witnesses for the state in exchange for which the authorities declined to prosecute them. In April 1889, the vigilantes Andrew Adams and Joseph Hyde reached an agreement with the prosecution to have the cases against them dropped as well.[94] By contrast, only one of the nine remaining prisoners, William Newton, saved himself by turning state's evidence and testifying against his comrades.[95] Four of the prisoners, including Dave Walker, William Walker, Wiley Mathews, and John Mathews, were later convicted of first-degree murder. Three more of them, Amos Jones, C. O. Simmons, and William Stanley later pled guilty to second-degree murder and received prison sentences, while James Mathews, John Mathews's teenage son, received probation on account of his youth.[96]

Preparations for the next term of the circuit court began on February 27, 1888. On that day Judge Hubbard arrived by train from Springfield, along with the other officers of the court and many attorneys. The large crowds which had accompanied the court to Ozark at the August term also showed up for this session. Sheriff Johnson allowed the families of the imprisoned vigilantes to visit them in jail, and dozens of women and children crowded into the brick structure to spend a few moments with their fathers, husbands, and brothers. At 2:30 in the afternoon Judge Hubbard ordered the sheriff to bring the Bald Knobber prisoners into the court room. At the prisoners' request, the court granted them a "severance," meaning that each defendant would stand trial separately. After a brief consultation, the attorneys for the defense and prosecution agreed to try the case of William Walker first.[97] So began one of the most famous courtroom battles in the history of the Ozarks, an event long remembered and debated among the people of that region.

# CHAPTER 6

# "A Scene of Ghastliness": The Tragic End of the Bald Knobbers in Christian County

T he trial of William Walker marked the beginning of a climactic phase in the history of the Bald Knobbers. Up to this point, local authorities in Christian County had adopted something like a "carpet bombing" approach to dealing with the Bald Knobber threat in their midst; they had brought a wide variety of charges against as many vigilantes as possible, thereby demoralizing the rank-and-file of the organization. In so doing, they had broken the back of the Bald Knobber conspiracy. Now, with the trial of William Walker, the first of four significant vigilante leaders to stand trial for murder, they aimed to cut off its head.

Appropriately, some of the most well known legal names in southwest Missouri represented either the state or the defense in this case. Four prominent attorneys from Springfield and Ozark represented Walker: David M. Payne, Sempronius H. Boyd, Thomas J. Delaney, and Oliver H. Travers.[1] D. M. Payne was a successful criminal attorney based in Ozark. Just a few months after the Bald Knobber trials, he became the first mayor of Ozark when the county court officially incorporated it as a city in August 1888.[2] S. H. Boyd was one of the more colorful figures in the legal history of southwest Missouri.

In addition to practicing law intermittently from 1857 until his death in 1894, he fought as a colonel in the Union army during the Civil War, served a brief stint as a circuit court judge, and won election to Congress twice in the 1860s. He co-owned and managed the Southwest Pacific Railroad Company in the 1860s and 1870s and founded a wagon factory in Springfield in 1874.[3] Boyd's son-in-law, T. J. Delaney, served for two years as Greene County's prosecuting attorney from 1883 to 1885, after which he practiced law for several years as a partner in his father-in-law's firm.[4] O. H. Travers, another notable lawyer from Springfield, came to southwest Missouri from Baltimore, Maryland, shortly after the Civil War. Like Delaney, Travers served two years as the county's prosecuting attorney, from 1879 to 1881.[5]

This same legal team represented not only William Walker, but also his father, Dave Walker, and John and Wiley Mathews. For the most part, they did so *pro bono*; the small fees they could collect from their clients did not even cover the hotel bills, train fare, and other costs associated with handling cases that eventually went all the way to the Missouri Supreme Court.[6] They probably did so for the recognition that came with handling such high-profile cases, although in the case of Delaney, a genuine friendship seemed to have developed between the lawyer and his clients. Not only did Delaney exhaust himself in the defense of the Bald Knobbers during their trial and subsequent appeals, he also made a point of visiting Dave and William Walker before their eventual executions. His efforts were not lost on Dave Walker, who mentioned the lawyer fondly in one of his last letters to his brother Joseph in Douglas County. "It is too bad for him to work so hard to try to save our lives at his own expense," Walker lamented, and he asked his brother to "get some money for him" and send it to him as soon as possible.[7]

Prosecutor G. A. Watson also headed up a four-man team of attorneys representing the state. The team included J. A. Hammond, Almus Harrington, and John J. Brown.[8] Hammond was a notable attorney based in Ozark as well as a founder and future alderman of that town.[9] Harrington learned about the law while working as a stage coach driver carrying lawyers from place to place on the twenty-first judicial circuit, which encompassed much of southwest Missouri. He passed the bar exam in 1879 and set up his own practice in Springfield. Although

**Fig. 6.1:** Prosecuting Attorney Gustavus A. Watson. Source: William L. Vandeventer, *Justice in the Rough*, 1937. Used by permission of the State Historical Society of Missouri Research Center, Rolla, MO.

Harrington never excelled as a student—a fellow attorney once said he "had ignorance reduced to an exact science"—he made up for it with colorful oratory designed to sway juries to his side.[10] Perhaps the most surprising member of the team was J. J. Brown, the former Taney County prosecutor, who helped found the Bald Knobbers in that county and wrote the original Bald Knobber oath.[11] Brown's motives for joining the prosecution remain somewhat unclear. Not long before the trials began he moved his law practice from Forsyth to Ozark, so he may have wished to distance himself from the Bald Knobbers in the minds of his neighbors in that community.

The trial of William Walker began on March 1, 1888. Prosecutor Watson delivered the opening argument for the state, while D. M. Payne opened for the defense, and the trial proceeded with the hearing of evidence. From the beginning it became clear who had the weight of evidence on their side. The prosecution had assembled an impressive list of twenty-eight witnesses, including eleven vigilantes, who testified for the state.[12] The most significant of these, in terms of the substance of their testimony, were James McGuire, Charles Graves, Joseph Newton, Lewis Davis, and William Newton. McGuire testified that William Walker had initiated him into the Bald Knobbers the day before the killing, which confirmed Walker's leadership position in the group. McGuire also identified Walker as the man wounded in the attack on James Edens's cabin. Charles Graves's testimony agreed with McGuire's on this point. Graves said that when the shooting at the cabin stopped, he saw two or three men carrying another away, and afterward discovered it was William Walker. Later that night he overheard a conversation between Dave and William Walker in which the younger man admitted that he had tried to shoot a woman in the cabin, most likely Melvina Greene, but that she had managed to deflect the gun with her hand. Joseph Newton recounted his role in the capture of William Walker and testified about the conversations he had with Walker. Newton said the young assistant chief told him about the night's events, including his struggle with James Edens and his attempt to shoot Melvina Greene. Lewis Davis identified William Walker as one of the men who went into the Edens cabin that night. Although Davis did not see what happened in the cabin himself, he said that he later overheard William Walker say that someone had shot him in the house, but that he had "gotten revenge on the sons of bitches." William Newton testified that he had gone to the Edens cabin but did not go into it. He did, however, see William Walker and other men enter the house, and when Walker came out the door he observed that one leg of Walker's pants had caught fire. Newton asked him if he had been shot, and Walker replied that he had. Newton also said that he saw Walker stand at the doorway to the cabin and fire one last shot inside, which presumably was the shot aimed at the prostrate form of William Edens.[13]

The testimony of these witnesses alone might have been enough to convict William Walker, but the state added to them witnesses such as James Edens, Emma Edens, and Melvina Greene, who described the desperate fight that went on in the cabin that night. The prosecution also called on Coroner J. P. Ralston, who described the physical evidence at the crime scene, and Sheriff Johnson, who explained how he had recovered Bald Knobber masks, weapons, and other equipment from the vicinity of the killings. Other witnesses such as Charles Greene's father, George W. Greene, and his wife, Mary, saw the crime scene not long after the killings and testified as to what they saw.[14]

Against this veritable mountain of evidence William Walker's defense attorneys could muster only three witnesses. The young man, not yet eighteen years old, testified in his own behalf and stubbornly maintained his innocence. He denied firing any shots at the house, denied trying to shoot anyone, denied fighting with a woman, and adamantly denied trying to shoot a woman. He further disclaimed any of the statements attributed to him by three of the state's key witnesses, Joseph Newton, Lewis Davis, and Charles Graves. The defense also called Lafayette Abbott, a Bald Knobber, who briefly testified that he saw Walker's shotgun the day after the killings, and it was broken and could not fire. He also mentioned, however, that the gun had blood on it and a load in one of the barrels suggesting that it may have recently been fired.[15]

Lastly, the defense called to the stand Lois Newton, William Walker's sweetheart. The young woman had remained steadfastly loyal to her beau throughout the ordeal, even though it caused her to become estranged from her family. Now, in what must have been a heartbreaking scene, she did what little she could to save him. She tried to impeach the testimony of her brothers, Joseph and William, saying that they had both told her they would "swear anything" to convict Walker because he "was a damn mean man." Her testimony probably failed to impress the jury, however, because of her obvious affection for her sweetheart. Under cross-examination, Lois acknowledged that William Walker had been courting her for roughly two months before the Edens-Greene shooting, though she denied that the two were engaged. She also admitted that she had gone to live at Dave Walker's residence because her father had threatened to throw her out if she testified against her brothers. Lastly, she probably undercut her own testimony when she claimed that she did not go with her brother Joseph into Arkansas to see her sweetheart, even though William Walker's sister Ellen accompanied them. When asked why then she did go, the poor girl could only say that her brother just "wanted me to go with him is all."[16] Given the weight of the evidence against the defendant, it probably surprised no one when the jury found William Walker guilty of murder in the first degree on March 9, 1888. Since Missouri law prescribed a sentence of death by hanging for this crime, the judge set the date for Walker's execution at May 18, 1888.[17]

The trial of Wiley Mathews began the same day the court found William Walker guilty. Most of the evidence that the prosecution presented in this trial had also been used in William Walker's trial, so the outcome was never much in doubt. Once again, the testimony of fellow Bald Knobbers, particularly William Newton, Charles Graves, and Lewis Davis, proved critical to the outcome. Newton testified that he saw Wiley Mathews batter down the western door of James Edens's cabin with an ax, and then saw him enter the cabin along with eight or ten other men. He further testified that Mathews was in the cabin when the firing started. Afterward, as the men made their way away from the crime scene, Newton talked with Mathews, who mentioned that he had an empty gun, which suggested that he had fired it inside the house.[18]

Charles Graves also testified that after the raid on the Edens house Wiley Mathews had talked with him about what happened inside the cabin. Mathews reportedly told Graves that he killed William Edens that night "to save his uncle John that he shot him in the back with a shot gun." Likewise, Lewis Davis recalled that the Sunday after the killing he had gone to John Mathews's house and heard Wiley Mathews telling his uncle John that he had shot William Edens in the back with a shotgun because he saw Edens aiming a pistol at John. Mathews reportedly told his uncle, "If I hadn't pulled down on him with my shotgun he would have got you." Other witnesses disagreed as to whether or not William Edens had a pistol that night, but in any event Davis's testimony clearly indicated that Wiley Mathews inflicted the fatal wound on Edens.[19]

In terms of evidentiary substance, the testimony of Newton, Graves, and Davis was probably most influential in securing Wiley Mathews's conviction. But perhaps the most powerful testimony in the trial came from sixty-five-year-old George W. Greene, father of the deceased Charles Greene. As it happened, the elder Mr. Greene lived but a short distance from James Edens's house. Around 11 o'clock that night he awoke to the sound of gunfire, and recognizing the general direction from which it came he set off on foot to discover its source. As he made his way up the railroad tracks toward the Edens cabin he met a party of Bald Knobbers coming the other way. One of them, whom he recognized by voice as Wiley Mathews, challenged him and demanded to know where he was headed. Greene replied evasively, saying, "I aint going but a little ways," and the men let him pass. As he approached the house he was alarmed to hear "the screaming of the women," and ran inside. The jury could hardly have been unmoved as they heard the old man recount how, taking hold of his son's arm he slightly lifted the body thinking "there may be, possibly a little life in him," only to be disappointed.[20]

Against this compelling evidence, Wiley Mathews's attorneys mustered only a meager response. They did manage to cast some doubt on George Greene's testimony. They introduced Greene's conflicting testimony from the trial of Gilbert Applegate in which he said that he only recognized the man's voice as being "one of the Mathews," but did not know which one. The defense also called the court stenographer, Arthur D. Allen, to confirm this point. It hardly mattered, though, since Charles Graves had already confirmed in his testimony that it was Wiley Mathews who had confronted Green that night. Other than that, the defense barely dented the prosecution's case against Mathews, and the jury found him guilty of first-degree murder on March 15, 1888. The judge set the date for his execution at May 18, 1888, the same day as William Walker.[21]

The trial of John Mathews came next on the court's docket. The account of the elder Mathews's trial is more difficult to narrate because the supreme court case file does not include transcripts of the witnesses' testimony. It does, however, include a table of contents that indicates that witnesses in this case were essentially the same people who had testified in the other murder trials.[22] None of the testimony given in those trials proved that John Mathews shot anybody on the night in question. Testimony from several witnesses, however, proved that Mathews accompanied the other men who went inside James Edens's house.[23] So even if he did not kill anybody, he did nothing to stop the killing and effectively aided those who did it. Nor did

Mathews do much to help his own cause. According to one newspaper account, at one point during his trial Mathews broke down and made a rambling, semi-coherent confession in which he admitted to entering the house, but said he did not go with the intention of killing anybody. He claimed that someone shot at him, the bullet grazing the back of his head, and that he clubbed the man (possibly James Edens) with his rifle to save his own life. He also claimed he tried to remonstrate with the other men, saying, "Stop that shooting, in the name of God what do you mean?" Finally, he said that after the killing William Walker told him, "I am shot, but while they were getting me I got three of them."[24]

Without having the full transcript of Mathews's trial, it is difficult to know what to make of this account, and one can only wonder what the jury made of it. Mathews's version of events diverges sharply from testimony taken in the other cases. No one else seemed to remember him pleading with other Bald Knobbers not to kill anybody, and no one else testified that Mathews was shot in the back of the head. William Walker may well have confided in Mathews after the killings, but it is hard to imagine him saying that he "got three of them" when only two men were killed, and Walker would have known that Wiley Mathews killed one of them. Perhaps Mathews's strange "confession" was the first instance of a pattern of bizarre behavior that led many people, including his own lawyers, to question his sanity in the coming months.[25] Shortly before his execution, Mathews's lawyers wrote a letter to Sheriff Johnson asking him to assemble a jury "to inquire into the sanity of John Mathews whom they believe insane." This last attempt to spare their client's life failed, but it also showed that the people closest to him had begun to question his mental stability.[26] In any event, the jury did not believe Mathews's story, and found him guilty of first-degree murder on Saturday, March 24, 1888.[27]

The trial of Dave Walker began on April 9, 1888. In this case the prosecution's most damaging evidence probably came from Joe Inman and Charles Graves. These men testified that after the killings took place Dave Walker conferred with other Bald Knobbers on the road leading away from James Edens's house and suggested going back to kill the women and children, thereby eliminating any evidence of the crime.[28] Walker's attorneys considered Graves's testimony particularly damning, so much so that during the trial they tried assiduously to undercut his credibility as a witness. They put Dave Walker on the stand to deny Graves's charge that he had suggested killing women and children. Walker declared that he had never even thought of such a thing "until I heard that Charles Graves' swore it."[29] The defense also introduced as witnesses William Stilliens and Frank Williams, two prisoners in the Greene County jail in Springfield at roughly the same time that many Bald Knobbers including Graves were held there. Stilliens and Williams swore that Charles Graves had told them in jail that the only way out of his predicament was to swear to whatever the prosecution wanted him to swear.[30] Given the outcome of the trial, however, these denials apparently carried little weight with the jury.

The trial differed from the other three in one key respect: unlike William Walker, Wiley Mathews, and John Mathews, Dave Walker never actually entered the house. Indeed, even the state's witnesses agreed that Walker actually tried to keep his men from going to James Edens's house, and after the shooting commenced he called to them to stop firing.[31] The prosecution, however, argued that Walker's leadership position within the Bald Knobber organization made him responsible for the raid on James Edens's house, because he could have prevented it. The judge helped the prosecution's case by handing down instructions to the jury telling them that the defendant did not actually have to kill anybody to be guilty of murder. Rather, they should find him guilty if the evidence showed that he was part of a group engaged "in a common design or agreement to kill either Greene or Edens." In that situation, the defendant would be "responsible for the acts of the others the same as if he had killed Greene [or Edens] with his own hand."[32] The jury found Dave Walker guilty of first-degree murder on April 12, 1888, and the judge set his execution date for May 18, the same date as the other condemned Bald Knobbers.[33]

This string of convictions must have come as dispiriting news to the other men in jail with the four condemned men. The prisoners knew that the evidence against each of them was pretty much the same, so with each new conviction they felt their own chances for acquittal rapidly diminishing. After the verdict in John Mathews's trial, William Stanley, Amos Jones, C. O. Simmons, and James Mathews pled guilty to second-degree murder. Judge Hubbard took pity on

James Mathews because of his youth—he was only sixteen years old at the time—and gave him probation. He made the young man sign a bond, with his attorneys S. H. Boyd and D. M. Payne as co-signers, as security for his future good behavior. Then the judge told him to go home, help support his family, and stay out of trouble in the future. Hubbard sentenced Stanley to a prison term of twenty-one years, and gave Jones and Simmons sentences of twenty-five years and twelve years, respectively.[34]

Nine years later, Judge Hubbard joined several other well-known Springfield lawyers, including T. J. Delaney, who had represented the Bald Knobbers and two members of the prosecuting team, G. A. Watson and Almus Harrington, in petitioning Gov. Lawrence V. Stephens to commute the sentences of Amos Jones and William Stanley.[35] In a separate letter to Governor Stephens, Hubbard wrote that at the time he gave Simmons a lighter sentence than the others because he still had "some *slight* doubt" about his guilt. A few months later, however, Hubbard had a private conversation with William Walker in jail, which removed any doubt about Simmons's guilt. He now believed "Stanley and Jones do not deserve any greater punishment than Simmons gets," and should be released at the same time as Simmons.[36] Responding to these requests, Governor Stephens commuted the sentences of Stanley and Jones on July 16, 1897.[37]

Almost immediately after their convictions, the four Bald Knobbers sentenced to death appealed to the state supreme court for a reversal of the lower court's decision. In preparation for the appeal the circuit clerk compiled lengthy transcripts of their trials totaling roughly 315,000 words, and forwarded them to the supreme court in early May. On Monday, May 14, Missouri's high court agreed to hear the Bald Knobber cases, which granted the condemned men a temporary reprieve from their appointment with the hangman that Friday.[38]

The supreme court considered the first three cases—those pertaining to William Walker, Wiley Mathews, and John Mathews—in November and December of 1888. The issues in these cases were relatively straightforward, and dwelt mainly on technical matters. For example, in William Walker's case, Walker's attorneys argued that the court erred in allowing certain witnesses, including Charles Graves, to testify even though they clearly had self-interested motives for doing so. They objected to some of the court's instructions given to the jury, which they said were worded in such a way as to sway the jurors in favor of conviction. They further objected that William Walker was forced to testify against himself in that he was compelled to undergo a medical examination to verify that he had sustained wounds consistent with other witnesses' testimony. Finally, they argued that Walker, if he was guilty of anything, had conspired only to whip William Edens and not to kill him, and therefore should have been charged with a lesser crime. On November 12, the supreme court rejected these arguments and upheld the decision of the lower court, setting a new date for Walker's execution on December 28.[39] The next two cases ended up much the same way. On November 26, the high court upheld the conviction and sentence of John Mathews, and on December 20 the court upheld the conviction of Wiley Mathews as well. The supreme court set a new execution date for these men of February 15, 1889. Gov. Albert P. Morehouse, who had assumed the governorship when John S. Marmaduke unexpectedly died in office, postponed their executions until after the court could rule on Dave Walker's case.[40]

The supreme court did not hear Dave Walker's case until March 1889. In the meantime the four condemned Bald Knobbers remained confined in the county jail in Ozark. The local government desperately wanted to ensure the security of their prisoners. They had built a new jail the previous summer in part because they knew they would need a safe place to keep their vigilante prisoners, lest their comrades on the outside attempt to mount some kind of rescue operation.[41] They also deputized many local residents of Ozark and the surrounding area to assist law enforcement officials in providing security. Years later one such resident, Andrew Jackson Whitehead, recalled that local authorities deputized around 100 men to serve as guards at the jail, because they believed that "some organized effort might be made by the Bald Knobbers to rescue the four" condemned men.[42]

The county put the same effort into making the jail itself as impervious to escape as possible. According to Judge William L. Vandeventer, who saw the structure while it was still standing, the new jailhouse served as both a jail and the sheriff's residence. It consisted of a two-story brick structure with four cells inside a large cage located

**Fig. 6.2:** The jail cells in
Ozark from which John
Mathews and Wiley
Mathews escaped. Source:
William L. Vandeventer,
*Justice in the Rough*, 1937.
Used by permission of the
State Historical Society of
Missouri Research Center,
Rolla, MO.

on the first floor. The doors to the cells could be locked or unlocked
using a lever located "inside a steel box, and this box was always kept
locked." Inside the box another padlock secured the lever itself. The
door to the cage around the cells was locked on the outside, while the
"outside door of the jail proper was also locked and bars were across all
the windows." Thus, four locks, thick brick walls, and barred windows
all separated the prisoners from freedom.[43]

In December 1888, around the time the supreme court rejected
the appeals submitted by the first three Bald Knobbers, John and
Wiley Mathews began planning their escape. They stole the keys to
the padlocks on the doors to the cells and the cage from one of the
sheriff's deputies who guarded the jail, and made impressions of
them on a bar of soap. Sheriff Johnson had allowed John Mathews,

a skilled woodcarver, to keep a pocketknife and some wood in order to make canes to sell to support his family. Mathews used his skill to carve keys to the padlocks on the cells and the cage. However, they still needed a way to get into the big steel box that held the levers. To do this, Mathews asked one of the guards for a bar of lead, ostensibly to make heads for his canes. Instead, he melted the lead together with some zinc from an old washboard they had in their possession, using the jail's woodstove for heat. He then poured the alloy into a mold carved in a pine board. This gave them a key they could use to unlock the box. Now the prisoners could get outside of their cells and the cage, but the door to the jail itself locked from the outside. Over several nights the prisoners surreptitiously overcame this obstacle by making a hole in the wall on the southern side of the jail where the jailer had stacked a pile of firewood. Each night the prisoners removed bricks from the inside of the wall by filing away the mortar between the bricks and pulling them out. When they stopped working they would put the bricks back in the hole without the mortar. They left the outside layer of bricks intact, knowing they could break through it when they needed. From the outside, the wall of the jail looked secure. On the inside, however, the pile of firewood concealed their progress on the hole.[44]

On the evening of December 28, 1888, John and Wiley Mathews made their escape from jail. The men made some noise breaking through the remaining bricks in the wall and scampering away from the jail, which awoke Sheriff Johnson sleeping in his quarters. When the sheriff went to check on the prisoners, he found that John and Wiley Mathews and five other prisoners had gone, and he saw Dave and William Walker dressed and standing outside of the cage. He also found the guard on duty that evening, J. C. Rucker, bound and gagged on the floor, having apparently been overpowered by the escapees. The Walkers claimed they had not tried to escape and had no intention of leaving, for, as Dave Walker laconically remarked, he had "not come into the jail by that hole, and he was not going out that way."[45] The circumstances notwithstanding, the Walkers may well have told the truth when they said that they did not wish to escape. The Missouri Supreme Court had not yet ruled on Dave Walker's appeal, so he had reason to hope that the law might yet vindicate him. Likewise, William

Walker probably hoped that an appeal to the governor for clemency would succeed given his youth.

In the wake of the escape, sensationalized stories appeared in newspapers across the country inaccurately attributing the escape to a Bald Knobber raiding party numbering as many as twenty-five men. The raiders supposedly broke through the brick walls and then used crowbars to pry open the doors to the cells, all the while failing to raise the alarm in Ozark and bring the sheriff and his many deputies running to intervene.[46] In Ozark, the public tended to suspect that the escaped prisoners had help from someone on the inside. Suspicion fell heavily on one of the guards, a sheriff's deputy named J. C. Rucker, who some believed had helped the escaped prisoners. At the next term of the circuit court, a grand jury actually indicted Rucker for assisting the escaped fugitives, and his case went to trial. The jury did not find the evidence persuasive enough to convict Rucker, however, and declared him not guilty.[47]

John Mathews did not fare well as a fugitive. Because of his long confinement, the older man had grown unused to outdoor conditions, and in the dead of winter he did not make it very far. One night he almost froze to death hiding in a corn field. Finally, he sought shelter at a nearby house.[48] The owner of the house, a farmer named James Collins, reportedly found the convict in a pitiful state, "almost exhausted by hunger and cold, having had but one meal since he left the jail." Collins turned Mathews over to the authorities, who took him back to jail.[49]

Unlike his uncle, the younger and more physically robust Wiley Mathews managed to evade capture and eventually made his way into the Oklahoma territory. Walker family tradition states that many years later, around 1930, Wiley Mathews returned to Christian County to visit his sister, who still lived in the area. After he arrived he checked into a hotel in Chadwick under an assumed name and claimed to be a "mineral man" from Oklahoma who had come to the Ozarks to conduct surveys. Shortly thereafter he went to visit his sister, and slept in the woods near her house in order to avoid arousing suspicion concerning his identity. During his stay he briefly met a small boy named Lloyd Walker, the grandson of Joseph Walker, Dave Walker's brother. When Mathews left the area, the boy's father asked him if he knew who the stranger was. When the boy replied that he did not, his father told him it was Wiley Mathews, "the Bald Knobber that escaped from jail in Christian County."[50]

The escape from the county jail in Ozark was one of many lurid and sensational aspects of the Bald Knobber story that had captured the attention of both state and national newspapers ever since the Edens-Greene killings two years before. It is likely impossible to express in quantitative terms how big a story the Bald Knobbers became in the late 1880s. One may safely say, however, that for a couple years after March 1887, most of the newspaper reading public in America had some knowledge of them. Major city newspapers greatly increased their coverage of the Bald Knobbers after the Edens-Greene murders. For example, prior to the killings the New York Times ran just four articles about the Bald Knobbers,[51] but over roughly the next two years the nation's newspaper of record published at least twenty-five articles on the topic.[52] Likewise, the Chicago Daily Inter-Ocean ran no articles on the Bald Knobbers prior to the Edens-Greene affair, but subsequently published no fewer than thirty-eight articles on them.[53] Many major newspapers sent reporters to southwest Missouri, especially when the circuit court convened in Ozark, to report on the Bald Knobber trials and collect information about the vigilante order disclosed in them. For example, in December 1888, local newspapers noted that a special correspondent for the New York Sun, William McMurtrie Speer, had come to visit Taney and Christian Counties to gather information for a series of articles for that newspaper.[54]

Correspondents like Speer produced a steady stream of Bald Knobber–related articles to satisfy the public's appetite for information about the colorful vigilantes. Much of the newspaper coverage in this period was responsible and accurate, but a substantial number of the articles published contained errors, distortions, and sometimes outright fabrications. The worst errors tended toward embellishment of the violent and sensational aspects of the vigilante saga. For example, in December 1886, a Philadelphia newspaper reported that a party of Bald Knobbers had whipped a black man in Miller County, which seems unlikely since the Bald Knobbers never organized in Miller County.[55] Likewise in June 1887, a Chicago newspaper reported as fact a story about the Bald Knobbers threatening to forcibly disband the Missouri General Assembly, a threat that somehow escaped the attention of the newspapers in Jefferson City.[56]

Perhaps the best example, however, comes from a story that began circulating in November 1888, beginning in Kansas City and then making its way through newspapers across the country. The story had it that on November 13 a band of night riders had lynched five witnesses in Christian County who had testified against "the Bald Knobber king Dave Walker" at his murder trial.[57] Variations of this tall tale appeared in newspapers in many parts of the country including South Dakota, Georgia, and Nebraska.[58] Even the well-respected *New York Times* ran the story, adding that "the action of the Supreme Court in sentencing Walker to death" had caused the lynchings.[59]

The story was completely false. The circuit court records for Christian County contain no reference to a quintuple lynching at that time or any other time, nor do the local newspapers in the area corroborate it. The *Springfield Daily Republican* did reprint a version of the story that had appeared in a newspaper published in Denver, Colorado. The *Republican* cited it as an example of the kind of "slanderous story" and "purely malicious invention" that often besmirched the reputation of southwest Missouri. The Springfield paper attributed the original source of the story to a Kansas City newspaper it sarcastically dubbed the "Kansas City Liar."[60]

Such sensational stories enjoyed widespread popularity among America's newspaper-reading public. The stories appealed to readers in part because they played upon generations of ingrained stereotypes about southern mountain people, particularly those who lived in the Appalachian or Ozark hill country.[61] The *Chicago Daily Inter-Ocean*, for example, expressed the conventional wisdom when it observed that groups like the Bald Knobbers "flourish where the newspaper and the railway and the telegraph have not shed their civilizing light."[62]

Nor did the press confine these stereotypes to coverage of the Bald Knobbers. Big city journalists, who cover episodes of social unrest in these regions, have often yielded to the temptation to fit their facts into preexisting narratives about savage "mountaineers" or "hillbillies" always ready to resort to violence at the slightest provocation. Historians who have written about such diverse events as the Hatfield-McCoy feud in the Tug Valley region of Kentucky and West Virginia, or the famous Arkansas "ghost trial" of 1929–30, have noted this tendency of reporters to shade the truth when dealing with southern hill folk as their subjects.[63] Likewise, during the infamous Scopes "Monkey Trial" in Dayton, Tennessee, newspaper coverage of the event tended to focus on not only the trial itself but also the character of Dayton's residents, usually to their detriment. Some of the most savage caricatures came from editorialist H. L. Mencken, whose portrayal of local mountain people as "yokels" and "morons" nearly provoked mob violence against him during the trial.[64]

Public interest in the Ozarks vigilantes remained high as the Missouri Supreme Court got ready to decide the last Bald Knobber murder case on its docket. On March 23, 1889, the court announced its decision on Dave Walker's appeal. Prior to this decision, the vigilante chief still had some reason to hope for a reversal of the lower court's judgment. After all, the testimony taken in his trial tended to show that unlike the other three condemned men he had not actually gone into James Edens's house where the killings occurred. Moreover, even some of the state's witnesses agreed that he had tried to call back the men headed toward the house before the killings happened and had ordered them to stop shooting once he heard shots fired.[65] The justices, however, did not consider these facts sufficient grounds for acquittal. The court ruled that Dave Walker's leadership role within the Bald Knobber organization made him responsible for the actions of his subordinates. Writing for the majority, Justice Theodore Brace declared that since Walker "was the leader and master spirit" of the vigilantes who did the killing, he "could be guilty of no less a crime than murder in the first degree and could have no ground or justification to stand upon."[66]

The supreme court set the date for Dave Walker's execution at May 10, and on April 17 Missouri's newly elected governor David R. Francis reset the execution dates for John Mathews and William Walker to coincide with that day as well.[67] The court's decision to uphold the convictions of the men sentenced to death for the Edens-Greene killings meant that the three vigilantes still in jail in Ozark had only one hope left to escape execution. That hope rested in Governor Francis, to whom the condemned men had to appeal for clemency if they wished to avoid the hangman's noose.

Even before the supreme court handed down its final decision in the Bald Knobber cases, the lawyers for the three men coordinated an ambitious public relations campaign aimed at persuading the governor to commute their sentences. Attorney T. J. Delaney took the lead in this campaign, penning a personal plea to Governor Francis in which he laid out several grounds on which clemency was justified.[68] Likewise, in November 1888, Delaney told the *Springfield Daily Republican* that a grassroots effort to spare his clients' lives had begun. This included a petition drive on behalf of William Walker, who many people believed merited clemency on account of his youth at the time the crime was committed. Many prominent persons in the local community, including even jurors in the Walker case, had signed these petitions.[69] The following February Governor Francis received a delegation of distinguished men from southwest Missouri, which included Delaney, S. H. Boyd, former secretary of state Martin K. McGrath, and other politicians and officeholders. The visitors pleaded with the governor to save the lives of the three condemned men and presented statements from officials in all of the counties affected by the Bald Knobber organization, who swore that it "had disbanded forever."[70] In April, as the deadline for the executions approached, Francis received several visits from delegations of "representative men from Christian, Douglas, Stone, Taney, and Greene counties," who called on him to express their support for clemency.[71] One such delegation included several prominent Springfield attorneys such as Delaney, O. H. Travers, and John Walker. Representative Alonzo Prather, the former Bald Knobber from Taney County now serving in the state legislature, also presented a petition "signed by 102 members of the [General] Assembly," which requested clemency for the Bald Knobber prisoners.[72]

Why the sudden outpouring of support for the convicted murderers? Strange as it might seem, given the initial public backlash against the vigilantes following the Edens-Greene killings, by the spring of 1889 southwest Missourians had softened their attitude toward the three condemned prisoners and support for clemency had grown. For example, one newspaper report estimated, likely with some exaggeration, that nine-tenths of the Christian County population would support the governor commuting the death sentences of the Bald Knobbers to life in prison.[73] The reasons for this shift in attitude were difficult to explain to people from outside the region. As one newspaper commented, most locals believed that although the vigilantes "were criminals in act, they were not so in motive or intent; that in spirit and purpose they do not possess the characteristics of the murderer." These ordinary citizens would have no sympathy at all for a "hardened criminal," but for the vigilantes they had made "earnest and numerous appeals for clemency."[74] Other people believed that the Bald Knobbers deserved clemency because they had maintained generally good reputations prior to becoming involved in vigilantism. For example, Greene County prosecutor James J. Gideon told an interviewer that he had served with Dave Walker during the Civil War, and he considered Walker "as good a citizen as we have had since the war, never getting into trouble until this thing came up."[75]

In the face of this outpouring of public sentiment, Governor Francis remained mostly silent and weighed his options carefully. On the one hand, he could appease public opinion in his own state if he commuted the death sentences of the vigilantes. On the other hand, if he did so, he would necessarily have to overturn the judgments of both a circuit court and the state supreme court. Moreover, as a businessman and former president of the St. Louis Merchant Exchange, Francis worried that a commutation would tend to reinforce the belief in the rest of the country that Missouri was a lawless and criminal state. This perception could discourage people from immigrating to Missouri or investing their money there. "The people of the East," he once remarked, "have an idea that lawlessness prevails here, and profess to believe that their lives and property would be unsafe within our borders."[76]

On Wednesday, May 8, Governor Francis made the decision not to intervene on behalf of the prisoners. He sent a letter explaining his decision to T. J. Delaney, the Bald Knobbers' ever-faithful attorney who had continued lobbying for a commutation until the last possible moment. The letter arrived just past midnight. In it the governor said that he had made his decision because the evidence in the cases indicated that the "crime was the result of deliberation," because Dave Walker could have stopped the killings if he wanted to, and because William Walker's leadership role among the vigilantes made him as responsible for the murders as anyone. Francis concluded, saying that "the crime must be expiated by the lives of the three men and that they must suffer on account thereof, I discover many reasons why the sentence of the law should be carried out."[77] The following morning the governor also sent a brief telegraph to Ozark announcing his decision to the authorities there. The message read, "I have declined to intervene," but in a cruel twist of fate the telegraph operator mistyped it as "I have *decided* to intervene." This erroneous report "raised the hopes of the three men to a high pitch." A few hours later, however, they received the disappointing news that the first message was a mistake, and that the three of them still faced execution.[78]

For the rest of the day the town of Ozark made preparations for the impending executions. Large crowds began arriving that morning from the surrounding countryside to witness the event, and by evening the town had completely filled up. Journalists from several major newspapers came to Ozark to watch the execution. Ozark had only one telegraph wire, however, so the reporters made arrangements with horsemen to take their manuscripts and "drive at full speed" to Springfield where they would wire their stories back to their editors.[79] A stockade had already been constructed around a space on the eastern side of the jail, and inside that area the sheriff and his deputies built a scaffold on which the executions would take place.[80] Sheriff Johnson had originally intended to hire a professional executioner named Daniel Binkley of Kansas City to do the job, but the prisoners objected to this plan. Dave Walker told the sheriff that he did not want to die at the hands of a stranger, and asked Johnson to perform the execution himself as a last favor to a friend. Johnson agreed, even though he had no experience with executions, a decision he later came to regret.[81]

The evening before the execution the three condemned men participated in a small religious service held at their request inside the jail. A local minister, T. B. Horn, officiated. William Walker had requested an opportunity for baptism, so the sheriff and his men procured a bathtub, and Reverend Horn performed the rite for the young man who emerged from the water "shouting, singing, and praying so loudly that he was heard for quite a distance."[82] Dave and William Walker seemed relatively composed that evening. They managed to fall asleep shortly before midnight and did not wake until dawn. By contrast, John Mathews spent most of the night awake, praying, singing hymns, and talking to the guard on duty in the jail, and "every now and then protesting that he was innocent" and did not deserve to be hanged. He finally fell asleep just before dawn. The other men in the jail decided not to wake him until necessary.[83]

At around six o'clock in the morning T. J. Delaney paid a last visit to his clients. Mathews had not yet wakened, but the Walkers received him warmly, and thanked him for all his work on their behalf. Half an hour later the men had their last meal, which they "ate heartily and with evident relish." John Mathews even requested a second pint of coffee to wash his food down. About an hour after they finished their meal, the men held devotional exercises with three local ministers who had come to witness the execution. The preachers prayed with the prisoners and joined them in singing several of their favorite religious songs.[84] Herbert Rogers, who had been a boy living in Ozark at that time, recalled hearing the words to the old hymns "Nearer My God to Thee," "Home Sweet Home," and "In the Sweet Bye and Bye" wafting through the windows of the jail.[85]

At about half past nine o'clock the sheriff and two of his deputies marched the three prisoners to the place where the executions would occur. The stockade that enclosed the yard and the gallows blocked the view of the crowd assembled outside. Only a small group of people, including the jurors in the case, the three ministers, three physicians, and a few journalists had been invited to witness the event. Before tying the nooses, the sheriff gave the prisoners a chance to say a few last words. The two Walkers both made terse statements, in which they repeated that they were innocent, but also said that they were ready to die. John Mathews made a long and rambling statement, loudly proclaiming his innocence, and bemoaning the plight of his poor wife and children who would soon lose their father. When the sheriff slipped the nooses over their heads Mathews "gave way to talking again." He asked the journalists present not to write ill of them, or to say "that we will take our dinners in hell today," and begged the witnesses to help support his wife and children after he died.[86]

**Fig. 6.3:** William Walker. Source: William L. Vandeventer, *Justice in the Rough*, 1937. Used by permission of the State Historical Society of Missouri Research Center, Rolla, MO.

Just before the sheriff pulled the black hoods over their heads, Dave and William Walker leaned close and kissed each other. As the hood went over John Mathews's head he yelled out a farewell to all the witnesses. Then, at six minutes before ten o'clock the sheriff pulled the lever and the three men fell through the trap door in the scaffold. From that point on, things went terribly wrong. Only John Mathews's execution went according to plan; his neck broke on the first drop and he died quickly. The Walkers, however, did not have it so easy. Sheriff Johnson had either misjudged the length of Dave Walker's rope, or else had not taken into account how far it would stretch, for the elder Walker was left dangling with his feet touching the ground, desperately trying to push himself up. Meanwhile, William Walker's

**Fig. 6.4:** John Mathews. Source: William L. Vandeventer, *Justice in the Rough*, 1937. Used by permission of the State Historical Society of Missouri Research Center, Rolla, MO.

rope had come undone, and he fell to his knees moaning in agony and spitting out blood and phlegm into his hood. The sheriff and his deputies left William there for the moment as they struggled to lift up his father, while shortening and readjusting the rope. After re-hanging Dave Walker the sheriff and his men attempted to do the same to his son. In the process William's noose slipped entirely off his head, and he fell to the ground on his face groaning in pain, and begging God to end his suffering. Finally, the sheriff and his men succeeded in hoisting William through the trap door and seated him on the scaffold. He remained there until the physicians present pronounced both his father and John Mathews dead. At sixteen minutes past ten o'clock the sheriff and his men finally lifted William up, retied the rope, and hung him a second time. Once again William's neck failed to break when he dropped through the trap door, and over the next sixteen minutes he slowly strangled to death. Finally, the sheriff and his deputies cut him down and laid him next to his father. They placed the bodies in walnut coffins each encased in a pine box.[87]

This "scene of ghastliness" reportedly had a sobering effect on everyone who witnessed it.[88] Some people blamed the tragedy on Sheriff Johnson, who had performed the execution without having sufficient knowledge or training to do so. In reality, however, the sheriff had only honored the wishes of the men in his charge, and could not have predicted the unfortunate outcome.[89] Most people, even some of the Bald Knobbers' "most bitter enemies," admitted that they wished the two Walkers "had died a less painful death."[90]

The deaths of the Walkers and John Mathews also left their families with the pressing problem of how to bury them. Before his death John Mathews expressed a desire to have his remains buried on his own property so as to be near his wife and children. So Mathews's family took his body and quietly buried it in a small plot on the family's farm.[91] Before the execution, the Walker family had relied on the members of the Sparta post 257 of the Grand Army of the Republic (GAR), a veteran's group to which Dave Walker belonged, to provide burials for him and his son. At the last minute, however, the other members changed their minds, and informed the family that they would not provide a funeral because they did not wish to be publicly associated with the Bald Knobbers. Finally, two GAR members volunteered to take the bodies in a wagon to a small cemetery behind the Baptist Church in Sparta. The Walker family buried the bodies without ceremony and with no minister present. Lois Newton, who had lived with the Walkers after becoming estranged from her family, accompanied them to the gravesite. The mourners placed their loved ones in a single large grave dug wide enough to accommodate both coffins. Since the family had no money for headstones, they placed two wooden boards at the top of the grave, on which they scrawled the names of the deceased.[92] Fortunately, the grave did not remain unmarked forever. A few years later, members of the GAR placed a small military headstone to mark Dave Walker's gravesite, which remains there to this day. For more than a century, however, the grave

**Fig. 6.5:** Author's photograph of the Walker gravesite. Taken by the author at Sparta, MO.

had no marker bearing William Walker's name. Finally, in the 1990s a descendant of Dave Walker placed a second, larger headstone at the gravesite with the names of both father and son inscribed on it.[93]

The executions of Dave Walker, William Walker, and John Mathews represented the culmination of a long chain of events that began with the murders of William Edens and Charles Greene. Those killings provoked a public outcry from the people of southwest Missouri who demanded prompt and forceful action from their courts and law enforcement officials to put down the dangerous vigilante movement in their midst. The legal crackdown on the Bald Knobbers that ensued resulted in a protracted legal battle that went all the way to the Missouri Supreme Court, and beyond to the office of Gov. David R. Francis, whose final decision sealed the fate of the men who died on the scaffold in Ozark on May 10, 1889. More important, the hangings in Ozark marked the effective end of the Bald Knobber movement in nearly all of southwest Missouri. With the exception of Taney County, where the summer of 1889 would bring one final spasm of violence, the masked night riders no longer haunted the Ozarks hills.

## CHAPTER 7

# The Death of Nat Kinney and a Duel on the Fourth of July

As discussed in chapter 2, the primary rationale behind the creation of a vigilance committee in Taney County was the perception of many residents that their community faced an epidemic of crime and violence, and that the local government lacked either the ability or the will to confront it. The elections of 1884 and 1886 handed control of local government to a political faction consisting of several leading Bald Knobbers and their allies, thereby giving the vigilantes the opportunity to govern as they wished. Once they held the reins of power, therefore, the Bald Knobber officials knew that they needed to demonstrate their capacity to enforce the law more effectively and aggressively than had their Democratic and Anti-Bald Knobber predecessors. Their first major challenge to prove that they could do so came on May 9, 1886, when in front of several witnesses Wash Middleton murdered Sam Snapp outside of John Kintrea's general store in Kirbyville.[1]

Since Middleton belonged to the Bald Knobbers, and because Snapp had witnessed Nat Kinney's shooting of Andrew Coggburn the year before, many Anti-Bald Knobbers concluded that the vigilantes had arranged for Snapp's death in order to protect their leader from prosecution. The Bald Knobber critics assumed that the vigilantes would always protect one of their own, even if that meant shielding a murderer from the law's consequences. Therefore, they appealed to the state government for help lest the county descend into anarchy and bloodshed.[2] Contrary to these dire predictions, the Bald Knobbers did not interfere on behalf of Middleton, and Prosecutor Harrison E. Havens built a successful case against him. On October 10, 1887, a jury in Forsyth found Middleton guilty of murder and sentenced him to forty years in the state penitentiary, a sentence which Judge Walter D. Hubbard later reduced to fifteen years.[3] Alas, Middleton escaped from the county jail before spending any time in the state penitentiary.[4]

Around the same time that the circuit court handed down its decision in the Wash Middleton case, it also had another sensational murder case on its docket. On June 6, 1887, a Christian County man named Robert Meadows was on his way to visit his brother John Meadows, who lived on Bull Creek in Taney County. His wife accompanied him. Just south of the county line, someone shot at him from cover with a rifle. The bullet struck Meadows through the heart, killing him instantly. His wife caught a glimpse of two men running from the scene, and later identified one of them as L. T. Matthews, also a resident of Christian County.[5] The initials L. T. referred to Lemuel T. Matthews, an Arkansas man who came to Missouri with his father, Enoch A. Matthews, and who does not appear to have had family connection to the Bald Knobbers John and Wiley Mathews.[6]

Some early reports of the murder speculated that the bushwhacking was linked in some way to the Bald Knobber troubles.[7] Other reports contradicted that idea, however, suggesting that a personal grievance rather than vigilantism explained the killing. As the *Taney County News* pointed out, a "feud has existed between the [Matthews and Meadows] families" stemming from circumstances surrounding the tragic death of Matthews's infant son.[8] The child died as the result of a botched ambush perpetrated by the "Payton boys," two malcontent teenage brothers who harbored a grudge against Matthews. In 1885, Matthews took his family north from Taney County to a new home near Chadwick. During the move, the Payton brothers tried to shoot him from ambush but killed his son instead.[9] Robert Meadows had apparently lent "considerable money" to the Payton brothers to help pay for their defense, which earned him the enmity of the Matthews clan.[10]

The preliminary hearing in the L. T. Matthews murder case took place in Forsyth about a week after the murder. Prosecutor Havens handled the case for the state, and Nat Kinney's stepson James A. DeLong assisted him.[11] The circuit court took up the case at its next regularly scheduled term in October. The jury retired to deliberate over the case on Monday, October 17, and returned a verdict of not guilty later that day "on the ground that the state's evidence failed to prove his identity as the murderer beyond a 'reasonable doubt.'"[12]

The prosecutions of Wash Middleton and Lemuel Matthews demonstrated the willingness of the county's pro-Bald Knobber government to bring alleged murderers before the bar of justice. They needed to do so in order to prove to the public that they would take a tougher stand on crime than had their predecessors. On some occasions, however, this aggressive approach to law enforcement could lead to unanticipated bloodshed. On Friday, August 12, 1886, at a dance held at a local residence in Forsyth, some of the rowdier participants became intoxicated and went into the public square where they fired their pistols into the air. Warrants were sworn out against several of the participants for disturbing the peace. Deputy Sheriff George L. Taylor, a Bald Knobber, and a local constable named Jerry Franklin took the warrants and went in search of the offenders. After arresting a number of suspects, they went to the home of Reuben Pruitt, one of the participants in the drunken revelries. Pruitt was an Anti-Bald Knobber, and several members of his family had already been driven from the county. The exact details of what happened next are somewhat murky, but it appears that Pruitt resisted arrest, and Taylor shot him in the chest. For a while many people believed that Pruitt would likely die of his wounds, but he eventually recovered and left the area never to return.[13]

Later that same month an outlaw named James Brown, who had escaped from the Greene County jail in Springfield a few months before, passed through Taney County. After Brown robbed a number of homes and farms in the area, local authorities formed a posse to pursue him. The posse caught up with Brown on the morning of August 20, and a shootout ensued in which the outlaw shot one of his pursuers, a man named James Manes, in the bowels, the shot piercing his bladder. Manes later died of his wound, but he managed to return fire and inflict several wounds on his killer. Nevertheless, Brown still managed to elude the posse. The following day they caught up with him again, and when he failed to surrender, one of the posse, James Bunch, killed the outlaw with a shot to the back.[14]

As the preceding examples attest, the new pro-Bald Knobber regime mostly kept its promise of a more vigorous approach to law enforcement, although the same incidents also show that violent crime and outlawry had not vanished from Taney County under Bald Knobber rule. Another key element of the Bald Knobber agenda was the promotion of economic development and population growth in their region. To that end, many former leaders of the Bald Knobbers participated in the Taney County Immigration Society, an organiza-tion created to promote "immigration into our county by bringing prominently before the public our wealth of resources and desirability of location."[15] A membership role of the Immigration Society, pub-lished in a local newspaper, showed that the organization had at least eight known Bald Knobbers on its roster, including Alonzo S. Prather, James A. DeLong, Charles H. Groom, Nat Kinney, John L. Cook, Joseph C. ("Cal") Parrish, John T. Dickenson, and D. F. McConkey.[16]

In addition to their promotional work on behalf of immigration to their county, the Bald Knobber officials also tried to attract settlers by cutting taxes. In 1887, the county court passed legislation that slashed property taxes by 30 percent from $2.35 per $100 of assessed property value, to $1.60 per $100 of property. The rationale for this move was to increase the economic incentive for new settlers to move to the county. "This move alone," proclaimed the *Taney County News*, a generally pro-Bald Knobber and pro-Republican newspaper, "will cause the population of this county to increase more rapidly than was ever known before."[17]

The tax cuts, however, accompanied a much stronger approach to enforcing tax collection. Before they seized control of the local government, the Bald Knobber faction had sharply criticized the old Democratic courthouse ring for their irresponsible handling of county finances. As Nat Kinney observed, Taney County had amassed "$42,000 in debt, and had not even a plank to show for it."[18] In order to reduce the county's indebtedness, not to mention pay for their tax cuts, the Bald Knobber officials needed to tackle aggressively the problem of tax evasion. In March 1887, the *Taney County News* published a brief announcement stating that Sheriff James K. Polk McHaffie, who also served as the county tax collector, "is now making preparations to institute suit against all delinquent tax payers. All those in arrears should take warning."[19]

True to their word, over the next couple of years county officials initiated scores of lawsuits against delinquent taxpayers. Those whom the court found to be in arrears either had to pay the balance of taxes owed or have their property seized and auctioned to cover the debt and court costs. The suits involved sums both large and small and targeted all sorts of people, including some former Bald Knobbers.[20] It comes as no surprise, however, that the names of individuals formerly associated with the Anti-Bald Knobber faction showed up more often as defendants in these cases. For example, in 1888, the government brought a suit against William H. Miles, the former leader of the Anti-Bald Knobber militia company, and three other individuals including Anti-Bald Knobber James S. B. Berry, for back taxes owed on several parcels of property near Forsyth. The case concluded with the auctioning of the property to pay for the debt in question.[21]

Likewise, in the late 1880s, the county brought suit against several other Anti-Bald Knobbers who had in some way antagonized the vigilantes and their friends in government. Sampson Barker and William Lunceford, both of whom had written to Governor Marmaduke in support of a militia company, had suits brought against them for sums ranging from two dollars to fifty-one dollars.[22] County officials also sued William Buck and William E. Moore, who had met with Adj. Gen. J. C. Jamison to complain about affairs in the county,[23] and they filed three suits against John S. Coggburn, Andrew Coggburn's uncle, for amounts up to thirty-three dollars.[24] They brought multiple lawsuits against Thomas A. Layton, the former Anti-Bald Knobber county clerk, and his father Thomas F. Layton.[25] Other Anti-Bald Knobbers who faced legal action for taxes owed to the county included K. L. Burdette and Jordan M. Haworth.[26]

Exactly what these defendants thought about the government's actions remains unknown, but they most likely resented the expropriation of their property. It also seems probable, given the history of antagonism between the two factions in the county, that they interpreted the government's efforts to retrieve the money owed to it as a form of persecution by their old political enemies.

Nor did the opponents of the Bald Knobbers have only tax lawsuits to worry about. In the years following the formal disbandment of the vigilante organization in 1886, the former vigilantes used their control of the local legal system to bring their erstwhile adversaries into court on a wide variety of charges. In April 1886, the county's grand jury indicted Thomas A. Layton, the Anti-Bald Knobber county clerk, for carrying a concealed weapon into the courthouse. While serving as clerk, Layton brought a revolver into the courthouse, allegedly for his own protection. Since he did not need to have a firearm to perform any of the lawful duties of his office, this act rendered him in violation of the law against carrying concealed weapons, a misdemeanor generally punished with a fine.[27]

Later that same year the grand jury indicted Sampson Barker, who had served as deputy clerk under Layton, for issuing a false witness certificate to one Price Wilson, a witness in the murder trial of William Taylor who had never actually testified. Barker allegedly sold the certificate to a man named D. R. Riggs, who used the document to claim $17.70 in travel and attendance fees from the circuit court.[28] Barker, who seemed to attract indictments like a magnet, also faced charges in 1887 and 1889 for embezzlement. In the first case he stole roughly $20 from Aurora Gallagher, a minor under the age of sixteen, who had entrusted him to act as her agent in paying certain taxes on property belonging to her. Instead of paying the taxes, Barker pocketed the money for himself. In the second case, he embezzled $133 from the estate of Thomas Snodgrass, another minor, of which Barker acted as the curator.[29] Two of Barker's sons, Rufus C. Barker and Edward E. Barker, also frequently ran afoul of the law. In 1888, a grand jury indicted Rufus of selling whiskey without a license. In 1893, Edward Barker faced charges for killing a cow belonging to Barnett P. Parrish, the father of the Bald Knobber Joseph Calvin ("Cal") Parrish.[30]

For certain former Anti-Bald Knobbers, their trouble with local law enforcement continued well into the 1890s. In that decade, a number of Anti-Bald Knobbers faced prosecution for violating Missouri's game and fishing laws. Almost all of these cases involved the illegal use of seines, or large fishing nets made to hang vertically across a body of water such as a river, creek, or stream. Once again, members of the Barker family, including Sampson Barker and his sons Edward and Rufus, frequently violated the law against this type of fishing. Between 1893 and 1897 each of the Barker men went to court multiple times to face charges of illegal seine fishing.[31] In 1897, the grand jury also indicted Elisha Miles, the son of Anti-Bald Knobber leader William H. Miles, for illegal seine fishing, and charged the Anti-Bald Knobber John Haworth with using an illegal fish trap to catch fish in the White River.[32]

The law forbade the use of seines and fish traps because those who used them depleted the stock of fish for everybody else. For the most part, however, the authorities only rarely enforced such laws, and many people who lived in the county at that time remembered using such methods without interference from the law. One elderly resident, Isaac Moore, recalled that "at that time they were allowed to seine all they wanted to. I saw seven thousand pounds seined out at one draw. . . . There were so many fish in the seine we could not draw it out."[33] Another old-timer, C. B. Stallcup, bragged, "I have helped to catch several hundred pounds at one haul with a seine. Some of the fish were big fellows, weighing twenty-five pounds or more. There were buffalo fish, drum, catfish, and many others."[34] Indeed, the circuit court records for Taney County in the nineteenth century contain only a handful of criminal cases pertaining to game and fishing laws, but a substantial number of that handful involved people who either belonged to the Anti-Bald Knobber faction or were related to someone who was. This does not mean that the charges against these people were false or trumped up, but it does show that local law enforcement officials paid close attention to any sort of criminal activity in which they might get involved. That in turn indicates that some of the old prejudice between the vigilante and anti-vigilante factions of the 1880s survived well into the next decade.

The Anti-Bald Knobbers directed much of their animus toward the person of Nathaniel Kinney himself. The huge vigilante captain had a polarizing effect on those around him, and few who knew him lacked an opinion about him. From the late 1880s until well into the twentieth century, many rumors circulated among the people of southwest Missouri that some members of the Anti-Bald Knobber militia faction conspired to have Kinney killed. One of the earliest of these rumors found its way onto the pages of the *Kansas City Journal.* This newspaper reported that one of its reporters had learned from a local resident that several militia men were plotting to murder Nat Kinney and several other leading vigilantes. According to the *Journal,* "Captain Kinney was to be the first one killed" followed by "Deputy [Galba] Branson and William P. Hensley . . . then Rube Isaacs, West Brooks, A. C. Kissee, [John] T. Dickenson, and Colonel Prather. Then Deputy [Arter] Kissee and Sheriff McHaffie."[35] Another story, recorded in Vance Randolph's account of the Bald Knobbers, stated that a group of Kinney's enemies put together "a purse of $2,000 in gold" as a bounty for anyone who would kill him.[36] Still another account, first published in the *Taney County Republican* in 1959 and later repeated in Elmo Ingenthron and Mary Hartman's book on the Bald Knobbers, stated that Kinney's killers decided his fate by a game of cards. According to this story, sometime after Sam Snapp's death a group of five Anti-Bald Knobbers, including Billy Miles and Matt Snapp, met in a barn and played a game of cards, with the loser agreeing to kill Nat Kinney. Since Miles lost the game, it fell to him to kill the vigilante captain, which he eventually did two years later.[37]

The common denominators of each of these conspiracy theories are their sensational character and lack of corroborating evidence. In all likelihood, none of these accounts describe something that actually happened. The first story posited a sequence of events that did not occur (only Nat Kinney was assassinated, not the other men mentioned), and the second and third seem like attempts to explain Nat Kinney's death after the fact. Moreover, even if Kinney's enemies had put a bounty on his head, it seems improbable that in a poor region like southwest Missouri they could have raised $2,000 *in gold* for that purpose. Finally, the story of the assassin's card game drew a strong rebuttal from Billy Miles's niece, Mrs. Ida Miles DeClue, in a 1995 interview with *Branson Living* magazine.[38]

At the same time, these stories do convey a sense of the extreme hostility that Kinney evoked on the part of many of his neighbors. The Anti-Bald Knobbers generally considered him a "bad man," and many doubted whether peace would ever return to their community so long as he remained among them.[39] Even among some vigilantes, Kinney's domineering personality had begun to create mixed feelings. As previously discussed, when Adj. Gen. James C. Jamison demanded that the Bald Knobbers disband, Kinney and a number of his followers initially wanted to continue their work as before, but a moderate faction led by Alonzo S. Prather opposed them and supported disbanding the group. The moderate position prevailed, indicating that most of the vigilantes had no desire to provoke a confrontation with the state.[40]

Opposition from fellow Bald Knobbers may explain why Kinney found his ambitions for political office frustrated, even as other leading vigilantes triumphed in local elections. In 1884, and again in 1886, Kinney lost elections for state representative from his county. In the first race, he lost to Republican and fellow Bald Knobber James C. Johnson. In the second campaign, the local Republican Party recruited Samuel Dial, a former Arkansas state representative and the receiver of the federal government's land office in Harrison, Arkansas, to run for state representative against him. In a very close contest, Dial prevailed over Kinney, winning by fewer than fifty votes.[41] Some Bald Knobbers probably opposed Kinney because of his political affiliation. He was a staunch Democrat, after all, and most of his fellow vigilantes sided with the Republicans. In the election of 1886, however, he was the only Bald Knobber candidate who lost. Fellow vigilantes James McHaffie, Reuben Branson, and Madison Day each won their contests for sheriff, county clerk, and coroner, respectively.[42] That Kinney could not win, even with his faction ascendant in the county, suggests that some of his comrades had reservations about trusting him with a political office.

The controversy that Kinney's polarizing personality so often engendered also showed up during the course of a bitter and protracted legal battle that the vigilante captain waged with the city of Springfield. The trouble started on the evening of September 12, 1885. Kinney had gone to Springfield on business, and late that afternoon he went to meet a train at the depot. Following that he went out for some supper, and then he went to a local bowling alley where he bowled three games of ten pins with a group of his friends from Taney County who were also in town. This group included the

Bald Knobbers Patterson Fickle, Clayton Stokely, Cal Parrish, and several others. After they finished bowling, Kinney and a number of his companions started walking toward a feed store. Before they had gone far Kinney fell into an uncovered pothole on a dimly lit thoroughfare known as South Alley (now called McDaniel Street), which ran between Campbell Street and South Street. It seems that for some time prior to the accident, city employees had kept the hole covered by putting a wood box over the opening, but that night someone had removed the box. As a result of his fall, Kinney suffered injuries to his left foot, leg, and hip, as well as his stomach and left testicle.[43]

After seeing a physician who gave him some bandages and liniments, Kinney spent the evening convalescing at a local hotel called the American House. His friend Clayton Stokely stayed with him, and the following day Stokely took him back home. The next month Kinney filed a lawsuit against the city of Springfield for $5,000 in damages for failing to cover properly the dangerous pothole. He claimed that the accident had left him permanently disabled, making it difficult for him to perform his ordinary labor as a farmer and stock raiser. The case first appeared on the circuit court docket in May 1886, but the court continued the case all the way to November 1887, when it finally came to trial. The attorneys for the city accused Kinney of contributory negligence, claiming that he was drunk at the time of the accident, a charge that he strongly denied. They also requested a court-appointed physician to examine Kinney in order to determine the extent of his injuries, which the court refused to do because they made the request too late. On November 17, 1887, the jury returned a verdict in favor of Nat Kinney and awarded him $1,500 for his injuries. The city naturally chaffed at this decision and appealed it all the way to the St. Louis Court of Appeals, which affirmed the lower court's decision on March 19, 1889. Kinney never received the money, however, having died almost seven months before the final decision occurred.[44]

The case merits discussion, not only because of the plaintiff, but also because of the people who testified in it. Not surprisingly, several men associated with the Anti-Bald Knobber faction, including the former Democratic officeholders Dr. K. L. Burdette, Leroy Thomas, Thomas A. Layton, and John Moseley, took advantage of the opportunity to get back at their nemesis by testifying against him. For example, Burdette testified that he had seen Nat Kinney at a Democratic barbeque in October 1884, during his first campaign for state representative, and that at that event he was "so lame that he could hardly walk" and had to use his cane in order to mount the podium to speak. Burdette also said that he believed Kinney suffered from rheumatism. He had seen Kinney several times since the barbeque. Sometimes Kinney used a cane and sometimes he did not, but in any event Burdette believed that he had gone lame before September 1885. Leroy Thomas attended the same barbeque and his observations generally confirmed Burdette's account. By contrast, Layton and Moseley testified that after Kinney's alleged injuries they had seen him engaging in wrestling matches and other "tests and trials of strength and activity," and that during these competitions he easily excelled his opponents. Moreover, since the accident they had seen him doing his "ordinary and usual amount of work" without any noticeable difficulty.[45]

At least one former Bald Knobber also testified against Captain Kinney. After the first trial, city attorney W. H. Johnson formally requested a new trial, supported with new affidavits from a number of witnesses including James R. Vanzandt. Vanzandt, a minister, Mexican and Civil War veteran, and former state representative, testified that after his accident Kinney performed his usual work around his home and farm just as before. Prior to the second trial, a member of the Hensley family also agreed to testify for the state against the captain. Unfortunately, the document that mentions the name, a motion for a continuance filed by the city's attorneys in December 1886, does not make it clear which Hensley wanted to testify. It may have been one of the Bald Knobbers, either Augustus C. ("Gus") Hensley or his brother William P. Hensley, or perhaps someone else from the same family. Since both Vanzandt and the Hensley family were well-known supporters of the Bald Knobber cause, the fact that one of them would testify against Kinney may indicate discontent with their controversial captain's leadership.[46]

Kinney's penchant for plunging into controversies ultimately got him involved in the situation that led to his death: a tawdry divorce scandal involving James S. B. Berry, a prosperous Forsyth merchant and Anti-Bald Knobber; Berry's wife, Ann E. Berry; and Kinney's friend and fellow Bald Knobber George Taylor. In early 1888, Mrs. Berry filed a petition for a divorce from her husband, accusing him of serial infidelity and physical abuse going back many years. She also requested that the court seize part of his assets, which she valued at around $5,000, in order to provide for her financial support after the marriage ended.[47] Mrs. Berry hired George Taylor as her lawyer to represent her in the case, and it appears that some sort of relationship developed between them, because he soon moved into a hotel that she managed in Forsyth. Despite his own numerous marital indiscretions, Berry accused his wife and Taylor of having an adulterous affair. At one point he even brandished a gun at the lawyer and threatened to shoot him. The incident resulted in formal charges against Berry for threatening Taylor, and against Taylor for illegal cohabitation with Mrs. Berry. The feud between the two men came to a head again on August 3, when Berry and Taylor ended up trading pistol shots with each other near the Hilsabeck Hotel close to the town square in Forsyth.[48]

The feud between Berry and Taylor originally had nothing to do with the old Bald Knobber troubles. Nevertheless, because Berry had been an Anti-Bald Knobber, and Taylor a Bald Knobber, their supporters tended to fall out along familiar factional lines. Billy Miles, for example, had been "a leading witness against Mrs. Berry and Taylor in the adultery case," and both Billy and James Miles for a time acted as Berry's body guards lest one of Taylor's friends try to kill him.[49] For his part, Kinney warmly supported his friend Taylor and testified on his behalf in the adultery case.[50] When circuit judge W. D. Hubbard put the Berry Brothers Store into receivership, pending the outcome of the divorce settlement, Kinney volunteered to serve as the firm's receiver. By assuming this responsibility he agreed to take charge of the store and make an inventory of its goods. He did so despite having heard reports that Berry and his business partner, a man named W. D. Webster, had publicly threatened to kill whomever the court appointed as receiver. Just before Kinney took responsibility for the Berry's store, his friend Charles Groom reportedly advised him not to do so. Groom argued that it might needlessly expose him to retaliation from the Berry-Miles camp. Kinney unwisely decided to ignore his advice.[51]

On Monday morning, August 20, Kinney was in the store performing his duties as receiver of the company. At about ten o'clock that
morning, Billy and James Miles walked into the store, ostensibly to
get a drink from the water barrel there. The only other person in the
building at the time was a bystander named William Beaman. Exactly
what happened next is subject to interpretation, and many versions
of that morning's events appeared in the press over the next few days,
but a few facts seem certain. At some point an argument developed
between the two men, and Kinney ordered Miles to leave the premises,
an order Miles refused. According to Miles, Kinney made a motion
to go for his gun, and both men drew their pistols. Miles got off the
first shot, which struck Kinney's forearm and ricocheted through
the muscle of the arm and into his body, causing the big man to roar
like "a wounded lion." Miles quickly fired off three more rounds in
succession. The bullets hit Kinney in the chest, stomach, and back,
killing him instantly. He never had the opportunity to return fire. Also
according to Miles, right before the shots were fired Kinney shouted
at him, "Billy Miles, you damned son of a bitch, I am going to kill
you." James Miles and William Beaman corroborated his version of
the events.[52]

Shortly before all of this took place, James Berry went to the office
of James DeLong's newspaper, the *Taney County News*, with a rifle in
his hands. The office was located about sixty feet from Berry's store on
the same side of the square. Berry entered the building and took a seat
behind the editor, who was talking with a customer about a newspaper
subscription. When the shots rang out from the Berry Brothers Store,
the men in the office jumped to their feet. According to some newspaper reports, Berry then ordered the editor to remain in his office,
and that command prevented him from coming to his stepfather's
aid. But James DeLong's own deposition, taken as evidence for Berry's
murder trial, does not bear out this version of events. According to
his testimony, when the shooting occurred, Berry simply followed the
others onto the porch in front of his office. He kept his firearm at the
ready, but did not try to stop anyone from leaving.[53] Thus, it remains
unclear exactly what Berry was doing on the day of the killing. Did
he really go to the office on that day just by coincidence, or did he go
there to keep watch on DeLong and make sure that he would not try

to avenge Kinney's death? In any event, the Taney County grand jury must have interpreted his actions suspiciously, for they later indicted him as an accessory to murder.[54]

After Miles shot Kinney, he reloaded his pistol and went outside. He tossed the spent shell casings aside and announced to the crowd gathering outside the store that he had killed Nat Kinney in self-defense. He kept his pistol until Sheriff McHaffie arrived, at which point he handed it to one of the bystanders and surrendered himself to the law.[55] When he left the scene several people went into the store to view the body. Accounts of the disposition of the crime scene differed widely among those who saw it. Some witnesses reported seeing Kinney's pistol lying on the floor next to him,[56] while others said that the big man still had it clenched tightly in his hand.[57] One of Kinney's friends, who viewed the crime scene, later claimed that the pistol found near his body belonged not to him, but to his son. This witness stated that shortly before the shooting both this weapon and Kinney's had been seen lying in the front of the store behind a prescription case some distance from the body.[58] The implication of this version of the story is that Miles shot Kinney in cold blood and later placed the pistol near his body to make it seem like self-defense. In any event, a coroner's jury soon assembled, which ruled the cause of death to be gunshot wounds produced by bullets from Billy Miles's pistol.[59]

The sudden death of the Bald Knobber chieftain produced electrifying headlines, followed sometimes by inaccurate stories, in newspapers across the state and country. Rumors circulated in some papers that Kinney's friends had already lynched Miles in retaliation for the killing.[60] The day after the shooting, the *St. Louis Post-Dispatch* ran a story, based on a hastily written telegraph report from a correspondent in Springfield, stating that the murder took place in Ozark, Missouri, and that both Miles and Kinney had gone there to attend a Republican political rally (both men were actually Democrats). The same report also erroneously referred to Nat Kinney as the leader of the vigilantes in Christian County.[61] Meanwhile, the *Springfield Republican* ran an article luridly titled "Blood Will Flow," which suggested that the Miles-Kinney shooting presaged "the beginning of another reign of terror and violence in the county."[62] A week later the *Springfield Leader* published an editorial by a Taney County resident strongly refuting this story, asserting that the county was still at peace and most people wanted the law to take its course.[63]

These comforting assurances notwithstanding, the situation in Taney County did become extremely tense in the days following Kinney's death. Shortly after surrendering to the authorities, Miles posted a $5,000 bond for his appearance in court and was released on his own recognizance. Posting the bond allowed him to enjoy his freedom for the time being, but it also raised the possibility of fresh bloodshed between the Miles family and any of Kinney's friends who might want revenge. A correspondent for a Springfield newspaper who visited the county a few days after the killing compared many of the residents he encountered to "walking arsenals" who traveled about heavily armed to ensure their safety. Billy Miles, the journal-ist reported, went about his business with a small group of seven or eight of his friends, heavily armed, acting as his body guards.[64] With this tense state of affairs, many people probably awaited the next session of the circuit court with anxious anticipation, hoping that the two sides would keep the peace long enough for the law to deal with the situation.

The court's next scheduled term began in October, so Billy Miles and James Berry did not have to wait long to learn their fate. On Tuesday, October 9, the grand jury handed down an indictment against Miles for murder in the first degree for the shooting of Nat Kinney. At the same time the grand jury also indicted Berry as an accessory to murder before the fact. The indictment specifically alleged that Berry had either persuaded or hired Miles to murder Kinney for him. At the request of both the state and the defense, the court then continued the cases until its next scheduled term. The sheriff then locked the prisoners in the county jail in Forsyth for safekeeping, but concerns about the safety of the jail led to their removal two days later to the new Christian County jail in Ozark. There they would remain until the circuit court reconvened in April 1889.[65]

Between the indictments of Berry and Miles for murder and the beginning of the new court term, Taney County held another election. On November 6, 1888, voters cast their ballots in state and federal elec-tions and also elected a new slate of county officials. The Republican

Party again dominated at the polls, sending Republican and former Bald Knobber Alonzo Prather to Jefferson City as state representative and delivering substantial majorities to the GOP candidates in the state senate and congressional races.[66] Once more, a number of known Bald Knobbers also won races for various local offices. Galba Branson won the election for county sheriff; Madison Day won his bid for reelection as county coroner; and James DeLong prevailed in the race for county prosecutor.[67] DeLong's victory put him in the awkward position of potentially having to prosecute the men allegedly responsible for his stepfather's death.

The election results reaffirmed the strong influence that the old Bald Knobber faction still had over county affairs, a fact which the accused murderers Miles and Berry surely understood. If they wanted any chance of acquittal, it would probably have to come from a trial held somewhere other than Taney County. Thus, at the beginning of the circuit court's term in April 1889, both defendants submitted requests for a change of venue to a neutral location, arguing that the minds of the local residents had become so prejudiced against them that they could not receive a fair trial in the county. Judge Hubbard must have found these arguments persuasive, for he granted the request and ordered the prisoners removed to the Greene County jail in Springfield to await trial there.[68]

Once in Springfield, Billy Miles posted a bond for $8,000 to secure his release from jail. James Berry, however, could not find sufficient funds or co-signers to make bail, and so he remained behind bars.[69] Miles had little property of his own to cover the bond and would have remained in jail as well had not several of his friends and family members co-signed his bond. Interestingly enough, the list of Miles's co-signers featured several known Anti-Bald Knobbers, including his father, William H. Miles, William E. Moore, John Moseley, and Robert Snapp. This provided more fodder for those of Kinney's friends inclined to believe that his death had been the result of an Anti-Bald Knobber conspiracy.[70]

After getting out on bail, Billy Miles returned to his family's farm in Taney County. For the next few months he managed to live quietly, avoiding conflict with any of his Bald Knobber neighbors. Around the same time, a man named Ed Funk arrived in Taney County. Funk's background and career prior to coming to the county are something of a mystery. Some newspaper accounts erroneously referred to Funk as a "deputy" (so far as I can tell, Branson never deputized him), but most described him as a private "detective" from Eureka Springs, Arkansas.[71] Although the term *detective* has since lost many of its negative connotations, at that time it often implied that a man was a hired gun.[72] Funk came to Taney County sometime in the spring of 1889, in the company of another private detective named James Dennis. The men came to the county to apprehend some dealers in "queer" money (i.e., counterfeit money), but they had no luck in making any arrests. In late June, they managed to convince the proprietor of a store located near the mouth of Bear Creek to help them catch two local thieves by allowing them to stage a robbery of his establishment. The sting operation did result in the apprehension of two thieves, a teenager named Albert Combs and another young man named Stansell, but it also cost Dennis his life when Combs shot and killed him while attempting to escape.[73]

Although destined to play a small but significant role in the Bald Knobber story in Taney County, Ed Funk had no apparent connection with either the Bald Knobber or Anti-Bald Knobber factions. Thus, his motivation for getting involved remains murky. In their book on the Bald Knobbers, Mary Hartman and Elmo Ingenthron write that the Bald Knobbers "allegedly sent fifteen hundred dollars to Ed Funk at Eureka Springs," in return for which he promised to kill Billy Miles. The money supposedly came from the cash settlement that Nat Kinney's widow had just received from the city of Springfield. The authors offer no evidence for this theory, however, and at this point it remains a supposition.[74]

On July 4, 1889, Ed Funk attended an Independence Day picnic at a campground near Kirbyville. Sheriff Galba Branson, and three of the Miles brothers, William, James, and Emanuel, also attended the festivities. The Miles brothers came to the party armed with pistols concealed on their persons, presumably to protect themselves from any Bald Knobbers who might be out for revenge. Around four or five o'clock in the afternoon the Miles brothers walked to a nearby spring to get a drink of water. Branson and Funk followed them, ostensibly to arrest them for carrying concealed weapons. Funk arrived at the spring shortly before the sheriff, and walked up to Billy Miles and drew his pistol. Leveling his weapon at the young man, Funk demanded to know if he carried a pistol. Billy replied that he did, and Funk ordered him to surrender. According to an interview Miles later gave to the *Springfield Leader* while in jail, Funk also cursed him and told him he would "shoot my brains out if I moved a muscle."[75]

At this point, Miles could not draw his weapon because Funk had the drop on him, but Funk had unwisely ignored Miles's brothers standing off some distance from him. When he saw Funk threaten his brother, James Miles drew his weapon and fired two shots into the detective's body, one bullet piercing his heart. Around this time Sheriff Branson came running up to that place, and seeing his companion fall he drew his revolver and began firing at James Miles. He fired between three and six shots, one of which struck James in the groin, passing through his scrotum and into his thigh. Billy Miles quickly returned fire. He shot the sheriff once in his leg, and once through his head, killing him instantly.[76]

As soon as the shooting stopped, Billy, James, and Emanuel Miles fled on foot eastward, away from the scene of the killing. They feared what might happen to them if they fell into the hands of any of Sheriff Branson's Bald Knobber friends. Billy and Emanuel helped carry their badly wounded brother until they reached the home of one of their friends, who offered James shelter and sent for Dr. K. L Burdette to come and treat his wounds. Perhaps realizing that he could not run forever, James Miles sent word to Madison Day, who became the interim sheriff following the death of Galba Branson, and Constable L. T. Richardson of Forsyth that he wanted to surrender. The two lawmen took him into custody on Saturday, July 6, just two days after the shooting. Meanwhile, Billy and Emanuel left their brother at the house and hid in the woods nearby. Emanuel Miles eventually went home, having less to fear than his brothers because he had taken no part in the shootings. Billy Miles fled north into Greene County, where he stopped at the home of James Barker a short distance from Springfield. From there he sent word to Sheriff J. C. Dodson of Greene County that he wanted to surrender, which he did on Tuesday morning, July 9.[77]

Apparently, Miles wanted to surrender to Sheriff Dodson rather than to the authorities in Taney County, because he did not wish to fall into the hands of Bald Knobbers in that county. In an interview with the *Springfield Republican*, Miles claimed that he fled to Springfield because he knew that "if I threw down my pistols and gave myself up in Taney County I would be killed."[78] He may have had good reason to feel that way. In an interview with the *Springfield Express*, Deputy Sheriff W. H. Manning of Taney County acknowledged that "having heard that Bill Miles was making for [Springfield] to surrender," he led a small posse in pursuit, hoping to catch the fugitive before he had a chance to surrender. He said he and his men arrived in Springfield "too late by ten minutes" to intercept Miles before he was taken into custody. Manning did not say what his posse would have done had they caught Miles, but he did say that the people of his county did not want the Miles brothers released on bail because they "don't want them loose to kill more good men under bond."[79]

In addition to the arrests of Billy and James Miles, authorities in Taney County also arrested two other men, Rufus Barker and J. W. Combs. These men were in the vicinity of the spring when the shootings occurred, and some people initially suspected them of having taken part in the killings. The vigilante element was especially suspicious of Barker because of his Anti-Bald Knobber sympathies. Some even suspected him of taking part in a conspiracy with the Miles brothers to murder the sheriff and Funk. The preliminary examinations, however, uncovered no evidence to connect them to the murders, and they were released.[80]

Before the Miles brothers could face charges for killing Branson and Funk, Billy Miles and James Berry still had to stand trial for killing Nat Kinney. Unfortunately for Prosecutor DeLong, who tried the cases, Judge Hubbard had already decided to change the venue of these trials to Springfield in Greene County. By 1889, both Kinney and the Bald Knobbers had become quite unpopular in Springfield. Their lack of popularity stemmed in part from the publicity surrounding the recent Edens-Greene killings in Christian County and partly from Nat Kinney's recent lawsuit, which had forced the city's taxpayers to cough up the $1,500 awarded to his widow and family.[81] The *Springfield Daily Republican* probably expressed the views of many residents when it termed Kinney's death a "good riddance" and commented that with his death southwest Missouri had been "cleared of the root of the evil which has been its curse."[82] Given the strength of public sentiment, a jury composed of Springfield men might have been expected to sympathize with the parties allegedly responsible for his death.

The first of the two men to stand trial was James Berry, whose case came before the circuit court in August 1889. The main problem for the prosecution stemmed from the lack of strong evidence supporting their fundamental contention: that Berry had either persuaded or hired Billy Miles to kill Nathaniel Kinney. To be sure, some circumstantial evidence pointed in that direction. Prosecutor Delong testified about how Berry came into his office carrying a rifle just before the time of Kinney's death and remained near him until after the shooting occurred. The county's probate judge, W. B. Burks, recalled having a conversation with Berry shortly before the shooting in which Berry told him, "'I'll die before he shall stay in that store,' or words to that effect." But the prosecution produced no hard evidence proving that Berry had conspired to have Kinney killed, and the jury found him not guilty on August 30, 1889.[83]

Prosecutor DeLong had better luck trying James Berry for his assault on George Taylor the previous summer. Berry had tried to shoot Taylor out of jealousy over the latter's alleged affair with his wife. Because public prejudice against Berry in Taney County had not abated, the circuit court granted his request for another change of venue to Greene County. This time, however, Berry did not find the jurors in Springfield sympathetic to his case. On February 28, 1890, the jury found him guilty of felonious assault and sentenced him to five years in the state penitentiary.[84] Ultimately, even this small victory for the prosecution proved fleeting. On June 5, Berry and several other prisoners in the Greene County jail in Springfield overpowered one of the guards and escaped.[85]

The trial of Billy Miles for the murder of Nat Kinney began on March 18, 1890. During the course of the trial the court recognized fifty-nine witnesses for the defense, along with forty-six for the state. Ultimately, however, it came down to whether the jurors would believe

Billy Miles, who claimed he shot Kinney in self-defense, or the prosecution, which insisted that he had killed Kinney in cold blood. On March 21, both sides concluded taking testimony from their witnesses. Judge Mordecai Oliver, who had recently replaced W. D. Hubbard as the trial judge for this case, set the following day for final arguments. Judge Oliver allotted four hours for each side to make its case. James H. Vaughan, H. E. Havens, and Benjamin B. Price each gave closing arguments for the state, while Almus Harrington, George Pepperdine, and O. H. Travers argued for the defense. James DeLong, who had led the prosecuting team, opted not to give a closing statement. The jurors listened to the lawyers for about eight hours. Shortly before ten o'clock that evening, they retired to consider the evidence. It took them only half an hour, however, to return a verdict of "not guilty," to the evident relief of the defendant. Miles received a hearty round of congratulations from his friends who had come to watch the trial. Nevertheless, he was soon returned to the jail to await trial for his part in the killing of Galba Branson and Ed Funk.[86]

Some former Bald Knobbers reacted sourly to the news of the acquittal. Alexander Kissee, editor of the *Taney County Times*, decried the verdict, which he attributed to the "considerable prejudice at Springfield and over Greene County against Captain Kinney (as well as against people that were Bald Knobbers of this county)."[87] Kissee may have had a point. As noted above, over the previous few years the people of Springfield had developed a decidedly poor opinion of Nat Kinney in particular and the Bald Knobbers in general. Thus, the Springfield residents on the jury may have felt predisposed to believe Miles's version of events over any other. Moreover, many of the instructions that Judge Oliver gave to the jury in Billy Miles's murder trial seemed weighted in the defendant's favor. The first instruction, for example, enjoined the jurors to remember that "self-defense is a lawful right" enjoyed by every person, and further stated that if Billy Miles had reasonable grounds to believe that Kinney was about to shoot him, then he "had the right to act upon appearances as they presented themselves to his mind." Subsequent instructions repeated the same basic idea in different words several times.[88]

If the verdicts in the Miles and Berry murder cases provided any indication, the prosecution could expect an equally difficult task in winning convictions against either William or James Miles for their role in the Fourth of July gunfight at Kirbyville the previous summer. Once again the circuit court changed the venue of these trials, this time to Ozark in Christian County, the scene of the recent execution of three Bald Knobbers convicted of murder. On September 4, 1890, almost six months after Billy Miles's acquittal in the Kinney murder case, he and his brother James stood trial again for the murder of Galba Branson. The judge had decided to hold a second trial for the murder of Ed Funk, if it became necessary. The actual trial lasted only one day. "The state," reported Alexander Kissee's *Taney County Times*, "made a much shorter case than was expected." The prosecution argued that the Miles brothers had gunned down Funk and Branson in cold blood after the sheriff and his companion had tried to arrest them for carrying concealed weapons. The defense claimed that the Bald Knobbers had conspired "to kill the Miles boys . . . and that Detective Funk was the hired agent of the murderous plot."[89] Overall, the defense got the better end of the argument. One local newspaper concluded that "the state has made about the weakest case we ever saw in a trial for murder." The prosecution's own witnesses "clearly show a case of self-defense, and no doubt by the time our readers get this paper the verdict will be in, and for an acquittal."[90]

At around four o'clock that afternoon the jurors retired to deliberate. They ended up taking far longer to reach a verdict than anyone anticipated. Only after more than fourteen hours of deliberations, which lasted straight through the night and into the next morning, did the jurors finally reach a decision. It turned out that eleven of the twelve jurors initially favored acquittal, while one holdout wanted to convict the defendants of murder in the second degree. Only after hours of debate did the stubborn juror at last acquiesce to the majority's opinion. Finally, at seven o'clock that morning the jury announced a verdict of "not guilty" on the charge of murder against Billy and James Miles. At this point Prosecutor DeLong, realizing that there was no point in pursuing further action against the brothers, dropped the remaining charges against them for killing Ed Funk.[91]

The deaths of Nat Kinney, Galba Branson, and Ed Funk, along with the subsequent court trials and the acquittal of their killers, marked the end of the Bald Knobber era in Taney County. For the remainder of its history, the county witnessed only one other vigilante incident involving the lynching of John Wesley Bright in 1892. Bright was a volatile man who killed his wife in a fit of jealousy because he suspected her of infidelity. The authorities charged him with murder, and opened a preliminary hearing into the case on March 12, 1892. The hearing did not conclude that day, however, and so Bright was returned to the county jail for the night. That evening a mob of around fifteen or twenty men entered Forsyth and broke into the jail. One of the sheriff's deputies, George L. Williams, attempted to intervene and was shot dead for his trouble. The mob then took Bright from the jail and hung him from the limb of an oak tree in a nearby cemetery.[92]

The lynching of Bright and the murder of Deputy Williams caused a brief furor in the press, with some newspapers linking the incident to the old feud between the Bald Knobber and militia factions and suggesting that it might reignite that conflict.[93] In retrospect, however, the Bright lynching appears to have been a spontaneous act of mob violence, not an attempt to revive the old Bald Knobber organization. Roughly two months after the raid, Missouri's attorney general John M. Wood visited Forsyth to investigate the Bright lynching. Although he expressed skepticism about the ability of local authorities to handle the situation properly, he also concluded "[i]t is not a Bald Knobber movement, of that I am sure."[94] Eventually Sheriff John L. Cook, himself a former Bald Knobber, managed to round up most of the men suspected of participating in the raid on the jail, including some former vigilantes like Madison Day, Rueben Isaacs, and D. F. McConkey. These men went to trial at a special term of the circuit court in July 1892. The prosecution's case fell apart, however, when their key witness, George Friend, one of the men who had participated in the raid on the jail and then turned state's evidence, reneged on his plea agreement and refused to testify. After that, the county prosecutor had to dismiss the cases against all of the defendants.[95]

The Bright lynching and the murder of Deputy Williams did not lead to a renewal of the feud between the Bald Knobber and Anti-Bald Knobber factions as some people had feared. That conflict remained buried with Nat Kinney, Galba Branson, and Ed Funk, though for a long time the memories of that turbulent period simmered in the minds of those who lived through it. Many years later, Anti-Bald Knobber John H. Haworth wrote about these killings with evident satisfaction: "we did get rid of three of the Bald-Nobbers [sic], Branson, Funk and Kinney. All of these cases came to trial . . . and in each case we came clear." If they had only had the opportunity, Haworth added, "there would have probably have been ten or fifteen Bald Nobbers [sic] to our credit."[96]

The shootings did not, however, put an end to the hegemony that the Bald Knobber-Republican faction enjoyed in local politics. Throughout the 1890s and well into the next century, former Bald Knobbers regularly won elections for offices in local government. For example, the aforementioned John L. Cook won the election for sheriff in 1890, a position that he had held since winning a special election to replace the deceased Galba Branson the previous year. Benjamin Price held the offices of prosecuting attorney (1892–94) and collector of revenue (1896–1902). Other former Bald Knobbers, including James B. Rice, George Taylor, James Johnson, and John Dickenson, also held multiple elected positions over the following two decades.[97] Moreover, the Republican Party, to which most Bald Knobbers belonged, continued to dominate local politics for well over a generation. Indeed, the most comprehensive history of the county states that the Democrats did not seriously contend for control of local government again until the election of 1928, on the eve of the New Deal era.[98] Thus, for the Anti-Bald Knobbers the Miles-Kinney shooting and the Fourth of July gunfight at Kirbyville amounted to Pyrrhic victories: events that offered them the satisfaction of revenge, but could not change the reality of their defeat.

# Conclusion

The Bald Knobber movement took shape at a critical juncture in the history of southwest Missouri, as the region was transformed by forces beyond the control of its inhabitants. By the 1880s, the vanguard of industrial capitalist expansion—railroads, mining and timber companies, businessmen, and investors—had made deep inroads into the Ozarks hinterland. They came to utilize the land and resources of the region for their benefit. Accompanying these changes was a new wave of settlers to the area, many from states in the North and Midwest, who slowly altered the demographic make-up of the region. The newcomers came from all walks of life. Some were simple farmers and homesteaders looking to take advantage of the large surplus of government land in the area. Others were shrewd businessmen like Cal Parrish, Alexander Kissee, and James K. Polk McHaffie or lawyers and aspiring politicians like Charles Groom and Alonzo Prather. Still others were restless wanderers like Nathaniel Kinney and Joe McGill, who had traveled across the United States, looking for a place to call home. The new men set out to remake Ozark society in their own image by promoting immigration and investment in the region and trying to create a new socioeconomic order centered around new roads, bridges, banks, railroads, responsible local government, and free-market prosperity.

The presence of the newcomers, and the many social and economic changes that accompanied them, prompted sharp reactions from the older settlers they encountered upon arrival. The older community composed primarily of poor immigrants from upper South states like Tennessee, Virginia, and Kentucky, had established a way of life based on close-knit communities, subsistence agriculture, stock raising, and hunting and fishing. Many felt threatened by their seem-ingly foreign neighbors and the changes to their way of life that the new socioeconomic order portended.

Often people perceived these differences through the prism of the Civil War, the salient event that had marked the lives of most adult men who lived through the chaotic Bald Knobber period. The Civil War helped create the necessary conditions for groups like the Bald Knobbers to exist by leaving a legacy of bitterness and mistrust between supporters of the Union and the Confederacy. In Taney County, for example, the vigilantes included in their ranks at least twelve Union veterans, including men like Nat Kinney, Augustus C. Hensley, Madison Day, Alexander Kissee, and George Washington ("Wash") Middleton. Many of these men had spent the war years serving in regiments that did most of their fighting in the Ozarks and witnessed the sort of vicious guerrilla warfare that typified the con-flict in this region. Among their opponents, the Anti-Bald Knobbers, Confederate veterans predominated. Consequently, the two sides looked on each other with mutual suspicion that grew out of their shared experiences as combatants. Thus, when Wash Middleton called Samuel Snapp a "bushwhacker" just before gunning him down on a public street in Kirbyville, he demonstrated that he had transferred the old hostility for his wartime enemies to his new adversaries in the Anti-Bald Knobber faction.[1] Likewise, when an Anti-Bald Knobber spokesman like Sampson Barker appealed to Gov. John S. Marmaduke to intervene on their behalf citing their shared experiences in the Confederate military, he showed the emotional resonance that the old cause still elicited among those who had fought for it.[2] Finally, when Andrew Coggburn antagonized Nat Kinney by singing "The Ballad of the Bald Knobbers," few listeners could have missed the line that referred to Kinney's "federal clothes" (i.e., federal uniform).[3] That lyric clearly marked Kinney as a former Union veteran, whom Taney County's ex-Confederates would have distrusted instinctively.

The hostility that the Civil War engendered also helped polar-ize the political culture of Taney County where the Bald Knobber organization originated. The county's political history after the Civil War went through three distinct phases. In the first phase, from the end of the Civil War through the early 1870s, the Republican Party dominated local politics largely because the state government had disfranchised most Democratic voters because of their previous support for the Confederacy. After intraparty discord within the state's Republican Party paved the way for the end of disfranchisement in 1872, Democrats in Taney County recaptured control of the county government. A Democratic courthouse ring composed of a small cadre of elected officials managed to maintain power for roughly a decade. Finally, a coalition of Republicans and Bald Knobbers drove the courthouse ring from power in the middle 1880s by blaming them for running up the county's debt and allowing the local criminal class to operate unchecked. Nat Kinney, the chieftain of the vigilantes, indicated the intensity of feeling on both sides when he described the struggle for control as "a war between civilization and barbarism."[4]

Finally, the Civil War led to a surge of lawlessness, both in southwest Missouri and the state at large, and an increased cultural acceptance of violence and vigilantism as a means of solving problems and deterring crime. Historians have described the post–Civil War period as a "reign of terror" in which former soldiers and guerrillas left the battlefields and faded into Missouri's countryside only to reemerge later as criminals and outlaws.[5] These included some of the most celebrated outlaws of the age, such as the members of the infamous James-Younger gang, whose apprenticeship in the outlaw trade came during the war.[6] The increase in crime swelled Missouri's prison population from 286 to 2,041 between 1860 and 1880.[7]

Many Missourians responded to this situation by turning to vigilante justice to deal with crime in their communities. Thus, nearly half of the documented lynchings in the state's history (112 out of 229) occurred within a twenty-year time span following the Civil War.[8] Likewise, during this period many vigilante groups organized in various parts of the state, such as the Anti-Horse Thief Association in Clark County in northeast Missouri, the Marmiton League in Vernon County, and the Honest Men's League in Greene County.[9] Groups like these set a precedent for vigilantism which the Bald Knobbers would follow in the 1880s.

Concern over crime led directly to the founding of the first Bald Knobber organization in Taney County. There the precipitating factors were the murders of James Everett and Amos Ring in 1883 and

1884, and the attempted murders of Mr. and Mrs. John T. Dickenson in 1885, three events that galvanized public sentiment in favor of vigilante justice. In 1885, a diverse coalition of middle-class and upper-class men came together to form a vigilance committee in Forsyth. They felt compelled to do so, not only by the prevalence of crime in their neighborhoods, but also by the perception that their elected officials did little or nothing to help prosecute or punish the perpetrators in their midst. As Bald Knobber Joe McGill later observed, criminals regularly trampled the law and taunted the county's lawmen, telling them that their "'authority reaches only to the bluffs,' and when they were once in the hills and brush, they defied the law—nothing and nobody were safe."[10] The failure of civil authorities to convict criminals accused of serious crimes only reinforced this perception, as when local roughneck Al Layton, cousin of county clerk Thomas A. Layton, was acquitted of the murder of James Everett.[11]

The Bald Knobbers' disenchantment with the performance of their local government extended to fiscal and economic matters as well. The vigilantes focused much of their criticism on the appalling condition of county finances. Over roughly a decade prior to the founding of the Bald Knobbers, Taney County accumulated tens of thousands of dollars in debt, reaching the once astounding figure of $42,000 in late 1883.[12] Since the Democratic courthouse ring controlled the local government for most of this period, an emerging coalition of Republicans and Bald Knobbers happily blamed the fiscal situation on their political enemies. Nathaniel Kinney charged that when he arrived "the county was $42,000 in debt, and had not even a plank to show for it. The money had simply been stolen."[13]

Behind the political rhetoric about crime and debt lay a genuine concern among the Taney County Bald Knobbers for the economic progress of their community. Since many of the vigilantes were prosperous businessmen and professionals, they felt they had an economic stake in the future of the county. They demonstrated this commitment by coming to Taney County in the first place, by investing their money in the local economy, and by participating in organizations like the Taney County Immigration Society, created to promote immigration to the area by advertising its resources and the advantages of settling there.[14] But if the county remained mired in debt and plagued by crime, how many people would want to move there or invest their money there? From the vigilantes' perspective, therefore, the failure of the local government to resolve these problems to their satisfaction directly threatened the future they had hoped to build for themselves and their families. It hardly comes as a surprise, then, that they sought a solution through extralegal measures. In a speech to his followers, Nat Kinney put the issue as follows, "What will become of our sons and daughters? Our lives, our property, and our liberty are at stake. I appeal to you, as citizens of Taney County, to say what we shall do. Shall we organize ourselves into a vigilant committee and see that when crimes are committed the laws are enforced, or shall we sit down and fold our arms and quietly submit?"[15]

Within a year of their founding in Taney County, new chapters of the Bald Knobber organization spread north to adjacent Christian and Douglas Counties. The members in these neighboring areas, however, did not follow the same pattern of vigilante activity that their counterparts to the south had practiced. The original vigilance committee had focused on protecting, in Nat Kinney's words, lives, property, and liberty. The Bald Knobbers in Christian and Douglas Counties, by contrast, were more concerned with enforcing morality than with protecting life, liberty, and property. In Taney County, the first recorded vigilante acts included the attempted lynching of Newton Herrell, a murderer, and the successful lynching of the Taylor brothers, two outlaws and attempted murderers. In Christian County, however, one of the earliest large-scale actions attributed to the Bald Knobbers was the raid on a saloon in Chadwick belonging to John Rhodes and Russell McCauley. During this raid they wrecked the place and destroyed the proprietors' stock of beer and whiskey.[16]

The Chadwick raid demonstrated the Bald Knobbers' commitment to regulating the morals and private lives of their neighbors. So too did many of the whippings that the vigilantes inflicted on their neighbors. These included the two floggings administered to Greene Walker, a local resident who had become notorious for his polygamous lifestyle,[17] and the two lashings of E. P. Helms, a homesteader who stood accused of such offenses as keeping "lewd women" in his home.[18] These men drew the Bald Knobbers' ire because they allegedly violated the accepted sexual mores of their community, though the vigilantes meted out similar punishment to people guilty of other offenses as well. For example, they applied the hickory switch to Horace Johnson for failing to support his family, and they flogged others like Clayton Whiteacre for disorderly public behavior including discharging a firearm in public and throwing rocks at people passing by on a public road.[19]

In addition to enforcing morality, the northern Bald Knobbers also aimed to protect the livelihoods of their members. In the 1880s, many of the vigilantes depended on making railroad ties to supplement their modest incomes earned from farming. With the completion of a railroad spur line to Chadwick, the dense forests of Christian County and the surrounding area became an important source of railroad ties for the St. Louis–San Francisco Railroad. At twenty cents a tie and eight to ten ties per day, a man could make a significant sum of money for himself and his family hewing ties.[20] Not surprisingly, the tie hackers (as the workers were called) felt keen to protect their earnings. So when a local timber company that purchased ties in the area refused to pay a price for the ties that their workers found equitable, a group of Bald Knobbers visited the company's office in Chadwick at night to intimidate the owner into raising the prices. Another time they threatened the manager of the company's commissary in Sparta, warning that if he culled too many ties belonging to vigilantes "the Bald Knobbers will call on you."[21] Although these threats did not result in any direct action against the company, they showed how serious the vigilantes took any threat to their way of life.

For the same reason, many Bald Knobbers resisted the arrival of new homesteaders who competed with them for the land and resources needed to make a living. Between 1887 and 1888, roughly three dozen vigilantes from Christian and Douglas Counties faced charges in federal court for intimidating homesteaders and driving them off their land. As discussed in chapter 4, their reasons for expelling individual homesteaders were not always clear. In general, however, it appears that the vigilantes targeted homesteaders who stole other people's timber or those who cut off access to timber that the Bald Knobbers wanted.

Because of their violent persecution of homesteaders and their interference in the private lives of their neighbors, the Bald Knobbers in Christian and Douglas Counties became the subject of frequent controversy, as well as the target of local and federal law enforcement. In the end, their intolerance of dissent and criticism proved their undoing. That intolerance led to the murders of Charles Greene and William Edens, the latter having provoked the vigilantes by speaking against them in public.[22] After the murders, a legal crackdown ensued that led to the arrest and conviction of scores of Bald Knobbers on various charges, including the conviction and death sentence of four Bald Knobber leaders for their role in the Edens-Greene killings. One of the four condemned men escaped from jail and evaded recapture, while the other three were executed in Ozark, Missouri, on May 10, 1889.[23] Their execution brought the Bald Knobber movement in the two northern counties to a bloody conclusion, as the vigilante organization thereafter ceased to exist.

The vigilance committee in Taney County came to a different end, though one no less bloody than its northern counterpart. There a new ruling faction composed of vigilantes and their Republican political allies had taken firm control of local government in the middle 1880s. Following Adj. Gen. James C. Jamison's visit to the county in April 1886, the Bald Knobbers officially disbanded their organization.[24] Although some of their enemies insisted that vigilante activity continued, it seems that most of the Bald Knobbers kept their promise to remain inactive. That did not, however, prevent them from using their newfound political power to persecute the supporters of the old militia faction that had opposed them. From the 1880s onward, former Anti-Bald Knobbers increasingly found themselves in court to face a variety of criminal charges ranging from the serious to the frivolous. These included tax evasion, embezzlement, and misconduct in office, violating game and fishing laws, and so on.

Such hostile treatment only further embittered the anti-vigilantes, who longed for any opportunity to strike back at their old enemies. One such opportunity came on August 20, 1888, when the Anti-Bald Knobber William ("Billy") Miles gunned down the Bald Knobber chieftain Nathaniel Kinney in a general store in Forsyth.[25] The following year Billy Miles and his brother James shot and killed Sheriff Galba Branson, a Bald Knobber, and a detective named Ed Funk at an Independence Day picnic near Kirbyville.[26] These two killings allowed the anti-vigilantes to savor a measure of revenge against their old nemeses, but did nothing to disturb Bald Knobber and Republican hegemony in Taney County politics. Former Bald Knobbers continued to hold various public offices well into the twentieth century, which indicated that they were the ultimate victors in the struggle over the county's future.

In this study we have seen how three small rural counties in southwest Missouri responded to the great social and economic changes facing their region in the late nineteenth century. The story of the Bald Knobbers illustrates why people living in communities like these often resorted to vigilantism to cope with problems that seemed beyond ordinary legal or political means of redress. In so doing, it makes a useful contribution, not only to the history of Missouri and the Ozarks, but also to the history of American vigilantism in general. In this present work, we have seen how the Bald Knobbers functioned as two separate and essentially different vigilante groups, one based in Taney County and the other in Christian and Douglas Counties. These groups shared a name but had very different motives, goals, and membership. When looked at in this way, the Bald Knobbers are especially valuable because they represent the diverse and versatile nature of American vigilantism.

Richard Maxwell Brown described the prototypical vigilante group as socially conservative, and committed to preserving respect for the law, property rights, and the three-tiered social hierarchy that he identified as the basic structure of American society in the eighteenth and nineteenth centuries. This social hierarchy included the upper and middle levels, from which vigilante groups drew most of their leaders and ordinary members, and a lower level composed of marginal or alienated people who often became the targets of vigilante action.[27] The classic example that Brown used to describe this type of organization was the South Carolina Regulators of 1767–69, one of the first vigilance committees in American history, and the one which he argued set the basic pattern that most subsequent vigilantes would follow.[28] Other vigilante groups that followed this pattern include the two San Francisco Committees of Vigilance formed in 1851 and 1856 and the vigilantes of southwestern Montana's Ruby River district in the 1860s. Each of these organizations formed in the wake of a mass migration prompted by a major mineral discovery: the California gold rush of 1849 in the case of San Francisco, and the Alder Gulch gold rush of 1863 in the case of Montana. Both groups drew members from the respectable elements of society, and portrayed themselves as alliances designed to protect honest men from the thieves and outlaws in their midst.[29]

For the most part, the Taney County Bald Knobbers conformed to Brown's basic model of vigilantism. Most of their leadership and rank-and-file members came from upper-class or middle-class backgrounds. They included in their ranks many lawyers, merchants, businessmen, and several political officeholders. Many of their victims, like the outlaws Frank and Tubal Taylor, or local ruffians like Andrew Coggburn, were just the sort of socially marginal people that Brown expected vigilantes to target. Although none of the Bald Knobbers would likely have articulated their goals in terms of preserving a social hierarchy or class structure, they clearly did have their own economic interests in mind. These included establishing an honest and thrifty local government and making the county safe for immigration, new businesses, and investment.

The Christian County Bald Knobbers shared their Taney County brethren's desire to create a strong social order through vigilante tactics, as well as a willingness to use those tactics to promote their own self-interests. In other respects, however, they diverged sharply from the pattern of vigilantism followed by their Taney County counterparts. Their members were overwhelmingly poor farmers of modest social standing and little connection to political power. So far from promoting new investment and immigration into southwest Missouri, many of their activities focused on limiting the power of large corporations over their lives and on limiting economic competition from outsiders. Thus, their contemporaries often accused them of retarding the socioeconomic progress of that area. In discussing the Bald Knobbers' anti-homesteader activities with a correspondent, U.S. commissioner McLain Jones wrote that the vigilantes did much harm to the region by "keeping back emigration, etc." For this reason, he recommended aggressive prosecutions of those who violated homesteader rights.[30]

The emphasis that the Christian County and Douglas County Bald Knobbers placed on moral regulation also set them apart from

the original vigilance committee in Taney County. Both groups wanted to use vigilantism to create a strong social order, but in the two
northern counties the vigilantes attempted to create a *moral* order
based on values derived from their religious convictions. In this
respect, the closest parallel to the Bald Knobber movement in these
two counties was the widespread "whitecap" movement that began in
Indiana and spread across the country in the 1880s and 1890s. The
phenomenon of whitecapping, so named because many of its prac-
titioners wore white hoods reminiscent of the Ku Klux Klan, varied
greatly from place to place. In its most prevalent form, however, it
was "a movement of violent moral regulation by local masked bands,"
aimed at punishing people who transgressed the moral standards of
their community.[31] Some notable examples of this kind of whitecapping include the first whitecap organization founded in southern
Indiana in the 1880s and similar groups created in eastern Tennessee
and Oklahoma's Indian territory around the same time.[32]

The distinctions made here between the two forms of Bald
Knobberism that existed in Taney County and Christian and Douglas
Counties are indicative of the multifaceted nature of vigilantism itself.
In some places, local elites used vigilante methods to advance their
own interests or to suppress people who opposed those interests. In
other places, nonelite actors used vigilantism to empower themselves
to pursue their interests against those of the elites or to rectify wrongs
they perceived in their society. In some cases, vigilantes used their
power to protect private property, prevent violent crime, and purge
their communities of criminal elements. In other cases, they focused
on enforcing morality and social mores in the face of social and economic trends that threatened their values. In each case, vigilantism
constituted an improvised solution to meet the needs of a particular
situation. In southwest Missouri in the 1880s, that solution was the
Bald Knobber movement, which became an enduring symbol of the
Ozark region from whence it sprang.

Beyond its implications for the study of vigilantism per se, the story of the Bald Knobbers also conveys a powerful moral message about
the enduring attraction that vigilante justice holds for Americans and
about the dangers of pursuing such a course. One of the basic assump-
tions of the American political creed is that all government derives

its authority from the people. Many times in our history, however, Americans have drawn from that assumption the faulty conclusion that the people may, whenever they deem it necessary, short circuit the legitimate institutions of self-government and law enforcement to carry out their will directly in their communities. Without denying that in some rare and extraordinary circumstances such methods might have been necessary, in most instances where Americans have fallen back on this expedient it has resulted in tragic consequences. The Bald Knobbers were no exception.

# Names of Bald Knobbers
# by County

## Taney County

1. Barger, Sam
2. Boothe, J. Columbus ("Lum")
3. Branson, Galba E.
4. Branson, Reuben S.
5. Brazeal, George W.
6. Brooks, John W.
7. Brown, John J.
8. Claflin, Elverton C.
9. Compton, Thomas F.
10. Connor, William G.
11. Cook, John Lafayette
12. Day, Madison
13. Delong, James A.
14. Dickenson, John T.
15. Everett, Barton Yell
16. Everett, Emmett R.
17. Fickle, Patterson F.
18. Groom, Charles H.
19. Haggard, John
20. Hensley, August C. ("Gus")
21. Hensley, William P.
22. Isaacs, Reuben
23. Johnson, James C.
24. Kinney, Nathaniel N. ("Nat")
25. Kissee, Alexander C.
26. Kissee, Arter
27. McConkey, D. F.
28. McGill, Joe
29. McHaffie, James K. Polk
30. Middleton, George Washington ("Wash")
31. Nagle, Louis
32. Parnell, James
33. Parrish, Joseph Calvin ("Cal")
34. Phillips, Thomas W.
35. Pollard, W. H.
36. Prather, Alonzo S.
37. Price, Benjamin B.
38. Price, T. W.
39. Rice, James B.
40. Stokely, Clayton
41. Vanzandt, "Jack"
42. Vanzandt, James R.

# Christian County

1. Abbott, Ed (or "Et")
2. Abbott, William
3. Adams, Andrew
4. Anderson, Hiram
5. Applegate, Gilbert
6. Applegate, Henry
7. Applegate, William
8. Bond, John William
9. Carr, James W.
10. Caudle, Newton
11. Caudle, William
12. Connor, N. B.
13. Dalton, Thomas A. ("Tandy")
14. Daugherty, Thomas Benton
15. Davis, Lewis
16. Davis, Peter
17. Elkins, Euclid
18. Forgey, Epsom
19. Fowler, Marion
20. Gann, James M. ("Bud")
21. Gardner, James M.
22. Garrison, Isaac
23. Gomann, Ike
24. Graves, Charles
25. Hale, Reuben L.
26. Harland, John
27. Hedgepeth, Cal
28. Hiles, Andrew Jackson ("Jack")
29. Hiles, John
30. Hobbs, Dowe
31. Humble, Martin T.
32. Humble, Michael M.
33. Hyde, Joseph
34. Inman, Joe
35. James, John
36. Johns, William
37. Johnson, James
38. Jones, Amos
39. Jones, Thomas K.
40. Kennedy, Ed
41. Kissee, Sylvanus
42. Linscott, Ed
43. Mapes, John
44. Mapes, William
45. Mathews, James
46. Mathews, John
47. Mathews, Thomas
48. Mathews, Wiley
49. McGinnis, Robert
50. McGuire, James R.
51. Meadows, John
52. Meyers, Newton
53. Morrisett, James
54. Nash, James M. ("Matt")
55. Nash, John
56. Nash, Thomas
57. Newton, Joseph
58. Newton, Samuel
59. Newton, William
60. Nix, Robert
61. Preston, George
62. Preston, James
63. Preston, Sam, Jr.
64. Preston, Sam, Sr.
65. Propst, Jacob
66. Ray, William J. ("Bud")
67. Roberts, Patterson
68. Roberts, William Jr.
69. Robertson, Jesse
70. Shelton, William H.
71. Shipman, John H.

72. Shipman, Reuben
73. Simmons, Pastor C. O.
74. Smith, William
75. St. John, Richard
76. Stanley, William
77. Stone, John E.
78. Stottle, Thomas Jefferson ("Jeff")
79. Todd, Walter
80. Vandeventer, Dr. Daniel
81. Walker, Charles Gatson ("Gat")
82. Walker, Dave
83. Walker, William
84. White, James T.
85. Wilson, John
86. Yeary, Fremont

## Douglas County

1. Casad, Joel
2. Denney, Calvin
3. Denney, Charles
4. Denney, Robert E.
5. Garrison, Jackson
6. Handcock, Benjamin ("Berry")
7. Johns, E. G.
8. Lakey, Simon
9. Lewis, William
10. Pruitt, Uriah
11. Sanders, George L.
12. Silvey, George W. ("Wash")
13. Silvey, Jackson, Jr.
14. Silvey, Jackson, Sr.
15. Silvey, William A.
16. Smith, William
17. Teal, Jonathan R.
18. Walker, Joseph
19. Wright, John
20. Wright, William F.

# Names of Anti-Bald Knobbers in Taney County

1. Barker, Rufus
2. Barker, Sampson
3. Berry, James S. B.
4. Buck, William
5. Burdette, Dr. K. L.
6. Coggburn, Robert
7. Dennison, Parson Henry
8. Everett, Henry C.
9. Haworth, John H.
10. Haworth, Rev. Jordan M.
11. Johnson, B. F.
12. Jones, William H.
13. Layton, Thomas A.
14. Lunceford, William H.
15. Miles, Jim
16. Miles, William H.
17. Miles, William M.
18. Moore, William E.
19. Moseley, John
20. Reynolds, John J.
21. Snapp, Lafayette
22. Snapp, Matt
23. Snapp, Robert
24. Snapp, Samuel H.
25. Spellings, T. C.
26. Stanley, Enos

# Notes

INTRODUCTION

1. Author's Interview with Lloyd Walker, Springfield, MO, January 2, 2009.

2. *Springfield Express*, January 4, 1889.

3. *Kansas City Star*, April 20, 1885.

4. *Springfield Daily Herald*, March 6, 1886; *New York Times*, March 5, 1885.

5. *Springfield Daily Herald*, May 13, 1886.

6. *Kansas City Star*, March 17, 1887; *St. Louis Post-Dispatch*, March 15, 1887.

7. *Springfield Express*, May 10, 1889; *Kansas City Star*, May 10, 1889.

8. Richard Maxwell Brown, *Strain of Violence: Historical Studies of American Violence and Vigilantism* (Oxford: Oxford University Press, 1975), 108, 313; Mary Hartman and Elmo Ingenthron, *Bald Knobbers: Vigilantes on the Ozarks Frontier* (Gretna, LA: Pelican Publishing Company, 1989), 8–9.

9. The Bald Knobbers in Taney and Christian Counties killed six victims, including Frank and Tubal Taylor, who were lynched, and Andrew Coggburn, Samuel Snapp, William Edens, and Charles Greene, who died of gunshot wounds. Additionally, three Bald Knobbers, George Washington Middleton, Nathaniel N. Kinney, and Galba Branson, died in gunfights, while three more, Dave Walker, William Walker, and John Mathews, died by hanging. Finally, a private detective named Ed Funk, who was not a vigilante, died in a gunfight in 1889 in which he apparently sided with the Bald Knobber Galba Branson against the Anti-Bald Knobbers William and James Miles.

10. Wayne Gard, *Frontier Justice* (Norman: University of Oklahoma Press, 1949), 152–67; Alan Valentine, *Vigilante Justice* (New York: Reynal & Company, 1956).

11. Richard Maxwell Brown, *The South Carolina Regulators* (Cambridge, MA: Harvard University Press, 1963); Marjoleine Kars, *Breaking Loose Together: The Regulator Rebellion in Pre-Revolutionary North Carolina* (Chapel Hill: University of North Carolina Press, 2002); Roger Ekirch, *Poor Carolina: Politics and Society in Colonial North Carolina* (Chapel Hill: University of North Carolina Press, 1981). Brown identifies the South Carolina Regulators as the first-ever vigilante organization, but pride of place is somewhat difficult to determine. The South Carolina Regulators formally organized sometime in October 1767 (Brown, 39), while Roger Ekirch points to the founding of the Sandy Creek Association of Orange County,

North Carolina, in August 1766, as the beginning of the North Carolina Regulators (Ekirch, 164–65). The simple solution is to call them contemporaneous.

12. John G. Cawelti, *Mystery, Violence, and Popular Culture* (Madison: University of Wisconsin Press, 2004), 163–65.

13. Brown, *Strain of Violence,* 22, 95–96. See also James E. Cutler, *Lynch-Law: An Investigation into the History of Lynching in the United States* (New York: Longmans, Green, and Company, 1905), 1. Cutler, for example, described lynching as "our national crime," one that was "peculiar to the United States."

14. Patrick Bates Nolan, "Vigilantes on the Middle Border: A Study of Self-Appointed Law Enforcement in the States of the Upper Mississippi from 1840 to 1880" (PhD Dissertation, University of Minnesota, 1971), 1; Arnold Madison, *Vigilantism in America* (New York: Seabury Press, 1973), 13; Richard Hofstadter and Michael Wallace, eds., *American Violence: A Documentary History* (New York: Alfred A. Knopf, 1970), 20. For example, Hofstadter and Wallace argue that "lynching and vigilantism … can be regarded as distinctively American institutions."

15. William C. Culberson, *Vigilantism: Political History of Private Power in America* (Westport, CT: Praeger Publishers, 1990), 1–43. Quote found on page 42.

16. Brown, *Strain of Violence,* 98–118.

17. Brown, *South Carolina Regulators,* 1–11, 45–52, 113–26.

18. Brown, *Strain of Violence,* 98–102; see also Brown, *South Carolina Regulators,* 135–42.

19. John W. Caughey, *Their Majesties the Mob: The Vigilante Impulse in America* (Chicago, IL: University of Chicago Press, 1960), 27–45; W. Eugene Hollon, *Frontier Violence: Another Look* (New York: Oxford University Press, 1974), 56–57, 63–67; Hubert Howe Bancroft, *Popular Tribunals,* vol. 1 (San Francisco: History Company, Publishers, 1887), 142–57.

20. George R. Steward, *Committee of Vigilance: Revolution in San Francisco* (Boston, MA: Houghton Mifflin, 1964); Alan C. Valentine, *Vigilante Justice* (New York: Reynal and Company, 1956); Barton Clark Olsen, "Lawlessness and Vigilantes in America: An Historical Analysis Emphasizing California and Montana" (PhD Dissertation, University of Utah, 1968).

21. Brown, *Strain of Violence,* 102, 108.

22. Lew L. Callaway, *Montana's Righteous Hangmen: The Vigilantes in Action* (Norman: University of Oklahoma Press, 1982); Frederick Allen, *A Decent and Orderly Lynching: The Montana Vigilantes* (Norman: University of Oklahoma Press, 2004).

23. Edward L. Ayres, *Vengeance and Justice: Crime and Punishment in the 19th-Century American South* (New York: Oxford University Press, 1984), 155–65; David M. Chalmers, *Hooded Americanism: The History of the Ku Klux Klan* (Durham, NC: Duke University Press, 1987), 8–21.

24. Eric Foner, *A Short History of Reconstruction, 1863–1877* (New York: Harper & Row, 1990), 184–91.

25. Ayers, *Vengeance and Justice,* 163–64; Heather Cox Richardson, *West from Appomattox: The Reconstruction of America after the Civil War* (New Haven, CT: Yale University Press, 2007), 90–91.

26. Richard Maxwell Brown, *No Duty to Retreat: Violence and Values in American History and Society* (New York: Oxford University Press, 1991), 44, 90–92.

27. Helena Huntington Smith, *The War on the Powder River: The History of an Insurrection* (Lincoln: University of Nebraska Press, 1967).

28. Wayne Gard, *Frontier Justice* (Norman: University of Oklahoma Press, 1949), 104–19.

29. Brown, *Strain of Violence*, 270–72.

30. Brown, *No Duty to Retreat*, 93–110.

31. Michael Walzer, "Puritanism as a Revolutionary Ideology," in *Studies in Social Movements: A Social Psychological Perspective*, ed. Barry McLaughlin (New York: Free Press, 1969), 118–54. The quotation comes from page 149.

32. Kars, *Breaking Loose Together*, 5–6, 215; Ekirch, *Poor Carolina*, 78–85, 182–92, 216–20. Taking a different approach than Kars, Ekirch attributes the Regulator violence to North Carolina's prolonged political instability during the colonial period owing to poor economic performance, corruption in colonial government, and a lack of qualified local elites to hold public office.

33. Brown, *Strain of Violence*, 24.

34. William F. Holmes, "Whitecapping: Agrarian Violence in Mississippi, 1902–06," *Journal of Southern History* 35, no. 2 (May 1969): 165–85; Pete Daniel, *Standing at the Crossroads: Southern Life since 1900* (New York: Hill and Wang, 1986), 54–55.

35. Andrew Bancroft Schlesinger, "Las Gorras Blancas, 1889–1891," *Journal of Mexican American History* 1, no. 2 (Spring 1971): 87–129; Robert J. Rosenbaum, *Mexicano Resistance in the Southwest: "The Sacred Right of Self-Preservation"* (Austin: University of Texas Press, 1981).

36. Brown, *Strain of Violence*, 150.

37. E. W. Crozier, *The White-Caps: A History of the Organization in Sevier County* (Knoxville, TN: Bean, Warters & Gaut, Printers and Binders, 1899), 180–88. In 1893 one of their female victims, Mrs. Mary Breeden, died of wounds sustained from a whitecap whipping. Thereafter the enemies of the whitecaps formed a rival organization called the "Blue-bills" to combat them, resulting in multiple skirmishes between the groups.

38. Robert E. Cunningham, *Trial by Mob* (Stillwater, OK: Redland Press, 1957), 10–12.

39. Madeleine M. Noble, "The White Caps of Harrison and Crawford County, IN: A Study in the Violent Enforcement of Morality" (PhD Dissertation, University of Michigan, 1973), 10.

40. Ibid., 102–3.

41. *Taney County News*, October 13, 1887; J. J. Bruton et al., *The Bald Knob Tragedy of Taney and Christian Counties* (Sparta, MO: The Authors, 1887).

42. Frank Luther Mott, *Golden Multitudes: The Story of Best Sellers in the United States* (New York: Macmillan, 1947), 225–33; See also Harold Bell Wright's obituary in the *New York Times*, May 24, 1944.

43. Harold Bell Wright, *The Shepherd of the Hills* (New York: A. L. Burt Company, 1907). Wright's Shepherd proved so popular that in the years following several film adaptations of it appeared, including a motion picture in 1941 starring John Wayne. See Randy Roberts and James S. Olson, *John Wayne: American* (New York: Free Press, 1995), 195–96.

44. Clyde Edwin Tuck, *The Bald Knobbers: A Romantic and Historical Novel*

(Indianapolis, IN: B. F. Bowen & Company, 1910); Anna M. Doling, *Brilla* (New York: Neal Publishing Company, 1913); Laura Johnson, *The Home-Coming in the Ozarks* (Chicago, IL: Glad Tidings Publishing, 1922); Vonda Wilson Sheets, *Absolution: A Bald Knobber Saga* (Kirbyville, MO: The Author, 2012).

45. Lynn Morrow and Linda Myers-Phinney, *Shepherd of the Hills Country: Tourism Transforms the Ozarks, 1880's–1930's* (Fayetteville: University of Arkansas Press, 1999), 25–36.

46. Aaron K. Ketchell, *Holy Hills of the Ozarks: Religion and Tourism in Branson, Missouri* (Baltimore, MD: Johns Hopkins University Press, 2007), 88–90.

47. A. M. Haswell, "The Story of the Bald Knobbers," *Missouri Historical Review* 18 (October 23, 1923): 28. In the 1880s, Haswell was a lead and zinc mine operator in Christian County where he came in contact with a number of people who belonged to the Bald Knobbers, including many of his employees.

48. William L. Vandeventer, *Justice in the Rough* (Springfield, MO: The Author, 1937).

49. John Ketchum, "Bald Knobbers," *Stone County News-Oracle*, September 6 to October 4, 1963: Reprint of an exposé originally published in the *New York Sun* in 1888; Robert L. Harper, *Among the Bald Knobbers: A History of the Desperadoes of the Ozark Mountains, Their Atrocious Deeds, Rendezvous, Homes and Habits, Their Arrest, and Conviction* (Clinton, MO: The Author, 1888). The book *Among the Bald Knobbers* was originally published under the pseudonym "Bob Sedgwick."

50. A. M. Haswell, "The Story of the Bald Knobbers," *MHR* 18 (October 23, 1923): 28.

51. Vandeventer, *Justice in the Rough*, 97.

52. Lucille Morris Upton, *Bald Knobbers* (Caldwell, ID: Caxton Printers, 1939), 15–20.

53. Vance Randolph, *The Bald Knobbers: The Story of the Lawless Night-Riders Who Ruled Southern Missouri in the 80's* (Girard, KS: Haldeman-Julius Publications, 1944).

54. Mary Hartman and Elmo Ingenthron, *The Bald Knobbers: Vigilantes of the Ozarks Frontier* (Gretna, LA: Pelican Publishing Company, 1989), ix.

55. Ibid., 12–16; Upton, *Bald Knobbers*, 25–31.

56. David Thelen, *Paths of Resistance: Tradition and Dignity in Industrializing Missouri* (New York: Oxford University Press, 1986), 92.

57. Kristen Kalen and Lynn Morrow, "Baldknobbers Sought to Bring Their Kind of Capitalism, Order to Ozarks Counties in the 1880's," *Springfield News-Leader*, December 19, 1989; Lynn Morrow, "Where Did All the Money Go?: War and the Economics of Vigilantism in Southern Missouri," *White River Valley Historical Quarterly* 34, no. 2 (Fall 1994): 2–15; Kristen Kalen and Lynn Morrow, "Nat Kinney's Sunday School Crowd," *White River Valley Historical Quarterly* 33, no. 1 (Fall 1993): 6–13.

58. Lawrence O. Christensen and Gary R. Kremer, *A History of Missouri: 1875–1919* (Columbia: University of Missouri Press, 2004), 23–24.

59. Thomas M. Spencer, "The Bald Knobbers, the Anti-Bald Knobbers, Politics, and the Culture of Violence in the Ozarks, 1860–1890," in *The Other Missouri History: Populists, Prostitutes, and Regular Folk*, ed. Thomas M. Spencer (Colombia: University of Missouri Press, 2004), 32.

60. Michael Fellman, *Inside War: The Guerrilla Conflict in Missouri during the American Civil War* (New York: Oxford University Press, 1989), 231–40; Jonathan Fairbanks and Clyde Edwin Tuck, *Past and Present of Greene County Missouri: Early and Recent History and Genealogical Records of Many of the Representative Citizens* (Indianapolis, IN: A. W. Bowen, 1915), 223–28; Return I. Holcombe, *History of Vernon County, Missouri: Written and Compiled from the Most Authentic Official and Private Sources, Including a History of its Townships, Towns and Villages* (St. Louis, MO: Brown & Company, 1887), 349–50; Minnie M. Brashear, "The Anti-Horse Thief Association of Northeast Missouri," *MHR* 45, no. 4 (July 1951): 346–47.

## CHAPTER 1

1. Milton D. Rafferty, *The Ozarks: Land and Life* (Fayetteville: University of Arkansas Press, 2001), 1–10. The quote is found on page 1.

2. Ibid., 15–17.

3. William E. Foley, *The Genesis of Missouri: From Wilderness Outpost to Statehood* (Columbia: University of Missouri Press, 1989), 4–5.

4. Foley, *The Genesis of Missouri*, 16–17, 24–25; Carl Ekberg, *Colonial St. Genevieve: An Adventure on the Mississippi Frontier* (Gerald, MO: Patrice Press, 1985), 2–25; Return I. Holcombe, *History of Greene County, MO* (St. Louis, MO: Western Historical Company, 1883), 125–26.

5. Holcombe, *History of Greene County, MO*, 125; Willard H. Rollings, *The Osage: An Ethnohistorical Study of Hegemony on the Prairie-Plains* (Columbia: University of Missouri Press, 1992), 5–12; Elmo Ingenthron, *Indians of the Ozark Plateau* (Point Lookout, MO: School of the Ozarks Press, 1970), 59.

6. Ingenthron, Indians, 59–60; Louis F. Burns, "Osage," *Encyclopedia of Oklahoma History and Culture*, http://digital.library.okstate.edu/encyclopedia/entries/O/OS001.html (accessed August 30, 2009).

7. Ingenthron, *Indians*, 60–61. The great nineteenth-century explorer, geographer, and folklorist Henry Rowe Schoolcraft observed three camps left by Osage hunting parties in the vicinity of Swan Creek in present-day Taney County during his visit to the region in 1818–19. Although the camps were deserted, Schoolcraft could identify them as Osage because their "method of building camps, and the order of encampment ... are different from anything of the kind I have noticed among the various tribes of aboriginal Americans." See Henry Rowe Schoolcraft, *Schoolcraft in the Ozarks: Reprint of a Journal of a tour into the Interior of Missouri and Arkansas in 1818 and 1819* (Van Buren, AR: Press-Argus, 1955), 107–9; Burns, "Osage," *Encyclopedia of Oklahoma History and Culture.*

8. Silas C. Turnbo, *The White River Chronicles of S. C. Turnbo: Man and Wildlife on the Ozarks Frontier*, ed. James F. Keefe and Lynn Morrow (Fayetteville: University of Arkansas Press, 1994), 15–19. Turnbo calls the Cokers one of the "first families" of the Ozarks. They were also one of the first families of Taney County and left their mark on the geography of that county. For example, Poor Joe Bald, a prominent hill in Taney County, took its name from William Coker's son, Joe Coker, and Katie's Prairie is named after William Coker's daughter Katie.

9. Early settlers did report seeing small herds of buffalo numbering sixty or more,

and they hunted them whenever they had the chance. See Turnbo, *The White River Chronicles*, 77–79. However, despite Pettijohn's optimistic assessment, buffalo were not especially numerous in the Ozarks, although the American black bear (*ursus americanus*) was far more common. See Charles and Elizabeth Swartz, *The Wild Mammals of Missouri* (Columbia: University of Missouri Press, 1981), 280, 350.

10. Holcombe, *History of Greene County, MO*, 126–27; Jonathan Fairbanks and Clyde Edwin Tuck, *Past and Present of Greene County, Missouri: Early and Recent History and Genealogical Records of Many of the Representative Citizens* (Indianapolis, IN: A. W. Bowen & Company, 1915), 129–30.

11. Holcombe, *History of Greene County, MO*, 131–35; Fairbanks and Tuck, *Past and Present of Greene County*, 131–32; Lynn Morrow, "Trader William Gillis and Delaware Migration in Southern Missouri," *Missouri Historical Review* 75 (January 1981): 152–60. James Wilson arrived with the Delaware Indians in 1822 and built a farm in present-day Christian County near the mouth of what became known as Wilson's Creek (where the famous Civil War battle occurred). During his time among the Delaware, Wilson married three different Indian women in succession before finally marrying his fourth wife, a French woman from St. Louis, who survived him. Likewise, trader William Gillis married at least two Indian women during his stay among the Delaware, and had at least one child, a daughter named Nancy.

12. Holcombe, *History of Greene County, MO*, 134-35; Fairbanks and Tuck, *Past and Present of Greene County*, 132.

13. Viola Hartman, "The Layton Story: Part II," *White River Valley Historical Quarterly* 7, no. 3 (Spring 1980): 3–6. Hereafter, the title of this journal shall be abbreviated *WRVHQ*.

14. The land office at Springfield, Missouri, issued Harrison Snapp his first four land patents on January 1, 1849. The patent numbers were 9143, 9144, 9145, 9208. His next two patents came on April 2, 1849, and July 1, 1852. Their numbers were 9122 and 10824. All land patents cited in this dissertation were obtained using the U.S. General Land Office Records database at Ancestry.com.

15. Ruth Gulls Ryser, "The Snapp Family," *WRVHQ* 4, no. 3 (Spring 1971): 2–3.

16. Janice Looney, "Andrew Coggburn," *WRVHQ* 9, no. 6 (Winter 1987): 9. For a description of the gunfight ending in James Coggburn's death, see the Springfield, Missouri, *Patriot Advertiser*, May 1, 1879. The land office in Fayette, Missouri, issued James Coggburn his land patent, number 34,801, on January 15, 1856.

17. Rafferty, *The Ozarks*, 41–46, 55–57; Russel L. Gerlach, *Settlement Patterns in Missouri: A Study of Population Origins, with a Wall Map* (Columbia: University of Missouri Press, 1986), 20–24. For an analysis of Scotch-Irish settlement in the Ozarks, see Russel L. Gerlach, "The Ozark Scotch-Irish," in *Cultural Geography of Missouri*, ed. Michael Roark (Cape Girardeau: Department of Earth Sciences, Southeast Missouri State University, 1983), 11–29.

18. U.S. Census Office, *The Statistics of the Population of the United States: embracing ... the original returns of the ninth census, (June 1, 1870,) under the direction of the Secretary of the Interior* (Washington, DC: Government Printing Office, 1872), 361–63.

19. U.S. Census Office, *Manufactures of the United States in 1860: compiled ... under the direction of the Secretary of the Interior* (Washington, DC: Government Printing Office, 1865), 315–16.

20. U.S. Census Office, *Agriculture of the United States in 1860: Compiled ... under the Direction of the Secretary of the Interior* (Washington, DC: Government Printing Office, 1864), 88–95. In 1860, the farmers in these counties grew 679,000 bushels of corn, 78,000 bushels of wheat, 34,000 bushels of oats, 13,600 bushels of Irish potatoes, and 6,300 bushels of sweet potatoes. The stock raisers in these counties raised herds of roughly 4,900 dairy cows, 7,500 beef cattle, 10,000 sheep, 4,000 oxen, and so on.

21. Ibid.

22. Silas C. Turnbo, *White River Chronicles*, 77–79; Turnbo, "Bruin Wallows a Hunter in Clay," in *The Turnbo Manuscripts*, Vol. 6, Springfield-Greene County Library, http://thelibrary.org/lochist/turnbo/v6/st173.html (accessed June 20, 2013); Turnbo, "An Interesting Time Among Game and Finding Bee Trees During the Pioneer Days of Ozark County, Missouri," in *Turnbo Manuscripts*, Vol. 14, Springfield-Greene County Library, http://thelibrary.org/lochist/turnbo/v14/st438.html (accessed June 20, 2013).

23. Hugh Crumpler, "Fishing the Wild Streams of the Ozarks," *Ozarks Watch* 4, no. 3 (Winter 1991): 3–6; James E. Price, "Bowin' and Spikin' in the Jillikins," *Ozarks Watch* 4, no. 3 (Winter 1991): 12–15; Elmo Ingenthron, *The Land of Taney: A History of an Ozark Commonwealth* (Branson, MO: Ozarks Mountaineer, 1983), 297–300.

24. Missouri House of Representatives, *Journal of the House of Representatives of the State of Missouri, at the Adjourned Session, Twentieth General Assembly* (Jefferson City, MO: W. G. Cheeney, Public Printer, 1860), 428–31.

25. U.S. Census Office, *Population of the United States in 1860: Compiled ... under the Direction of the Secretary of the Interior* (Washington, DC: Government Printing Office, 1864), 281–83. The counties included in these statistics are Jasper, Newton, McDonald, Dade, Lawrence, Barry, Greene, Christian, Stone, Webster, Douglas, and Taney.

26. U.S. Census Office, *Agriculture of the United States in 1860*, 89–91, 93–95. Hemp was the predominant "slave crop" in antebellum Missouri. According to R. Douglas Hurt, in 1850 the three largest hemp-producing counties were also "the counties with the largest slave populations," and without slaves, large-scale hemp production "would not have been economically viable." See R. Douglas Hurt, *Agriculture and Slavery in Missouri's Little Dixie* (Columbia: University of Missouri Press, 1992), 123. See also "The Lost Missouri Hemp Industry," *Missouri Historical Review* 37, no. 1 (October 1942): 57–65. Hereafter, the title of this periodical shall be abbreviated *MHR*.

27. U.S. War Department, *The War of the Rebellion: A Compilation of the Official Records of the Union and Confederate Armies*, Ser. 1, Vol. 22, Part 2, 604–5. Hereafter, the title of this series shall be abbreviated *O.R.*

28. Holcombe, *History of Greene County, Missouri*, 277.

29. The state convention, which met in March 1861, was not a typical secession convention in that it was not empowered to pass ordinances of secession, but only to make recommendations. If they had recommended secession, the voters would have had to approve that action in a statewide referendum. See Duane G. Meyer, *The Heritage of Missouri*, 3rd ed. (Springfield, MO: Emden Press, 1982), 350–51.

30. William E. Parrish, *A History of Missouri, Vol. III, 1860–1875* (Columbia: University of Missouri Press, 1973), 2; Meyer, *Heritage of Missouri*, 343–44. For

a more comprehensive discussion of the internal divisions within the Missouri Democratic Party in 1860, see J. F. Snyder, "The Democratic State Convention of Missouri in 1860," *MHR* 2, no. 2 (January 1908): 112–30.

31. Holcombe, *History of Greene County, Missouri, 269–70; Parrish, History of Missouri*, 2. For the descriptions of Orr, and the 1860 gubernatorial race in general, see B. B. Lightfoot, "Nobody's Nominee: Sample Orr and the Election of 1860," *MHR* 60, no. 2 (January 1966): 127–48. The quotes appear on pages 136 and 138.

32. 1860 Election Returns for Greene, Christian, Lawrence, Ozark, Taney, and Stone Counties, Missouri State Archives, Record Group 5, Box 8, Folders 4–6, 8–10. Hereafter, "Missouri State Archives" shall be abbreviated MSA.

33. Parrish, *History of Missouri*, 3; Lightfoot, "Nobody's Nominee," 147.

34. Goodspeed, *History of Southeast Missouri: Embracing and Historical Account of the Counties of St. Genevieve, St. Francois, Perry, Cape Girardeau, Bollinger, Madison, New Madrid, Pemiscot, Dunklin, Scott, Mississippi, Stoddard, Butler, Wayne, and Iron* (Chicago: Goodspeed Publishing Company, 1888), 165–67. It appears that the 1860 presidential election returns for Douglas County were not preserved.

35. Meyer, *Heritage of Missouri*, 350; Parish, *History of Missouri*, 6.

36. Holcombe, *History of Greene County, Missouri*, 276.

37. Jay Monaghan, *Civil War on the Western Border, 1854–1865* (Boston: Little, Brown and Company, 151–58.

38. Monaghan, *Civil War*, 170–81; For the most comprehensive history of the Battle of Wilson's Creek, see William Garrett Piston, *Wilson's Creek: The Second Battle of the Civil War and the Men Who Fought It* (Chapel Hill: University of North Carolina Press, 2000). For a list of casualties suffered on both sides, see Edwin C. Bearss, *The Battle of Wilson's Creek*, 4th ed. (Cassville, MO: Wilson's Creek National Battlefield Foundation, 1992), 161–64.

39. Paul Robinett, "Marmaduke's Expedition into Missouri: The Battle's of Springfield and Hartville, January, 1863," *MHR* 58, no. 2 (January 1964): 151–73; O.R., Series 1, Vol. 22, Part 1, 179–87. For a comprehensive analysis of this campaign, see Frederick W. Goman, *Up From Arkansas: Marmaduke's First Missouri Raid Including the Battles of Springfield and Hartville* (Springfield, MO: Wilson's Creek National Battlefield Foundation, 1999).

40. Examples: Michael Fellman, *Inside War: The Guerrilla Conflict in Missouri during the Civil War* (Oxford: Oxford University Press, 1989); Richard S. Brownlee, *Gray Ghosts of the Confederacy: Guerrilla Warfare in the West, 1861–65* (Baton Rouge: Louisiana State University Press, 1984); Bruce Nichols, *Guerrilla Warfare in Civil War Missouri*, 2 Vols. (Jefferson, NC: McFarland & Company, 2004–7); Daniel E. Sutherland, *A Savage Conflict: The Decisive Role of Guerrillas in the American Civil War* (Chapel Hill: University of North Carolina Press, 2009).

41. William E. Parrish et al., *Missouri: The Heart of the Nation* (St. Louis, MO: Forum Press, 1980), 181–82.

42. Thomas M. Spencer, "The Bald Knobbers, the Anti-Bald Knobbers, Politics, and the Culture of Violence in the Ozarks, 1860–1890," in *The Other Missouri History: Populists, Prostitutes, and Regular Folk* (Colombia: University of Missouri Press, 2004), 37–38. Spencer's essay says that there were nine Union veterans among the Taney County Bald Knobbers, but does not name them. My own research also shows that

eleven Bald Knobbers fought for the Union during the Civil War. Their names are Samuel Barger, Galba E. Branson, John J. Brown, John Lafayette Cook, Madison Day, August C. Hensley, Nathaniel N. Kinney, Alexander C. Kissee, George W. Middleton, W. H. Pollard, Alonzo Prather, and James R. VanZandt. These individuals were identified using Alexander Street Press, LLC, "The American Civil War Research Database," http://asp6new.alexanderstreet.com.libezp.lib.lsu.edu/cwdb/, and Ancestry.com, "Civil War Collection," http://www.ancestry.com/search/rectype/grouplist.aspx?group=CivilWar.

43. For example, Sam H. Snapp, the Anti-Bald Knobber who died at the hands of George W. Middleton, had three older brothers—David, LaFayette, and Andrew—who fought for the Confederacy. See Ruth Gulls Ryser, "The Snapp Family," *WRVHQ* 4, no. 3 (Spring 1971): 2. Similarly, James A. DeLong's stepfather (Nathaniel Kinney) and father-in-law (Alonzo Prather) were both Union veterans.

44. Nola A. James, "The Civil War Years in Independence County," *Arkansas Historical Quarterly* 28, no. 3 (Autumn 1969): 245–49.

45. Elmo Ingenthron, *Borderland Rebellion: A History of the Civil War on the Missouri-Arkansas Border* (Branson, MO: Ozarks Mountaineer, 1980), 196–98, 285. See also Dennis K. Boman, *Lincoln's Resolute Unionist: Hamilton Gamble, Dred Scott Dissenter and Missouri's Civil War Governor* (Baton Rouge: Louisiana State University Press, 2006), 175–76, 201–3. Missouri's pro-Union militia structure went through several incarnations during the Civil War. In January 1862, Missouri's loyalist state government created the Missouri State Militia (M.S.M.), a replacement for the older, chaotic, and disorganized Six Months' Militia units. In July 1862, Brig. Gen. John M. Schofield organized the Enrolled Missouri Militia (E.M.M.), an expanded version of the M.S.M. that could call up any able-bodied man of military age to bear arms in service to the Union. Finally, in February 1863 Gov. Hamilton Gamble organized the Provisional Enrolled Missouri Militia, a smaller, elite contingent of the E.M.M. that took over much of the day-to-day responsibility for guerrilla fighting.

46. Parrish et al., *Missouri*, 178.

47. "William Reed," *United States Provost Marshal Papers*, MSA, Reel No. F 1205.

48. U.S. Census Office, *Agriculture of the United States in 1860*, 92; Missouri General Assembly, *Second Annual Report of the Commissioner of Statistics to the General Assembly of the State of Missouri for the Year 1867* (Jefferson City, MO: Ellwood Kirby, Public Printer, 1868), 47.

49. *Nelson Burkhart vs. Samuel Miller, et al.*, in *Civil War Related Court Files*, located at the Greene County Archives and Records Center, Springfield, MO, folder 66CW. Hereafter, "Greene County Archives and Records Center" shall be abbreviated as "GCA."

50. "Mrs. L. A. Vance," *United States Provost Marshal Papers*, MSA, Reel No. F 1273.

51. Mark W. Geiger, "Indebtedness and the Origins of Guerrilla Violence in Civil War Missouri," *Journal of Southern History* 75, no. 1 (February 2009): 49–82. A map on page 52 of this article shows that the highest number of these foreclosures occurred, as we might expect, in Missouri's central-western counties near the Missouri-Kansas border. However, a significant number also occurred in the southwestern counties of Greene, Lawrence, and Dade.

52. "Thomas Barker," *United States Provost Marshal Papers*, MSA, Reel No. F 1183.

This file contains a copy of Barker's loyalty oath, which follows the basic format common to such documents. In this particular oath, Barker promises to remain within the confines of Taney County, where he lived, for the remainder of the war. His bond pledged up to $2,000 of his property as security for his loyalty.

53. Thomas F. Layton, *United States Provost Marshal Papers*, MSA, Reel No. F 1360. The fact that Thomas Layton claimed that he did not actually belong to the rebel army, despite fighting on their side at Pea Ridge, raises the possibility that he belonged to an independent company. Otherwise, it is hard to explain in what capacity he fought at Pea Ridge.

54. Ibid. In her statement, Mrs. Layton says that she "suspicioned [*sic*] that her husband was going to try to get her away, because he tried to hire her from me, and I would not let her go."

55. Viola Hartman, "The Layton Story, Part 2," *White River Valley Historical Quarterly* 7, no. 3 (Spring 1980): 2–3. Hereafter, this journal's title shall be abbreviated *WRVHQ*.

56. Fellman, *Inside War*, 51–52.

57. Ingenthron, *Borderland Rebellion*, 128–32, 293.

58. William Monks, *A History of Southern Missouri and Northern Arkansas: Being an Account of the Early Settlements, the Civil War, the Ku-Klux, and Times of Peace*, ed. John F. Bradbury Jr. and Lou Wehmer (Fayetteville: University of Arkansas Press, 2003), 105.

59. "Thomas Budd," *United States Provost Marshal Papers*, MSA, Reel No. F 1477.

60. "Madison Day," *United States Provost Marshal Papers*, MSA, Reel No. F 1226.

61. Elmo Ingenthron, "Guerrillas, Jayhawkers, and Bushwackers," *WRVHQ* 2, no. 4 (Summer 1965): 2.

62. William Neville Collier, "Ozark and Vicinity in the Nineteenth Century," *WRVHQ* 2, no. 10 (Winter 1966): 20. This article consists of an excerpt from William Neville Collier's 1946 manuscript of the same title. The manuscript was published as a series of articles in the *White River Valley Historical Quarterly*.

63. Ingenthron, *Borderland Rebellion*, 285–86.

64. Faun I. Hill, "William Jeptha Johnson," *WRVHQ* 1, no. 3 (Spring 1962): 8. Willis Kissee led a violent and dissipated life after the war. On January 21, 1884, he died in Gunnison, Colorado, in a gunfight with a gambler named John Kellogg, which stemmed from a dispute over a game of cards. During his time in Colorado Kissee had often faced charges for assault and for carrying weapons. See *Springfield Express*, January 25, 1884. For the family relationship between Alexander C. Kissee and Willis Kissee, see *Taney County News*, June 2, 1887.

65. Ingenthron, *Borderland Rebellion*, 287–89. Viola Hartman, "The Layton Story: Part 2," *WRVHQ* 7, no. 3 (Spring 1980): 4; "Madison Day," *United States Provost Marshal Papers*, MSA, Reel No. F 1226; Nichols, *Guerrilla Warfare*, Vol. 2, 17.

66. Collier, "Ozark and Vicinity," *WRVHQ* 2, no. 10 (Winter 1966): 20.

67. Holcombe, *History of Greene County, Missouri*, 476. For a summary of Burch's military exploits, see Howard V. Canan, "Milton Burch: Anti-Guerrilla Fighter," *Missouri Historical Review* 59, no. 2 (January 1965): 223–42. Hereafter, *Missouri Historical Review* shall be abbreviated as *MHR*.

68. Elmo Ingenthron, "The Civil War 1862: Skirmishes at Ozark and Snapp's

Farm," *WRVHQ* 1, no. 5 (Fall 1962): 10–13; Canan, "Milton Burch," *MHR* 59, no. 2 (January 1865): 226–28.

69. *O.R.*, Series 1, Vol. 12, Part 1, 38–39; *O.R.*, Series 1, Vol. 22, Part 1, 159; Lee Carson Davis, "Bean Cave: Marion County, Arkansas," *WRVHQ* 2, no. 11 (Spring 1967): 3–4.

70. Holcombe, *History of Greene County*, Missouri, 476–77; Collier, "Ozark and Vicinity," *WRVHQ* 2, no. 10 (Winter 1966): 20–22. For the quote on Kelso's attitude toward rebels, see Holcombe, page 477. For the quote about Kelso's unique method of bushwhacking, see Collier, page 21.

71. Collier, "Ozark and Vicinity," *WRVHQ* 2, no. 10 (Winter 1966): 21–22; Holcombe, *History of Greene County, Missouri*, 477–78; Nichols, *Guerrilla Warfare*, Vol. 2, 169–70.

72. Ingenthron, *Borderland Rebellion*, 292–94.

73. *O.R.* Series 1, Vol. 48, Part 1, 37, 578. See also Turnbo, "The Alph Cook Cave," *Turnbo Manuscripts*, Vol. 1, Springfield-Greene County Library, http://thelibrary. org/lochist/turnbo/V1/ST002.html (accessed September 11, 2009). The Turnbo account of this incident says that a fourth man, named "Alph Dean," also died at the cave.

74. U.S. Census Office, *Agriculture of the United States in 1860*, 88, 92; Missouri General Assembly, *Second Annual Report of the Commissioner of Statistics ... for the Year 1867*, 45.

75. Turnbo, "Depriving Children of the Last Morsel of Food," in *Turnbo Manuscripts*, Vol. 4, Springfield-Greene County Library, http://thelibrary.org/lochist/turnbo/v4/st105.html (accessed September 26, 2009).

76. Turnbo, "Hardships and Starvation in the Turbulent Days of War," in *Turnbo Manuscripts*, Vol. 23, Springfield-Greene County Library, http://thelibrary.org/lochist/turnbo/V23/ST684.html (accessed September 27, 2009).

77. Ingenthron, *Borderland Rebellion*, 303; Monks, *A History of Southern Missouri*, 141–42; Ingenthron, *Land of Taney*, 123–34.

78. Holcombe, *History of Greene County, Missouri*, 459, 480.

79. Harriet C. Frazier, *Lynchings in Missouri, 1803–1981* (Jefferson, NC: McFarland & Company, 2009), 191–97.

80. Meyer, *Heritage of Missouri*, 506–8.

81. Patrick Bates Nolan, "Vigilantes on the Middle Border: A Study of Self-Appointed Law Enforcement in the States of the Upper Mississippi from 1840 to 1880" (PhD Dissertation, University of Minnesota, 1971), 134–50; Minnie M. Brashear, "The Anti-Horse Thief Association of Northeast Missouri," *MHR* 45, no. 4 (July 1951): 346–47. Some historians, notably Richard Maxwell Brown, argue that "protective associations" like the Anti-Horse Thief Association (AHTA) do not count as vigilance committees because they only apprehended criminals and turned them over to the legal authorities, rather than punishing the criminals themselves. Nolan disagrees (p. 235). I tend to agree with Nolan, but here I use the AHTA as an example of citizens organizing to combat crime, so the question of definition is nonessential.

82. Holcombe, *History of Greene County, Missouri*, 497–501; Fairbanks and Tuck, *Past and Present of Greene County*, 223–26.

83. Return I. Holcombe, *History of Vernon County, Missouri: Written and Compiled from the Most Authentic Official and Private Sources, Including a History of its Townships, Towns and Villages* (St. Louis, MO: Brown & Company, 1887), 349–50.

84. Lynn Morrow, "George Caleb Bingham's Ride into the Ozarks: Confronting the Sons of Honor," *WRVHQ* 36, no. 1 (Summer 1996): 4–9.


## CHAPTER 2

1. Mary Hartman and Elmo Ingenthron, *The Bald Knobbers: Vigilantes of the Ozarks Frontier* (Gretna, LA: Pelican Publishing Company, 1989), 27. Vance Randolph, *The Bald Knobbers: The Story of the Lawless Night-Riders Who Ruled Southern Missouri in the 80's* (Girard, KS: Haldeman-Julius Publications, 1944), 8–9.

2. Milton D. Rafferty, *The Ozarks: Land and Life* (Fayetteville: University of Arkansas Press, 2001), 62.

3. U.S. Census Office, *The Statistics of the Population of the United States: embracing ... the original returns of the ninth census, (June 1, 1870,) under the direction of the Secretary of the Interior* (Washington, DC: Government Printing Office, 1872), 361–63. Since the census compendiums for the 1900 U.S. Census do not have nativity statistics, I compiled the figures for 1900 using Janice Soutee Looney's transcription of the Taney County census manuscripts for that year. See Janice Soutee Looney, *Taney County, Missouri: 1900 Federal Census* (Walnut Grove, MO: The Author, 1986).

4. Rafferty, *The Ozarks*, 62.

5. Barnett Parrish, 1870 U.S. Census, Taney County, Swan Township, p. 4; Sibyl Parrish, "Joseph Calvin Parrish," *WRVHQ* 1, no. 6 (Winter 1962): 15.

6. Parrish, "Joseph Calvin Parrish," 15.

7. Goodspeed Brothers, *A Reminiscent History of the Ozarks Region: Comprising a Condensed General History ... of Prominent citizens* (Chicago: Goodspeed Brothers, Publishers, 1894), 103–5. The 1880 census does not show Charles H. Groom living in Taney County, even though his Goodspeed biography says he should have been there at that time. In 1900 he appears in the Taney County census, living in Forsyth with his wife, Tremandria, and two of his children. See Charles Groom, 1900 U.S. Census, Taney County, Forsyth, District 132, p. 1.

8. Goodspeed Brothers, *Reminiscent History*, 349–53.

9. Ibid., 196, 350–53.

10. *A. C. Kissee vs. Rosa M. Kissee*, 1899, Missouri State Archives, *Taney County Circuit Court Files*, Reel No. C 37196, Box 14, Folder 66. Hereafter, "Missouri State Archives" shall be abbreviated as MSA.

11. Alexander Kissee, 1900 U.S. Census, Missouri, Taney County, Swan Township, District 132, p. 35. In this case, the surname is rendered as "Kinner," which is a corruption of Kissee. Sarah J. Kissee, 1910 U.S. Census, Missouri, Taney County, Swan Township, District 208, p. 7. The 1910 census lists Sarah Kissee as a widow, living with four children, and one stepson, Alfred C. Kissee, who was born to Alexander and Cordelia Kissee twenty-one years earlier. This establishes that Sarah Kissee was Alexander Kissee's widow.

12. Goodspeed Brothers, *Reminiscent History*, 195–96.

13. See John T. Dickenson, 1900 U.S. Census, Missouri, Taney County, Swan Township, District 132, p. 30.

14. Roy E. Stout, "The Eglinton Colony in Missouri, 1882," *WRVHQ* 2, no. 12 (Summer/Fall 1967): 1–3; Roger H. Grant, "Missouri's Utopian Communities," *MHR* 66, no. 1 (October 1971): 20–48.

15. Douglas Mahnkey, Alonzo Prather's grandson, says that the Prather family moved from Mulverd, Kansas, to Taney County in 1880. However, in 1880 the U.S. Census lists the Prather family as living in Springfield, Missouri, although it seems they did not stay there very long. See Alonzo S. Prather, *1880 U.S. Census, Greene County, Springfield, District 44*, p. 34.

16. Douglas Mahnkey, "The Mahnkey and Prather Families," *WRVHQ* 4, no. 2 (Winter 1970–71): 5.

17. Ibid., 5–6. For the information concerning Prather's political career, and his career as publisher of the *Home and Farm*, see Elmo Ingenthron, *The Land of Taney: A History of an Ozark Commonwealth* (Branson, MO: Ozarks Mountaineer, 1983), 334, 463. For information concerning Prather's activities in the GAR, see *Taney County News*, June 2, 1887. See also *Taney County News*, September 22, 1887, quoted in Ingenthron, *Land of Taney*, 409–11.

18. The Sixth West Virginia Infantry spent most of the war installations along the Baltimore and Ohio Railroad. As a result, it served in no major battles, but did engage in constant skirmishing with small parties of Confederate raiders. See Theodore F. Lang, *Loyal West Virginia from 1861 to 1865* (Baltimore, MD: Deutsch Publishing Company, 1895), 258–60.

19. Nathaniel Kinney served in Companies M and L of the Sixth West Virginia Infantry. He held the rank of private when enlisted and still held that rank at the end of his service. See National Park Service, "Civil War Soldiers and Sailors," http://www.itd.nps.gov/cwss/soldiers.cfm (accessed October 18, 2009); Kristen Kalen and Lynn Morrow, "Nat Kinney's Sunday School Crowd," *WRVHQ* 33, no. 1 (Fall 1993): 6.

20. Samuel Radges, *Radges Bienniel Directory to the Inhabitants, Institutions, Manufacturing Establishments, Business Firms, etc. of the City of Topeka, for 1876–77* (Topeka, KS: Commonwealth Job Printing Establishment, 1875), 88; Samuel Radges, *Radges Bienniel Directory to the Inhabitants, Institutions, Manufacturing Establishments, Business Firms, etc. of the City of Topeka, for 1878–79* (Topeka, KS: Commonwealth Job Printing Establishment, 1877), 103.

21. Ibid., 242–43.

22. Kalen and Morrow, "Kinney's Sunday School Crowd," 7–8; Randolph, *Bald Knobbers*, 6; Richard Prather, "'Cap' Kinney, Bald Knobber Chief'" (Typed Manuscript, n.d.), 1, from the Lynn Morrow Collection. Prather's essay on Nat Kinney was later published in the *Taney County Republican* as a series of articles from June 6 to June 27, 1957. Concerning Kinney's size, Prather, who as a young boy knew Kinney personally, says he was six feet, six inches tall. Kalen and Morrow put the likely range at between six feet, two inches and six feet, five inches, with emphasis on the lower figure. Vance Randolph says he measured six feet and seven inches. Estimates of his weight also vary widely. However, all the sources agree that

by the standards of the day Kinney was a massive specimen, powerfully built, with a personality to match his physique.

23. N. N. Kinney, *1880 U.S. Census, Kansas, Shawnee County, Auburn Township, District 12*, p. 15. Kinney's stepson is not mentioned in this census record, but he definitely came to Taney County later.

24. A list of homicides printed in the *Springfield Express* on October 28, 1887, listed two murders that occurred in Kinney's saloon in 1883 and 1884.

25. Kalen and Morrow, "Kinney's Sunday School Crowd," 8-9. The description of Kinney's income and farming activities comes from his deposition in his lawsuit against the City of Springfield. See *Nat N. Kinney vs. City of Springfield*. Circuit Court of Greene CO, docket # 5902. Greene County Archives. Folder: "Nat Kinney / Bald Knobbers." Hereafter, Greene County Archives will be abbreviated as GCA.

26. William E. Parrish, *A History of Missouri, Vol. 3: 1860 to 1875* (Columbia: University of Missouri Press, 2001), 198-200.

27. *Springfield Missouri Weekly Patriot*, May 5, 1870.

28. Wilson Nicely, *The Great Southwest, or Plain Guide for Emigrants and Capitalists Embracing a Description of the States of Missouri and Kansas ... with Incidents of Two Years Travel and Residence in Missouri and Kansas and other Valuable Information* (St. Louis, MO: R. P. Studley and Company, 1867), 15-21.

29. Parrish, *History of Missouri*, 200.

30. Nicely, *Great Southwest*, 26. Not surprisingly, the narrow corridor of counties along the Arkansas border, which had suffered the worst tribulations during the war, also had the largest number of acres in public land. In addition to Taney County, these included the counties of McDonald (200,000 acres), Barry (300,000 acres), Stone (200,000 acres), and Ozark (300,000 acres).

31. The Bald Knobbers who had homesteads in Taney County included the following persons (the dates and patent numbers are in parentheses): Benjamin Price (1900, 33,995), James R. Vanzandt (1898, 11,141), Thomas W. Phillips (1886, 32,234), Barton Y. Everett (1890, 6,388), James Columbus Boothe (1901, 11,301), Galba Branson (1890, 9,197), Reuben S. Branson (1891, 7,242), Charles H. Groom (1905, 34,928), John M. Haggard (1888, 5,301), William P. Hensley (1881, 4,162), Reuben Isaacs (1881, 4,166), Alexander C. Kissee (1884, 31,823; 1888, 32,693; 1890, 32,864), Arter Kissee (1892, 8,658), James K. Polk McHaffie (1871, 30,515; 1882, 31,375; 1888, 32,699; 1892, 33,245), John T. Dickenson (1895, 10,267), D. F. McConkey (1901, 34,470), James B. Rice (1873, 956; 1881, 31,357), Louis Nagle (1892, 9,717), and Clayton Stokely (1886, 32,174).

32. Mabel West, "Jacksonport, Arkansas: Its Rise and Decline," *Arkansas Historical Quarterly* 9, no. 4 (Winter 1950): 235-36; Elmo Ingenthron, *The Land of Taney: A History of an Ozarks Commonwealth* (Branson, MO: Ozarks Mountaineer, 1883), 55-60; Don A. Sullenberger, "Forsyth Steamboat Landing," *WRVHQ* 8, no. 12 (Summer 1985): 12-16.

33. Return I. Holcombe, *History of Greene County, Missouri* (St. Louis, MO: Western Historical Company, 1883), 222-23.

34. *Taney County Republican*, April 26, 1956, quoted in Elmo Ingenthron, *Land of Taney*, 58. As an example of the dangers involved in commerce on the White River, in December 1870 the keelboat *J. F. Allen* sank with its cargo of 80 bales of cotton,

and that same month the steamboat *Batesville* sank with a cargo of 475 bales of cotton. See West, "Jacksonport, Arkansas," *AHQ* 9, no. 4 (Winter 1950): 237.

35. In 1860, the Census Office reported that Christian, Douglas, and Taney Counties ginned no cotton that year. See U.S. Census Office, *Agriculture of the United States in 1860*, 89, 93.

36. U.S. Census Office, *Report on the Productions of Agriculture as Returned at the Tenth Census* (reprint; New York: Norman Ross Publishing, 1991), 232–33.

37. *Taney County Times*, November 24, 1887. This figure is probably an exaggeration, given that Taney County would have had to produce far more cotton than reported in either the tenth or eleventh census to reach that total. Nevertheless, the *Taney County Times*'s report underscores the growing significance of cotton to the local economy.

38. U.S. Census Office, *Report on the Statistics of Agriculture in the United States at the Eleventh Census, 1890* (Washington, DC: Government Printing Office, 1895), 395.

39. Ibid.

40. Ingenthron, *Land of Taney*, 319–21. Ingenthron gives William Connor's name as "W. G. Conner." However, I can find no entry in the census records matching that name. The closest match is William Connor, who lived in Taney County in 1880. See William Connor, 1880 U.S. Census, Missouri, Taney County, Swan Township, District 124, p. 8.

41. *Taney County Republican*, December 31, 1903, cited in Ingenthron, *Land of Taney*, 325; W. D. Cameron, "History and Hearsay," *WRVHQ* 5, no. 7 (Spring 1975): 19.

42. Goodspeed Brothers, *Reminiscent History*, 126; Mary Lou Boswell, "The Levi Boswell Family of Taney County, Missouri," *WRVHQ* 9, no. 12 (Summer 1988): 11.

43. U.S. Census Office, *Report on the Mining Industries of the United States (exclusive of precious metals): with Special Investigations into the Iron Resources of the Republic and into the Cretaceous coals of the Northwest* (reprint; New York: Norman Ross Publishing, 1991), 804. Jasper County was easily the biggest mining county in Missouri in 1880, producing nearly 11,000 tons of lead ore and 21,000 tons of zinc ore, followed by Newton, which mined roughly 1,300 tons of lead and 10,000 tons of zinc. The other counties discussed here produced far less.

44. U.S. Census Office, *Report on Mineral Industries in the United States at the Eleventh Census, 1890* (Washington, DC: Government Printing Office, 1892), 166. According to the report on mineral industries in 1890, Taney County mined no lead or zinc that year, although this is hardly definitive since the report includes the disclaimer that the "difficulty of collecting data for the lead and zinc mining industry in Southwest Missouri was insuperable." Moreover, only the larger mining companies kept records, and even these often proved incomplete.

45. Ingenthron, *Land of Taney*, 206–10; *Taney County Times*, March 26, 1891; *Taney County Republican*, June 4, 1903; Walter Williams, ed., *The State of Missouri: An Autobiography* (Columbia, MO: E. W. Stephens, 1904), 526. Williams lists the sites of successful lead prospecting as "Turkey, Bylin, Swan, Bull, Bear, Beaver, and Short creeks." Bylin Creek does not appear on any map, recent or contemporary, but the other creeks are all in western Taney County.

46. Douglas County's population increased from 2,414 to 14,111; Stone County's population increased from 2,400 to 7,090; Christian County expanded

its population from 5,491 to 14,017; Ozark County's population climbed from 2,447 to 9,795. U.S. Census Office, *Population of the United States in 1860: Compiled ... under the Direction of the Secretary of the Interior* (reprint; New York: Norman Ross Publishers, 1990), 286–87; U.S. Census Office, *Report on Population of the United States at the Eleventh Census, 1890* (Washington, DC: Government Printing Office, 1895).

47. U.S. Census Office, *Agriculture of the United States in 1860: Compiled ... under the Direction of the Secretary of the Interior* (reprint; New York: Norman Ross Publishers, 1990), 91–92; *Report on the Statistics of Agriculture in the United States at the Eleventh Census, 1890* (Washington, DC: Government Printing Office, 1895), 216–17.

48. Edith S. McCall, *English Village in the Ozarks: The Story of Hollister, Missouri* (Hollister, MO: The Author, 1969), 24.

49. Lynn Morrow, "Where Did All the Money Go?" *WRVHQ* 34, no. 2 (Fall 1994): 7.

50. Goodspeed Brothers, *History of Southeast Missouri*, 169; Ingenthron, *Land of Taney*, 216–18.

51. *St. Louis Daily Dispatch*, March 4, 1865, quoted in David D. March, "Charles Drake and the Constitutional Convention of 1865," *Missouri Historical Review* 47, no. 2 (January 1953): 112–13. Hereafter, the title *Missouri Historical Review* shall be abbreviated as *MHR*.

52. William E. Parrish, *Missouri under Radical Rule, 1865–1870* (Columbia: University of Missouri Press, 1965), 32–33; Duane G. Meyer, *The Heritage of Missouri*, 3rd ed. (Springfield, MO: Emden Press, 1982), 407–8.

53. Missouri Secretary of State's Office, *Register of Civil Officers, Vol. 5: Reynolds–Wright Counties, 1865–1904*, MSA, Record Group 5, Reel No. S83, p. 319. George Meyers served as sheriff; James Morrow, Henry Loughlin, and Thomas Maynard served as justices of the county court. As previously mentioned, William L. Fennix was appointed both county clerk and circuit clerk. The offices of county clerk and circuit clerk were often combined to save money.

54. Meyer, *Heritage of Missouri*, 408–9; Thomas S. Barclay, "Test Oath for the Clergy in Missouri," *MHR* 18, no. 3 (April 1924): 345–81.

55. 1868 Election Returns for Taney County, MSA, Record Group 5, Box 12, Folder 5.

56. Ibid.; Missouri Secretary of State's Office, *Register of Civil Officers, Vol. 5: Reynolds–Wright Counties, 1865–1904*, MSA, Record Group 5, Reel No. S83, p. 319.

57. Parrish, *History of Missouri*, 274; Richardson, *West from Appomattox*, 108–10; Lucius E. Guese, "St. Louis and the Great Whiskey Ring," *MHR* 36 (April 1942): 160–83.

58. Thomas S. Barclay, "The Liberal Republican Movement in Missouri," *MHR* 21, no. 1 (October 1926): 67–68.

59. Charles Drake, *The Betrayal of the Republican Party in Missouri*, in *Congressional Globe*, 41st Congress, 3rd Session, Appendix No. 1, p. 3.

60. Barclay, "Liberal Republican Movement," *MHR* 21, no. 1 (October 1926): 72–75.

61. Meyer, *Heritage of Missouri*, 415–17.

62. Ibid., 418–22.

63. 1870 Election Returns for Taney County, MSA, Record Group 5, Box 13, Folder 2. At the 1870 Republican Convention in St. Louis Harrison E. Havens

had served as one of the floor leaders for the Radical faction. See Barclay, "Liberal Republican Movement," *MHR* 21, no. 1 (October 1926): 68.

64 Goodspeed Brothers, *History of Southeast Missouri*, 169–72. Grant's margin of victory in Taney County (128 votes) might have been even smaller if he had been running against an actual Democrat. Greeley had the endorsement of both the Liberal Republicans and the Democrats in 1872, but his abolitionist past may have put off many of Taney County's newly enfranchised Democrats. In the 1876 presidential election only seventeen votes separated Democrat Samuel Tilden from Republican Rutherford B. Hayes in Taney County, and in 1880 Democrat Winfield S. Hancock won the county by a large margin over the Republican candidate James A. Garfield.

65. 1872 Election Returns for Taney County, MSA, Record Group 5, Box 14, Folder 9.

66. Missouri Secretary of State's Office, *Register of Civil Officers, Vol. 5: Reynolds—Wright Counties, 1865–1904*, MSA, Record Group 5, Reel No. S83, p. 320; Morrow, "Where Did All the Money Go?" *WRVHQ* 34, no. 2 (Fall 1994): 10. Prior to 1985 the county court was the main legislative body and administrative body at the county level, empowered by state law to handle the county's "budget, its business, and its road system." Most small counties, such as Taney, had three judges on their county courts, although larger counties sometimes had different arrangements. In 1985 the name of this body was changed to the "county commission," but its function remained the same. See Richard J. Hardy et al., eds., *Missouri Government and Politics*, rev. ed. (Colombia: University of Missouri Press, 1995), 308.

67. *New York Sun*, December 23, 1888.

68. Missouri Secretary of State's Office, *Register of Civil Officers, Vol. 5: Reynolds—Wright Counties, 1865–1904*, MSA, Record Group 5, Reel No. S83, p. 320. In Missouri at that time, the positions of sheriff and collector of revenue were often combined and held by the same person, as were the positions of county clerk and circuit clerk. See Hardy, *Missouri Government and Politics*, 309–11.

69. This aspect of the history of Taney County, and of the Bald Knobbers, was first examined by Lynn Morrow in his article published in 1994 in the *WRVHQ* titled "Where Did All the Money Go?: War and the Economics of Vigilantism in Southern Missouri," which I have already cited. In addition to providing me with excellent research advice, Mr. Morrow graciously gave me access to his personal research collection, including many of the state government documents upon which the following analysis is based.

70. Missouri General Assembly, *Laws of the State of Missouri, Passed at the First Session of the Eighteenth General Assembly, Begun and Held at the City of Jefferson* (Jefferson City, MO: James Lusk, Public Printer, 1855), 475–76; Missouri General Assembly, *Laws of the State of Missouri, Passed at the Regular Session of the 21st General Assembly, Begun and Held at the City of Jefferson, on Monday, December 31, 1860* (Jefferson City, MO: W. G. Cheeney, Public Printer, 1861), 463–64.

71. Ingenthron, *Land of Taney*, 95–96.

72. Missouri House of Representatives, *Journal of the House of Representatives of the State of Missouri, at the Regular Session of the Twenty-Third General Assembly* (Jefferson City, MO: W. A. Curry, Public Printer, 1865), 38–47.

73. Missouri General Assembly, *Second Annual Report of the Commissioner of Statistics*

*to the General Assembly of the State of Missouri for the Year 1867* (Jefferson City, MO: Ellwood Kirby, Public Printer, 1868), 70.

74. Missouri General Assembly, *Report of the State Auditor to the Twenty-Seventh General Assembly of the State of Missouri, for the Two Years, from January 1, 1871 to December 31, 1872* (Jefferson City, MO: Regan & Carter, State Printers, 1873), 116, 125, 132–33; Missouri General Assembly, *Report of the State Auditor to the Thirty-Second General Assembly of the State of Missouri, for the Two Fiscal Years Beginning January 1, 1881, and Ending December 31, 1882* (Jefferson City, MO: State Journal Company, State Printers, 1883), ii–v; See also Morrow, "Where Did All the Money Go?" *WRVHQ* 34, no. 2 (Fall 1994): 11–12.

75. Missouri Secretary of State's Office, *Register of Civil Officers, Vol. 5: Reynolds–Wright Counties, 1865–1904*, MSA, Record Group 5, Reel No. S83, p. 319.

76. Missouri General Assembly, *Report of the State Auditor to the Thirty-First General Assembly of the State of Missouri for the Two Fiscal Years, January 1, 1879 to December 31, 1880* (Jefferson City, MO: Tribune Printing Company, State Printers, 1881), lx–lxi; Missouri General Assembly, *Report of the State Auditor to the Thirty-Second General Assembly ... Beginning January 1, 1881, and Ending December 31, 1882*, lxx, lxxiv, xc, xcviii; Missouri General Assembly, *Report of the State Auditor to the Thirty-Third General Assembly of the State of Missouri, for the Two Fiscal Years Beginning January 1, 1883, and Ending December 31, 1884* (Jefferson City, MO: Tribune Printing Company, State Printers, 1885), 197.

77. Ingenthron, *Land of Taney*, 226.

78. Marian M. Ohman, *Encyclopedia of Missouri Courthouses* (Columbia: University of Missouri, Columbia Extension Division, 1981). See entries for Crawford, Taney, and Texas Counties.

79. Meyer, *Heritage of Missouri*, 423, 540–45; Lawrence O. Christensen and Gary R. Kremer, *A History of Missouri: 1875–1919* (Columbia: University of Missouri Press, 2004), 4, 51–52; Morrow, "Where Did All the Money Go?" *WRVHQ* 34, no. 2 (Fall 1994): 8–9.

80. Ingenthron, *Land of Taney*, 225; Thomas M. Spencer, "The Bald Knobbers, the Anti-Bald Knobbers, Politics, and the Culture of Violence in the Ozarks, 1860–1890," in *The Other Missouri History: Populists, Prostitutes, and Regular Folk*, ed. Thomas M. Spencer (Colombia: University of Missouri Press, 2004), 36–37.

81. *Springfield Weekly Republican*, May 16, 1889; *Stone County News Oracle*, September 13, 1963.

82. Meyer, *Heritage of Missouri*, 506–8.

83. U.S. Census Office, *A Compendium of the Ninth Census (June 1, 1870) Compiled Pursuant to a Concurrent Resolution of Congress and under the Direction of the Secretary of the Interior* (Washington, DC: Government Printing Office, 1872), 531–33. U.S. Census Office, *A Compendium of the Tenth Census (June 1, 1880) Compiled Pursuant to an Act of Congress Approved August 7, 1882*, Part 2 (Washington, DC: Government Printing Office, 1888), 1676.

84. Henry Sinclair Drago, *Outlaws on Horseback: The History of the Organized Bands of Bank and Train Robbers Who Terrorized the Prairie Towns of Missouri, Kansas, Indian Territory, and Oklahoma for Half a Century* (Lincoln: University of Nebraska Press, 1988), 19–28.

85.  Charles Groom and D. F. McConkey, *The Bald Knobbers or Citizens Committee of Taney and Christian Counties, Missouri* (Forsyth, MO: The Authors, 1887), 4.

86.  *Jefferson City Daily Tribune*, September 19, 1888; *Taney County News*, September 27, 1888; *New York Sun*, December 23, 1888; *Stone County News Oracle*, September 13, 1963.

87.  The following cases involved homicides taking place in Christian County: *State of Missouri vs. J. H. Shipman*, 1868, MSA, *Christian County Circuit Court Files*, Reel No. C 44339, Box 18, Folder 82; *State of Missouri vs. John Bolton*, 1869, MSA, *Christian County Circuit Court Files*, Reel No. C 44378, Box 48, Folder 5; *State of Missouri vs. Andrew J. Walker*, 1871, MSA, *Christian County Circuit Court Files*, Reel No. C 44361, Box 37, Folder 15; *State of Missouri vs. Roswell K. Hart, et al.*, 1874, MSA, *Christian County Circuit Court Files*, Reel No. C 44378, Box 48, Folder 23; *State of Missouri vs. M. H. Kerr, et al.*, 1876, MSA, *Christian County Circuit Court Files*, Reel No. C 44336, Box 16, Folder 82; *State of Missouri vs. John Bowman*, 1876, MSA, *Christian County Circuit Court Files*, Reel No. 44327, Box 10, Folder 77; *State of Missouri vs. John Fugitt*, 1876, MSA, *Christian County Circuit Court Files*, Reel No. C 44327, Box 10, Folder 78; *State of Missouri vs. W. D. Wilson and A. J. Inman*, 1882, MSA, *Christian County Circuit Court Files*, Reel No. C 44365, Box 10, Folder 82; *State of Missouri vs. William R. Beeler*, 1883, MSA, *Christian County Circuit Court Files*, Reel No. C 44319, Box 4, Folders 127 and 128; *State of Missouri vs. William Magill*, 1883, MSA, *Christian County Circuit Court Files*, Reel No. C 44369, Box 42, Folder 9; *State of Missouri vs. A. R. Gonce*, 1884, MSA, *Christian County Circuit Court Files*, Reel No. C 44374, Box 35, Folder 29; *State of Missouri vs. G. W. Whiteside, et al.*, 1884, MSA, *Christian County Circuit Court Files*, Reel No. C 44333, Box 14, Folder 40; *State of Missouri vs. William R. Payton*, 1886, MSA, *Christian County Circuit Court Files*, Reel No. 44373, Box 44, Folder 126; *State of Missouri vs. John T. Swearengen*, 1886, MSA, *Christian County Circuit Court Files*, Reel No. C 44350, Box 27, Folder 23; *State of Missouri vs. James S. Payten*, 1886, MSA, *Christian County Circuit Court Files*, Reel No. 44367, Box 40, Folder 130.

88.  *Springfield Patriot Advertiser*, May 1, 1879, quoted in Janice Looney, "Andrew Coggburn, 1866–86," *WRVHQ* 9, no. 6 (Winter 1987): 8–9.

89.  Robert L. Harper, *Among the Bald Knobbers: A History of the Desperadoes of the Ozark Mountains, Their Atrocious Deeds, Rendesvous, Homes and Habits, the Arrest and Conviction* (Clinton, MO: The Author, 1888), 13–14; William L. Vandeventer, *Justice in the Rough* (Ozark, MO: The Author, 1937), 12–13, 21. William L. Vandeventer was born in 1889, the son of Dr. Daniel Vandeventer, a Christian County Bald Knobber. Vandeventer served for many years as the prosecuting attorney for Christian County, an assistant U.S. attorney in Kansas City, and finally as a judge on the Springfield Court of Appeals from 1944 until his death in 1953. His manuscript, *Justice in the Rough*, consists of his recollections of the Bald Knobber movement as told to him by several of the participants, including his father, as well as research he did in many of the court cases involving the Bald Knobbers. For Judge Vandeventer's obituary, see *Christian County Republican*, November 12, 1953.

90.  *Kansas City Journal*, April 13, 1886; E. J. and L. S. Hoenshel, *Stories of the Pioneers: Incidents, Adventures and Reminiscences as Told by Some of the Old Settlers of Taney County, Missouri* (Point Lookout, MO: School of the Ozarks Press, 1915), 54, 60.

91.  *Kansas City Journal*, April 13, 1886.

92. Ibid.; *New York Sun*, December 23, 1888.
93. Hoenshel, *Stories of the Pioneers*, 54–55.
94. W. B. Flippin, "The Tutt and Everett War in Marion County," *Arkansas Historical Quarterly* 17, no. 3 (Summer 1958): 155–63.
95. *New York Sun*, December 23, 1888; *Stone County News Oracle*, September 13, 1963, and September 20, 1963; Hartman and Ingenthron, *Bald Knobbers*, 18–19. In the terminology of the day, "forty rod" whiskey meant whiskey with a "reputation for being lethal at forty rods," or about 200 meters. See John Ayto and John Simpson, comps., *The Oxford Dictionary of Modern Slang* (Oxford: Oxford University Press, 2005), 77.
96. *New York Sun*, December 23, 1888; *Stone County News Oracle*, September 20, 1963; *New York Times*, December 11, 1886; *Springfield Express*, September 28, 1883; Groom and McConkey, *The Bald Knobbers*, 4–5. According to another version of this story, Al Layton made his escape not on his own horse, but on a horse belonging to a "Dr. Hensley." See Vandeventer, *Justice in the Rough*, 22.
97. *New York Sun*, December 23, 1888; *Stone County News Oracle*, September 20, 1963; *Springfield Express*, October 5, 1883. Whereas the *Sun* states that Layton surrendered to the sheriff, the *Springfield Express* states that Layton surrendered to his brother-in-law, who then turned him over to the authorities.
98. *New York Sun*, December 23, 1888; *New York Times*, December 11, 1886; *Springfield Express*, October 10, 1884.
99. Vandeventer, *Justice in the Rough*, 22–23.
100. *New York Sun*, December 23, 1888; *Stone County News Oracle*, September 20, 1963; *Springfield Express,* October 23, 1884.
101. Goodspeed Brothers, *History of Southeast Missouri*, 172; Michael K. McGrath, *Official Directory of the State of Missouri, 1885* (St. Louis, MO: John J. Daley Stationary & Printing Company, 1885), 16. The *Official Directory* lists Blaine's vote total in Taney County as 617, not 640. Either figure could be correct, but I have chosen to use the figure in Goodspeed for the sake of consistency, since I have used it for presidential votes throughout chapters 1 and 2.
102. McGrath, *Official Directory*, 18.
103. Missouri Secretary of State's Office, *Register of Civil Officers, Vol. 5: Reynolds–Wright Counties, 1865–1904*, MSA, Record Group 5, Reel No. S83, pp. 321–22; Hartman and Ingenthron, *Bald Knobbers*, 32. The partisan affiliations of Groom, McHaffie, and Branson are found in Goodspeed Brothers, *Reminiscent History of the Ozark Region*, 104, 195, 301. Hartman and Ingenthron say that a "slate of Republican candidates" was victorious in the local races, which would mean that Keithley, Underwood, and Burns were also Republicans. However, Burns also won the race for county prosecutor in the Democratic years of 1874 and 1876, which is why I think he was probably a Democrat.
104. McGrath, *Official Directory*, 38.
105. Vandeventer, *Justice in the Rough*, 23; Randolph, *Bald Knobbers*, 7–8; *New York Sun*, December 23, 1888. For the quotation, see the *New York Times*, December 11, 1886.
106. Douglas Mahnkey, "A Bald Knobber Badge," *Ozarks Mountaineer* 32 (April

1984): 54. See also Lucille Morris Upton, *Bald Knobbers* (Caldwell, ID: Caxton Printers, 1939), 58–60.

107. Randolph, *Bald Knobbers,* 9.

108. *New York Sun*, December 23, 1888; *Stone County News Oracle*, October 4, 1963.

109. *Taney County News*, September 27, 1888; *Jefferson City Daily Tribune*, September 19, 1888; *New York Sun*, December 23, 1888; *Stone County News Oracle*, October 4, 1963. James A. Delong was the editor of the *Taney County News* at that time. The story quoted here first appeared in the *Jefferson City Daily Tribune*. Delong reprinted the story in his own paper noting that it was an accurate account "barring three or four slight errors." He made one significant change, correcting the *Tribune*'s misspelling of Kinney's name from "Capt. J. B. Kinney" to "Capt. N. N. Kinney." The *New York Sun* noted that opponents of the Bald Knobbers disputed the accuracy of this account of the meeting, saying that the men who attended it arrived on horseback, not bothering to conceal their approach, nor showing any fear for their safety.

110. *New York Sun*, December 23, 1888; *Stone County News Oracle*, October 4, 1963; Randolph, *Bald Knobbers*, 8–9. These quotations are found in both sources.

111. *New York Times*, December 11, 1886; *New York Sun*, December 23, 1888; *Stone County News Oracle*, October 4, 1963.

112. Vandeventer, *Justice in the Rough*, 23; Groom and McConkey, *The Bald Knobbers*, 6; *New York Sun*, December 23, 1888; *Kansas City Star*, December 11, 1886.

113. *New York Sun*, December 23, 1888.

114. Ibid.; Groom and McConkey, *The Bald Knobbers*, 6.

115. *Kansas City Star*, September 7, 1887.

116. *Taney County Home and Farm*, April 16, 1885.

117. Vandeventer, *Justice in the Rough*, 27–28; Groom and McConkey, *The Bald Knobbers*, 8; *New York Sun*, December 23, 1888.

118. Ibid.; Groom and McConkey, *The Bald Knobbers*, 8–9.

119. *New York Sun*, December 23, 1888; Groom and McConkey, *The Bald Knobbers*, 9; Vandeventer, *Justice in the Rough*, 28.

120. *New York Sun*, December 23, 1888; *Kansas City Star*, December 11, 1886; *New York Times*, December 11, 1886; *Springfield Express*, April 17, 1885. The sources used here agree concerning the injuries to John T. Dickenson, but they disagree concerning the injuries to his wife. The *Times* and the *Star* say she was wounded in the "cheek and head," the *Express* says she received a "scalp wound," and the *Sun* says that a bullet took of the tip of her finger, while another grazed her neck. Moreover, it is unclear who fired which shot.

121. *Kansas City Star*, December 11, 1886.

122. Vandeventer, *Justice in the Rough*, 29.

123. *New York Times*, December 11, 1886; *New York Sun*, December 23, 1888.

124. *Kansas City Star*, December 11, 1886.

125. *New York Sun*, December 23, 1888; *Jefferson City Daily Tribune*, September 19, 1888; *Taney County News*, September 27, 1888.

126. Groom and McConkey, *The Bald Knobbers*, 10.

## CHAPTER 3

1. Mary Hartman and Elmo Ingenthron, *Bald Knobbers: Vigilantes on the Ozarks Frontier* (Gretna, LA: Pelican Publishing Company, 1989), 60.

2. William L. Vandeventer, *Justice in the Rough* (Springfield, MO: The Author, 1937), 39–40.

3. Estimates of the numerical strength of the Bald Knobbers in Taney County vary greatly depending on the source. On March 6, 1886, the *Jefferson City Daily Tribune* estimated that the vigilantes numbered around three hundred men out of around twelve hundred males of voting age in the county. By contrast, the Bald Knobber chroniclers Charles H. Groom and D. F. McConkey estimated that the Taney County vigilantes numbered around one thousand at the height of their influence. See Charles H. Groom and D. F. McConkey, *The Bald Knobbers or Citizen's Committee of Taney and Christian Counties, Missouri: A History of Southwest Missouri's Famous Organization, Its Origin, Object, Workings, and Final Termination* (Forsyth, MO: The Authors, 1887), 5. Additionally, the *Springfield Daily Herald* (March 13, 1886) estimated that around three hundred Bald Knobbers attended a mass meeting at Forsyth on March 10, 1886, and the *New York Times* (December 11, 1886) and the *New York Sun* (December 23, 1888) both estimated that around five hundred Bald Knobbers attended the final public meeting of the Bald Knobbers on April 10, 1886. Since the Bald Knobbers kept no membership records, their exact numerical strength can never be firmly established. I lean toward the lower end of the numerical spectrum, however, because of the relatively small population of the county and because of the tendency of observers to overstate the number of people in crowds. An even lower estimate comes from historian Thomas Spencer, who suggested that the Taney County Bald Knobbers numbered only "eighty to one hundred active members." See Thomas M. Spencer, "The Bald Knobbers, the Anti-Bald Knobbers, Politics, and the Culture of Violence in the Ozarks, 1860-1890." In Thomas M. Spencer, ed., *The Other Missouri History: Populists, Prostitutes, and Regular Folk* (Columbia: University of Missouri Press, 2004), 37. Spencer does not fully explain how he arrived at this estimate, however, and I believe it is too low in light of the evidence cited above.

4. *Taney County Times*, November 17, 1887. The words "raising more hemp" in this context appear to be a play on words suggesting the use of hemp for making nooses.

5. Groom and McConkey, *The Bald Knobbers*, 10. For the members of the Taylor household in 1880, see "Francis Taylor," 1880 U.S. Census, Missouri, Taney County, Swan Township, District 124, p. 21.

6. Vance Randolph, *The Bald Knobbers: The Story of the Lawless Night-Riders Who Ruled Southern Missouri in the 80's* (Girard, KS: Haldeman-Julius Publications, 1944), 11–12.

7. Vandeventer, *Justice in the Rough*, 74–75.

8. *Jefferson City Daily Tribune*, November 10, 1885; Sampson Barker to Gov. John S. Marmaduke, Forsyth, MO, March 20, 1886, Missouri State Archives, *Adjutant General's Papers*, Box 88, Folder 7. Hereafter, Missouri State Archives will be abbreviated MSA. The *Tribune* article spells the names of William H. Pruitt and Reuben Pruitt as "Pruet," but the correct spelling can be found in Sampson Barker's letter to Governor Marmaduke and in the 1880 census records.

9. *Jefferson City Daily Tribune*, November 10, 1885; Barker to Governor Marmaduke, Forsyth, MO, March 20, 1886, MSA, *Adjutant General's Papers*, Box 88, Folder 7. The reference to the three Orr brothers probably refers to James, Lewis, George, and Brazzeal Orr, four brothers who lived in Taney County in the 1880s. Census records show that all four were born and in Maries County, Missouri, to James and Temperance Orr. It is not clear, however, which three of the four brothers were expelled from Taney County. See "James Orr," 1860 U.S. Census, Missouri, Maries County, Boone Township, p. 9.

10. *Jefferson City Daily Tribune*, November 10, 1885.

11. Ibid.; Janice Looney, "Andrew Coggburn, 1866–1886," *White River Valley Historical Quarterly* 9, no. 6 (Winter 1987): 8–9. Hereafter, the *White River Valley Historical Quarterly* shall be abbreviated WRVHQ. The *Daily Tribune* does not identify the father of the two Coggburn boys by name, but John S. Coggburn is the most likely candidate since he was the only male head of a household named Coggburn who would have had two adult sons in 1885. See "John Coggburn," 1880 U.S. Census, Missouri, Taney County, Oliver Township, District 124, p. 10.

12. Barker to Governor Marmaduke, Forsyth, MO, March 20, 1886, MSA, *Adjutant General's Papers*, Box 88, Folder 7; Barton C. Everett, "'Uncle Jurd' Haworth," *WRVHQ* 4, no. 7 (Spring 1972): 16; *Jefferson City Daily Tribune*, December 16, 1876.

13. J. H. Haworth, "Taney County Bald Knobbers," *WRVHQ* 3, no. 9 (Spring 1986): 20–21. This article was published posthumously after Mr. Haworth's death in 1942. A description of this incident is also found in the *Jefferson City Daily Tribune*, March 7, 1886.

14. Robert L. Harper, *Among the Bald Knobbers: A History of the Desperadoes of the Ozark Mountains, Their Atrocious Deeds, Rendezvous, Homes and Habits, the Arrest and Conviction* (Clinton, MO: The Author, 1888), 19.

15. Richard Prather, "Cap' Kinney, Bald Knobber Chief," 2. This is a typed manuscript from the Lynn Morrow Collection. It appears to be the rough draft for a series of three articles published by Richard Prather in the *Taney County Republican*, June 6–27, 1957. Hereafter, the Lynn Morrow Collection shall be abbreviated LMC.

16. Groom and McConkey, *The Bald Knobbers*, 14; *New York Sun*, December 23, 1888; *Kansas City Star*, September 30, 1885.

17. *Kansas City Journal*, April 13, 1886.

18. Interview with *Springfield Daily Herald*, March 6, 1886, quoted in Groom and McConkey, *The Bald Knobbers*, 36.

19. *Kansas City Journal*, April 13, 1886. The articles in the *Kansas City Journal* and the *Springfield Daily Herald* disagree on two small but interesting points. The *Daily Herald* only mentions the miniature coffin, not the coat with the placard, and whereas the Journal says that the miniature coffin was placed on the coat, the *Daily Herald* says that it was affixed to the front door of the schoolhouse. Since the *Daily Herald* drew its information from an interview with Nathaniel Kinney, the *Journal*'s description of the coat with the threatening placard may have been an invention added after the fact. I have left it in my account, however, because it could just as easily be a true detail which the *Daily Herald* left out.

20. Vance Randolph, *The Devil's Pretty Daughter: and Other Ozark Folk Tales* (New York: Columbia University Press, 1955), 39–42; Hartman and Ingenthron, *Bald Knobbers*, 97–100. Randolph attributed the song to Coggburn alone, but Hartman

and Ingenthron suggested that other individuals such as Andrew Coggburn's uncle, Robert Coggburn, or Aunt Matt Moore, may have contributed verses to it as well. Additionally, the version of the song found in Hartman and Ingenthron's book has several more verses than the version in Randolph's *The Devil's Pretty Daughter*.

21. Goodspeed Brothers, *A Reminiscent History of the Ozark Region: Comprising A Condensed General History, A Brief Descriptive History of Each County, and Numerous Biographical Sketches of Prominent Citizens of such Counties* (Chicago: Goodspeed Brothers, Publishers, 1894), 105; *New York Sun*, December 23, 1888.

22. *New York Sun*, December 23, 1888; *Taney County News*, September 27, 1888; *Jefferson City Daily Tribune*, September 19, 1888; Randolph, *Bald Knobbers*, 12.

23. Marian M. Ohman, *Encyclopedia of Missouri Courthouses* (Columbia: University of Missouri, Columbia Extension Division, 1981). See entries for Douglas, Christian, Reynolds, and Shannon Counties.

24. According to a 1944 article in the *Journal of Southern History* on the state of record keeping in the South, virtually every state "has had many and disastrous courthouse fires." For example, North Carolina and Arkansas have had fifty-four and thirty-five courthouse fires, respectively. See J. G. De Roulhac Hamilton, "Three Centuries of Southern Records, 1607–1907," *Journal of Southern History* 10, no. 1 (February 1944): 15.

25. Elmo Ingenthron, *The Land of Taney: A History of an Ozark Commonwealth* (Branson, MO: Ozarks Mountaineer, 1983), 36–37.

26. Groom and McConkey, *The Bald Knobbers*, 10–12; Vandeventer, *Justice in the Rough*, 34–35; *State of Missouri vs. William Taylor*, 1886, MSA, *Taney County Circuit Court Files*, Reel No. C 37192, Box 1, Folder 5. Both the accounts by Groom and McConkey and Vandeventer describe Stafford as a "detective," but the circuit court records clearly state that he was a "deputy sheriff."

27. Vandeventer, 35–36; Groom and McConkey, *The Bald Knobbers*, 12.

28. *New York Times*, March 5, 1886; *Jefferson City Daily Tribune*, March 7, 1886; *Springfield Daily Herald*, March 11, 1886; *Springfield Express*, March 5, 1886. Some historians mistakenly give the date of this event as March 12, 1886, a mistake that stems from Charles H. Groom and D. F. McConkey's usually reliable narrative (see p. 20).

29. Groom and McConkey, *The Bald Knobbers*, 20–21; Richard Prather, "Cap' Kinney, Bald Knobber Chief," 3, LMC; *Taney County Republican*, June 20, 1957; *Springfield Daily Herald*, March 11, 1886.

30. Richard Prather, "Cap' Kinney, Bald Knobber Chief," 3, LMC; *Taney County Republican*, June 20, 1957; Groom and McConkey, *The Bald Knobbers*, 21.

31. *New York Times*, March 5, 1886; *Jefferson City Daily Tribune*, March 7, 1886.

32. *Springfield Daily Herald*, March 11, 1886.

33. Statement of Samuel H. Snapp to Adj. Gen. J. C. Jamison, Forsyth, MO, April 9, 1886, MSA, *Adjutant General's Papers*, Box 88, Folder 7. Jamison made a report on his trip to Taney to Gov. John S. Marmaduke, which includes statements he took from many individuals including Samuel Snapp.

34. Ibid.

35. During the Civil War the term "bushwhacker" was generally defined as a stealthy assassin who fired from cover at an unsuspecting and unprepared victim. See Leo E. Huff, "Guerrillas, Jayhawkers and Bushwhackers in Northern Arkansas

during the Civil War," *Arkansas Historical Quarterly* 24, no. 3 (Summer 1965): 130–31. If Coggburn and Snapp were indeed trying to ambush or "bushwhack" Kinney in the typical Ozarks fashion, Coggburn's greeting would have surrendered the critical element of surprise.

36. Many of these names, particularly those of the Anti-Bald Knobbers, can be found in a large file of correspondence pertaining to the troubles in Taney County found in Adj. Gen. James C. Jamison's public papers. See MSA, *Adjutant General's Papers*, Box 88, Folder 7. Others can be found using articles from contemporary newspapers such as the Springfield, Missouri, *Daily Herald*, the Springfield, Missouri, *Daily Republican,* the Kansas City, Missouri, *Star*, and the Jefferson City, Missouri, *Daily Tribune*. Still others can be found using primary source materials such as Robert L. Harper's *Among the Bald Knobbers*, William L. Vandeventer's *Justice in the Rough*, and Charles H. Groom and D. F. McConkey's *The Bald Knobbers*, all of which are already cited here. Additionally, I have used Elmo Ingenthron and Mary Hartman's *Bald Knobbers: Vigilantes on the Ozarks Frontier*, and Lucille Morris Upton's *Bald Knobbers* to confirm the identity of many of these individuals.

37. The information related to the place of birth of both Bald Knobbers and Anti-Bald Knobbers is based on federal census records for the years 1870, 1880, and 1900. The 1890 census records are unavailable because nearly the entire 1890 census was destroyed as a result of a fire at the National Archives in 1921. See Kellee Blake, "'First in the Path of the Firemen': The Fate of the 1890 Population Census," *Prologue: Quarterly of the National Archives* 28, no. 1 (Spring 1996): 64–81.

38. Viola Hartman, "The Layton Story: Part II," *WRVHQ* 7, no. 3 (Spring 1980): 3–6; Ruth Gulls Ryser, "The Snapp Family," *WRVHQ* 4, no. 3 (Spring 1971): 2–3; Janice Looney, "Andrew Coggburn," *WRVHQ* 9, no. 6 (Winter 1987): 9.

39. Goodspeed Brothers, *Reminiscent History*, 576–77; Claude Hibbard, "The Story of Two Pioneer Families Whose Lives Intertwined," *WRVHQ* 2, no. 8 (Summer 1966): 3.

40. Kristen Kalen and Lynn Morrow, "Nat Kinney's Sunday School Crowd," *WRVHQ* 33, no. 1 (Fall 1993): 8–9; Douglas Mahnkey, "The Mahnkey and Prather Families," *WRVHQ* 4, no. 2 (Winter 1970–71): 5; Hoenshel, *Stories of the Pioneers*, 31; Goodspeed Brothers, *Reminiscent History*, 103–4; 195–96.

41. Individuals who served in the Civil War were identified using Alexander Street Press, LLC, "The American Civil War Research Database," http://asp6new.alexanderstreet.com.libezp.lib.lsu.edu/cwdb/, and Ancestry.com, "Civil War Collection," http://www.ancestry.com/search/rectype/grouplist.aspx?group=CivilWar.

42. Ibid.

43. The occupational statistics cited here are based primarily on federal census records for the years 1870, 1880, and 1900. The census records for 1890 are unavailable because they were destroyed by fire. In addition to census records, I have gleaned occupational data from the Goodspeed Brothers, *Reminiscent History of the Ozarks Region*, and E. J. and L. S. Hoenshel, *Stories of the Pioneers*, both of which are already cited here. I have also consulted several articles from the *White River Valley Historical Quarterly*.

44. Ibid. In addition to surveying the occupational pursuits of the Bald Knobbers and Anti-Bald Knobbers, an attempt was made to ascertain the relative wealth of the two groups using Taney County's personal property tax records for 1883 and

1885. Those records, however, are terribly incomplete, and I was unable to find enough Bald Knobbers and Anti-Bald Knobbers to form the basis of an adequate comparison.

45. Missouri Secretary of State's Office, *Register of Civil War Officers, Vol. 5: Reynolds–Wright Counties, 1865–1904*, MSA, Record Group 5, Reel No. S83, pp. 319–23. See also Ingenthron, *The Land of Taney*, 457–63.

46. Ibid.

47. *Jefferson City Daily Tribune*, November 10, 1885. Many of the specific acts mentioned in McGrath's editorial, such as the eviction of the Pruitts and Orrs, Jefferson Weaver, and Jerome Winslow, are also mentioned in Sampson Barker's March 20, 1886, letter to Gov. John S. Marmaduke. Additionally, letters to Secretary of State McGrath from Thomas A. Layton (March 4) and J. J. Reynolds (March 12) are also found in MSA, *Adjutant General's Papers*, Box 88, Folder 7. Although neither of these letters could have been the source of McGrath's editorial published on November 10, 1885, they do show that he kept in contact with several of the Anti-Bald Knobber leaders in Taney County, which means that he probably got his source material from them.

48. William A. Settle Jr., "The James Boys and Missouri Politics," *MHR* 36, no. 4 (July 1942): 412–29. In addition to becoming a political issue between Republicans and Democrats, the James gang and other ex-Confederate outlaws became a source of controversy within the Democratic Party itself, which was divided between rival factions of ex-Confederates who sympathized with the James gang and ex-Unionists who did not. See T. J. Stiles, *Jesse James: Last Rebel of the Civil War* (New York: Vintage Books, 2003), 260–63, 286–91.

49. Michael K. McGrath, ed., *Directory of Missouri, 1887–88* (Jefferson City, MO: Tribune Printing Company, 1888), 179.

50. Cook and Vanzandt were both originally Democrats, though Vanzandt briefly joined the Greenback-Labor Party when he won the race for state representative in 1882, and Cook joined the Republicans when he ran for sheriff to replace the deceased Galba Branson in 1889. See Goodspeed Brothers, *Reminiscent History*, 284, E. J. and L. S. Hoenshel, *Stories of the Pioneers: Incidents, Adventures and Reminiscences as Told by Some of the Old Settlers of Taney County, Missouri* (Branson, MO: White River Leader, 1915), 4, and *Springfield Express*, July 26, 1889.

51. *Springfield Daily Herald*, March 6, 1886.

52. Ibid., March 16, 1886. Both Anti-Bald Knobber editorials mistakenly referred to Andrew Coggburn as "Joe Cogburn," a mistake the editor of the *Herald* did not correct, even though the newspaper printed his name correctly in other issues.

53. *Jefferson City Daily Tribune*, March 7, 1886. There are no extant copies of the actual pro-militia petition or the list of signatures. For a similar account of Kinney's threats against the militia supporters, see Statement of H. C. Everett, Anti-Bald Knobber, to Adj. Gen. J. C. Jamison, Forsyth, MO, April 9, 1886, MSA, *Adjutant General's Papers*, Box 88, Folder 7.

54. Thomas A. Layton to Gov. John S. Marmaduke, Forsyth, MO, March 1, 1886, MSA, *Adjutant General's Papers*, Box 88, Folder 7. Layton curiously does not mention Reynolds, even though he was the one who actually brought the petition to the governor.

55.  Thomas A. Layton to Gov. John S. Marmaduke, Forsyth, MO, March 4, 1886, MSA, *Adjutant General's Papers*, Box 88, Folder 7.

56.  *Jefferson City Daily Tribune*, March 7, 1886.

57.  J. J. Reynolds to Gov. John S. Marmaduke, Forsyth, MO, March 11, 1886, MSA, *Adjutant General's Papers*, Box 88, Folder 7.

58.  Ibid.; Thomas A. Layton to Adj. Gen. J. C. Jamison, Forsyth, MO, March 15, 1886, MSA, *Adjutant General's Papers*, Box 88, Folder 7; *Springfield Daily Herald*, March 14, 1886. Both Layton and Reynolds put the number of participants in the Bald Knobber meeting at the surprisingly exact figure of 154, while the *Daily Herald* estimated that around 300 Bald Knobbers attended the meeting.

59.  J. J. Reynolds to Secretary of State Michael K. McGrath, Forsyth, MO, March 11, 1886, MSA, *Adjutant General's Papers*, Box 88, Folder 7.

60.  *Springfield Daily Herald*, March 14, 1886. A handwritten copy of the Forsyth antimilitia resolutions was also made available to me by Lynn Morrow, along with a list of 234 signatures of people who endorsed them.

61.  Sampson Barker to Gov. John S. Marmaduke, Forsyth, MO, March 20, 1886, MSA, *Adjutant General's Papers*, Box 88, Folder 7.

62.  W. H. Lanceford to Gov. John S. Marmaduke, Forsyth, MO, March 27, 1886, MSA, *Adjutant General's Papers*, Box 88, Folder 7.

63.  Sampson Barker to Gov. John S. Marmaduke, Forsyth, MO, March 20, 1886, MSA, *Adjutant General's Papers*, Box 88, Folder 7.

64.  Robert L. Williams, "James Carson Jamison, 1830–1916," *Chronicles of Oklahoma* 21, no. 1 (March 1943): 3–7; "James Carson Jamison: A Filibusterer in Nicaragua, Pike County Man Became Missouri's Adjutant-General," *MHR* 25, no. 4 (July 1931): 623–26; Later in life, Jamison wrote a memoir detailing his experiences as a filibusterer in Nicaragua. See James Carson Jamison, *With Walker in Nicaragua: Reminiscences of an Officer of the American Phalanx* (Columbia, MO: E. W. Stephens Publishing Company, 1909).

65.  Williams, "James Carson Jamison, 1830–1916," *Chronicles of Oklahoma* 21, no. 1 (March 1943): 5–7; "James Carson Jamison," *MHR* 25, no. 4 (July 1931): 623–26. For Jamison's role in settling the 1885 railroad strike, see *New York Times*, March 16, 1886.

66.  James C. Jamison, *Report of the Adjutant General of Missouri for 1886* (Jefferson City, MO: Tribune Printing Company, 1887), 6.

67.  Hoenshel, *Stories of the Pioneers*, 57.

68.  Richard Prather, "'Cap' Kinney, Bald Knobber Chief," 4, LMC; *Taney County Republican*, June 27, 1957.

69.  *Springfield Daily Herald*, April 14, 1886.

70.  Jamison, *Report of the Adjutant General of Missouri for 1886*, 7.

71.  Statement of Dr. K. L. Burdette, Anti-Bald Knobber, to Adj. Gen. J. C. Jamison, Forsyth, MO, April 9, 1886, MSA, *Adjutant General's Papers*, Box 88, Folder 7.

72.  Statement of H. C. Everett, Anti-Bald Knobber, to Adj. Gen. J. C. Jamison, Forsyth, MO, April 9, 1886, MSA, *Adjutant General's Papers*, Box 88, Folder 7.

73.  Report of Adj. Gen. J. C. Jamison to Gov. John S. Marmaduke, Forsyth, MO, April 9, 1886, MSA, *Adjutant General's Papers*, Box 88, Folder 7.

74.  *Springfield Daily Herald*, April 14, 1886.

75. Statement of R. V. Burns, Neutral, to Adj. Gen. J. C. Jamison, Forsyth, MO, April 9, 1886, MSA, *Adjutant General's Papers*, Box 88, Folder 7.

76. *State of Missouri vs. William Taylor*, 1886, MSA, *Taney County Circuit Court Files*, Reel No. 37192, Box 1, Folder 5.

77. Groom and McConkey, *The Bald Knobbers*, 13–14; Vandeventer, *Justice in the Rough*, 37–38; *Springfield Express*, October 15, 1886; *Springfield Express*, November 5, 1885.

78. *Springfield Daily Herald*, April 14, 1886.

79. Hoenshel, *Stories of the Pioneers*, 34.

80. Ibid., 57.

81. *Springfield Daily Herald*, May 13, 1886. The "Dr. Anderson" referred to here is probably Elisha T. Anderson, a physician found on the 1900 federal census for Taney County. See "Elisha T. Anderson," 1900 U.S. Census, Missouri, Taney County, Oliver Township, District 131, p. 14.

82. J. J. Reynolds to Adj. Gen. J. C. Jamison, Forsyth, MO, May 10, 1886, MSA, *Adjutant General's Papers*, Box 88, Folder 7.

83. *Springfield Daily Herald*, May 13, 1886; *Springfield Leader*, May 12, 1886; *Springfield Express*, May 21, 1886.

84. *State of Missouri vs. George Washington Middleton*, 1886, Forsyth, MO, LMC.

85. Ibid.

86. Alonzo Prather to Adj. Gen. J. C. Jamison, Kirbyville, MO, June 11, 1886, MSA, *Adjutant General's Papers*, Box 88, Folder 7.

87. Ibid.

88. Mrs. James S. B. Berry to Adj. Gen. J. C. Jamison, Taney County, May 10, 1886, MSA, *Adjutant General's Papers*, Box 88, Folder 7. According Sam Snapp's great-granddaughter, Ruth Ryser, at her great-grandfather's funeral the minister asked people to "step forward and take Sam's children and they were divided up there at the cemetery." See Ruth Ryser, "Ninety-One Years Ago," *WRVHQ* 6, no. 2 (Winter 1977): 1–2.

89. J. J. Reynolds to Adj. Gen. J. C. Jamison, Forsyth, MO, May 10, 1886, MSA, *Adjutant General's Papers*, Box 88, Folder 7.

90. W. H. Jones to Adj. Gen. J. C. Jamison, Forsyth, MO, May 10, 1886, and K. L. Burdette to Adj. Gen. J. C. Jamison, Forsyth, MO, May 12, 1886, MSA, *Adjutant General's Papers*, Box 88, Folder 7.

91. Prather to Jamison, Kirbyville, MO, June 11, 1886, MSA, *Adjutant General's Papers*, Box 88, Folder 7.

92. *State of Missouri vs. George Washington Middleton*, 1886, Forsyth, MO, LMC; *Springfield Express*, October 14, 1887.

93. *Springfield Daily Herald*, October 19, 1887.

94. Douglas Mahnkey, "Who Killed Wash Middleton?" *Ozarks Mountaineer* 21, no. 4 (May 1973): 23. Hereafter, the Ozarks Mountaineer will be abbreviated OM.

95. *Springfield Daily Herald*, October 19, 1887.

96. Ibid.

97. Hartman and Ingenthron, *Bald Knobbers*, 204–5; John S. Marmaduke, "Offering a Reward, October 20, 1887," *WRVHQ* 6, no. 2 (Winter 1977): 3; Mahnkey, "Who Killed Wash Middleton?" *OM* 21, no. 4 (May 1973): 23.

98. *Springfield Express*, February 24, 1888.

99. *Springfield Express,* July 20, 1888; Mahnkey, "Who Killed Wash Middleton?" *OM* 21, no. 4 (May 1973): 23.
100. McGrath, ed., *Directory of Missouri, 1887–88,* 114. In this race, Republican Samuel R. Dial defeated Nat Kinney with 398 votes to Kinney's 319 votes.
101. James C. Jamison, *Report of the Adjutant General of Missouri for 1886* (Jefferson City, MO: Tribune Printing Company, 1887), 7.

CHAPTER 4

1. William L. Vandeventer, *Justice in the Rough* (Springfield, MO: The Author, 1937), 85; see also Author's Interview with Lloyd Walker, Springfield, MO, January 2, 2009. Lloyd Walker is Joseph Walker's grandson. In my interview with him he stated that his grandfather was the chieftain of the Bald Knobbers in Douglas County, which agrees with Vandeventer's account.
2. For Dave Walker's enlistment information, see "The American Civil War Research Database," http://asp6new.alexanderstreet.com.libezp.lib.lsu.edu/cwdb/cwdb.index.map.aspx (accessed April 5, 2010). For information concerning the Sixteenth Missouri Cavalry, see Selwyn A. Brant et al., eds., *The Union army: a history of military affairs in the loyal states, 1861–65—records of the regiments in the Union army—cyclopedia of battles—memoirs of commanders and soldiers,* Vol. 4 (Madison, WI: Federal Publishing Company, 1908), 279.
3. *State of Missouri vs. Wiley Mathews,* 1888, Missouri State Archives, *Missouri Supreme Court Files,* Box 1144, Case 8. Hereafter, Missouri State Archives shall be abbreviated MSA.
4. Vandeventer, *Justice in the Rough,* 85. For Dave Walker's leadership status, see *St. Louis Post-Dispatch,* April 20, 1887.
5. *New York Times,* August 25, 1887.
6. Robert L. Harper, *Among the Bald Knobbers: A History of the Desperadoes of the Ozark Mountains, Their Atrocious Deeds, Rendezvous, Homes and Habits, the Arrest and Conviction* (Clinton, MO: The Author, 1888), 30.
7. Harper, *Among the Bald Knobbers,* 65; Mary Hartman and Elmo Ingenthron, *Bald Knobbers: Vigilantes on the Ozarks Frontier* (Gretna, LA: Pelican Publishing Company, 1989), 147.
8. Wayne Glenn, *Christian County Memories, 1819–Present* (Nixa, MO: The Author, 2009), 136, 143; Harper, *Among the Bald Knobbers,* 101.
9. Glenn, *Christian County Memories,* 137; Wiley Mathews, 1880 U.S. Census, Missouri, Christian County, Linden Township, District 11, p. 26.
10. Gilbert Applegate, 1850 U.S. Census, Missouri, Greene County, Dallas Township, p. 2; Gilbert Applegate, 1860 U.S. Census, Missouri, Taney County, Buchanan Township, p. 87.
11. *Springfield Express,* May 13, 1887.
12. Gilbert Applegate, 1880 U.S. Census, Missouri, Douglas County, Buchanan Township, District 27, p. 5; Glenn, *Christian County Memories,* 129.
13. *Jefferson City Daily Tribune,* April 14, 1887; *Dallas Morning News,* April 14, 1887. Both of these articles consist of information gleaned from a story that originally ran in the *St. Louis Globe-Democrat,* April 12, 1887.
14. *Dallas Morning News,* December 15, 1886.

15. *Springfield Daily Republican*, September 27, 1887.

16. *Dallas Morning News*, March 24, 1887.

17. Mary Hartman and Elmo Ingenthron, *Bald Knobbers: Vigilantes of the Ozarks Frontier* (Gretna, LA: Pelican Publishing Company, 1989), 192. Hartman and Ingenthron cite the *Marshfield Chronicle* for this information. I have been unable to find the original issue that contains this story.

18. *U.S. vs. Granville Vanbiber*, 1887, National Archives at Kansas City, MO, Southern Division of the Western District of Missouri, Docket # 7. Hereafter, the National Archives at Kansas City shall be referred to as KCA.

19. *Springfield Daily Herald*, October 1, 1887.

20. *U.S. vs. John James*, 1887, KCA, Southern Division of the Western District of Missouri, Docket # 82; *Springfield Daily Herald*, September 28, 1887.

21. *State of Missouri vs. William Newton, et al.*, 1887, MSA, *Christian County Circuit Court Files*, Reel No. C 44349, Box 26, Folder 49; Harriet C. Frazier, *Lynchings in Missouri, 1803–1981* (Jefferson, NC: McFarland & Company, 2009), 96.

22. *Springfield Daily Herald*, September 28, 1887.

23. Vandeventer, *Justice in the Rough*, 90–91; *State of Missouri vs. David Walker, et al.*, 1887, MSA, *Christian County Circuit Court Files*, Reel No. C 44327, Box 10, Folder 62.

24. *Kansas City Star*, August 24, 1887.

25. Vandeventer, *Justice in the Rough*, 89–90.

26. Ibid., 92; See also Charles H. Groom and D. F. McConkey, *The Bald Knobbers or Citizen's Committee of Taney and Christian Counties, Missouri: A History of Southwest Missouri's Famous Organization, Its Origin, Object, Workings, and Final Termination* (Forsyth, MO: The Authors, 1887), 46.

27. *State of Missouri vs. M. M. Humble, et al.*, 1887, MSA, *Christian County Circuit Court Files*, Reel No. C 44328, Box 10, Folder 120; *Kansas City Star*, August 24, 1887.

28. *State of Missouri vs. David Walker, et al.*, 1887, MSA, *Christian County Circuit Court Files*, Reel No. 44339, Box 18, Folder 99; *Springfield Leader*, August 26, 1887.

29. Christian County Centennial, Inc., *Christian County: Its First 100 Years* (Jefferson City, MO: Von Hoffman Press, 1959), 16; Christian County Museum Historical Society, *Christian County, Missouri: History and Families* (Paducah, KY: Turner Publishing Company, 1998), 30.

30. Christian County Centennial, *Christian County*, 136; Christian County Museum Historical Society, *Christian County*, 25.

31. Edith McCall, *English Village in the Ozarks: The Story of Hollister, Missouri* (Hollister, MO: The Author, 1969), 18.

32. Dave Walker to Joseph Walker, Chadwick, MO, April 8, 1886, in the "Lloyd Walker Collection," at the Greene County Archives in Springfield, MO.

33. Harper, *Among the Bald Knobbers*, 36–37.

34. *State of Missouri vs. John Rhodes*, 1885, MSA, *Christian County Circuit Court Files*, Reel No. C 44313, Box 1, Folder 103; *State of Missouri vs. John Rhodes*, 1886, MSA, *Christian County Circuit Court Files*, Reel No. C 47704, Box 66, Folder 127; *State of Missouri vs. H. R. H. McCauley*, 1886, MSA, *Christian County Circuit Court Files*, Reel No. C 44320, Box 5, Folders 67 and 68.

35. *State vs. David Walker, et al.*, 1887, MSA, *Christian County Circuit Court Files*, Reel No. C 44318, Box 4, Folder 72; Groom and McConkey, *The Bald Knobbers*, 45–46.

36. *New York Times*, November 13, 1886.

37. Curtis H. Synhorst, "Antebellum Vigilantes: The Slicker War in Missouri," *Gateway Heritage* 3 (Summer 1982): 34–48; J. W. Vincent, "The 'Slicker War' and Its Consequences," *Missouri Historical Review* 7 (April 1913): 138–45.

38. Vandeventer, *Justice in the Rough*, 91.

39. *State vs. David Walker, et al.*, 1887, MSA, *Christian County Circuit Court Files*, Reel No. C 44318, Box 4, Folder 33; Hartman and Ingenthron, Bald Knobbers, 150.

40. Harper, Among the *Bald Knobbers*, 107–8.

41. *State vs. David Walker, et al.*, 1887, MSA, *Christian County Circuit Court Files*, Reel No. C 44318, Box 4, Folder 32; Vandeventer, *Justice in the Rough*, 134–35.

42. Some members, including Dave Walker, boasted that the organization had between 700 and 800 members, and these figures were widely quoted in the press. See *Kansas City Star*, April 15, 1887, and April 22, 1887. The Bald Knobber trials of 1887, however, shed greater light on the inner workings of the Bald Knobber organization, which caused many journalists to revise those estimates down to between 200 and 250. See *Kansas City Star*, April 28, 1887; *New York Times*, March 21, 1887.

43. Harper, *Among the Bald Knobbers*, 106.

44. *Kansas City Star*, April 15, 1887, and April 22, 1887.

45. A photocopy of this oath can found in a file labeled "Lloyd Walker Collection," at the Greene County Archives in Springfield, Missouri. Lloyd Walker also showed me the original copy when I interviewed him on January 2, 2009.

46. The data concerning occupation, age distribution, and place of birth for the Bald Knobbers in Christian and Douglas Counties come primarily from federal census records for the years 1870, 1880, 1900, and beyond. These records were accessed using Ancestry.com.

47. The individual Bald Knobbers who fought during the Civil War were identified using Alexander Street Press, LLC, "The American Civil War Research Database," http://asp6new.alexanderstreet.com.libezp.lib.lsu.edu/cwdb/, and Ancestry.com, "Civil War Collection," http://www.ancestry.com/search/rectype/grouplist.aspx?group=CivilWar.

48. *Christian County Land Assessment*, 1885, MSA, Reel No. C 1649; *Taney County Land Assessment*, 1886, MSA, Reel No. C 14339. I was unable to find a majority of the names of the Bald Knobbers who lived in these counties, partly because the records cited here were handwritten and not always legible, and because they may not have been complete to begin with. In the case of Taney County, the courthouse fire in 1885 probably destroyed many records that would otherwise have been available. The observations made here are based on the records for those individuals that I could find, which I believe constitute a large enough sample to make some general observations, even though they do not encompass every Bald Knobber property owner. Additionally, I compare only Christian and Taney Counties because no land assessment records were available for Douglas County during this period.

49. Vandeventer, *Justice in the Rough*, 85–86.

50. Douglas Mahnkey, "A Bald Knobber Badge," *Ozarks Mountaineer* 32 (April 1984): 54; Lucille Morris Upton, *Bald Knobbers* (Caldwell, ID: Caxton Printers, 1939), 58–60.

51. *New York Times*, March 21, 1887. When rumors of Hale's involvement with

the Bald Knobbers became public in 1887 they nearly cost Hale his job, as angry citizens submitted petitions demanding his resignation.

52. *U.S. vs. Joel Casad*, 1887, KCA, Southern Division of the Western District of Missouri, Docket # 99; *U.S. vs. George L. Sanders*, 1887, KCA, Southern Division of the Western District of Missouri, Docket # 107.

53. *New York Sun*, August 23, 1888; *Stone County News-Oracle*, October 4, 1963.

54. Harper, *Among the Bald Knobbers*, 50.

55. Ibid., 79.

56. *Columbus Enquirer-Sun*, March 18, 1887. This story also ran in the *New York Times* on March 18, 1887. However, the *Times* version replaces Joseph Hyde with "Joseph Kyes," which appears to be an error.

57. *Jefferson City Daily Tribune*, May 10, 1887.

58. Walter D. Hubbard to Gov. Lon V. Stephens, Springfield, MO, March 1, 1897, *Western Historical Manuscripts Collection* at Columbia, Missouri. Collection # 1725: Lon V. Stephens Papers, Folder 1.

59. Groom and McConkey, *The Bald Knobbers*, 44–45.

60. Ibid., 45–46.

61. Douglas Mahnkey, "Captain Kinney and the Bald Knobbers," *Ozarks Mountaineer* 26 (August 1978): 16–17; Goodspeed Brothers, *A Reminiscent History of the Ozarks Region: Comprising a Condensed General History ... of Prominent citizens* (Chicago: Goodspeed Brothers, Publishers, 1894), 126.

62. E. W. Crozier, *The White-Caps: A History of the Organization in Sevier County* (Knoxville, TN: Bean, Warters & Gaut, Printers and Binders, 1899); Robert E. Cunningham, *Trial by Mob* (Stillwater, OK: Redland Press, 1957); Madeleine M. Noble, "The White Caps of Harrison and Crawford County, IN: A Study in the Violent Enforcement of Morality" (PhD Dissertation, University of Michigan, 1973).

63. Walter B. Stevens, *Missouri: The Center State, 1821–1915*, Vol. 3 (St. Louis, MO: S. J. Clarke Publishing Company, 1915), 186; Jonathan Fairbanks and Clyde Edwin Tuck, *Past and Present of Greene County, Missouri: Early and Recent History and Genealogical Records of Many of the Representative Citizens* (Indianapolis, IN: A. W. Bowen & Company, 1915), 1666; Milton D. Rafferty, "The Ozark Forest: Its Exploitation and Restoration," *Ozarks Watch* 6, no. 2 (Summer 1992): 24.

64. Upton, *Bald Knobbers*, 110–12.

65. Christopher Waldrep, *Night Riders: Defending Community in the Black Patch, 1890–1915* (Durham, NC: Duke University Press, 1993).

66. *Springfield Daily Herald*, September 16, 1887. This article discusses the origins of the homesteader intimidation cases and includes a copy of a letter sent from McLain Jones to Arnold Krekel.

67. *U.S. vs. John James*, 1887, KCA, Southern Division of the Western District of Missouri, Docket # 82; *U.S. vs. James T. White*, 1887, KCA, Southern Division of the Western District of Missouri, Docket # 111; *U.S. vs. William Applegate*, 1887, KCA, Southern Division of the Western District of Missouri, Docket # 113; *U.S. vs. William Smith*, 1887, KCA, Southern Division of the Western District of Missouri, Docket # 116; *U.S. vs. James Morrisett*, 1887, KCA, Southern Division of the Western District of Missouri, Docket # 121; *U.S. vs. Jack Hiles*, 1887, KCA, Southern Division of the Western District of Missouri, Docket # 122; *U.S. vs. Henry Applegate*, 1887,

KCA, Southern Division of the Western District of Missouri, Docket # 123; *U.S. vs. William Roberts & Jack Hiles*, 1887, KCA, Southern Division of the Western District of Missouri, Docket # 126; *U.S. vs. Sam Newton & James Morrisett*, 1887, KCA, Southern Division of the Western District of Missouri, Docket # 128; *U.S. vs. Gat Walker*, 1887, KCA, Southern Division of the Western District of Missouri, Docket # 130; *U.S. vs. Matt Nash & Gilbert Applegate*, 1887, KCA, Southern Division of the Western District of Missouri, Docket # 133; *U.S. vs. Andy Adams & C.O. Simmons*, 1887, KCA, Southern Division of the Western District of Missouri, Docket # 134; *U.S. vs. William Newton & Matt Shipman*, 1887, KCA, Southern Division of the Western District of Missouri, Docket # 135; *U.S. vs. Wylie Mathews & Ed Linscott*, 1887, KCA, Southern Division of the Western District of Missouri, Docket # 136; *U.S. vs. Amos Jones & Henry Applegate*, 1887, KCA, Southern Division of the Western District of Missouri, Docket # 137; *U.S. vs. Newton Myers*, 1887, KCA, Southern Division of the Western District of Missouri, Docket # 323.

68. *U.S. vs. John James*, 1887, KCA, Southern Division of the Western District of Missouri, Docket # 82; *U.S. vs. Thomas K. Jones*, 1887, KCA, Southern Division of the Western District of Missouri, Docket # 78; *U.S. vs. Dr. Daniel Vandeventer*, 1887, KCA, Southern Division of the Western District of Missouri, Docket # 85. Hursh's name was spelled "Heursh" in some of the court documents.

69. *U.S. vs. John Denney*, 1887, KCA, Central Division of the Western District of Missouri, Docket # 2520.

70. Ibid.

71. *New York Times*, December 30, 1886; *Jefferson City Daily Tribune*, December 14, 1886.

72. *Kansas City Star*, September 10, 1887; *Taney County News*, September 22, 1887; *New York Times*, March 12, 1888; *Dallas Morning News*, March 12, 1888. The names of the men sentenced included John Wright, William Silvey, George Silvey, Jackson Silvey Sr., Jackson Silvey Jr., John Denney, Elliot Denney, John Wright, Benjamin ("Berry") Handcock, and W. F. Wright.

73. *U.S. vs. J.L. Garrison*, 1888, KCA, Southern Division of the Western District of Missouri, Docket # 260; *U.S. vs. David Hunter*, 1888, KCA, Southern Division of the Western District of Missouri, Docket # 309.

74. Ibid.

75. *U.S. vs. Simon Lakey*, 1887, KCA, Southern Division of the Western District of Missouri, Docket # 97; *U.S. vs. Uriah Pruitt*, 1887, KCA, Southern Division of the Western District of Missouri, Docket # 98; *U.S. vs. Joel Casad*, 1887, KCA, Southern Division of the Western District of Missouri, Docket # 99; *U.S. vs. George L. Sanders*, 1887, KCA, Southern Division of the Western District of Missouri, Docket # 99.

76. *U.S. vs. James W. Carr*, 1887, KCA, Southern Division of the Western District of Missouri, Docket # 88.

77. *Dallas Morning News*, December 9, 1887.

78. *Springfield Daily Republican*, September 9, 1887.

79. The U.S. General Land Office at Springfield, Missouri, issued David Walker patent number 410 for 160 acres in Christian County in 1871 and patent number 32171 for 33 acres in 1886. The same office issued patent number 2956 for 40 acres to James Gann in 1876 and patent number 7463 for 160 acres to Gilbert Applegate in 1891.

80. Vandeventer, *Justice in the Rough*, 20.

81. J. J. Bruton et al., *The Bald Knob Tragedy of Taney and Christian Counties* (Sparta, MO: The Authors, 1887), 19–20.

82. *Springfield Daily Herald*, September 28, 1887.

83. *U.S. vs. James W. Carr*, 1887, KCA, Southern Division of the Western District of Missouri, Docket # 88.

84. All information about the location and layout of James Edens's home comes from John C. Rogers, the former county clerk, who testified in the Edens-Greene murder case. Rogers identified the precise location of the home as the northwest quarter of section 5, township 26, and range 19 of Christian County. See *State of Missouri vs. Wiley Mathews*, 1888, MSA, *Missouri Supreme Court Files*, Box 1144, Case 8; *State of Missouri vs. David Walker*, 1888, MSA, *Missouri Supreme Court Files*, Box 1144, Case 4.

85. *State of Missouri vs. Wiley Mathews*, 1888, MSA, *Missouri Supreme Court Files*, Box 1144, Case 8.

86. Vandeventer, *Justice in the Rough*, 3, 122.

87. According to the various court records pertaining to this incident, the men who attended the meeting included Dave Walker, William Walker, James McGuire, John Mathews, James Mathews, Wiley Mathews, C. O. Simmons, Gilbert Applegate, William Stanley, William Newton, Charles Graves, Joseph Inman, Joseph Hyde, Andrew Adams, Amos Jones, Lewis Davis, Peter Davis, John Hiles, Jack Hiles, William Johns, James Preston, William J. ("Bud") Ray, William Abbot, Jesse Robertson, Matt Nash, and John Nash.

88. Vandeventer, *Justice in the Rough*, 97; Harper, *Among the Bald Knobbers*, 88–89. This explanation also appears in Hartman and Ingenthron, *Bald Knobbers*, 151.

89. *State of Missouri vs. David Walker*, 1888, MSA, *Missouri Supreme Court Files*, Box 1144, Case 4.

90. *State of Missouri vs. Wiley Mathews*, 1888, MSA, *Missouri Supreme Court Files*, Box 1144, Case 8; *State of Missouri vs. David Walker*, 1888, MSA, *Missouri Supreme Court Files*, Box 1144, Case 4.

91. *State of Missouri vs. Wiley Mathews*, 1888, MSA, *Missouri Supreme Court Files*, Box 1144, Case 8; *State of Missouri vs. David Walker*, 1888, MSA, *Missouri Supreme Court Files*, Box 1144, Case 4; *State of Missouri vs. William Walker*, 1888, MSA, *Missouri Supreme Court Files*, Box 1144, Case 1. McGuire testified in all four trials involving the Bald Knobbers sentenced to death. This included the John Mathews trial, but that case file is incomplete and his testimony is missing. William Newton testified in the Wiley Mathews and William Walker trials.

92. Ibid.

93. Ibid.

94. Ibid. Coroner Ralston testified in all four cases, as did James Edens.

95. Ibid. Melvina Greene later identified her assailant as William J. ("Bud") Ray, although subsequent testimony demonstrated that Ray had gone home after the meeting and had not gone to the Edens's house. In retrospect, her assailant was most likely William Walker, whose was also a young man and clean shaven.

96. Ibid.

CHAPTER 5

1. *St. Louis Republican*, December 12, 1886.
2. *Springfield Leader*, December 13, 1886.
3. William L. Vandeventer, *Justice in the Rough* (Springfield, MO: The Author, 1937), 99.
4. *Springfield Leader*, December 17, 1886.
5. Robert L. Harper, *Among the Bald Knobbers: A History of the Desperadoes of the Ozark Mountains, Their Atrocious Deeds, Rendezvous, Homes and Habits, the Arrest and Conviction* (Clinton, MO: The Author, 1888), 57.
6. *St. Louis Post-Dispatch*, March 14, 1887.
7. Vandeventer, *Justice in the Rough*, 100.
8. *New York Times*, March 21, 1887.
9. Missouri Secretary of State's Office, *Register of Civil Officers, Vol. 1: Adair—Christian Counties, 1865–1904*, MSA, Record Group 5, Reel No. S82, pp. 422.
10. *State of Missouri vs. Wiley Mathews*, 1888, MSA, *Missouri Supreme Court Files*, Box 1144, Case 8.
11. Vandeventer, *Justice in the Rough*, 99–100; *St. Louis Post-Dispatch*, March 15, 1887; *Springfield Express*, March 18, 1887.
12. *State of Missouri vs. Wiley Mathews*, 1888, MSA, *Missouri Supreme Court Files*, Box 1144, Case 8; *State of Missouri vs. David Walker*, 1888, MSA, *Missouri Supreme Court Files*, Box 1144, Case 4. James McGuire and Joseph Inman later testified that Ray had gone home after the meeting at the old smelter. In light of this, Mrs. Greene's assailant was most likely William Walker, who was also a young, clean-shaven man.
13. Vandeventer, *Justice in the Rough*, 98.
14. *St. Louis Post-Dispatch*, March 15, 1887.
15. *Springfield Express*, March 18, 1887; *New York Times*, March 18, 1887.
16. *St. Louis Post-Dispatch*, March 16, 1887; *Springfield Express*, March 18, 1887.
17. *St. Louis Post-Dispatch*, March 17, 1887; *New York Times*, March 18, 1887.
18. *St. Louis Post-Dispatch*, March 18, 1887.
19. *New York Times*, August 24, 1887; *New York Times*, August 28, 1887; *Dallas Weekly Herald*, August 27, 1887; Omaha, Nebraska, *Daily Herald*, December 30, 1888.
20. Harper, *Among the Bald Knobbers*, 68.
21. *Kansas City Star*, March 21, 1887.
22. *St. Louis Post-Dispatch*, March 18, 1887. "Anvil shooting" is a celebratory frontier custom in which two anvils are placed one on top of the other and an explosive charge is detonated between them causing the top anvil to launch high into the air. See Arthur Woodard, "Anvil Firing Launches Seward's July 4th Celebration," *Lincoln Journal Star*, http://journalstar.com/news/local/anvil-firing-launches-seward-s-july-celebration/article_db9e4a77-debb-5b8f-8679-656a74d42434.html (accessed July 8, 2013).
23. *Springfield Leader*, March 19, 1887.
24. *Kansas City Star*, March 29, 1887.
25. Ibid., March 21, 1887.
26. *St. Louis Post-Dispatch*, March 18, 1887.
27. *Kansas City Star*, March 17, 1887.

28. William Vandeventer wrote that "it was generally understood that she and William were engaged." See Vandeventer, *Justice in the Rough*, 107.

29. Ibid., 106-7.

30. *Springfield Leader*, April 21, 1887; *Springfield Daily Republican*, September 7, 1887.

31. See testimony of Joseph Newton in *State of Missouri vs. William Walker*, 1888, MSA, *Missouri Supreme Court Files*, Box 1144, Case 1; Vandeventer, *Justice in the Rough*, 106-8.

32. Vandeventer, *Justice in the Rough*, 108-9; See also testimony of Joseph Newton in *State of Missouri vs. William Walker*, 1888, MSA, *Missouri Supreme Court Files*, Box 1144, Case 1. In his testimony, Newton explains how he enticed Walker and Bean to head toward West Plains with the intent of delivering them to the law. It is Vandeventer, however, who supplies the information that their ultimate destination was Batesville via Jonesboro. It remains unclear why they chose such a circuitous route rather than cutting across directly from Baxter County to Batesville.

33. Ibid.

34. See testimony of Charles Graves and Joe Inman in *State of Missouri vs. David Walker*, 1888, MSA, *Missouri Supreme Court Files*, Box 1144, Case 4.

35. *Kansas City Star*, April 15, 1887.

36. Dave Walker to Joseph Walker, Ozark, MO, October 16, 1887, in the "Lloyd Walker Collection," at the Greene County Archives in Springfield, MO.

37. Amos Jones to Brother, Ozark, MO, n.d., in the "Lloyd Walker Collection," at the Greene County Archives in Springfield, MO.

38. *Kansas City Star*, March 17, 1887; *St. Louis Post-Dispatch*, March 18, 1887; Testimony of Joe Inman in *State of Missouri vs. David Walker*, 1888, MSA, *Missouri Supreme Court Files*, Box 1144, Case 4.

39. *Kansas City Star*, March 21, 1887; Testimony of James McGuire in *State of Missouri vs. Wiley Mathews*, 1888, MSA, *Missouri Supreme Court Files*, Box 1144, Case 8.

40. Testimony of William Abbott in *State of Missouri vs. Wiley Mathews*, 1888, MSA, *Missouri Supreme Court Files*, Box 1144, Case 8.

41. Testimony of Charles Graves in *State of Missouri vs. Wiley Mathews*, 1888, MSA, *Missouri Supreme Court Files*, Box 1144, Case 8.

42. Testimony of Charles Graves in *State of Missouri vs. David Walker*, 1888, MSA, *Missouri Supreme Court Files*, Box 1144, Case 4.

43. *St. Louis Post-Dispatch*, April 23, 1887; *Springfield Leader*, April 23, 1887.

44. *Springfield Leader*, April 21, 1887; *Albuquerque Morning Democrat*, April 22, 1887. *Kansas City Star*, September 6, 1887.

45. *Springfield Daily Republican*, September 7, 1887.

46. Testimony of William Newton in *State of Missouri vs. Wiley Mathews*, 1888, MSA, *Missouri Supreme Court Files*, Box 1144, Case 8.

47. *St. Louis Post-Dispatch*, April 22, 1887; *St. Louis Post-Dispatch*, April 23, 1887.

48. Vandeventer, *Justice in the Rough*, 117-18.

49. *St. Louis Post-Dispatch*, April 28, 1887; *Kansas City Star*, April 28, 1887; *New York Times*, April 29, 1887.

50. *State of Missouri vs. David Walker, et al.*, 1887, MSA, *Christian County Circuit Court Files*, Reel No. C 44318, Box 4, Folder 30.

51. *State of Missouri vs. David Walker, et al.*, 1887, MSA, *Christian County Circuit Court Files*, Reel No. C 44327, Box 10, Folder 62.

52. *State of Missouri vs. David Walker, et al.*, 1887, MSA, *Christian County Circuit Court Files*, Reel No. C 44327, Box 10, Folder 59.

53. *State of Missouri vs. William Newton, et al.*, 1887, MSA, *Christian County Circuit Court Files*, Reel No. C 44349, Box 26, Folder 49.

54. *State of Missouri vs. M. M. Humble, et al.*, 1887, MSA, *Christian County Circuit Court Files*, Reel No. C 44328, Box 10, Folder 120; Vandeventer, *Justice in the Rough*, 92.

55. *State of Missouri vs. David Walker, et al.*, 1887, MSA, *Christian County Circuit Court Files*, Reel No. C 44318, Box 4, Folder 33; Hartman and Ingenthron, *Bald Knobbers*, 150.

56. *State of Missouri vs. David Walker, et al.*, 1887, MSA, *Christian County Circuit Court Files*, Reel No. C 44318, Box 4, Folder 31.

57. *State of Missouri vs. David Walker, et al.*, 1887, MSA, *Christian County Circuit Court Files*, Reel No. 44339, Box 18, Folder 99; *Springfield Leader*, August 26, 1887.

58. *State of Missouri vs. David Walker, et al.*, 1887, MSA, *Christian County Circuit Court Files*, Reel No. C 44318, Box 4, Folder 72.

59. *State of Missouri vs. David Walker, et al.*, 1887, MSA, *Christian County Circuit Court Files*, Reel No. C 44318, Box 4, Folder 32.

60. *State of Missouri vs. M. M. Humble, et al.*, 1887, MSA, *Christian County Circuit Court Files*, Reel No. C 44328, Box 11, Folder 10; *State of Missouri vs. David Walker, et al.*, 1887, MSA, *Christian County Circuit Court Files*, Reel No. C 44336, Box 16, Folder 32; *State of Missouri vs. David Walker, et al.*, 1887, MSA, *Christian County Circuit Court Files*, Reel No. C 44318, Box 4, Folder 31.

61. *State of Missouri vs. T. B. Daugherty*, 1887, MSA, *Christian County Circuit Court Files*, Reel No. C 44328, Box 11, Folder 28.

62. *State of Missouri vs. Joseph Garrison*, 1887, MSA, *Christian County Circuit Court Files*, Reel No. C 44374, Box 45, Folder 116; *Kansas City Star*, August 30, 1887.

63. *St. Louis Post-Dispatch*, April 20, 1887.

64. *Kansas City Star*, April 28, 1887.

65. Ibid., April 22, 1887.

66. *St. Louis Post-Dispatch*, April 28, 1887.

67. *New York Times*, April 28, 1887.

68. *St. Louis Post-Dispatch*, April 23, 1887.

69. *Springfield Leader*, August 23, 1887; *Springfield Daily Republican*, August 24, 1887.

70. U.S. Census Office, *Report on Population of the United States at the Eleventh Census: 1890* (Washington, DC: Government Printing Office, 1895), 213. The population of Ozark in 1890 was 490 people.

71. *Kansas City Star*, August 23, 1887; *New York Times*, August 25, 1887.

72. *Springfield Leader*, August 28, 1887.

73. Ibid., August 26, 1887.

74. Ibid., August 25, 1887; *Kansas City Star*, August 23, 1887.

75. *New York Times*, August 25, 1887.

76. *Springfield Leader*, August 25, 1887.

77. Ibid., August 26, 1887, August 28, 1887.

78. Ibid., August 23, 1887; *Kansas City Star*, August 23, 1887.

79. *Kansas City Star*, August 24, 1887; *Springfield Leader*, August 24, 1887.

80. *Springfield Leader*, August 25, 1887; *New York Times*, August 25, 1887; *Kansas City Star*, August 27, 1887.

81. *State of Missouri vs. David Walker, et al.*, 1887, MSA, *Christian County Circuit Court Files*, Reel No. C 44336, Box 16, Folder 42.

82. Testimony of James Edens and Emma Edens in *State of Missouri vs. Wiley Mathews*, 1888, MSA, *Missouri Supreme Court Files*, Box 1144, Case 8, and *State of Missouri vs. David Walker*, 1888, MSA, *Missouri Supreme Court Files*, Box 1144, Case 4.

83. *U.S. vs. Gat Walker*, 1887, National Archives at Kansas City, MO, Southern Division of the Western District of Missouri, Docket # 130.

84. Testimony of James Edens and J. P. Ralston in *State of Missouri vs. David Walker*, 1888, MSA, *Missouri Supreme Court Files*, Box 1144, Case 4.

85. Testimony of Mary J. Greene, and A. E. Lasley in *State of Missouri vs. David Walker*, 1888, MSA, *Missouri Supreme Court Files*, Box 1144, Case 4. Lasley was a member of the coroner's jury that saw the crime scene.

86. *Kansas City Star*, August 23, 1887.

87. *Springfield Daily Herald*, September 3, 1887.

88. *Springfield Daily Herald*, September 3, 4, and 6, 1887. No transcripts were made of this trial, but according to newspaper accounts the following people testified: James Edens, Melvina, Greene Emma Edens, George W. Greene, Mary J. Greene, Arch Mayden, Nancy Bridges, A. E. Lasley, J. P. Ralston, George F. Greene, Elizabeth Edens, James McGuire, W. J. Johns, W. J. Ray, James Preston, Jack Hiles, John Hiles, Mat Nash, John Nash, Nelson Fischer, Thomas Wendle, Sheriff Zachary Johnson, Charles Graves, E. B. Brown, William Newton, and Lewis Davis. Of these, only Wendle and Brown did not testify in the cases involving Dave Walker, William Walker, Wiley Mathews, or John Mathews.

89. Testimony of Gilbert Applegate in *State of Missouri vs. David Walker*, 1888, MSA, *Missouri Supreme Court Files*, Box 1144, Case 4.

90. *Springfield Daily Herald*, September 7, 1887; *Springfield Daily Herald*, September 8, 1887; *Kansas City Star*, September 7, 1887, *Taney County News*, September 8, 1887.

91. *Springfield Leader*, August 28, 1887; *Springfield Daily Republican*, August 28, 1887; *New York Times*, August 28, 1887.

92. *Springfield Leader*, August 30, 1887; *Springfield Daily Republican*, August 30, 1887; *Kansas City Star*, August 30, 1887.

93. *Springfield Daily Herald*, September 8, 1887; *Springfield Leader*, September 26, 1887.

94. *Springfield Weekly Republican*, March 14, 1889; *Chicago Daily Inter-Ocean*, August 29, 1889. The *Weekly Republican* reported on March 11 that the attorneys for the state and the defendants Andrew Adams and Joseph Hyde had reached a mutual agreement that the cases against them would be continued to the next term, "which means that these two members of Walker's band will never be tried for their part in the last raid." Not until August 28, however, did the state actually drop the cases against them. The reason for the interval is unclear.

95. *State of Missouri vs. Wiley Mathews*, 1888, MSA, *Missouri Supreme Court Files*, Box 1144, Case 8. The prosecution in this case issued a *nolle prosequi* order concerning the indictments against Charles Graves and William Newton, allowing them to testify.

96. Vandeventer, *Justice in the Rough*, 137–38.
97. *Springfield Leader*, February 29, 1888.


CHAPTER 6
1. *State of Missouri vs. William Walker*, 1888, MSA, *Missouri Supreme Court Files*, Box 1144, Case 1.
2. William N. Collier, "Ozark and Vicinity in the Nineteenth Century," *White River Valley Historical Quarterly* 2, no. 11 (Spring 1967): 14. Hereafter, this publication shall be abbreviated as *WRVHQ*.
3. Goodspeed Brothers, *A Reminiscent History of the Ozarks Region: Comprising a Condensed General History ... of Prominent citizens* (Chicago, IL: Goodspeed Brothers, Publishers, 1894), 180–81.
4. Goodspeed Brothers, *Reminiscent History*, 786–87.
5. Goodspeed Brothers, *Pictorial and Genealogical Record of Greene County, Missouri: together with biographies of prominent men of other portions of the state, both living and dead* (Chicago, IL: Goodspeed Brothers, Publishers, 1893), 106.
6. *Springfield Leader*, May 9, 1889.
7. *Springfield Express*, May 10, 1889; Dave Walker to Joseph Walker, Ozark, MO, April 23, 1889, in the "Lloyd Walker Collection," at the Greene County Archives in Springfield, MO.
8. *State of Missouri vs. William Walker*, 1888, MSA, *Missouri Supreme Court Files*, Box 1144, Case 1.
9. Collier, "Ozark and Vicinity in the Nineteenth Century," *WRVHQ* 2, no. 11 (Spring 1967): 14.
10. William L. Vandeventer, *Justice in the Rough* (Springfield, MO: The Author, 1937), 114–15; Goodspeed Brothers, Pictorial and Genealogical Record, 73–74.
11. *New York Sun*, December 23, 1888; Vance Randolph, *The Bald Knobbers: The Story of the Lawless Night-Riders Who Ruled Southern Missouri in the 80's* (Girard, KS: Haldeman-Julius Publications, 1944), 8–9.
12. *State of Missouri vs. William Walker*, 1888, MSA, *Missouri Supreme Court Files*, Box 1144, Case 1. The Bald Knobbers who testified for the state included William J. Ray, James McGuire, William J. Johns, John Hiles, William Abbott, John Nash, Charles Graves, Joseph Newton, Gilbert Applegate, Lewis Davis, and William Newton. A list of the witnesses in this case is located in the table of contents near the end of the file.
13. Testimony of James McGuire, Charles Graves, Joseph Newton, Lewis Davis, and William Newton in *State of Missouri vs. William Walker*, 1888, MSA, *Missouri Supreme Court Files*, Box 1144, Case 1.
14. Testimony of J. P. Ralston, Zachary Johnson, George W. Greene, and Mary J. Greene in *State of Missouri vs. William Walker*, 1888, MSA, *Missouri Supreme Court Files*, Box 1144, Case 1.
15. Testimony of William Walker and Lafayette Abbott in *State of Missouri vs. William Walker*, 1888, MSA, *Missouri Supreme Court Files*, Box 1144, Case 1.
16. Testimony of Lois Newton in *State of Missouri vs. William Walker*, 1888, MSA, *Missouri Supreme Court Files*, Box 1144, Case 1.

17. *State of Missouri vs. William Walker*, 1888, MSA, *Missouri Supreme Court Files*, Box 1144, Case 1; *Springfield Leader*, March 10, 1888.
18. Testimony of William Newton in *State of Missouri vs. Wiley Mathews*, 1888, MSA, *Missouri Supreme Court Files*, Box 1144, Case 8.
19. Testimony of Charles Graves, Lewis Davis, and James Edens in *State of Missouri vs. Wiley Mathews*, 1888, MSA, *Missouri Supreme Court Files*, Box 1144, Case 8. During cross-examination, D. M. Payne asked James Edens if his son owned a pistol. Edens replied that he did, and he kept it at his own house, but he did not have it with him on the night he was murdered.
20. Testimony of George W. Greene in *State of Missouri vs. Wiley Mathews*, 1888, MSA, *Missouri Supreme Court Files*, Box 1144, Case 8.
21. Testimony of Charles Graves, George W. Greene (from Gilbert Applegate trial), and Arthur Allen in *State of Missouri vs. Wiley Mathews*, 1888, MSA, *Missouri Supreme Court Files*, Box 1144, Case 8.
22. *State of Missouri vs. John Mathews*, 1888, MSA, *Missouri Supreme Court Files*, Box 1144, Case 7.
23. Testimony of Charles Graves and Lewis Davis in *State of Missouri vs. Wiley Mathews*, 1888, MSA, *Missouri Supreme Court Files*, Box 1144, Case 8, and *State of Missouri vs. William Walker*, 1888, MSA, *Missouri Supreme Court Files*, Box 1144, Case 1; Testimony of Joseph Inman in *State of Missouri vs. David Walker*, 1888, MSA, *Missouri Supreme Court Files*, Box 1144, Case 4.
24. *Springfield Leader*, March 26, 1888.
25. *Springfield Daily Republican*, April 16, 1889.
26. *Springfield Leader*, May 9, 1889.
27. Ibid., March 26, 1888.
28. Testimony of Joe Inman and Charles Graves in *State of Missouri vs. David Walker*, 1888, MSA, *Missouri Supreme Court Files*, Box 1144, Case 4.
29. Testimony of David Walker in *State of Missouri vs. David Walker*, 1888, MSA, *Missouri Supreme Court Files*, Box 1144, Case 4.
30. Testimony of William Stilliens and Frank Williams in *State of Missouri vs. David Walker*, 1888, MSA, *Missouri Supreme Court Files*, Box 1144, Case 4.
31. Testimony of Joe Inman, Charles Graves, and James McGuire in *State of Missouri vs. David Walker*, 1888, MSA, *Missouri Supreme Court Files*, Box 1144, Case 4.
32. Instructions to the jury in *State of Missouri vs. David Walker*, 1888, MSA, *Missouri Supreme Court Files*, Box 1144, Case 4. The jury instruction quoted here is instruction number eleven.
33. *State of Missouri vs. David Walker*, 1888, MSA, *Missouri Supreme Court Files*, Box 1144, Case 4.
34. *Springfield Daily Herald*, March 28, 1888; *Springfield Leader*, March 26, 1888; Vandeventer, *Justice in the Rough*, 137–38.
35. A Petition from the members of the Springfield Bar to Gov. Lon V. Stephens, Springfield, MO, June 14, 1897, *Western Historical Manuscripts Collection* at Columbia, Missouri. Collection # 1725: Lon V. Stephens Papers, Folder 1. Hereafter, the words *Western Historical Manuscript Collection* shall be abbreviated WHMC.
36. Walter D. Hubbard to Gov. Lon V. Stephens, Springfield, MO, March 1, 1897, WHMC at Columbia, Missouri. Collection # 1725: Lon V. Stephens Papers, Folder 1.

37. Emporia, Kansas, *Daily Gazette*, July 16, 1897.
38. *Springfield Leader*, May 14, 1888; *Kansas City Star*, May 14, 1888.
39. Brief and Argument in support of Motion for a Rehearing in *State of Missouri vs. William Walker*, 1888, MSA, *Missouri Supreme Court Files*, Box 1144, Case 1; *Springfield Daily Republican*, November 14, 1888; *Aberdeen*, South Dakota, *Daily News*, November 15, 1888.
40. *State of Missouri vs. John Mathews*, 1888, MSA, *Missouri Supreme Court Files*, Box 1144, Case 7; *State of Missouri vs. Wiley Mathews*, 1888, MSA, *Missouri Supreme Court Files*, Box 1144, Case 8; *Chicago*, Illinois, *Daily Intelligencer*, December 30, 1888.
41. *Springfield Daily Republican*, August 24, 1887.
42. Statement of Andrew Jackson Whitehead, Springfield, MO, November 28, 1932. WHMC at Columbia, Collection # 3551: *WPA, Historical Records Survey, Missouri, 1935–42*, Folder 5237.
43. Vandeventer, *Justice in the Rough*, 140.
44. Ibid., 141–42; *State of Missouri vs. J. C. Rucker*, 1889, MSA, *Christian County Circuit Court Files*, Reel No. C 44361, Box 36, Folder 115.
45. Vandeventer, *Justice in the Rough*, 143; *Springfield Express*, January 4, 1889; *Springfield Weekly Republican*, February 21, 1889; the quotation comes from the Statement of Andrew Jackson Whitehead, Springfield, MO, November 28, 1932. WHMC at Columbia, Collection # 3551: *WPA, Historical Records Survey, Missouri, 1935–42*, Folder 5237.
46. *New York Times*, December 30, 1888; *Omaha*, Nebraska, *Daily Herald*, December 30, 1888.
47. *State of Missouri vs. J. C. Rucker*, 1889, MSA, *Christian County Circuit Court Files*, Reel No. C 44361, Box 36, Folder 115.
48. Statement of Andrew Jackson Whitehead, Springfield, MO, November 28, 1932. WHMC at Columbia, Collection # 3551: *WPA, Historical Records Survey, Missouri, 1935–42*, Folder 5237.
49. *New York Times*, January 2, 1889.
50. Author's Interview with Lloyd Walker, Springfield, MO, January 2, 2009. The date of this meeting is estimated. In my interview with him, Lloyd Walker remembered being about six years old when he met Wiley Mathews. Since Walker was born in 1924, he probably met the fugitive around 1930.
51. *New York Times*, March 5, 1886, November 13, 1886, December 11, 1886, December 30, 1886.
52. Ibid., March 14, 1887, March 18, 1887, March 21, 1887, April 14, 1887, April 24, 1887, April 28, 1887, April 29, 1887, May 27, 1887, May 30, 1887, August 24, 1887, August 25, 1887, August 28, 1887, September 7, 1887, March 12, 1888, March 19, 1888, May 15, 1888, August 22, 1888, August 23, 1888, November 16, 1888, December 17, 1888, December 30, 1888, January 2, 1889, February 25, 1889, April 14, 1889, July 27, 1889.
53. *Chicago Daily Inter-Ocean*, May 30, 1887, June 18, 1887, July 16, 1887, August 11, 1887, August 23, 1887, August 24, 1887, August 26, 1887, August 27, 1887, August 28, 1887, August 19, 1887, August 31, 1887, September 4, 1887, September 9, 1887, September 10, 1887, September 11, 1887, September 14, 1887, September 30, 1887, November 5, 1887, November 6, 1887, February 13, 1888, February 18, 1888, February 25, 1888, February 26, 1888, February 29, 1888, March 10, 1888,

March 12, 1888, April 10, 1888, April 13, 1888, May 14, 1888, July 9, 1888, July 24, 1888, August 22, 1888, November 13, 1888, December 30, 1888, January 2, 1889, February 9, 1889, February 10, 1889, August 29, 1889.

54. *Springfield Daily Republican*, December 29, 1888; *Taney County Times*, December 13, 1888. Speer was a prominent political reporter for the *Sun*, who spent several years reporting on the state government in Albany, New York. See *New York Times*, April 12, 1893.

55. *Philadelphia Inquirer*, December 1, 1886.

56. *Chicago Daily Inter-Ocean*, June 18, 1887.

57. *Kansas City Star*, November 15, 1888.

58. *Aberdeen*, South Dakota, *Daily News*, November 17, 1888; *Columbus*, Georgia, *Enquirer-Sun*, November 16, 1888; *Omaha*, Nebraska, *Daily Herald*, November 16, 1888.

59. *New York Times*, November 16, 1888. The *Times* apparently did not know that the Missouri Supreme Court had not yet ruled on Dave Walker's case.

60. *Springfield Daily Republican*, November 24, 1888.

61. For a comprehensive analysis of the evolving stereotypes concerning southern mountain people, see Anthony Harkins, *Hillbilly: A Cultural History of an American Icon* (New York: Oxford University Press, 2004).

62. *Chicago Daily Inter-Ocean*, September 10, 1887.

63. Altina L. Waller, *Feud: Hatfields, McCoys, and Social Change in Appalachia, 1860–1900* (Chapel Hill: University of North Carolina Press, 1988), 206–34; Brooks Blevins, "The Arkansas Ghost Trial: The Connie Franklin Case and the Ozarks in the National Media," *Arkansas Historical Quarterly* 68, no. 3 (Autumn 2009): 245–71. See also Brooks Blevins, *Ghost of the Ozarks: Murder and Memory in the Upland South* (Chicago: University of Illinois Press, 2012), 36–43.

64. S. L. Harrison, "The Scopes 'Monkey Trial' Revisited: Mencken and the Editorial Art of Edmund Duffy," *Journal of American Culture* 17, no. 4 (1994): 55–63; Edward J. Larsen, *Summer for the Gods: The Scopes Trial and America's Continuing Debate over Science and Religion* (New York: Basic Books, 1997), 164–65, 175, 179, 182.

65. Testimony of James McGuire, Joe Inman, and Charles Graves in *State of Missouri vs. David Walker*, 1888, MSA, *Missouri Supreme Court Files*, Box 1144, Case 4.

66. Opinion of the Court, filed March 23, 1889, in *State of Missouri vs. David Walker*, 1888, MSA, *Missouri Supreme Court Files*, Box 1144, Case 4.

67. *Springfield Daily Republican*, April 18, 1889; *Columbus*, Georgia, *Enquirer-Sun*, April 18, 1887.

68. Thomas J. Delaney, "Plea for Clemency for the Bald Knobbers," in the "Lloyd Walker Collection," at the Greene County Archives in Springfield, MO. In his appeal, Delaney pled for clemency on the basis of age, arguing that William Walker had only been a boy "under the age of eighteen at the time of the offense commit-ted." Likewise, Dave Walker and John Mathews were both "old men" (between forty and fifty years old), and had maintained excellent reputations prior to their involve-ment in vigilantism. Delaney also invoked recent history, comparing the Bald Knobbers to the "anarchists" involved in the Haymarket Square riot in Chicago and the Molly Maguires of eastern Pennsylvania. He argued that whereas both of these

groups were founded for violent and criminal purposes, the Bald Knobbers had organized to enforce the law and regulate public morals. He also noted approvingly that the governor had commuted the sentences of two of the anarchists involved in the Haymarket Square incident.

69. *Springfield Daily Republican*, November 28, 1888.
70. *Springfield Express*, February 15, 1889.
71. *Springfield Daily Republican*, April 13, 1889.
72. Ibid., April 14, 1889.
73. *Springfield Express*, May 10, 1889.
74. *Springfield Daily Republican*, April 16, 1889.
75. *Springfield Weekly Republican*, April 4, 1889.
76. Harper Barnes, *Standing on a Volcano: The Life and Times of David Rowland Francis* (St. Louis, MO: Missouri Historical Society Press, 2001), 72–73; Quotation in David Thelen, *Paths of Resistance: Tradition and Dignity in Industrializing Missouri* (Oxford: Oxford University Press, 1986), 91.
77. *Springfield Weekly Republican*, May 9, 1889.
78. *Springfield Daily Republican*, May 10, 1889.
79. *Springfield Leader*, May 9, 1889. Ozark was located abreast the short railroad line that ran approximately thirty-five miles from Springfield to Chadwick, so some of the journalists may have been able to get to Springfield by train. At that time, however, the Chadwick train made only one trip a day, leaving Springfield in the morning and departing Chadwick on the return leg around noon, so any person leaving Ozark for Springfield later in the day would have had to go by horseback. See Christian County Centennial, Inc., *Christian County: Its First 100 Years* (Jefferson City, MO: Von Hoffman Press, 1959), 137–38.
80. *Springfield Express*, May 10, 1889.
81. *Kansas City Star*, January 5, 1889; Vandeventer, *Justice in the Rough*, 152–53.
82. *Springfield Daily Republican*, May 10, 1889.
83. *Springfield Express*, May 10, 1889.
84. Ibid.
85. Will Townsend, "Now 92, Herbert Rogers Rubbed Horses' Noses Nearby as Grisly Scene Unfolded," *Springfield News-Leader*, November 23, 1975. This article is based on an interview that Will Townsend conducted with Herbert Rogers in 1975.
86. *Springfield Express*, May 10, 1889; Vandeventer, *Justice in the Rough*, 165–67.
87. *Springfield Express*, May 10, 1889; *Kansas City Star*, May 10, 1889.
88. *Kansas City Star*, May 10, 1889.
89. *Springfield Express*, May 10, 1889.
90. Ibid., May 17, 1889.
91. Vandeventer, *Justice in the Rough*, 173. See also John H. Mitchell, *Tales of Bull Creek Country* (Cassville, MO: The Author, 1990), 21.
92. Vandeventer, *Justice in the Rough*, 172–23; *Springfield Express*, May 17, 1889.
93. Author's Interview with Sharon Maggard, Sparta, Missouri, August 9, 2010. Mrs. Maggard is the great-granddaughter of Dave Walker. She related to me the information given here concerning the gravesite of Dave and William Walker, and also gave me directions to the cemetery so that I could visit it myself.

CHAPTER 7

1. *Springfield Daily Herald*, May 13, 1886; *Springfield Leader*, May 12, 1886.
2. W. H. Jones to Adj. Gen. J. C. Jamison, Forsyth, MO, May 10, 1886, and K. L. Burdette to Adj. Gen. J. C. Jamison, Forsyth, MO, May 12, 1886, Missouri State Archives, *Adjutant General's Papers*, Box 88, Folder 7, MSA. Hereafter, the Missouri State Archives shall be abbreviated as MSA.
3. *Springfield Express*, October 14, 1887; *Springfield Leader*, October 12, 1887, and October 17, 1887.
4. *Springfield Daily Herald*, October 19, 1888.
5. *Kansas City Star*, June 8, 1887; *Taney County News*, June 9, 1887, and June 16, 1887; *Springfield Leader*, October 13, 1887, and October 17, 1887. Only the *Taney County News* and *Springfield Leader* refer to the perpetrator of this crime as "L. T. Matthews." Other sources refer to him as "Bud" or "Bob" Matthews, but these are probably nicknames.
6. For L. T. Matthews's census information, see Lemuel T. Matthews, 1880 U.S. Census, Taney County, Jasper Township, District 123, p. 19.
7. *Chicago Daily Inter-Ocean*, July 9, 1887.
8. *Taney County News*, June 9, 1887.
9. *Springfield Express*, April 17, 1885.
10. *Taney County News*, June 9, 1887. One of the Payton brothers, James S. Payton, was sentenced to be hanged for his role in the murder of the Matthews boy. Payton appealed his case all the way to the Missouri Supreme Court, which affirmed the lower court's ruling. See *Springfield Express*, December 10, 1886; *San Jose, California, Daily News*, December 8, 1886.
11. *Taney County News*, June 16, 1887.
12. *Springfield Leader*, October 17, 1887, and October 19, 1887.
13. Charles Groom and D. F. McConkey, *The Bald Knobbers or Citizens Committee of Taney and Christian Counties, Missouri* (Forsyth, MO: The Authors, 1887), 33; *Springfield Express*, August 20, 1886. Reports differ as to exactly how the shooting occurred. Groom and McConkey say that Pruitt drew his revolver first and that he and Taylor fired at about the same time. The *Express* states that Taylor drew and fired first. As with most of the violent acts in this narrative, different people often told conflicting stories about the same event.
14. Groom and McConkey, *The Bald Knobbers*, 34; *Springfield Express*, August 27, 1886.
15. *Taney County News*, June 16, 1887.
16. Ibid., June 23, 1887.
17. Ibid., May 5, 1887. The editor of the *News* was James A. DeLong, Nat Kinney's stepson, and so its comments on the Bald Knobbers generally favored the vigilantes. The newspaper had no official partisan affiliation, but in its news coverage and its editorial comments it generally supported positions held by the Republican Party. For example, in the same issue quoted here it defended its opposition to increased railroad regulation, a position held by the Republican Party, stating that "until we are thoroughly convinced that further legislation will not discourage railroad building in Missouri we shall remain earnestly opposed to it."
18. *Springfield Weekly Republican*, May 16, 1889.

19. *Taney County News*, March 17, 1887.

20. The Bald Knobbers whom the county sued for back taxes included Charles H. Groom, John J. Brown, Alonzo S. Prather, John L. Cook, and John Haggard. See *State ex rel. vs. C. H. Groom*, 1888, MSA, *Taney County Circuit Court Files*, Reel No. C 37196, Box 15, Folder 4; *State ex rel. vs. Charles H. Groom*, 1888, MSA, *Taney County Circuit Court Files*, Reel No. C 37196, Box 16, Folders 6 and 14; *State ex rel. vs. J. J. Brown*, 1888, MSA, *Taney County Circuit Court Files*, Reel No. C 37196, Box 15, Folder 23; *State ex rel. vs. J. L. Cook*, 1888, MSA, *Taney County Circuit Court Files*, Reel No. C 37196, Box 15, Folder 62; *State ex rel. vs. A. S. Prather*, 1888, MSA, *Taney County Circuit Court Files*, Reel No. C 37196, Box 15, Folder 147; *State ex rel. vs. John Haggard*, 1888, MSA, *Taney County Circuit Court Files*, Reel No. C 37196, Box 16, Folder 61.

21. *State ex rel. vs. William H. Miles, et al.*, 1888, MSA, *Taney County Circuit Court Files*, Reel No. C 37196, Box 16, Folder 107.

22. *State ex rel. vs. Sampson Barker*, 1887, MSA, *Taney County Circuit Court Files*, Reel No. C 37196, Box 15, Folder 26; *State ex rel. vs. Sampson Barker*, 1888, MSA, *Taney County Circuit Court Files*, Reel No. C 37196, Box 15, Folders 3 and 37; *State ex rel. vs. William Lunceford*, 1888, MSA, *Taney County Circuit Court Files*, Reel No. C 37196, Box 16, Folder 138; *State ex rel. vs. William Lunceford*, 1888, MSA, *Taney County Circuit Court Files*, Reel No. C 37197, Box 17, Folder 57; Sampson Barker to Gov. John S. Marmaduke, Forsyth, MO, March 20, 1886, and W. H. Lanceford to Gov. John S. Marmaduke, Forsyth, MO, March 27, 1886, in MSA, *Adjutant General's Papers*, Box 88, Folder 7.

23. *State ex rel. vs. William M. Buck*, 1888, MSA, *Taney County Circuit Court Files*, Reel No. C 37196, Box 15, Folder 60; *State ex rel. vs. W. E. Moore*, 1888, MSA, *Taney County Circuit Court Files*, Reel No. C 37196, Box 16, Folders 170 and 171; Report of Adj. Gen. J. C. Jamison to Gov. John S. Marmaduke, Forsyth, MO, April 9, 1886, MSA, *Adjutant General's Papers*, Box 88, Folder 7.

24. *State ex rel. vs. John Coggburn*, 1887, MSA, *Taney County Circuit Court Files*, Reel No. C 37196, Box 15, Folder 64; *State ex rel. vs. John Coggburn*, 1888, MSA, *Taney County Circuit Court Files*, Reel No. C 37196, Box 15, Folder 96; *State ex rel. vs. Thomas A. Layton and J. S. Coggburn*, 1888, MSA, *Taney County Circuit Court Files*, Reel No. C 37197, Box 17, Folder 59.

25. *State ex rel. vs. Thomas A. Layton*, 1889, MSA, *Taney County Circuit Court Files*, Reel No. C 37196, Box 16, Folder 140; *State ex rel. vs. Thomas A. Layton*, 1888, MSA, *Taney County Circuit Court Files*, Reel No. C 37197, Box 17, Folders 55 and 60; *State ex rel. vs. Thomas A. Layton and J. S. Coggburn*, 1888, MSA, *Taney County Circuit Court Files*, Reel No. C 37197, Box 17, Folder 59; *State ex rel. vs. Thomas F. Layton*, 1888, MSA, *Taney County Circuit Court Files*, Reel No. C 37197, Box 17, Folder 60; *State ex rel. vs. Thomas F. Layton*, 1888, MSA, *Taney County Circuit Court Files*, Reel No. C 37196, Box 16, Folder 142.

26. *State ex rel. vs. K. L. Burdette and Michael Bowerman*, 1888, MSA, *Taney County Circuit Court Files*, Reel No. C 37196, Box 15, Folders 49 and 54; *State ex rel. vs. J. M. Haworth*, 1888, MSA, *Taney County Circuit Court Files*, Reel No. C 37196, Box 16, Folders 55 and 84.

27. *State of Missouri vs. Thomas A. Layton*, 1886, MSA, *Taney County Circuit Court Files*, Reel No. C 37192, Box 1, Folder 6.

28. *State of Missouri vs. Sampson Barker*, 1886, MSA, *Taney County Circuit Court Files*, Reel No. C 37192, Box 1, Folder 15.

29. *State of Missouri vs. Sampson Barker*, 1887, MSA, *Taney County Circuit Court Files*, Reel No. C 37192, Box 1, Folder 8; *State of Missouri vs. Sampson Barker*, 1889, MSA, *Taney County Circuit Court Files*, Reel No. C 37192, Box 1, Folder 32.

30. *State of Missouri vs. Rufus Barker*, 1888, MSA, *Taney County Circuit Court Files*, Reel No. C 37192, Box 1, Folder 24; *State of Missouri vs. Ed Barker*, 1893, MSA, *Taney County Circuit Court Files*, Reel No. C 37192, Box 2, Folder 22.

31. *State of Missouri vs. Rufus C. Barker, et al.*, 1893, MSA, *Taney County Circuit Court Files*, Reel No. C 37192, Box 2, Folder 21; *State of Missouri vs. Rufus C. Barker, et al.*, 1893, MSA, *Taney County Circuit Court Files*, Reel No. C 37192, Box 2, Folder 47; *State of Missouri vs. Edward E. Barker, et al.*, 1893, MSA, *Taney County Circuit Court Files*, Reel No. C 37192, Box 2, Folder 49; *State of Missouri vs. Edward E. Barker, et al.*, 1894, MSA, *Taney County Circuit Court Files*, Reel No. C 37192, Box 2, Folder 68; *State of Missouri vs. Sampson Barker, et al.*, 1897, MSA, *Taney County Circuit Court Files*, Reel C 37193, Box 4, Folder 45; *State of Missouri vs. Edward E. Barker, et al.*, 1897, MSA, *Taney County Circuit Court Files*, Reel C 37193, Box 5, Folder 2.

32. *State of Missouri vs. J. M. Kinyon, et al.*, 1897, MSA, *Taney County Circuit Court Files*, Reel No. C 37193, Box 5, Folder 7; *State of Missouri vs. John Haworth*, 1897, MSA, *Taney County Circuit Court Files*, Reel No. C 37193, Box 5, Folder 7.

33. E. J. and L. S. Hoenshel, *Stories of the Pioneers: Incidents, Adventures and Reminiscences as Told by Some of the Old Settlers of Taney County, Missouri* (Branson, MO: White River Leader, 1915), 77.

34. Ibid., 26.

35. *Kansas City Journal*, April 13, 1886.

36. Vance Randolph, *The Bald Knobbers: The Story of the Lawless Night-Riders Who Ruled Southern Missouri in the 80's* (Girard, KS: Haldeman-Julius Publications, 1944), 27.

37. Mary Hartman and Elmo Ingenthron, *Bald Knobbers: Vigilante on the Ozarks Frontier* (Gretna, LA: Pelican Publishing Company, 1989), 136–37.

38. Gaye Lisby, "Bald Knobbers Exposed: Taney Countian Shares for the First Time Her Family's Experiences with Bald Knobber Treachery and Murder," *Branson Living* (Summer 1995): 24–25.

39. Report of Adj. Gen. J. C. Jamison to Gov. John S. Marmaduke, Forsyth, MO, April 9, 1886, MSA, *Adjutant General's Papers*, Box 88, Folder 7.

40. Richard Prather, "'Cap' Kinney, Bald Knobber Chief," 4, Lynn Morrow Collection. Hereafter, the Lynn Morrow Collection shall be abbreviated LMC.

41. Michael K. McGrath, *Official Directory of the State of Missouri, 1885* (St. Louis, MO: John J. Daley Stationary & Printing Company, 1885), 38; Michael K. McGrath, ed., *Directory of Missouri, 1887–88* (Jefferson City, MO: Tribune Printing Company, 1888), 114; Kristen Kalen and Lynn Morrow, "Nat Kinney's Sunday School Crowd," *WRVHQ* 33, no. 1 (Fall 1993): 12.

42. Missouri Secretary of State's Office, *Register of Civil Officers, Vol. 5: Reynolds–Wright Counties, 1865–1904*, Record Group 5, Reel No. S83, p. 322, MSA.

43. *Nathaniel Kinney vs. the City of Springfield*, 1887, GCA, Greene County Circuit Court, Case # 5902, Springfield, MO. Hereafter, the Greene County Archives shall

be abbreviated GCA. See also, Kristen Kalen and Lynn Morrow, "A Bald Knobber Sues Springfield," *WRVHQ* 32, no. 3 (Spring 1993): 12.

44. *Taney County Times*, November 24, 1887; *Springfield Leader*, August 22, 1888; *Nathaniel Kinney vs. the City of Springfield*, 1887, GCA, Greene County Circuit Court, Case # 5902.

45. *Nathaniel Kinney vs. City of Springfield*, 1887, GCA, Greene County Circuit Court, Case # 5902; Kalen and Morrow, "A Bald Knobber Sues Springfield," *WRVHQ* 32, no. 3 (Spring, 1993): 13–14.

46. *Nathaniel Kinney vs. City of Springfield*, 1887, GCA, Greene County Circuit Court, Case # 5902.

47. *Ann E. Berry vs. J. S. B. Berry,* 1888, MSA, *Taney County Circuit Court Files*, Reel No. C 37195, Box 10, Folder 70.

48. Hartman and Ingenthron, *Bald Knobbers*, 210–12; Vandeventer, *Justice in the Rough*, 81; *Taney County News*, August 5, 1888.

49. Vandeventer, *Justice in the Rough*, 81; *Taney County Times*, August 30, 1888.

50. *Springfield Daily Republican*, August 24, 1888.

51. Vandeventer, *Justice in the Rough*, 81–82; *Springfield Daily Republican*, August 22, 1888; *New York Times*, August 23, 1888; *Taney County Times*, August 30, 1888.

52. *Taney County Times*, August 22, 1888, and August 30, 1888; *Springfield Daily Herald*, August 22, 1888; *Springfield Leader*, August 22, 1888; *New York Times*, August 23, 1888; *Taney County Republican*, June 27, 1957. Some accounts say Miles fired five or six shots, but the indictment makes it clear that he fired four shots, each producing "mortal wounds" on his body. See *State of Missouri vs. William Miles, Jr.*, 1889, GCA, Greene County Circuit Court, Case # 2662.

53. *Springfield Daily Republican*, August 24, 1888; Deposition of James A. Delong in *State of Missouri vs. James S. B. Berry*, 1889, GCA, Greene County Circuit Court, Case # 2648.

54. *State of Missouri vs. James S. B. Berry*, 1889, MSA, *Taney County Circuit Court Files*, Reel No. C 37192, Box 1, Folder 22.

55. *Springfield Leader*, August 22, 1888; *Taney County Times*, August 23, 1888.

56. *Springfield Daily Republican*, August 24, 1888; *Taney County Times*, August 23, 1888; *Taney County Republican*, June 27, 1957.

57. *Springfield Leader*, August 22, 1888; *Taney County Times*, August 30, 1888.

58. *Springfield Daily Republican*, August 24, 1888. In his 1957 retrospective articles on the Bald Knobbers, Richard Prather tells a similar story. According to Prather, next to Kinney's body "lay 'Long Tom,' a gun Kinney never carried. On a desk lay 'Short Tom' his constant companion. Form your own opinion. It looked like deliberate murder to most of us." See *Taney County Republican*, June 27, 1957.

59. *Taney County Times*, August 23, 1888.

60. Ibid., August 30, 1888.

61. *St. Louis Post-Dispatch*, August 21, 1888. A version of this story was later republished in the *New Orleans Times-Picayune*, August 22, 1888.

62. *Springfield Daily Republican*, August 23, 1888.

63. *Springfield Leader*, September 1, 1888.

64. *Springfield Daily Republican*, August 24, 1888, and August 26, 1888.

65. *Springfield Daily Republican*, October 12, 1888; *Chicago Daily Inter-Ocean*, October 11, 1888; *State of Missouri vs. James S. B. Berry*, 1889, MSA, *Taney County Circuit Court Files*, Reel No. C 37192, Box 1, Folder 22.

66. 1888 Election Returns for Senatorial Districts and U.S. Congressional Districts, Record Group 5, Box 16, Folders 1 and 2, MSA.

67. Missouri Secretary of State's Office, *Register of Civil Officers, Vol. 5: Reynolds–Wright Counties, 1865–1904*, Record Group 5, Reel No. S83, pp. 322, MSA.

68. *State of Missouri vs. William Miles, Jr.*, 1889, GCA, Greene County Circuit Court, Case # 2662; *State of Missouri vs. James S. B. Berry*, 1889, MSA, *Taney County Circuit Court Files*, Reel No. C 37192, Box 1, Folder 22; *Springfield Daily Republican*, April 6, 1889.

69. *Springfield Daily Republican*, April 9, 1889.

70. *State of Missouri vs. William Miles, Jr.*, 1889, GCA, Greene County Circuit Court, Case # 2662.

71. *Springfield Leader*, July 9, 1889; *Taney County Times*, July 11, 1889; *Springfield Express*, July 12, 1889.

72. In the late nineteenth century, individual detectives and detective agencies, such as the famed Pinkerton National Detective Agency, often hired themselves out to railroads, mining companies, and other industrial concerns to act as a kind of corporate police force. For example, private detectives played a key role in the infiltration and prosecution of the secretive Irish coal miner association in eastern Pennsylvania known as the Molly Maguires, and in suppressing labor unrest during the railroad strikes of 1877. For a discussion of the reputation of detectives and detective agencies in the late nineteenth century, and their role as hired guns for large corporations, see William R. Hunt, *Front Page Detective: William J. Burns and the Detective Profession, 1880–1930* (Bowling Green, OH: Bowling Green State University Popular Press, 1990), 95–110. See also Frank Morn, *The Eye That Never Sleeps: A History of the Pinkerton National Detective Agency* (Bloomington: Indiana University Press, 1982), 68–109.

73. *Springfield Leader*, July 2, 1889; *Springfield Express*, July 12, 1889.

74. Hartman and Ingenthron, *Bald Knobbers*, 246.

75. *Springfield Leader*, July 9, 1889; *Taney County Times*, July 11, 1889; *Springfield Express*, July 12, 1889.

76. *Springfield Leader*, July 9, 1889; *Taney County Times*, July 11, 1889; *Springfield Express*, July 12, 1889.

77. *Springfield Leader*, July 9, 1889; *Taney County Times*, July 11, 1889; *Springfield Express*, July 12, 1889. The newspaper accounts cited here give the name of the man who sheltered James Miles as "Cal Adkinson," "T. C. Adkinson," or "Calvin Atkins." It remains unclear which of these names is correct.

78. *Springfield Weekly Republican*, July 18, 1889.

79. *Springfield Express*, July 12, 1889.

80. *Springfield Daily Republican*, July 25, 1889, and July 26, 1889.

81. *Springfield Leader*, August 22, 1888.

82. *Springfield Daily Republican*, August 22, 1888.

83. See depositions of James A. DeLong and W. B. Burks in *State of Missouri vs. James S. B. Berry*, 1889, GCA, Greene County Circuit Court, Case # 2648.

84. *Springfield Daily Republican*, February 28, 1890, and February 29, 1890.
85. *Springfield Express*, June 6, 1890.
86. *State of Missouri vs. William Miles, Jr.*, 1889, GCA, Greene County Circuit Court, Case # 2662, GCA; *Springfield Daily Republican*, March 19, 1890, March 22, 1890, and March 23, 1890; *Springfield Express*, March 28, 1890.
87. *Taney County Times*, March 27, 1890.
88. *State of Missouri vs. William Miles, Jr.*, 1889, GCA, Greene County Circuit Court, Case # 2662.
89. *Taney County Times*, September 5, 1890.
90. *Ozark Mail*, September 5, 1890, quoted in Hartman and Ingenthron, *Bald Knobbers*, 268.
91. *Springfield Express*, September 12, 1890; *St. Louis Globe-Democrat*, September 6, 1890.
92. Douglas Mahnkey, "Dark Day in Old Forsyth," *Ozarks Mountaineer* 31, no. 1 (February 1983): 42–44.
93. *Kansas City Star*, March 16, 1892, March 18, 1892; *Springfield Leader*, March 14, 1892.
94. *Springfield Leader*, May 6, 1892. In his article on the Bright lynching, Douglas Mahnkey agreed with Wood's conclusion that the killing was not "a Bald Knobber lynching." See Mahnkey, "Dark Day in Old Forsyth," 43.
95. Mahnkey, "Dark Day in Old Forsyth," 45–46.
96. John H. Haworth, "Taney County Bald Knobbers," *WRVHQ* 9, no. 3 (Spring 1986): 27.
97. Missouri Secretary of State's Office, *Register of Civil Officers, Vol. 5: Reynolds–Wright Counties, 1865–1904*, Record Group 5, Reel No. S83, pp. 323–25, MSA.
98. Elmo Ingenthron, *The Land of Taney: A History of an Ozark Commonwealth* (Branson, MO: Ozarks Mountaineer, 1953), 234.

CONCLUSION
1. Alonzo Prather to Adj. Gen. J. C. Jamison, Kirbyville, MO, June 11, 1886, Missouri State Archives, *Adjutant General's Papers*, Box 88, File 7. Hereafter, Missouri State Archives shall be abbreviated as MSA.
2. Sampson Barker to Gov. John S. Marmaduke, Forsyth, MO, March 20, 1886, MSA, *Adjutant General's Papers*, Box 88, File 7.
3. Vance Randolph, *The Devil's Pretty Daughter: and Other Ozark Folk Tales* (New York: Columbia University Press, 1955), 39–42; Hartman and Ingenthron, *Bald Knobbers*, 97–100.
4. *Springfield Weekly Republican*, May 16, 1889.
5. Duane G. Meyer, *The Heritage of Missouri*, 3rd ed. (Springfield, MO: Emden Press, 1982), 506–8.
6. Henry Sinclair Drago, *Outlaws on Horseback: The History of the Organized Bands of Bank and Train Robbers Who Terrorized the Prairie Towns of Missouri, Kansas, Indian Territory, and Oklahoma for Half a Century* (Lincoln: University of Nebraska Press, 1988), 19–28.
7. U.S. Census Office, *A Compendium of the Ninth Census (June 1, 1870) Compiled*

*Pursuant to a Concurrent Resolution of Congress and under the Direction of the Secretary of the Interior* (Washington, DC: Government Printing Office, 1872), 531–33; U.S. Census Office, *A Compendium of the Tenth Census (June 1, 1880) Compiled Pursuant to an Act of Congress Approved August 7, 1882,* Part 2 (Washington, DC: Government Printing Office, 1888), 1676.

    8. Harriet C. Frazier, *Lynchings in Missouri, 1803–1981* (Jefferson, NC: McFarland & Company, 2009), 191–97.

    9. Patrick Bates Nolan, "Vigilantes on the Middle Border: A Study of Self-Appointed Law Enforcement in the States of the Upper Mississippi from 1840 to 1880" (PhD Dissertation, University of Minnesota, 1971), 134–50; Jonathan Fairbanks and Clyde Edwin Tuck, *Past and Present of Greene County, Missouri: Early and Recent History and Genealogical Records of Many of the Representative Citizens* (Indianapolis, IN: A. W. Bowen, 1915), 223–28; Return I. Holcombe, *History of Vernon County, Missouri: Written and Compiled from the Most Authentic Official and Private Sources, Including a History of its Townships, Towns and Villages* (St. Louis, MO: Brown & Company, 1887), 349–50.

    10. E. J. and L. S. Hoenshel, *Stories of the Pioneers: Incidents, Adventures and Reminiscences as Told by Some of the Old Settlers of Taney County, Missouri* (Point Lookout, MO: School of the Ozarks Press, 1915), 54.

    11. *Springfield Express,* October 23, 1884; *New York Sun,* December 23, 1888.

    12. Missouri General Assembly, *Report of the State Auditor to the Thirty-Third General Assembly of the State of Missouri, for the Two Fiscal Years Beginning January 1, 1883, and Ending December 31, 1884* (Jefferson City, MO: Tribune Printing Company, State Printers, 1885), 197, LMC.

    13. *Springfield Weekly Republican,* May 16, 1889.

    14. *Taney County News,* June 16, 1887.

    15. *New York Sun,* December 23, 1888; Vance Randolph, *The Bald Knobbers: The Story of the Lawless Night-Riders Who Ruled Southern Missouri in the 80's* (Girard, KS: Haldeman-Julius Publications, 1944), 8–9.

    16. *New York Times,* November 13, 1886.

    17. *Kansas City Star,* August 24, 1887.

    18. *Springfield Daily Herald,* September 28, 1887.

    19. Charles H. Groom and D. F. McConkey, *The Bald Knobbers or Citizen's Committee of Taney and Christian Counties, Missouri: A History of Southwest Missouri's Famous Organization, Its Origin, Object, Workings, and Final Termination* (Forsyth, MO: The Authors, 1887), 46; *Springfield Leader,* August 26, 1887.

    20. Edith McCall, *English Village in the Ozarks: The Story of Hollister, Missouri* (Hollister, MO: The Author, 1969), 18.

    21. Lucille Morris Upton, *Bald Knobbers* (Caldwell, ID: Caxton Printers, 1939), 110–12.

    22. *Springfield Express,* March 18, 1887; William L. Vandeventer, *Justice in the Rough* (Springfield, MO: The Author, 1937), 3, 122.

    23. *Springfield Leader,* January 1, 1889; *Springfield Express,* May 10, 1889; *Kansas City Star,* May 10, 1889.

    24. *Springfield Daily Herald,* April 14, 1886, and April 17, 1886; *New York Times,* December 11, 1886.

25. *Springfield Leader*, August 22, 1888; *Kansas City Star*, August 21, 1888; *New York Times*, August 23, 1888.

26. *Springfield Leader*, July 9, 1889; *Springfield Express*, July 12, 1889; *Kansas City Star*, July 9, 1889.

27. Richard Maxwell Brown, *Strain of Violence: Historical Studies of American Violence and Vigilantism* (Oxford: Oxford University Press, 1975), 98–118.

28. Ibid., 98–102; See also Richard Maxwell Brown, *The South Carolina Regulators* (Cambridge, MA: Harvard University Press, 1963), 135–42.

29. George R. Stewart, *Committee of Vigilance: Revolution in San Francisco, 1851* (Boston, MA: Houghton Mifflin, 1964); Alan C. Valentine, *Vigilante Justice* (New York: Reynal and Company, 1956); Lew L. Callaway, *Montana's Righteous Hangmen: The Vigilantes in Action* (Norman: University of Oklahoma Press, 1982); Frederick Allen, *A Decent, Orderly Lynching: The Montana Vigilantes* (Norman: University of Oklahoma Press, 2004).

30. *Springfield Daily Herald*, September 16, 1887.

31. Brown, *The South Carolina Regulators*, 150.

32. Madeleine M. Noble, "The White Caps of Harrison and Crawford County, IN: A Study in the Violent Enforcement of Morality" (Ph.D. Dissertation, University of Michigan, 1973); E. W. Crozier, *The White-Caps: A History of the Organization in Sevier County* (Knoxville, TN: Bean, Warters & Gaut, Printers and Binders, 1899); Robert E. Cunningham, *Trial by Mob* (Stillwater, OK: Redland Press, 1957).

# Bibliography

## PRIMARY SOURCES

### MANUSCRIPT COLLECTIONS

*MISSOURI STATE ARCHIVES, JEFFERSON CITY, MO:*
1860 Election Returns, Record Group 5, Box 8, Folders 4–10.
1868 Election Returns, Record Group 5, Box 12, Folder 5.
1870 Election Returns, Record Group 5, Box 13, Folder 2.
1872 Election Returns, Record Group 5, Box 14, Folder 9.
*Adjutant General's Papers*, Box 88, Folder 7.
*Christian County Land Assessment*, 1885, Reel No. C 1649.
*Register of Civil Officers, Vol. 1: Adair—Christian Counties, 1865–1904*, Record Group 5, Reel No. S82.
*Register of Civil Officers, Vol. 5: Reynolds—Wright Counties, 1865–1904*, Record Group 5, Reel No. S83.
*Taney County Land Assessment*, 1886, Reel No. C 14339.
*United States Provost Marshal Papers*, Reel No. F1183.
*United States Provost Marshal Papers*, Reel No. F1205.
*United States Provost Marshal Papers*, Reel No. F1226.
*United States Provost Marshal Papers*, Reel No. F1273.
*United States Provost Marshal Papers*, Reel No. F1360.
*United States Provost Marshal Papers*, Reel No. F1477.

*WESTERN HISTORICAL MANUSCRIPT COLLECTION, COLUMBIA, MO:*
Collection 1041: *E. Y. Mitchell Papers.*
Collection 1725: *Lon V. Stephens Papers.*
Collection 3551: *WPA Historical Records Survey, Missouri, 1935–42.*

*WESTERN HISTORICAL MANUSCRIPT COLLECTION, ROLLA, MO:*
Audio Recording of Lucille Morris Upton Interview, Springfield, Missouri, July 25, 1979. R669: *Bittersweet Collection.* Box 7, Folder 237.
Bald Knobber Photographs. R 669: *Bittersweet Collection.* Box 16, Photo box 2.

**GREENE COUNTY ARCHIVES AND RECORD CENTER, SPRINGFIELD, MO:**
Civil War Related Court Files
Lloyd Walker Collection

**LYNN MORROW COLLECTION, PRIVATE COLLECTION, JEFFERSON CITY, MO:**

**Unpublished Court Cases**

**CHRISTIAN COUNTY CIRCUIT COURT RECORDS AT THE MISSOURI STATE ARCHIVES, JEFFERSON CITY, MO:**

*State of Missouri vs. Andrew J. Walker*, 1871. *Christian County Circuit Court Files*, Reel No. C 44361, Box 37, Folder 15.

*State of Missouri vs. A. R. Gonce*, 1884. *Christian County Circuit Court Files*, Reel No. C 44374, Box 35, Folder 29.

*State of Missouri vs. David Walker, et al.*, 1887. *Christian County Circuit Court Files*, Reel No. C 44318, Box 4, Folder 30.

*State of Missouri vs. David Walker, et al.*, 1887. *Christian County Circuit Court Files*, Reel No. C 44318, Box 4, Folder 31.

*State of Missouri vs. David Walker, et al.*, 1887. *Christian County Circuit Court Files*, Reel No. C 44318, Box 4, Folder 32.

*State of Missouri vs. David Walker, et al.*, 1887. *Christian County Circuit Court Files*, Reel No. C 44318, Box 4, Folder 33.

*State of Missouri vs. David Walker, et al.*, 1887. *Christian County Circuit Court Files*, Reel No. C 44318, Box 4, Folder 72.

*State of Missouri vs. David Walker, et al.*, 1887. *Christian County Circuit Court Files*, Reel No. C 44327, Box 10, Folder 59.

*State of Missouri vs. David Walker, et al.*, 1887. *Christian County Circuit Court Files*, Reel No. C 44327, Box 10, Folder 62.

*State of Missouri vs. David Walker, et al.*, 1887. *Christian County Circuit Court Files*, Reel No. C 44336, Box 16, Folder 32.

*State of Missouri vs. David Walker, et al.*, 1887. *Christian County Circuit Court Files*, Reel No. C 44336, Box 16, Folder 42.

*State of Missouri vs. David Walker, et al.*, 1887. *Christian County Circuit Court Files*, Reel No. 44339, Box 18, Folder 99.

*State of Missouri vs. G. W. Whiteside*, et al., 1884. *Christian County Circuit Court Files*, Reel No. C44333, Box 14, Folder 40.

*State of Missouri vs. H. R. H. McCauley*, 1886. *Christian County Circuit Court Files*, Reel No. C 44320, Box 5, Folders 67 and 68.

*State of Missouri vs. James S. Payten*, 1886. *Christian County Circuit Court Files*, Reel No. 44367, Box 40, Folder 130.

*State of Missouri vs. J. C. Rucker*, 1889. *Christian County Circuit Court Files*, Reel No. C 44361, Box 36, Folder 115.

*State of Missouri vs. J. H. Shipman*, 1868. *Christian County Circuit Court Files*, Reel No. C 44339, Box 18, Folder 82.

*State of Missouri vs. John Bolton*, 1869. *Christian County Circuit Court Files*, Reel No. C 44378, Box 48, Folder 5.

*State of Missouri vs. John Bowman*, 1876. *Christian County Circuit Court Files*, Reel No. 44327, Box 10, Folder 77.

*State of Missouri vs. John Fugitt,* 1876. *Christian County Circuit Court Files,* Reel No. C 44327, Box 10, Folder 78.

*State of Missouri vs. Joseph Garrison,* 1887. *Christian County Circuit Court Files,* Reel No. C 44374, Box 45, Folder 116.

*State of Missouri vs. John Rhodes,* 1885. *Christian County Circuit Court Files,* Reel No. C 44313, Box 1, Folder 103.

*State of Missouri vs. John Rhodes,* 1886. *Christian County Circuit Court Files,* Reel No. C 47704, Box 66, Folder 127.

*State of Missouri vs. John T. Swearengen,* 1886. *Christian County Circuit Court Files,* Reel No. C 44350, Box 27, Folder 23.

*State of Missouri vs. M. H. Kerr,* et al., 1876. *Christian County Circuit Court Files,* Reel No. C 44336, Box 16, Folder 82.

*State of Missouri vs. M. M. Humble, et al.,* 1887. *Christian County Circuit Court Files,* Reel No. C 44328, Box 10, Folder 120.

*State of Missouri vs. M. M. Humble, et al.,* 1887. *Christian County Circuit Court Files,* Reel No. C 44328, Box 11, Folder 10.

*State of Missouri vs. Roswell K. Hart, et al.,* 1874. *Christian County Circuit Court Files,* Reel No. C 44378, Box 48, Folder 23.

*State of Missouri vs. T. B. Daugherty,* 1887. *Christian County Circuit Court Files,* Reel No. C 44328, Box 11, Folder 28.

*State of Missouri vs. William Magill,* 1883. *Christian County Circuit Court Files,* Reel No. C 44369, Box 42, Folder 9.

*State of Missouri vs. William Newton, et al.,* 1887. *Christian County Circuit Court Files,* Reel No. C 44349, Box 26, Folder 49.

*State of Missouri vs. William R. Beeler,* 1883. *Christian County Circuit Court Files,* Reel No. C 44319, Box 4, Folders 127 and 128.

*State of Missouri vs. William R. Payton,* 1886. *Christian County Circuit Court Files,* Reel No. 44373, Box 44, Folder 126.

*State of Missouri vs. W. D. Wilson and A. J. Inman,* 1882. *Christian County Circuit Court Files,* Reel No. C 44365, Box 10, Folder 82.

TANEY COUNTY CIRCUIT COURT RECORDS AT THE MISSOURI STATE ARCHIVES, JEFFERSON CITY, MO:

*Ann E. Berry vs. J. S. B. Berry,* 1888. *Taney County Circuit Court Files,* Reel No. C 37195, Box 10, Folder 70.

*State ex rel. vs. A. S. Prather,* 1888. *Taney County Circuit Court Files,* Reel No. C 37196, Box 15, Folder 147.

*State ex rel. vs. Charles H. Groom,* 1888. *Taney County Circuit Court Files,* Reel No. C 37196, Box 16, Folders 6 and 14.

*State ex rel. vs. C. H. Groom,* 1888. *Taney County Circuit Court Files,* Reel No. C 37196, Box 15, Folder 4.

*State ex rel. vs. J. J. Brown,* 1888. *Taney County Circuit Court Files,* Reel No. C 37196, Box 15, Folder 23.

*State ex rel. vs. J. L. Cook,* 1888. *Taney County Circuit Court Files,* Reel No. C 37196, Box 15, Folder 62.

*State ex rel. vs. J. M. Haworth,* 1888. *Taney County Circuit Court Files,* Reel No. C 37196, Box 16, Folders 55 and 84.

*State ex rel. vs. John Coggburn,* 1887. *Taney County Circuit Court Files,* Reel No. C 37196, Box 15, Folder 64.

*State ex rel. vs. John Coggburn,* 1888. *Taney County Circuit Court Files,* Reel No. C 37196, Box 15, Folder 96.

*State ex rel. vs. John Haggard,* 1888. *Taney County Circuit Court Files,* Reel No. C 37196, Box 16, Folder 61.

*State ex rel. vs. K. L. Burdette and Michael Bowerman,* 1888. *Taney County Circuit Court Files,* Reel No. C 37196, Box 15, Folders 49 and 54.

*State ex rel. vs. Sampson Barker,* 1887. *Taney County Circuit Court Files,* Reel No. C 37196, Box 15, Folder 26.

*State ex rel. vs. Sampson Barker,* 1888. *Taney County Circuit Court Files,* Reel No. C 37196, Box 15, Folders 3 and 37.

*State ex rel. vs. Thomas A. Layton,* 1889. *Taney County Circuit Court Files,* Reel No. C 37196, Box 16, Folder 140.

*State ex rel. vs. Thomas A. Layton,* 1888. *Taney County Circuit Court Files,* Reel No. C 37197, Box 17, Folders 55 and 60.

*State ex rel. vs. Thomas A. Layton and J. S. Coggburn,* 1888. *Taney County Circuit Court Files,* Reel No. C 37197, Box 17, Folder 59.

*State ex rel. vs. Thomas F. Layton,* 1888. *Taney County Circuit Court Files,* Reel No. C 37196, Box 16, Folder 142.

*State ex rel. vs. Thomas F. Layton,* 1888. *Taney County Circuit Court Files,* Reel No. C 37197, Box 17, Folder 60.

*State ex rel. vs. W. E. Moore,* 1888. *Taney County Circuit Court Files,* Reel No. C 37196, Box 16, Folders 170 and 171.

*State ex rel. vs. William H. Miles, et al.,* 1888. *Taney County Circuit Court Files,* Reel No. C 37196, Box 16, Folder 107.

*State ex rel. vs. William M. Buck,* 1888. *Taney County Circuit Court Files,* Reel No. C 37196, Box 15, Folder 60.

*State ex rel. vs. William Lunceford,* 1888. *Taney County Circuit Court Files,* Reel No. C 37196, Box 16, Folder 138.

*State of Missouri vs. Ed Barker,* 1893. *Taney County Circuit Court Files,* Reel No. C 37192, Box 2, Folder 22.

*State of Missouri vs. Edward E. Barker, et al.,* 1893. *Taney County Circuit Court Files,* Reel No. C 37192, Box 2, Folder 49.

*State of Missouri vs. Edward E. Barker, et al.,* 1894. *Taney County Circuit Court Files,* Reel No. C 37192, Box 2, Folder 68.

*State of Missouri vs. Edward E. Barker, et al.,* 1897. *Taney County Circuit Court Files,* Reel C 37193, Box 5, Folder 2.

*State of Missouri vs. James S. B. Berry,* 1889. *Taney County Circuit Court Files,* Reel No. C 37192, Box 1, Folder 22.

*State of Missouri vs. J. M. Kinyon, et al.,* 1897. *Taney County Circuit Court Files,* Reel No. C 37193, Box 5, Folder 7.

*State of Missouri vs. John Haworth,* 1897. *Taney County Circuit Court Files,* Reel No. C 37193, Box 5, Folder 7.

*State of Missouri vs. Rufus Barker,* 1888. *Taney County Circuit Court Files,* Reel No. C 37192, Box 1, Folder 24.

*State of Missouri vs. Rufus C. Barker, et al.,* 1893. *Taney County Circuit Court Files,* Reel No. C 37192, Box 2, Folder 21.

*State of Missouri vs. Rufus C. Barker, et al.,* 1893. *Taney County Circuit Court Files,* Reel No. C 37192, Box 2, Folder 47.

*State of Missouri vs. Sampson Barker,* 1887. *Taney County Circuit Court Files,* Reel No. C 37192, Box 1, Folder 8.

*State of Missouri vs. Sampson Barker,* 1886. *Taney County Circuit Court Files,* Reel No. C 37192, Box 1, Folder 15.

*State of Missouri vs. Sampson Barker,* 1889. *Taney County Circuit Court Files,* Reel No. C 37192, Box 1, Folder 32.

*State of Missouri vs. Sampson Barker, et al.,* 1897. *Taney County Circuit Court Files,* Reel No. C 37193, Box 4, Folder 45.

*State of Missouri vs. Thomas A. Layton,* 1886. *Taney County Circuit Court Files,* Reel No. C 37192, Box 1, Folder 6.

**GREENE COUNTY CIRCUIT COURT RECORDS AT THE GREENE COUNTY ARCHIVES AND RECORDS CENTER, SPRINGFIELD, MO:**

*Nathaniel Kinney vs. the City of Springfield,* 1887. Greene County Circuit Court, Case # 5902.

*State of Missouri vs. James S. B. Berry,* 1889. Greene County Circuit Court, Case # 2648.

*State of Missouri vs. William Miles, Jr.,* 1889. Greene County Circuit Court, Case # 2662.

**MISSOURI SUPREME COURT RECORDS AT MISSOURI STATE ARCHIVES, JEFFERSON CITY, MO:**

*State of Missouri vs. David Walker,* 1888. *Missouri Supreme Court Files,* Box 1144, Case 4.

*State of Missouri vs. John Mathews,* 1888. *Missouri Supreme Court Files,* Box 1144, Case 7.

*State of Missouri vs. Wiley Mathews,* 1888. *Missouri Supreme Court Files,* Box 1144, Case 8.

*State of Missouri vs. William Walker,* 1888. *Missouri Supreme Court Files,* Box 1144, Case 1.

**U.S. DISTRICT COURT RECORDS AT THE NATIONAL ARCHIVES IN KANSAS CITY, MO:**

*U.S. vs. Amos Jones and Henry Applegate,* 1887. Southern Division of the Western District of Missouri, Docket # 137.

*U.S. vs. Andy Adams and C. O. Simmons,* 1887. Southern Division of the Western District of Missouri, Docket # 134.

*U.S. vs. David Hunter,* 1888. Southern Division of the Western District of Missouri, Docket # 309.

*U.S. vs. Dr. Daniel Vandeventer,* 1887. Southern Division of the Western District of Missouri, Docket # 85.

*U.S. vs. Gat Walker,* 1887. Southern Division of the Western District of Missouri, Docket # 130.

*U.S. vs. George L. Sanders*, 1887. Southern Division of the Western District of Missouri, Docket # 99.

*U.S. vs. Granville Vanbiber*, 1887. Southern Division of the Western District of Missouri, Docket # 7.

*U.S. vs. Henry Applegate*, 1887. Southern Division of the Western District of Missouri, Docket # 123.

*U.S. vs. Jack Hiles*, 1887. Southern Division of the Western District of Missouri, Docket # 122.

*U.S. vs. James Morrisett*, 1887. Southern Division of the Western District of Missouri, Docket # 121.

*U.S. vs. James T. White*, 1887. Southern Division of the Western District of Missouri, Docket # 111.

*U.S. vs. James W. Carr*, 1887. Southern Division of the Western District of Missouri, Docket # 88.

*U.S. vs. J. L. Garrison*, 1888. Southern Division of the Western District of Missouri, Docket # 260.

*U.S. vs. Joel Casad*, 1887. Southern Division of the Western District of Missouri, Docket # 99.

*U.S. vs. John Denney*, 1887. Central Division of the Western District of Missouri, Docket # 2520.

*U.S. vs. John James*, 1887. Southern Division of the Western District of Missouri, Docket # 82.

*U.S. vs. Matt Nash and Gilbert Applegate*, 1887. Southern Division of the Western District of Missouri, Docket # 133.

*U.S. vs. Newton Myers*, 1887. Southern Division of the Western District of Missouri, Docket # 323.

*U.S. vs. Sam Newton and James Morrisett*, 1887. Southern Division of the Western District of Missouri, Docket # 128.

*U.S. vs. Simon Lakey*, 1887. Southern Division of the Western District of Missouri, Docket # 97.

*U.S. vs. Thomas K. Jones*, 1887. Southern Division of the Western District of Missouri, Docket # 78.

*U.S. vs. Uriah Pruitt*, 1887. Southern Division of the Western District of Missouri, Docket # 98.

*U.S. vs. William Applegate*, 1887. Southern Division of the Western District of Missouri, Docket # 113.

*U.S. vs. William Newton and Matt Shipman*, 1887. Southern Division of the Western District of Missouri, Docket # 135.

*U.S. vs. William Roberts and Jack Hiles*, 1887. Southern Division of the Western District of Missouri, Docket # 126.

*U.S. vs. William Smith*, 1887. Southern Division of the Western District of Missouri, Docket # 116.

*U.S. vs. Wylie Matthews and Ed Linscott*, 1887. Southern Division of the Western District of Missouri, Docket # 136.

## NEWSPAPERS

Aberdeen, South Dakota, *Aberdeen Daily News*, 1888
*Albuquerque Morning Democrat*, 1887
*Chicago Daily Intelligencer*, 1888
*Chicago Daily Inter-Ocean*, 1886 to 1889
*Christian County Republican*, 1953
Columbus, Georgia, *Columbus Enquirer-Sun*, 1887 to 1889
*Dallas Morning News*, 1886 to 1888
Emporia, Kansas, *Emporia Daily Gazette*, 1897
*Jefferson City Daily Tribune*, 1885 to 1888
*Jefferson City State Times*, 1887
*Kansas City Journal*, 1886
*Kansas City Star*, 1885 to 1913
*New York Sun*, 1888
*New York Times*, 1886 to 1944
Omaha, Nebraska, *Omaha Daily Herald*, 1888
*Philadelphia Inquirer*, 1885 to 1889
San Jose, California, *San Jose Daily News*, 1886
*Springfield Daily Herald*, 1886 to 1888
*Springfield Daily Republican*, 1887 to 1890
*Springfield Express*, 1883 to 1889
*Springfield Leader*, 1886 to 1889
Springfield, *Missouri Weekly Patriot*, 1870
*Springfield News-Leader*, 1975 to 1989
*Springfield Patriot Advertiser*, 1879
*Springfield Weekly Republican*, 1889
*St. Louis Daily Dispatch*, 1865
*St. Louis Post-Dispatch*, 1886 to 1889
*St. Louis Republican*, 1886
*Stone County News Oracle*, 1963
*Taney County News*, 1887 to 1888
*Taney County Republican*, 1903 to 1956
*Taney County Times*, 1887 to 1891

## AUTHOR'S INTERVIEWS

Maggard, Sharon. Recorded Interview with author. Sparta, Missouri, August 9, 2010.
Walker, Lloyd. Recorded Interview with author. Springfield, Missouri, January 2, 2009.

## PUBLISHED PRIMARY SOURCES

Lang, Theodore F. *Loyal West Virginia from 1861 to 1865*. Baltimore, MD: Deutsch Publishing Company, 1895.
Nicely, Wilson. *The Great Southwest, or Plain Guide for Emigrants and Capitalists Embracing a Description of the States of Missouri and Kansas Showing their Topographical Features, Climate, Soil, Timber, Prairie, Minerals, Water, Amount of*

Government Lands, Location of Valuable Mineral Lands, the Various Railroad Lines
Completed and Projected, Table of Distances, Homestead Law, with Incidents of Two
Years Travel and Residence in Missouri and Kansas and other Valuable Information.
St. Louis, MO: R. P. Studley and Company, 1867.

Radges, Samuel. *Radges Bienniel Directory to the Inhabitants, Institutions,
Manufacturing Establishments, Business Firms, etc. of the City of Topeka, for 1876–
77*. Topeka, KS: Commonwealth Job Printing Establishment, 1875.

———. *Radges Bienniel Directory to the Inhabitants, Institutions, Manufacturing
Establishments, Business Firms, etc. of the City of Topeka, for 1878–79*. Topeka, KS:
Commonwealth Job Printing Establishment, 1877.

## U.S. GOVERNMENT PUBLICATIONS

U.S. Census Office. *A Compendium of the Ninth Census (June 1, 1870) Compiled
Pursuant to a Concurrent Resolution of Congress and under the Direction of the
Secretary of the Interior*. Washington, DC: Government Printing Office, 1872.

———. *A Compendium of the Tenth Census (June 1, 1880) Compiled Pursuant to an Act
of Congress Approved August 7, 1882*, Part 2. Washington, DC: Government
Printing Office, 1888.

———. *Agriculture of the United States in 1860: Compiled ... under the Direction of the
Secretary of the Interior*. Washington, DC: Government Printing Office, 1864.

———. *Agriculture of the United States in 1860: Compiled ... under the Direction of the
Secretary of the Interior*. Reprint, New York: Norman Ross Publishers, 1990.

———. *Manufactures of the United States in 1860: compiled ... under the direction of the
Secretary of the Interior*. Washington, DC: Government Printing Office, 1865.

———. *Population of the United States in 1860: Compiled ... under the Direction of the
Secretary of the Interior*. Washington, DC: Government Printing Office, 1864.

———. *Population of the United States in 1860: Compiled ... under the Direction of the
Secretary of the Interior*. Reprint, New York: Norman Ross Publishers, 1990.

———. *Report on Mineral Industries in the United States at the Eleventh Census, 1890*.
Washington, DC: Government Printing Office, 1892.

———. *Report on the Mining Industries of the United States (exclusive of precious metals): with Special Investigations into the Iron Resources of the Republic and into the
Cretaceous coals of the Northwest*. Reprint, New York: Norman Ross Publishing,
1991.

———. *Report on Population of the United States at the eleventh census, 1890*.
Washington, DC: Government Printing Office, 1895.

———. *Report on the Productions of Agriculture as Returned at the Tenth Census*. Reprint,
New York: Norman Ross Publishing, 1991.

———. *Report on the Statistics of Agriculture in the United States at the Eleventh Census,
1890*. Washington, DC: Government Printing Office, 1895.

———. *The Statistics of the Population of the United States: embracing ... the original
returns of the ninth census, (June 1, 1870,) under the direction of the Secretary of the
Interior*. Washington, DC: Government Printing Office, 1872.

U.S. War Department. *The War of the Rebellion: A Compilation of the Official Records of
the Union and Confederate Armies*, Series 1, Vol. 12, Part 1.

———. *The War of the Rebellion: A Compilation of the Official Records of the Union and*

*Confederate Armies*, Series 1, Vol. 22, Part 1.

——. *The War of the Rebellion: A Compilation of the Official Records of the Union and Confederate Armies*, Series 1, Vol. 22, Part 2.

——. *The War of the Rebellion: A Compilation of the Official Records of the Union and Confederate Armies*, Series 1, Vol. 48, Part 1.

## MISSOURI GOVERNMENT PUBLICATIONS

Jamison, James C. *Report of the Adjutant General of Missouri for 1886*. Jefferson City, MO: Tribune Printing Company, 1887.

McGrath, Michael K., ed. *Official Directory of the State of Missouri, 1885*. St. Louis, MO: John J. Daley Stationary & Printing Company, 1885.

——, ed. *Directory of Missouri, 1887–88*. Jefferson City, MO: Tribune Printing Company, 1888.

Missouri General Assembly. *Laws of the State of Missouri, Passed at the First Session of the Eighteenth General Assembly, Begun and Held at the City of Jefferson*. Jefferson City, MO: James Lusk, Public Printer, 1855.

——. *Laws of the State of Missouri, Passed at the Regular Session of the 21st General Assembly, Begun and Held at the City of Jefferson, on Monday, December 31, 1860*. Jefferson City, MO: W. G. Cheeney, Public Printer, 1861.

——. *Report of the State Auditor to the Thirty-First General Assembly of the State of Missouri for the Two Fiscal Years, January 1, 1879 to December 31, 1880*. Jefferson City, MO: Tribune Printing Company, State Printers, 1881.

——. *Report of the State Auditor to the Thirty-Second General Assembly of the State of Missouri, for the Two Fiscal Years Beginning January 1, 1881, and Ending December 31, 1882*. Jefferson City, MO: State Journal Company, State Printers, 1883.

——. *Report of the State Auditor to the Thirty-Third General Assembly of the State of Missouri, for the Two Fiscal Years Beginning January 1, 1883, and Ending December 31, 1884*. Jefferson City, MO: Tribune Printing Company, State Printers, 1885.

——. *Report of the State Auditor to the Twenty-Seventh General Assembly of the State of Missouri, for the Two Years, from January 1, 1871 to December 31, 1872*. Jefferson City, MO: Regan & Carter, State Printers, 1873.

——. *Second Annual Report of the Commissioner of Statistics to the General Assembly of the State of Missouri for the Year 1867*. Jefferson City, MO: Ellwood Kirby, Public Printer, 1868.

Missouri House of Representatives. *Journal of the House of Representatives of the State of Missouri, at the Adjourned Session, Twentieth General Assembly*. Jefferson City, MO: W. G. Cheeney, Public Printer, 1860.

——. *Journal of the House of Representatives of the State of Missouri, at the Regular Session of the Twenty-Third General Assembly*. Jefferson City, MO: W. A. Curry, Public Printer, 1865.

## LETTERS, DIARIES, AND MEMOIRS

Groom, Charles, and D. F. McConkey. *The Bald Knobbers or Citizen's Committee of Taney and Christian Counties*. Forsyth, MO: The Authors, 1887.

Harper, Robert L. *Among the Bald Knobbers: A History of the Desperadoes of the Ozark*

*Mountains, Their Atrocious Deeds, Rendezvous, Homes and Habits, Their Arrest, and Conviction.* Clinton, MO: The Author, 1888. The book *Among the Bald Knobbers* was originally published under the pseudonym "Bob Sedgwick."

Hoenshel, E. J., and L. S. Hoenshel. *Stories of the Pioneers: Incidents, Adventures and Reminiscences as Told by Some of the Old Settlers of Taney County, Missouri.* Point Lookout, MO: School of the Ozarks Press, 1915.

Jamison, James Carson. *With Walker in Nicaragua: or, Reminiscences of an Officer of the American Phalanx.* Columbia, MO: E. W. Stephens Publishing Company, 1909.

Schoolcraft, Henry Rowe. *Schoolcraft in the Ozarks: Reprint of a Journal of a tour into the Interior of Missouri and Arkansas in 1818 and 1819.* Van Buren, AR: Press-Argus, 1955.

Turnbo, Silas C. *The White River Chronicles of S. C. Turnbo: Man and Wildlife on the Ozarks Frontier.* Edited by James F. Keefe and Lynn Morrow. Fayetteville: University of Arkansas Press, 1994.

## SECONDARY SOURCES

### BOOKS

Allen, Frederick. *A Decent, Orderly Lynching: The Montana Vigilantes.* Norman: University of Oklahoma Press, 2004.

Ayres, Edward L. *Vengeance and Justice: Crime and Punishment in the 19th-Century American South.* New York: Oxford University Press, 1984.

Ayto, John, and John Simpson, comps. *The Oxford Dictionary of Modern Slang.* Oxford: Oxford University Press, 2005.

Bancroft, Hubert Howe. *Popular Tribunals,* Vol. 1. San Francisco: The History Company, Publishers, 1887.

Barnes, Harper. *Standing on a Volcano: The Life and Times of David Rowland Francis.* St. Louis: Missouri Historical Society Press, 2001.

Bearss, Edwin C. *The Battle of Wilson's Creek*, 4th ed. Cassville, MO: Wilson's Creek National Battlefield Foundation, 1992.

Benac, David. *Conflict in the Ozarks: Hillfolk, Industrialists, and Government in Missouri's Courtois Hills.* Kirksville, MO: Truman State University Press, 2011.

Blevins, Brooks. *Ghost of the Ozarks: Murder and Memory in the Upland South.* Chicago: University of Illinois Press, 2012.

Boman, Dennis K. *Lincoln's Resolute Unionist: Hamilton Gamble, Dred Scott Dissenter and Missouri's Civil War Governor.* Baton Rouge: Louisiana State University Press, 2006.

Brant, Selwyn A., et al., eds. *The Union army: a history of military affairs in the loyal states, 1861–65—records of the regiments in the Union army—cyclopedia of battles—memoirs of commanders and soldiers,* Vol. 4. Madison, WI: Federal Publishing Company, 1908.

Brown, Richard Maxwell. *No Duty to Retreat: Violence and Values in American History and Society.* Oxford: Oxford University Press, 1992.

———. *Strain of Violence—A History of American Violence and Vigilantism*. New York: Oxford University Press, 1975.

———. *The South Carolina Regulators*. Cambridge, MA: Harvard University Press, 1963.

Brownlee, Richard S. *Gray Ghosts of the Confederacy: Guerrilla Warfare in the West, 1861–65*. Baton Rouge: Louisiana State University Press, 1984.

Bruton, J. J., et al. *Bald Knob Tragedy of Taney and Christian Counties*. Sparta, MO: The Authors, 1887.

Callaway, Lew L. *Montana's Righteous Hangmen: The Vigilantes in Action*. Norman: University of Oklahoma Press, 1982.

Castleman, Harvey N. *The Bald Knobbers: Story of the Lawless Night Riders Who Ruled Southern Missouri in the 80's*. Girard, KS: Haldeman-Julius Publications, 1944.

Caughey, John W. *Their Majesties the Mob: The Vigilante Impulse in America*. Chicago: University of Chicago Press, 1960.

Cawleti, John G. *Mystery, Violence, and Popular Culture*. Madison: University of Wisconsin Press, 2004.

Chalmers, David M. *Hooded Americanism: The History of the Ku Klux Klan*. Durham, NC: Duke University Press, 1987.

Christensen, Lawrence O., and Gary R. Kremer. *A History of Missouri: 1875–1919*. Columbia: University of Missouri Press, 2004.

Christian County Centennial, Inc. *Christian County, Its First 100 Years*. Jefferson City, MO: Van Hoffman Press, 1959.

Collier, William Neville. *Ozark and Vicinity in the Nineteenth Century*. Ozark, MO: Christian County Library, 1946.

Crozier, E. W. *The White-Caps: A History of the Organization in Sevier County*. Knoxville, TN: Bean, Warters & Gaut, Printers and Binders, 1899.

Culberson, William G. *Vigilantism: Political History of Private Power in America*. Westport, CT: Praeger Publishers, 1990.

Cunningham, Robert E. *Trial by Mob*. Stillwater, OK: Redland Press, 1957.

Daniel, Pete. *Standing at the Crossroads: Southern Life since 1900*. New York: Hill and Wang, 1986.

Doling, Anna M. *Brilla*. New York: Neal Publishing Company, 1913.

Drago, Henry Sinclair. *Outlaws on Horseback: The History of the Organized Bands of Bank and Train Robbers Who Terrorized the Prairie Towns of Missouri, Kansas, Indian Territory, and Oklahoma for Half a Century*. Lincoln: University of Nebraska Press, 1988.

Ekberg, Carl. *Colonial St. Genevieve: An Adventure on the Mississippi Frontier*. Gerald, MO: Patrice Press, 1985.

Ekirch, Roger A. *Poor Carolina: Politics and Society in Colonial North Carolina, 1729–1776*. Chapel Hill: University of North Carolina Press, 1981.

Fairbanks, Jonathan, and Clyde Edwin Tuck. *Past and Present of Greene County, Missouri: Early and Recent History and Genealogical Records of Many of the Representative Citizens*. Indianapolis, IN: A. W. Bowen & Company, 1915.

Fellman, Michael. *Inside War: The Guerrilla Conflict in Missouri during the Civil War*. Oxford: Oxford University Press, 1989.

Foley, William E. *The Genesis of Missouri: From Wilderness Outpost to Statehood.* Columbia: University of Missouri Press, 1989.

Foner, Eric. *A Short History of Reconstruction, 1863–1887.* New York: Harper & Row, Publishers, 1990.

Frazier, Harriet C. *Lynchings in Missouri, 1803–1981.* Jefferson, NC: McFarland & Company, 2009.

Gard, Wayne. *Frontier Justice.* Norman: University of Oklahoma Press, 1949.

Gerlach, Russel L. "The Ozark Scotch-Irish." In *Cultural Geography of Missouri.* Edited by Michael Roark. Cape Girardeau: Department of Earth Sciences, Southeast Missouri State University, 1983.

———. *Settlement Patterns in Missouri: A Study of Population Origins, with a Wall Map.* Columbia: University of Missouri Press, 1986.

Glenn, Wayne. *Christian County Memories, 1819–Present.* Nixa, MO: The Author, 2009.

Goman, Frederick W. *Up From Arkansas: Marmaduke's First Missouri Raid Including the Battles of Springfield and Hartville.* Springfield, MO: Wilson's Creek National Battlefield Foundation, 1999.

Goodspeed Brothers. *History of Southeast Missouri: Embracing an Historical Account of the Counties of St. Genevieve, St. Francois, Perry, Cape Girardeau, Bollinger, Madison, New Madrid, Pemiscot, Dunklin, Scott, Mississippi, Stoddard, Butler, Wayne, and Iron.* Chicago: Goodspeed Brothers, Publishers, 1888.

———. *Pictorial and Genealogical Record of Greene County, Missouri: together with Biographies of Prominent Men of other Portions of the State, both Living and Dead.* Chicago: Goodspeed Brothers, Publishers, 1893.

———. *A Reminiscent History of the Ozarks Region: Comprising a Condensed General History, a Brief Descriptive History of Each County, and Numerous Biographical Sketches of Prominent Citizens of Such Counties.* Chicago: Goodspeed Brothers, Publishers, 1894.

Hardy, Richard J., et al., ed. *Missouri Government and Politics,* rev. ed. Colombia: University of Missouri Press, 1995.

Harkins, Anthony. *Hillbilly: A Cultural History of an American Icon.* New York: Oxford University Press, 2004.

Hartman, Mary, and Elmo Ingenthron. *Bald Knobbers: Vigilantes on the Ozarks Frontier.* Gretna, LA: Pelican Publishing, 1989.

Hofstadter, Richard, and Michael Wallace, eds. *American Violence: A Documentary History.* New York: Alfred A. Knopf, 1970.

Holcombe, Return I. *History of Vernon County, Missouri: Written and Compiled from the Most Authentic Official and Private Sources, Including a History of its Townships, Towns and Villages.* St. Louis, MO: Brown & Company, 1887.

———, ed. *History of Greene County, Missouri.* St. Louis, MO: Western Historical Company, 1883.

Hollon, W. Eugene. *Frontier Violence: Another Look.* New York: Oxford University Press, 1974.

Hunt, William R. *Front Page Detective: William J. Burns and the Detective Profession, 1880–1930.* Bowling Green, OH: Bowling Green State University Popular Press, 1990.

Hurt, R. Douglas. *Agriculture and Slavery in Missouri's Little Dixie.* Columbia: University of Missouri Press, 1992.

Ingenthron, Elmo. *Borderland Rebellion: A History of the Civil War on the Missouri-Arkansas Border.* Branson, MO: Ozarks Mountaineer, 1980.

———. *Indians of the Ozark Plateau.* Point Lookout, MO: School of the Ozarks Press, 1970.

———. *The Land of Taney: A History of an Ozark Commonwealth.* Point Lookout, MO: School of the Ozarks Press, 1974.

———. *The Land of Taney: A History of an Ozark Commonwealth.* Branson, MO: Ozarks Mountaineer, 1983.

Johnson, Laura. *The Home-Coming in the Ozarks.* Chicago: Glad Tidings Publishing, 1922.

Kars, Marjoleine. *Breaking Loose Together: The Regulator Revolution in Pre-Revolutionary North Carolina.* Chapel Hill: University of North Carolina Press, 2001.

Ketchell, Aaron K. *Holy Hills of the Ozarks: Religion and Tourism in Branson, Missouri.* Baltimore: Johns Hopkins University Press, 2007.

Larsen, Edward J. *Summer for the Gods: The Scopes Trial and America's Continuing Debate over Science and Religion.* New York: Basic Books, 1997.

Madison, Arnold. *Vigilantism in America.* New York: Seabury Press, 1973.

McCall, Edith S. *English Village in the Ozarks: The Story of Hollister, Missouri.* Hollister, MO: The Author, 1969.

Meyer, Duane G. *The Heritage of Missouri,* 3rd ed. Springfield, MO: Emden Press, 1982.

Mitchell, John H. *Tales of Bull Creek Country.* Cassville, MO: The Author, 1990.

Monaghan, Jay. *Civil War on the Western Border, 1854–1865.* Boston: Little, Brown and Company.

Monks, William. *A History of Southern Missouri and Northern Arkansas: Being an Account of the Early Settlements, the Civil War, the Ku-Klux, and Times of Peace.* Edited by John F. Bradbury Jr. and Lou Wehmer. Fayetteville: University of Arkansas Press, 2003.

Morn, Frank. *The Eye That Never Sleeps: A History of the Pinkerton National Detective Agency.* Bloomington: Indiana University Press, 1982.

Morrow, Lynn, and Linda Myers-Phinney. *Shepherd of the Hills Country: Tourism Transforms the Ozarks, 1880's–1930's.* Fayetteville: University of Arkansas Press, 1999.

Mott, Frank Luther. *Golden Multitudes: The Story of Best Sellers in the United States.* New York: Macmillan, 1947.

Nichols, Bruce. *Guerrilla Warfare in Civil War Missouri,* 2 Vols. Jefferson, NC: McFarland & Company, 2004–7.

Ohman, Marian M. *Encyclopedia of Missouri Courthouses.* Columbia: University of Missouri, Columbia Extension Division, 1981.

Parrish, William E. *A History of Missouri: 1860 to 1875.* Columbia: University of Missouri Press, 2001.

———. *Missouri under Radical Rule, 1865–1870.* Columbia: University of Missouri Press, 1965.

Piston, William Garrett. *Wilson's Creek: The Second Battle of the Civil War and the Men Who Fought It.* Chapel Hill: University of North Carolina Press, 2000.

Rafferty, Milton D. *The Ozarks: Land and Life.* Fayetteville: University of Arkansas Press, 2001.

Randolph, Vance. *The Bald Knobbers: The Story of the Lawless Night-Riders Who Ruled Southern Missouri in the 80's.* Girard, KS: Haldeman-Julius Publications, 1944.

———. *The Devil's Pretty Daughter: and Other Ozark Folk Tales.* New York: Columbia University Press, 1955.

Richardson, Heather Cox. *West from Appomattox: The Reconstruction of America after the Civil War.* New Haven, CT: Yale University Press, 2007.

Roberts, Randy, and James S. Olson. *John Wayne: American.* New York: Free Press, 1995.

Rollings, Willard H. *The Osage: An Ethnohistorical Study of Hegemony on the Prairie-Plains.* Columbia: University of Missouri Press, 1992.

Rosenbaum, Robert J. *Mexicano Resistance in the Southwest: "The Sacred Right of Self-Preservation."* Austin: University of Texas Press, 1981.

Sheets, Vonda Wilson. *Absolution: A Bald Knobber Saga.* Kirbyville, MO: The Author, 2012.

Smith, Helena Huntington. *The War on the Powder River: The History of an Insurrection.* Lincoln: University of Nebraska Press, 1967.

Spencer, Thomas M. "The Bald Knobbers, the Anti-Bald Knobbers, Politics, and the Culture of Violence in the Ozarks, 1860-1890." In *The Other Missouri History: Populists, Prostitutes, and Regular Folk.* Edited by Thomas M. Spencer. Columbia: University of Missouri Press, 2004.

Stevens, Walter B. *Missouri: The Center State, 1821–1915,* Vol. 3. St. Louis, MO: S. J. Clarke Publishing Company, 1915.

Stewart, George R. *Committee of Vigilance: Revolution in San Francisco, 1851.* Boston, MA: Houghton Mifflin, 1964.

Stiles, T. J. *Jesse James: Last Rebel of the Civil War.* New York: Vintage Books, 2003.

Sutherland, Daniel E. *A Savage Conflict: The Decisive Role of Guerrillas in the American Civil War.* Chapel Hill: University of North Carolina Press, 2009.

Swartz, Charles and Elizabeth. *The Wild Mammals of Missouri.* Columbia: University of Missouri Press, 1981.

Thelen, David R. *Paths of Resistance: Tradition and Dignity in Industrializing Missouri.* New York: Oxford University Press, 1986.

Tuck, Clyde Edwin. *The Bald Knobbers: A Romantic and Historical Novel.* Indianapolis, IN: B. F. Bowen & Company, 1910.

Upton, Lucille Morris. *Bald Knobbers.* Caldwell, ID: Caxton Printers, 1939.

Valentine, Alan. *Vigilante Justice.* New York: Reynal and Company, 1956.

Vandeventer, William L. *Justice in the Rough.* Springfield, MO: The Author, 1937.

Waldrep, Christopher. *Night Riders: Defending the Community in the Black Patch, 1890–1915.* Durham, NC: Duke University Press, 1993.

Waller, Altina L. *Feud: Hatfields, McCoys, and Social Change in Appalachia, 1860–1900.* Chapel Hill: University of North Carolina Press, 1988.

Walzer, Michael. "Puritanism as a Revolutionary Ideology." In *Studies in Social Movements: A Social Psychological Perspective,* edited by Barry McLaughlin. New York: Free Press, 1969.

Williams, Walter, ed. *The State of Missouri: An Autobiography.* Columbia, MO: E. W. Stephens, 1904.

Wright, Harold Bell. *The Shepherd of the Hills.* New York: A. L. Burt Company, 1907.

**ARTICLES**

Barclay, Thomas S. "Test Oath for the Clergy in Missouri." *Missouri Historical Review* 18, no. 3 (April 1924): 345–81.

———. "The Liberal Republican Movement in Missouri." *Missouri Historical Review* 21, no. 1 (October 1926): 59–108.

Blake, Kellee. "'First in the Path of the Firemen': The Fate of the 1890 Population Census." *Prologue: Quarterly of the National Archives* 28, no. 1 (Spring 1996): 64–81.

Blevins, Brooks. "The Arkansas Ghost Trial: The Connie Franklin Case and the Ozarks in the National Media." *Arkansas Historical Quarterly* 68, no. 3 (Autumn 2009): 245–71.

Boswell, Mary Lou. "The Levi Boswell Family of Taney County, Missouri." *White River Valley Historical Quarterly* 9, no. 12 (Summer 1988): 10–11.

Brashear, Minnie M. "The Anti-Horse Thief Association of Northeast Missouri." *Missouri Historical Review* 45, no. 4 (July 1951): 341–38.

Cameron, W. D. "History and Hearsay." *White River Valley Historical Quarterly* 5, no. 7 (Spring 1975): 19–20.

Canan, Howard V. "Milton Burch: Anti-Guerrilla Fighter." *Missouri Historical Review* 59, no. 2 (January 1965): 223–42.

Collier, William Neville. "Ozark and Vicinity in the Nineteenth Century," Part 1. *White River Valley Historical Quarterly* 2, no. 9 (Fall 1966): 22–27.

———. "Ozark and Vicinity in the Nineteenth Century," Part 2. *White River Valley Historical Quarterly* 2, no. 10 (Winter 1966): 15–24.

———. "Ozark and Vicinity in the Nineteenth Century," Part 3. *White River Valley Historical Quarterly* 2, no. 11 (Spring 1967): 11–17.

Crumpler, Hugh. "Fishing the Wild Streams of the Ozarks." *Ozarks Watch* 4, no. 3 (Winter 1991): 3–6.

Davis, Lee Carson. "Bean Cave: Marion County, Arkansas." *White River Valley Historical Quarterly* 2, no. 11 (Spring 1967): 3–4.

Everett, Barton C. "'Uncle Jurd' Haworth." *White River Valley Historical Quarterly* 4, no. 7 (Spring 1972): 16.

Flippin, W. B. "The Tutt and Everett War in Marion County." *Arkansas Historical Quarterly* 17, no. 3 (Summer 1958): 155–63.

Geiger, Mark W. "Indebtedness and the Origins of Guerrilla Violence in Civil War Missouri." *Journal of Southern History* 75, no. 1 (February 2009): 49–82.

Grant, Roger H. "Missouri's Utopian Communities." *Missouri Historical Review* 66, no. 1 (October 1971): 20–48.

Guese, Lucius E. "St. Louis and the Great Whiskey Ring." *Missouri Historical Review* 36 (April 1942): 160–83.

Hamilton, J. G. De Roulhac. "Three Centuries of Southern Records, 1607–1907." *Journal of Southern History* 10, no. 1 (February 1944): 3–36.

Harrison, S. L. "The Scopes 'Monkey Trial' Revisited: Mencken and the Editorial Art of Edmund Duffy." *Journal of American Culture* 17, no. 4 (1994): 55–63.

Hartman, Viola. "The Layton Story: Part II." *White River Valley Historical Quarterly* 7, no. 3 (Spring 1980): 3-6.

Haswell, A. M. "The Story of the Bald Knobbers." *Missouri Historical Review* 18 (October 23, 1923): 27-35.

Haworth, J. H. "Taney County Bald Knobbers." *White River Valley Historical Quarterly* 3, no. 9 (Spring 1986): 20-27.

Hibbard, Claude. "The Story of Two Pioneer Families Whose Lives Intertwined." *White River Valley Historical Quarterly* 2, no. 8 (Summer 1966): 3-4.

Hill, Faun I. "William Jeptha Johnson." *White River Valley Historical Quarterly* 1, no. 3 (Spring 1962): 8-9.

Holmes, William F. "Whitecapping: Agrarian Violence in Mississippi, 1902-06." *Journal of Southern History* 35, no. 2 (May 1969): 165-85.

Huff, Leo E. "Guerrillas, Jayhawkers and Bushwhackers in Northern Arkansas during the Civil War." *Arkansas Historical Quarterly* 24, no. 3 (Summer 1965): 127-48.

Ingenthron, Elmo. "Guerrillas, Jayhawkers, and Bushwackers." *White River Valley Historical Quarterly* 2, no. 4 (Summer 1965): 2-3.

———. "The Civil War 1862: Skirmishes at Ozark and Snapp's Farm." *White River Valley Historical Quarterly* 1, no. 5 (Fall 1962): 10-13.

James, Nola A. "The Civil War Years in Independence County." *Arkansas Historical Quarterly* 28, no. 3 (Autumn 1969): 234-74.

"James Carson Jamison." *Missouri Historical Review* 25, no. 4 (July 1931): 623-26.

Kalen, Kristin, and Lynn Morrow. "A Bald Knobber Sues Springfield." *White River Valley Historical Quarterly* 32, no. 3 (Spring 1993): 12-14.

———. "Nat Kinney's Sunday School Crowd." *White River Valley Historical Quarterly* 33, no. 1 (Fall 1993): 6-13.

Lightfoot, B. B. "Nobody's Nominee: Sample Orr and the Election of 1860." *Missouri Historical Review* 60, no. 2 (January 1966): 127-48.

Lisby, Gaye. "Bald Knobbers Exposed: Taney Countian Shares for the First Time Her Family's Experiences with Bald Knobber Treachery and Murder." *Branson Living* (Summer 1995): 24-25.

Looney, Janice. "Andrew Coggburn, 1866-86." *White River Valley Historical Quarterly* 9, no. 6 (Winter 1987): 9.

"The Lost Missouri Hemp Industry." *Missouri Historical Review* 37, no. 1 (October 1942): 57-65.

Mahnkey, Douglas. "A Bald Knobber Badge." *Ozarks Mountaineer* 32, no. 2 & 3 (April 1984): 54.

———. "Captain Kinney and the Bald Knobbers." *Ozarks Mountaineer* 26 (August 1978): 16-17.

———. "The Mahnkey and Prather Families." *White River Valley Historical Quarterly* 4, no. 2 (Winter 1970-71): 4-6.

———. "Who Killed Wash Middleton?" *Ozarks Mountaineer* 21, no. 4 (May 1973): 22-41.

March, David D. "Charles Drake and the Constitutional Convention of 1865." *Missouri Historical Review* 47, no. 2 (January 1953): 110-23.

Marmaduke, John S. "Offering a Reward, October 20, 1887." *White River Valley Historical Quarterly* 6, no. 2 (Winter 1977): 3.

Morrow, Lynn. "George Caleb Bingham's Ride into the Ozarks: Confronting the Sons of Honor." *White River Valley Historical Quarterly* 36, no. 1 (Summer 1996): 4–9.

———. "Trader William Gillis and Delaware Migration in Southern Missouri." *Missouri Historical Review* 75, no. 2 (January 1981): 147–67.

———. "Where Did All the Money Go?: War and the Economics of Vigilantism in Southern Missouri." *White River Valley Historical Quarterly* 34, no. 2 (Fall 1994): 2–15.

Parrish, Sibyl. "Joseph Calvin Parrish." *White River Valley Historical Quarterly* 1, no. 6 (Winter 1962): 15.

Price, James E. "Bowin' and Spikin' in the Jillikins." *Ozarks Watch* 6, no. 2 (Winter 1991): 12–15.

Rafferty, Milton D. "The Ozark Forest: Its Exploitation and Restoration." *Ozarks Watch* 6, no. 2 (Summer 1992): 23–29.

Robinett, Paul. "Marmaduke's Expedition into Missouri: The Battle's of Springfield and Hartville, January, 1863." *Missouri Historical Review* 58, no. 2 (January 1964): 151–73.

Ryser, Ruth Gulls. "The Snapp Family." *White River Valley Historical Quarterly* 4, no. 3 (Spring 1971): 2–3.

Schlesinger, Andrew Bancroft. "Las Gorras Blancas, 1889–1891." *Journal of Mexican American History* 1, no. 2 (Spring 1971): 87–129.

Settle, William A., Jr. "The James Boys and Missouri Politics." *Missouri Historical Review* 36, no. 4 (July 1942): 412–29.

Snyder, J. F. "The Democratic State Convention of Missouri in 1860." *Missouri Historical Review* 2, no. 2 (January 1908): 112–30.

Stout, Roy E. "The Eglinton Colony in Missouri, 1882." *White River Valley Historical Quarterly* 2, no. 12 (Summer/Fall 1967): 1–3.

Sullenberger, Don A. "Forsyth Steamboat Landing." *White River Valley Historical Quarterly* 8, no. 12 (Summer 1985): 12–16.

West, Mabel. "Jacksonport, Arkansas: Its Rise and Decline." *Arkansas Historical Quarterly* 9, no. 4 (Winter 1950): 231–58.

Williams, Robert L. "James Carson Jamison, 1830–1916." *Chronicles of Oklahoma* 21, no. 1 (March 1943): 3–7.

## THESES AND DISSERTATIONS

Noble, Madeline M. "The White Caps of Harrison and Crawford County, IN: A Study in the Violent Enforcement of Morality." Ph.D. Dissertation, University of Michigan, 1973.

Nolan, Patrick B. "Vigilantes on the Middle Border: A Study of Self-Appointed Law Enforcement in the States of the Upper Mississippi from 1840 to 1880." Ph.D. Dissertation, University of Minnesota, 1971.

Olsen, Barton C. "Lawlessness and Vigilantes in American: An Historical Analysis Emphasizing California and Montana." Ph.D. Dissertation, University of Utah, 1968.

**ONLINE MATERIALS**

Alexander Street Press, LLC. "The American Civil War Research Database." http://asp6new.alexanderstreet.com.libezp.lib.lsu.edu/cwdb/ (accessed January 3, 2011).

Ancestry.com. "Civil War Collection." http://search.ancestry.com/search/grouplist.aspx?group=CivilWar (accessed January 3, 2011).

———. "U.S. Federal Census Collection." http://search.ancestry.com/search/grouplist.aspx?group=USFEDCEN (accessed January 3, 2011).

———. "U.S. General Land Office Records, 1796–1907." http://search.ancestry.com/iexec/?htx=List&dbid=1246&offerid=0%3a7858%3a0 (accessed January 3, 2011).

Burns, Louis F. "Osage." *Encyclopedia of Oklahoma History and Culture.* http://digital.library.okstate.edu/encyclopedia/entries/O/OS001.html (accessed August 30, 2009).

National Park Service. "Civil War Soldiers and Sailors." http://www.itd.nps.gov/cwss/soldiers.cfm (accessed October 18, 2009).

Turnbo, Silas C. "An Interesting Time Among Game and Finding Bee Trees During the Pioneer Days of Ozark County, Missouri." *The Turnbo Manuscripts*, Vol. 14. Springfield-Greene County Library. http://thelibrary.org/lochist/turnbo/v14/st438.html (accessed June 20, 2013).

———. "The Alph Cook Cave." *The Turnbo Manuscripts*, Vol. 1. Springfield-Greene County Library. http://thelibrary.org/lochist/turnbo/V1/ST002.html (accessed September 11, 2009).

———. "Bruin Wallows a Hunter in Clay." *The Turnbo Manuscripts,* Vol. 6. Springfield-Greene County Library. http://thelibrary.org/lochist/turnbo/v6/st173.html (accessed June 20, 2013).

———. "Depriving Children of the Last Morsel of Food." *The Turnbo Manuscripts,* Vol. 4. Springfield-Greene County Library. http://thelibrary.org/lochist/turnbo/v4/st105.html (accessed September 26, 2009).

———. "Hardships and Starvation in the Turbulent Days of War." *The Turnbo Manuscripts*, Vol. 23. Springfield-Greene County Library. http://thelibrary.org/lochist/turnbo/V23/ST684.html (accessed September 27, 2009).

# Index

Johnson, Horace, 18, 153, 154, 156, 216

Johnson, James, Bald Knobber, 224

Johnson, James C., political activities, 61, 71; Bald Knobber, 195, 210, 223

Johnson, Zachariah A., Sheriff, Edens-Greene murder, 141–51; feared for prisoner's safety and allowed gifts to be brought to them, 155, 160; testimony at William Walker's trial, 165; request for him to inquire into Mathews' sanity, 168; jailbreak, 172–73; execution of Walkers, 180–84

Jones, Amos, Bald Knobber, 224; Helms wouldn't sell land to, 117, 135; request to commute his sentence, 127, 170; letter to his brother, 150; indicted, 152; incarcerated, 159; pled guilty, 169

Jones, McLain; U.S. commissioner, 130, 131, 142, 219

Jones, Thomas K., Bald Knobber, 224

Jones, William H., Anti-Bald Knobber, 107, 227

Jonesboro AR, 148

*Kansas City Journal* newspaper, 194

*Kansas City Star* newspaper, 154

Kansas (state), 101, 157; Osage moved to reservation there, 22; turmoil in counties bordering it, 33; immigrants from, 46–47, 50; Kinney from, 51, 92; Bald Knobbers from, 93, 123

Keithley, Francis M., 71

Keithley, James, 59

Kelso, John R., Union militia officer, 40–41; as congressman, 57

Kennedy, Ed, Bald Knobber, 224

Kentucky (state), Osage and Iroquois in, 22; emigrants from, 25–26, 42, 46–47, 67, 92, 124, 211; night riders of the "black patch," 129; Hatfield-McCoy feud, 176

King Solomon Mine, 56

Kinney, Georgia, 51

Kinney, J.C.F., 52

Kinney, Margaret (DeLong), 51

Kinney, Nathaniel N. ("Nat"), 223; killed Andrew Coggburn, 2, 82, 88–93, 187; killed by Billy Miles, 3; background on, 50–52; opposed to debt, 65; friend of James Everett, 68; member of grand jury, 70; ran for state representative, 71, 109; organized Bald Knobbers, 71–74, 112; lynching of Taylor brothers, 77–78; taught Sunday school class, 83; run-in with Andrew Coggburn, 84–85; was a Democrat, 96, 195; intimidated opponents, 97–99; said he would disband Bald Knobbers, 102–3; Snapp's death, 107–8; influence over his men, 122; former saloon keeper, 127; Immigration Society, 190; animosity towards him, 193–95; injury lawsuit against Springfield, 195–97; Berry's divorce, 197–98; shooting of, 199–201, 205–15, 217

Kinney, Paul, 51, 88–90

Kintrea, John; General Store, 105–6, 187

Kirbyville, MO, Snapp killed there, 3, 105, 106, 109, 212; "Murder Rock" south of, 39; Kinney lived near, 52, 112; "Snapp's Bald" near there, 73; Independence Day shootings near, 203, 208, 210, 217

Kissee, Alexander C., Bald Knobber, 39, 56, 223; fought in Union militia unit, 33, 48, 212; marriages and children, 49; Taylor gang maimed cattle of, 68, 76; brother of Arter, 84; wealth of, 124; on list of Bald Knobbers to be killed, 194; editor of *Taney County Times*, 207, 208; shrewd businessman, 211

Kissee, Arter, Bald Knobber, 84, 95, 223; property of, 124; on list of Bald Knobbers to be killed

McCauley, Russell, 119, 127, 153, 156, 215
McClurg, Joseph W., 60
McConkey, D. F., Bald Knobber, 190, 209, 223; wrote history of Bald Knobbers, 66, 127
McGinnis, Robert, Bald Knobber, 224
McGrath, Michael K., newspaper editor, 96
McGuire, James R., Bald Knobber, 136–37, 149, 224; arrested, 145; testimony, 149–51, 164
McGill, Joe, Bald Knobber, 67–68, 102, 104, 211, 214, 223; raid on John Haworth's house, 83
McHaffie, David, 49
McHaffie, Catherine, 49
McHaffie, James K. Polk, Bald Knobber, 223; member of Republican Party and Free Masons, 49; elected sheriff and collector of revenue, 71; attended meeting to organize vigilance committee, 71; prevented lynching of Newton Herrell, 74–75; Tubal Taylor's escape, 76; surrender of Taylor brothers, 77; settled in Taney County, 93; Bald Knobber and sheriff, 95, 98–99, 195; Middleton's escape, 108; wealthy, 124; instituted suit against delinquent tax payers, 191; on list of people to be killed, 194; Miles surrendered to him, 200; shrewd businessman, 211
McKee, David, founded Anti-Horse Thief Association, 44
Meadows, John, Bald Knobber,188, 224
Meadows, Robert, 188
Mencken, H. L., 177
Mercer, Buck, killed by Arter Kissee, 84
Mexican War, 101, 197
Meyers, E. W., 62
Meyers, Newton, Bald Knobber, 224

Middleton, George Washington ("Wash"), killed Samuel Snapp, 3, 24, 105–9, 187, escape from jail in Forsyth, 108; killed in Arkansas, 109; property owned by,124, trial of, 187–89, Union veteran, 106–07, 212; Bald Knobber, 223
Miles, Elisha, 193
Miles, Jim, Anti-Bald Knobber, 227
Miles, William H., Anti-Bald Knobber, 98, 101, 191, 193, 202, 227
Miles, William M., Anti-Bald Knobber, 227; killed Nat Kinney, 3, 194, 199–200, 217; involvement in Berry-Taylor dispute, 198; arrested and indicted, 201; bail, 202; alleged plot to kill, 203; shooting of Branson and Funk, 203–04; arrested in Greene County, 205; murder trials, 206–08;
Miller County, MO, 24, 175
Miller, Samuel, confederate guerrilla, 35
Missouri General Assembly, 31, 50, 62, 83, 87, 176
Missouri State Penitentiary in Jefferson City, 108
Monks, Captain William, Union militia officer, 38, 43
Montgomery County, AL, 22
Moore, Isaac, 193
Moore, William E., Anti-Bald Knobber, 191, 202, 227
Morehouse, Albert P.; Governor, 171
Morrisett, James, Bald Knobber, 224
Moseley, John, sheriff and collector of revenue, 61, 67; Layton surrendered to, 69; lost race for sheriff and collector of revenue, 71; father-in-law of Jefferson Weaver, 82; member of the old Democratic courthouse ring, 86; Anti-Bald Knobber, 95, 227; testified against Nat Kinney, 196–97, co-signed for Miles' bond, 202
Mulverd, KS, 50